CADOGANbritain

THE LAKE DISTRICT

'...a landscape of deep, dark lakes and glittering, mirror-like tarns crouching at the foot of small but perfectly formed craggy mountains where red deer roam.'

Vivienne Crow

About the Guide

The **full-colour introduction** gives the author's overview of the region, together with suggested **itineraries** and a regional **'where to go' map** and **feature** to help you plan your trip.

Enticing **cultural chapters** on the rich local history, food, arts and wildlife give you a full flavour of the region and what makes it so special.

Planning Your Trip gives you all the useful information you need before you go and the **Practical A–Z** deals with all the **essential information** and **contact details** that you may need while you are away.

The **regional chapters** are arranged in a loose touring order, with plenty of public transport and driving information. The author's top **'Don't Miss'** ❶ sights are highlighted at the start of each chapter.

Although everything listed in this guide is **personally recommended**, our author inevitably has her own favourite places to eat and stay. Whenever you see this **Author's Choice** ★ icon beside a listing, you will know that it is a little bit out of the ordinary.

Hotel Price Guide (*see also* p.45)

Luxury	over £200
Expensive	£120-£200
Moderate	£55-£120
Budget	under £55

Restaurant Price Guide (*see also* p.48)

Very expensive	cost no object
Expensive	£35-60
Moderate	£18-35
Budget	under £18

About the Author

Based in Cumbria, **Vivienne Crow** is a freelance journalist specializing in travel and outdoor writing. She is passionate about the Lake District and when not writing about the area she spends her time walking in the National Park's fells and photographing its serene landscapes.

1st Edition published 2010

01 INTRODUCING THE LAKE DISTRICT

Top: Catbells ridge
Above: Rowing boats on Ullswater

For hundreds of years, the Lake District has been an inspiration for writers and artists, moved by its tremendous views and its ever-changing patterns of light; today it inspires many hundreds of thousands of tourists who come seeking tranquillity and the great outdoors. Tucked away in the far northwest corner of England, hugging the Scottish border, this relatively remote spot contains some of the most spectacular scenery in the whole of the British Isles. Carved by glaciers that once covered this region in immense sheets of ice, it is a landscape of deep, dark lakes and glittering, mirror-like tarns crouching at the foot of small but perfectly-formed craggy mountains where red deer roam. Tumultuous waterfalls and fast-flowing becks come crashing down through the ancient woods that cloak the valley sides. Here, an assortment of wildlife live, including some of England's last red squirrels as well as rare plants and butterflies.

Beyond the Lake District itself, which is England's largest National Park, Cumbria is home to a huge variety of landscapes, including the lonely moorlands of the North Pennines, the rolling hills of the Howgills, the idyllic Eden Valley, the Solway Plain and a stretch of lovely coast.

For anyone who loves walking, kayaking, mountain-biking, climbing, paragliding – anything to do with the great outdoors – this is heaven on Earth. There are paths and trails everywhere, and a huge number of guides, instructors and hire companies are available to help visitors get the most out of their trip.

Yet this isn't an entirely natural landscape; since the ice sheets departed, it has been moulded by man – mining, water mills, cottage industries and farming have all left their mark. The Romans

Above: Wastwater, England's deepest lake

Opposite: The Langdale Pikes with Dungeon Ghyll in the foreground

were here, as were the 'beaker' people, the Celts, the Norsemen and, of course, the Anglo-Saxons, all adding to a colourful historical tapestry, the remains of which are scattered throughout the county. Enigmatic stone circles and henges from prehistoric times brush shoulders with stunningly located Roman forts and medieval castles. The far north of Cumbria also contains sections of Hadrian's Wall, a UNESCO World Heritage site.

Some of Britain's best-loved figures from the worlds of art and literature, including the poet William Wordsworth, the children's book writer and illustrator Beatrix Potter and the Victorian essayist, artist and social commentator John Ruskin, made their homes here, and many of these are open to the public today. There are also galleries, museums and art centres galore, all adding to the potential for enjoying a rich cultural experience.

Farming remains an important part of the local economy and it is partly this that has helped give Cumbria a first-class reputation where food is concerned. Michelin-starred restaurants, gastro-pubs and classy cafés serve up the best of local produce, while hundreds of small-scale entrepreneurs use secret recipes and home-grown ingredients to conjure up tasty sausages, delicious gingerbread, mouth-watering fudge and that most marvellous of Cumbrian inventions, sticky toffee pudding. A burgeoning micro-brewery scene adds an extra special ingredient to the region's increasingly diverse menu.

Above: Derwent Water

*Below: Lake
Windermere at sunset*

Where to Go

The regional chapters of this guide are ordered roughly according to the route of a traveller entering the Lake District from the south, and the final chapter covers areas outside the National Park.

South Lakes covers Kendal, Windermere and Bowness as well as Coniston, Hawkshead and the southern peninsulas that jut out into the immense sands of Morecambe Bay. Cruises on England's largest lake start from Bowness, and the area is also home to a number of interesting historical attractions such as Sizergh Castle, Levens Hall, Townend, Furness Abbey, Brantwood (the former home of John Ruskin) and Beatrix Potter's farm, Hill Top. This is a 'softer' landscape than the central Lakes, with gently rolling hills and wooded valleys only slowly giving way to higher fells as the visitor heads north and west.

Ambleside and Grasmere are at the physical and spiritual hub of the Lake District – it's where the mountains proper begin and, for many years, was the home of William Wordsworth. The spectacular scenery of Langdale is also accessible from here.

Beyond Kirkstone Pass is **Ullswater and the North East Lakes**, a quieter corner of the Lake District. Ullswater winds for miles through the mountains to the very foot of the craggy Helvellyn range. To the northeast is the town of Penrith, and hidden between Ullswater and the M6 are the remote eastern fells around Haweswater.

Keswick and the North Lakes is home to the Lake District's largest town, the towering mountain, Skiddaw, one of the largest and most beautiful of the lakes, Derwent Water, and probably the most popular of the Lakeland valleys, Borrowdale. Heading north is Bassenthwaite Lake, where the Lake District's only ospreys can be seen, and where tiny, scattered villages lie at the base of the grassy Northern Fells.

Crossing Honister Pass, the visitor reaches the **Western Lakes and the Coast** – Buttermere, Loweswater, Ennerdale, Wasdale, Eskdale and a long stretch of the Irish Sea and Solway coast that is beloved of bird-watchers. The most inaccessible of the western dales contain some of the wildest scenery, as well as fascinating historical sites. There are also some lovely old settlements, including Whitehaven, with its attractive harbour, and the colourful Georgian town of Cockermouth.

East Cumbria is often overlooked in favour of the National Park, but this area is worth a visit in its own right. Carlisle, with Hadrian's Wall nearby, is a must, as are the many gorgeous villages of the Eden Valley. Alston, close to the county's border with Northumberland and County Durham, is surrounded by the wild, lonely moorland of the North Pennines Area of Outstanding Natural Beauty. Further south still and there is a surprise in store – a chunk of the Yorkshire Dales National Park that falls within Cumbria's borders. The main settlements here are the quaint old market towns of Kirkby Stephen, Sedbergh and Kirkby Lonsdale.

Chapter Divisions

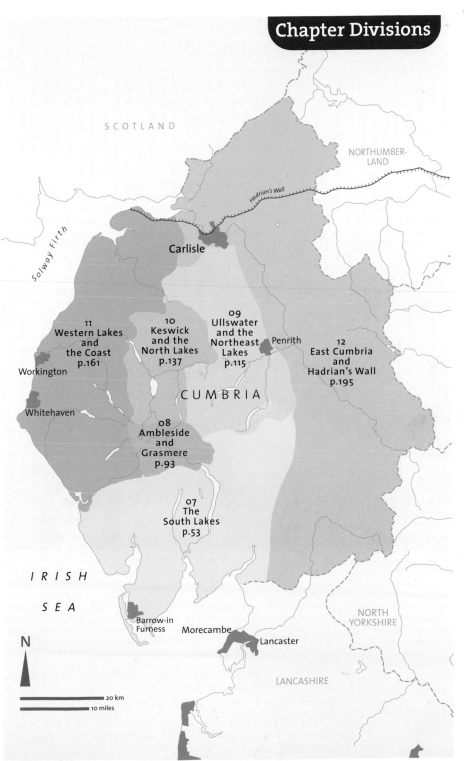

SCOTLAND

NORTHUMBER-
LAND

Hadrian's Wall

Solway Firth

Carlisle

11
Western Lakes
and
the Coast
p.161

Workington

Whitehaven

10
Keswick
and the
North Lakes
p.137

09
Ullswater
and the
Northeast
Lakes
p.115

Penrith

12
East Cumbria
and
Hadrian's Wall
p.195

C U M B R I A

08
Ambleside
and
Grasmere
p.93

07
The
South Lakes
p.53

I R I S H

S E A

Barrow-in
Furness   Morecambe   Lancaster

NORTH
YORKSHIRE

LANCASHIRE

N

20 km
10 miles

The Natural World

Craggy mountains, dramatic waterfalls, dark, narrow gorges, tumultuous rivers and becks, shimmering lakes and sparkling tarns – these are what most visitors come to see, and the Lake District has them in abundance. The National Park is also home to ancient woodland and wildlife that you won't see anywhere else in England.

- **Aira Force.** One of the most spectacular waterfalls in the Lake District, located in a stunning gorge, p.124
- **Great Gable.** An iconic mountain with far-ranging views from its summit, p.177

Above: Reflections of Fleetwith Pike in Buttermere

Opposite, clockwise from top left: Aira Force; Red squirrel sign on a Cumbrian country lane; Wasdale Head with Great Gable in the distance

- **Ospreys.** These magnificent birds of prey can be seen fishing in Bassenthwaite Lake during the summer, p.154
- **Easedale Tarn.** A crystal-clear mountain pool high up in the fells, p.111
- **Red squirrels.** These cute, bushy-tailed animals are increasingly confined to the northern parts of the county, p.152
- **Wasdale.** Where the lake and mountains meet to create Britain's favourite view, p.174
- **Bowder Stone.** An enormous Borrowdale boulder balanced precariously on one edge, p.148
- **Buttermere.** A beautiful lake surrounded by steep-sided, craggy mountains, p.167

Literary Lakeland

Attracted by the mountain scenery and the peaceful, laid-back atmosphere of the fell country, poets and writers have been flocking to the Lake District for years. Visitors can see the locations that inspired their writing and visit the homes where they lived and worked.

Top: Beatrix Potter's Hill Top farm

Above: Museum of Lakeland Life, Kendal

- **Wordsworth House.** The Cockermouth birthplace of the Romantic poet William Wordsworth, p.164
- **Rydal Mount.** One of the many homes occupied by the adult Wordsworth and now owned by one of his direct descendants, p.107
- **Hill Top.** Beatrix Potter's farm in Near Sawrey and the setting for several of her books, p.73
- **Watendlath.** The pretty, unspoilt setting for Hugh Walpole's 1931 novel *Judith Paris*, p.149
- **Museum of Lakeland Life, Kendal.** Home to a collection of the original sketches and manuscripts for Arthur Ransome's *Swallows and Amazons*, p.57

Cumbria's Galleries and Museums

With a fascinating history and many different cultural influences down the centuries, it is hardly surprising that Cumbria is home to some great museums and art galleries. Visitors can find out about anything from the Romans to the Arts and Crafts movement – often in some beautiful locations.

Below: Inside Tullie House Museum, Carlisle

Bottom: Abbot Hall, Kendal

- **Tullie House Museum and Art Gallery, Carlisle.** Award-winning museum with a huge range of interesting archaeological artefacts and superb galleries, p.197
- **Abbot Hall Art Gallery, Kendal.** British art from the 18th century to the modern day, housed in an elegant riverside villa, p.56
- **Senhouse Roman Museum, Maryport.** A huge number of inscribed altar stones forms part of one of the largest private archaeological collections in the country, p.190
- **Blackwell, near Windermere.** Britain's finest surviving Arts and Crafts house with a collection of work by artists including John Ruskin and Eric Gill, p.67
- **The Beacon, Whitehaven.** Award-winning visitor attraction with great interactive displays, p.185
- **High Head Sculpture Valley, Ivegill.** Life-size creations located in pretty meadows alongside the River Ive, p.121

Top Ten Picnic Spots

1. **Low Ling Crag, Crummock Water.** Enjoy spellbinding views across the lake whilst dipping your feet in the cool water, p.168

2. **Sale Fell, near Embleton.** The summit is a lovely spot for a picnic. Watch the sun set over the west coast, while its dying rays lend a pinkish glow to nearby Skiddaw, p.140

3. **Bowscale Tarn.** Tucked away in a secluded mountain basin, this is a great spot for a romantic picnic, p.158

4. **Moor Top, Grizedale Forest.** Roadside picnic benches surrounded by tall conifers, p.76

5. **Jenkyn's Crag, near Ambleside.** Views across Windermere to the sylvan countryside around Wray Castle and the craggy Coniston and Furness fells, p.98

Above: Long Meg, matriarch of one of England's largest stone circles

Below: Tarn Hows

6. **Tarn Hows.** Popular beauty spot surrounded by woodland, p.80

7. **Loughrigg Terrace.** A high-level path that provides breathtaking views across Grasmere, p.98

8. **Moss Eccles Tarn.** Beatrix Potter and her husband kept a boat on the tarn and spent many happy summer evenings here, p.73

9. **Robin Hood's Chair, Ennerdale Water.** A small headland with a few grassy ledges where you can sit almost completely hidden from the world, p.172

10. **Long Meg and Her Daughters.** Tuck into your lunch in the middle of one of England's largest and most enigmatic stone circles, p.205

Above: Wordsworth Street, Hawkshead

Below: Cartmel

Top Ten Towns and Villages

1. **Grasmere**. Great places to stay and eat, interesting cultural attractions and all surrounded by fantastic mountain scenery, p.109
2. **Hawkshead**. The quintessential Lakeland village with lots of interesting nooks and crannies, p.74
3. **Caldbeck**. A quiet conservation village with duck pond and pretty walks, p.158
4. **Cartmel**. Narrow, winding streets and a 12th-century priory, p.84
5. **Sedbergh**. Attractive old market town with lots of book shops, p.215
6. **Keswick**. Popular slate-built town at the base of mighty Skiddaw, p.139
7. **Ravenglass**. A sweet little seaside village made up of a motley collection of well-kept old cottages, p.186
8. **Troutbeck**. Fascinating buildings of all shapes and sizes half-way up the side of a lovely valley, p.64
9. **Cockermouth**. Pleasant town with hidden courtyards and colourful Georgian buildings, p.163
10. **Watendlath**. A cosy collection of cottages and farmhouses built beside a sparkling tarn high up in the fells, p.149

Itinerary 1: Lake District Highlights (One Week)

Day 1 Arrive in **Bowness-on-Windermere** and take a cruise on the lake. Stroll around the lovely fellside village of **Troutbeck**, visiting the 17th-century farmhouse of **Townend** and the church.

Day 2 Cross the lake via the vehicle ferry and visit Beatrix Potter's old farm, **Hill Top**, at Near Sawrey. Wander the narrow lanes and cobbled courtyards of delightful **Hawkshead**. Continue down to **Grizedale Forest** and hire mountain bikes for an energetic ride along specially constructed trails.

Day 3 Head north into **Langdale** via **Coniston**. Have lunch in one of **Ambleside**'s great cafés and then continue north to **Grasmere**, visiting **Rydal Mount** and **Dove Cottage** along the way.

Day 4 Return to Ambleside and then drive across **Kirkstone Pass** and down into **Patterdale**, stopping briefly in **Hartsop** for some interesting vernacular architecture. Enjoy a cruise on beautiful **Ullswater** and visit **Aira Force** and its arboretum.

Day 5 Have a day off from sight-seeing by tackling a walk in the fells above **Ullswater**. If you're feeling fit, try **Helvellyn**, but there are plenty of other interesting – and easier – routes. Drive to **Keswick**, stopping at **Castlerigg stone circle**.

Day 6 Visit some of the attractions in Keswick and then get the 74/74A bus up to **Dodd Wood** for a chance to spot the ospreys. Drive into **Borrowdale** to see the **Bowder Stone** and **Watendlath**.

Day 7 Drive the tortuous road up to **Honister Pass** and visit the slate mine. Drop down to **Buttermere** and then on to **Loweswater** to walk the Corpse Road above the Lake. Conclude your visit with **Wastwater**, Britain's favourite view.

Above: Former yeoman's cottage of Townend and gardens, Troutbeck

Below: Yachts on Windermere

Opposite: Castlerigg stone circle; Striding Edge from Helvellyn

Itinerary 2: Two Week Historical Tour of Cumbria

Day 1 Starting in **Carlisle**, visit the 12th-century castle, the award-winning **Tullie House Museum** and the red sandstone cathedral. Get the Hadrian's Wall bus out to the Roman fort at **Birdoswald**.

Day 2 Drive down through the **Eden Valley** to visit England's largest stone circle, **Long Meg and Her Daughters**. Continue to **Brougham** to see the castle and then on to nearby **Eamont Bridge** to visit **Mayburgh Henge**. Finish the day with a stroll around **Penrith**.

Day 3 Drive to **Pooley Bridge** via the **Rheged Centre** and then walk up to **Moor Divock** to see the **Cockpit stone circle**.

Day 4 Visiting **Aira Force** and its arboretum along the way, drive to **Keswick** to visit **Castlerigg stone circle** and the museums.

Day 5 Enjoy a morning walk up **Latrigg** and along the route of the old railway line. After lunch in one of Keswick's many cafés or restaurants, get the 74/74A bus to **Dodd Wood** to visit **Mirehouse**.

Day 6 Drive into **Borrowdale** to see the **Bowder Stone** and **Watendlath**, and then up to **Honister Pass** for an underground tour of the slate mine. Continue to **Buttermere**.

Day 7 Spend the morning in **Cockermouth**, including a visit to the National Trust's **Wordsworth House**. Drive out to **Maryport** to visit the **Senhouse Roman Museum** and then head down the coast to **Whitehaven**, to visit the **Rum Story** and **The Beacon**.

Day 8 Continue south to **Ravenglass**, stopping at the church in **Gosforth** where there are interesting Norse artefacts. After a stroll around the former port of Ravenglass and a visit to the Roman remains at **Walls Castle**, walk to majestic **Muncaster Castle**.

Day 9 Drive through Eskdale to the spectacularly located Roman fort at **Hardknott** via the waterfall at **Stanley Force**. Continue across the hair-raising passes of Hardknott and Wrynose to enjoy a few hours in **Ambleside** before heading to **Grasmere**.

Day 10 Walk to **Dove Cottage** and the **Wordsworth Museum and Art Gallery**. From here, continue along the old corpse road to **Rydal Mount**, another of Wordsworth's homes.

Day 11 Drive to **Coniston** and visit **Brantwood**, John Ruskin's home. Stroll around **Hawkshead**, with its many links with both Wordsworth and Beatrix Potter. Catch the bus to **Near Sawrey** to visit Beatrix Potter's farm, **Hill Top**.

Day 12 Visit the monastic remains on Cumbria's southern peninsulas. **Furness Abbey** and **Cartmel Priory** are both beautiful.

Day 13 Holker Hall, **Levens Hall** and **Sizergh Castle** are all within a short distance of each other. Choose one, or visit all three.

Day 14 Unwind in **Kendal**, visiting the galleries and museums including the **Quaker Tapestry** and the **Museum of Lakeland Life**.

Above: Topiary Garden, Levens Hall

Below: Rural scene, Langdale

CONTENTS

The Guide

Acknowledgements

The author wishes to thank the following: Brian Porter, Jean Cowgill, David Ramshaw, Richard Pratt and Mike Gardner for expert help in their various specialist fields; Julie Darroch and Nicola Hewitson at Cumbria Tourism; Liz Houseman at the National Trust; the ever friendly and helpful assistants at Cumbria's tourist information centres, especially the superb offices run by Eden District Council; the editorial staff at Cumbrian Newspapers; Terry Marsh for his guidance and encouragement; Lesley Anne Rose for her ideas and advice; Guy Hobbs for not hassling me too much; and, last but certainly not least, Heleyne for her seemingly infinite patience.

History

O2

From the moment the glaciers of the last Ice Age disappeared, man has been leaving his mark on the landscape of the Lake District, from Langdale's Neolithic 'axe factory' and the Roman forts to the castles and peel towers built to protect against the Scots, and the German copper and lead mines of the Elizabethan era. In place names too, settlers have left their calling cards – the names of the mountains, rivers and towns originated with the Celts, the Norsemen and the Anglo-Saxons. This chapter only skims the surface of Cumbria's history; the best way to understand it is to go and see what's left of it.

Warmer Climes – the Ice Sheets Disappear

Man probably first made an appearance in what is today called Cumbria towards the end of the last **Ice Age**. Palaeolithic hunters are thought to have reached the Morecambe Bay area, the edge of the great ice sheets, about 10,000 years ago.

As the ice receded, the glaciers left a barren landscape that was slowly colonized by hardy plants such as juniper, mosses and grasses. It was only by about 5,500 BC that the area's natural vegetation cover would have established itself: oak forest on the lower fells and then pine and birch woodland up to an altitude of about 2,000ft. If it hadn't been for man's intervention, that is exactly what you would see in Cumbria today – not the grassy, open fellsides that attract thousands of outdoor enthusiasts every year, but a mass of trees with just the rocky tops of the mountains poking through the woods.

It was also about this time, as the climate warmed up, that humans first began to turn their attentions to Cumbria, not just skirting the southern edge of the area as the Palaeolithic hunters did. Evidence of Mesolithic man, in the form of tiny flint chippings, has been found on the coast at Eskmeals and Walney near Barrow-in-Furness. These people would have been hunter-gatherers and, as such, would have had little noticeable impact on the environment.

The First Farmers – From Neolithic Man to the Iron Age

Up until Neolithic times, Mother Nature had been in charge of sculpting the landscape and clothing it as she saw fit, but the late **Stone Age** heralded a massive revolution as humans began to settle and farm. As well as growing crops, Neolithic man created clearings in the forest for his pigs and goats and cattle. These, in turn, chomped on the natural vegetation, restricting its growth and slowing the rate of natural regeneration, a process that has continued ever since. Solid evidence of Neolithic man in Cumbria is hard to find, but the most famous site is the Langdale axe factory (see p.103), where early quarrymen braved the steep, rugged slopes of Pike o' Stickle for the volcanic rock used in high-quality axe heads that were subsequently traded throughout the country.

The arrival of the 'Beaker' people in the Eden Valley early in the second millennium BC heralded the start of the **Bronze Age**. These were the people who left us some of the most enigmatic of prehistoric remains – stone circles such as mysterious **Castlerigg** (see p.140) and, Cumbria's largest, **Long Meg and Her Daughters** (see p.205). The henge at **Mayburgh** (see p.120) is thought to date from the early Bronze Age. But what were these stone monuments for? Were they religious sites, trading posts, calendars? We may never know for sure.

The climate was considerably warmer and calmer in the early to mid-Bronze Age, allowing man to move onto the fells. Many Bronze Age sites in Cumbria are located at about 150–300m (500–1,000ft) above sea level – cairnfields at places such as **Barnscar** near Devoke Water and **Burnmoor** above Eskdale are among the 60 or so sites that have been excavated. Today, they are lonely, moody spots that receive surprisingly few visitors.

The next group to arrive in Cumbria were the **Celts**, who crossed the Pennines from Yorkshire in about 300 BC. These Iron Age people were more sophisticated. They

The Modern County

Cumbria as we know it today was set up during the local government reorganization of 1974. Before that time, the area now covered by the modern county was made up of the historic counties of Cumberland and Westmorland as well as parts of Lancashire and Yorkshire. But that's not to say that Cumbria is a 20th-century invention. The word 'Cumbria' has its origins in the Celtic words 'Cymri' or 'Cumber', meaning the 'brothers' or 'countrymen'; and the borders of modern-day Cumbria roughly equate to those of the Celtic kingdom of Rheged (although the latter also incorporated parts of modern-day Yorkshire and Dumfries & Galloway).

introduced advanced mixed farming techniques and their Brythonic language – a predecessor of modern Welsh. Many names for the county's topographical features are Celtic in origin: 'blain' meaning summit gives rise to 'blen' as in Blencathra; and 'creic' becomes crag. The Cumbrian dialect sheep counting system, – yan, tan etc. – also comes from the Celtic language and bears striking similarities to Cornish and Breton.

At this time, the British Isles were divided amongst tribes, the Carvetti dominating most of Cumbria and the Setantii being confined to the far south of the county. They were eventually incorporated into the huge **Brigantes** tribe, which ruled most of northern England. There is some evidence of **Iron Age** settlements throughout the county, but more dramatic are the remains of the Celts' early hill forts, including the largest, on top of **Carrock Fell** near Caldbeck.

Hadrian's Wall – the Romans Arrive

The **Roman** invaders arrived in Britain in AD 43 and, at first, the Brigantes co-operated with the new rulers, living autonomously in their northern kingdom. When the Brigantes began fighting among themselves though, the Romans became increasingly involved in the affairs of this remote corner of the empire until the Celts were finally subdued in about AD 71.

The historian Professor R. G. Collingwood once said that Cumbria was 'almost at vanishing point in the scale of Romanisation'. There is plenty of evidence of Roman roads, forts and other defensive structures in the county, but this was purely a military zone and, as such, you won't find villas or markets or even Roman place names. But the military establishment was an impressive one and many of the forts survive today as do the roads that link them. One of the most dramatic of forts is at **Hardknott** (*see* p.181), high above Eskdale on the road linking the port of Ravenglass (*see* p.186) with the fort near Ambleside (*see* p.95). The road crossed the Hardknott and Wrynose passes and the modern road, with its many hairpin bends, still uses part of it (*see* p.181). Just as famous today is High Street (*see* p.119), the road crossing the high fells between Ambleside and Brougham (*see* p.120). Much of it is still used as a right of way popular with fell-walkers and cyclists.

Further north and the Romans constructed one of the most abiding images of their occupation of Britain – **Hadrian's Wall** (*see* p.201). This was built under the orders of the Emperor Hadrian after his visit to Britain in AD 122. He wanted, according to his biographer, to 'separate the Romans from the barbarians'. It ran for 73 miles (117 km) from Wallsend on the River Tyne to Bowness-on-Solway in Cumbria.

Northern Folk – the Dark Ages

Towards the end of Roman rule, Britain was pretty much ruling itself, but it wasn't until AD 410 that the conquerors finally left this far northwestern outpost of the empire to itself. So began the **Dark Ages**, a period of few historical documents and little archaeological evidence, when fact and fiction become intertwined and semi-mythological figures such as King Arthur and Urien of Rheged appear.

Even before the Romans left, the armies of the north were commanded by **Cole Hen**, who became king on their departure – probably the 'Old King Cole' of the nursery rhyme. On his death, his huge kingdom was carved into ever smaller territories by his descendants. One of these was **Urien** who ruled the kingdom of Rheged in the sixth century, a kingdom that covered much of modern-day Cumbria and may also have incorporated parts of southern Scotland, Yorkshire and north Lancashire. From his base in the Lyvennet valley (centred on the area around modern-day Crosby Ravensworth), he led other northern kings in battle against the **Anglo-Saxons** who were hammering hard on the door of the Celtic kingdoms. All that we know of this legendary figure comes from the verse of the Welsh bard Taliesin, who was appointed to Urien's court.

It was also during the Dark Ages that Christianity first came to Cumbria – brought by the saints such as Patrick, Ninian, Kentigern (*see* p.159) and, later, Cuthbert.

The power of the Celts began to decline in the early seventh century and, before long, the Anglo-Saxons held power in much of lowland Cumbria. Their influence can be seen in the intricately carved crosses at places such as **Bewcastle** and in some place names. Towns and villages ending in 'ingham' and 'ham' are Anglo-Saxon in origin. The most common is 'ton' from the Anglian word 'tun' meaning farmstead.

While the Germanic settlers farmed the valleys, the pastoralist **Vikings** began settling in the uplands of the Lake District towards the end of the ninth century. These weren't the raping, pillaging Danish raiders of modern mythology, but Norse settlers who had come from Norway via Ireland and the Isle of Man. Like the Anglo-Saxons, they too left their carved stone crosses, the most impressive of which can be seen at **Gosforth** (*see* p.174) and their place names. Ambleside, for example, is 'Hamal's saeter', or summer pasture. Look at a modern map of Norway and you will quickly discover why the Cumbrians call their hills and mountains 'fells' – 'fjell' means mountain in Norwegian. The Norse word for waterfall is 'foss', which becomes 'force' in the Lake District; 'tjorn' becomes 'tarn'; 'dalr' becomes 'dale'; and 'bekkr': 'beck'.

The last Celtic king, Dunmail, was defeated by **Edmund I** of England in AD 954, and his lands were ceded to the Scottish king **Malcolm I**, marking the start of centuries of bloody border conflict.

Scotland or Not – the Border Conflicts

Very little of Cumbria, except the far south, made it into the Domesday Book; in fact, it wasn't until 1092 that the Normans, under **William Rufus**, decided to take control of the area by building a castle at Carlisle. The son of William the Conqueror, he brought in English settlers who owed their allegiance to the Normans and divided the region up among his barons, who built castles in the Eden Valley (e.g. **Brougham**) and on the coastal plain (e.g. **Egremont**). The monasteries soon followed – the Benedictines at Wetheral some time between 1106 and 1112, Augustinians in Carlisle and Lanercost and, one of the most powerful monastic houses, the Furness Cistercians in 1127 (*see* p.88).

Meanwhile, throughout the 12th century and the early 13th century, the stronghold of Carlisle passed from Scottish to English hands and back again several times. It wasn't until 1216 that the English finally gained control and, except for a brief interlude when Bonnie Prince Charlie captured the city, it has remained in English hands ever since.

The 13th century marked a period of relative peace and prosperity. The wealth of the monastic houses grew tremendously as they acquired huge tracts of land. The monks farmed sheep, giving birth to the area's woollen trade. Packhorse routes and bridges, still in use today as part of the county's immense network of public rights of way, started appearing. The monks also knew about coppicing – for timber and for charcoal destined for the growing number of iron-smelting bloomeries – and they were keen brewers.

Sadly, the peace didn't last long; **Edward I**'s determination to impose English sovereignty on Scotland marked a resurgence in border difficulties, which continued long after his death at **Burgh by Sands** in 1307 (*see* p.193). In the early part of the 14th century, Scottish raiders, led by **Robert the Bruce**, ransacked much of the county – towns were burned, churches destroyed and villagers slaughtered. It was a truly grim century for the area, which also had to cope with famines and the Black Death. And, as if all that wasn't enough, this was also the time of the Border Reivers – the clans that carried out cross-border raids, looting and pillaging and bringing new, bleak words to the English language such as 'bereaved' and 'blackmail'. These families of the border's 'Debatable Lands' owed their allegiance to neither England nor Scotland; their loyalty was to their clan names – names that still dominate local phone books: Beattie, Armstrong, Little, Storey, Graham...

A period of great instability, the fear and insecurity engendered by these bloody times is reflected in the architecture of the era. The wealthy families built themselves stout, sturdy refuges attached to their homes. Known as peel towers, these had walls up to 10ft thick and would be inhabited by entire families – and some of their livestock – in the event of attack. There are examples of peel towers all over Cumbria. Some, such as **Kentmere Hall**, are used mostly for agricultural purposes; others, such as **Muncaster Castle**, have been incorporated into large stately homes.

Powerful families, known as the Wardens of the Marches, were installed by the English and Scottish monarchs to deal with the Reivers, but it wasn't until the border effectively ceased to exist – with the coronation of **James I** as the first joint ruler of England and Scotland in 1603 – that the people of Cumbria could begin to relax their guard.

Making the Most of Natural Resources – Early Industries

We have already seen how the rich monastic houses helped the development of trade and industry in Cumbria. Although the Dissolution of the Monasteries in the 16th century was a social disaster for Cumbria – schools were closed and poor relief abandoned – the economy didn't collapse. In fact, this was about the time that the woollen industry really began to peak, centred largely on Kendal and its surrounding towns (*see* p.55). The area had an abundance of resources that made it ideal for this cottage industry: there were the sheep, of course, and the power of the fast-flowing becks was harnessed to operate the fulling mills. In addition, lichen and broom provided colour for dyes, and bracken was used to create a soap for washing the wool.

It was also in the 16th century that the county's mining industry took off, encouraged by a national policy of fostering defence and industry. An influx of German miners, centred on the Keswick area, had a lasting impact on both the physical landscape and the social make-up of the area as they dug deep for copper, lead, silver and even gold (*see* p.142). The scars of their industry – and the subsequent mining operations, some of which lasted well into the 20th century – still litter the fellsides.

The '15 and the '45 – the Jacobites

Cumbria again became the focus of unwanted Scottish attention in the Jacobite uprisings of 1715 and 1745. In the first, the rebels bypassed Carlisle and instead proclaimed **King James III** in Brampton, Penrith, Appleby and Kendal. They got as far as Preston on this occasion.

The 1745 rebellion was an altogether more serious affair. Led by Prince Charles Edward Stuart, more commonly known today as **Bonnie Prince Charlie** or the Young Pretender, the Jacobites on this occasion seized **Carlisle Castle** before progressing as far south as Derby. It is said that the royal family had packed up the crown jewels and were preparing to flee to Germany, but the Jacobites then decided to retreat. The **Duke of Cumberland** chased them from English soil and the final skirmish of the uprising was at **Clifton** near Penrith, the last military battle on English soil (*see* p.120). The Jacobite garrison at Carlisle Castle finally surrendered on 29 December 1745 after a 10-day siege, the last siege in the castle's long history.

Winds of Change – Agriculture and Industry

Cumbria was slow to pick up on the changes that swept the rest of England during the **Agricultural Revolution** – partly because of its isolation and partly because its mountainous landscape made its circumstances very different from those in the arable south. Even the rebuilding of wooden farmhouses in stone came later than it did to the rest of the country, finally occurring in the late 17th and early 18th centuries. These sometimes quaint buildings, often in beautiful surroundings, are still dotted around the modern county and are now listed buildings, protected from development and adding to the image of the Lake District as a land caught in a time warp. Also much in evidence today are the drystone walls that started appearing from about 1750. Snaking up and down even the steepest of fellsides, these 'enclosures' were stimulated by a combination of factors. While the ever-rising and increasingly urban-based population needed more and more food, Britain's ability to import was restricted by the Napoleonic Wars of 1793–1815. With rising food prices, farmers were encouraged to reclaim wasteland and commons.

If Cumbria was a little slow to join the Agricultural Revolution, it was one of the first in line when it came to the **Industrial Revolution**. Mining for lead and copper had been thriving in the Lake District for some time, but it was the exploitation of west Cumbria's rich coal seams, particularly by the Lowther family in the **Whitehaven** area (*see* p.184), that brought a new type of prosperity to the area. In east Cumbria too, especially in the North Pennines around **Alston Moor**, lead mining provided employment for hundreds of people (*see* p.213). In the south of the county, in what was then Lancashire, **Barrow-in-Furness** had the largest steelworks in the world and was a major player in the shipbuilding industry. Meanwhile, the area's wealth of water, in the form of fast-flowing rivers and becks, allowed it to play a significant role in the textile industry – either by providing bobbins for the huge mills of Lancashire and Yorkshire, or, in the case of the Carlisle area, joining the big boys in the making of cloth.

The coming of the railways was one of the main catalysts for industrial development on such a massive scale. Cumbria's first public railway, connecting Carlisle with Newcastle, was completed in 1838, but it was in the 1840s that what we know today as the West Coast Main Line first sliced through the Lune Gorge, up and over the 914ft Shap Summit and on to Carlisle. The city promptly became one of Britain's busiest railway junctions, handling thousands of tonnes of cargo every week. But the new-fangled steam trains didn't only carry industrial goods; in 1847, despite much opposition, the railway reached Windermere, opening up the Lake District proper to mass tourism.

The Wonder of it All – Tourists Arrive

Few braved the wilds of Cumberland and Westmorland purely for the pleasure of it before the second half of the 18th century. Celia Fiennes, who undertook a horseback journey through the region in 1698, came across a miserable corner of the country:

'Here I came to villages of sad little hutts made up of drye walls, only stones piled together and the roofs of same slatt; there seemed to be little or noe tunnells for their chimneys and have no morter or plaister within or without; for the most part I tooke them at first sight for a sort of houses or barns to fodder cattle in, not thinking them to be dwelling houses, they being scattering houses here one there another, in some places there may be 20 or 30 together, and the Churches the same. It must needs be very cold dwellings but it shews something of the lazyness of the people; indeed here and there there was a house plaister'd, but there is sad entertainment, that sort of clap bread and butter and cheese and a cup of beer all one can have, they are 8 mile from a market town and their miles are tedious to go both for illness of way and length of the miles.'

The improvement of the turnpike roads in the middle of the century brought the first travellers, soon to be inspired by Father Thomas West's *A Guide to the Lakes*, published in 1778. But it was only with the opening of the railways in the 19th century that travel ceased to be the preserve of only the wealthiest in British society.

The prospect of railways and mass tourism wasn't to everyone's liking though. The Romantic poet **William Wordsworth**, who was born and lived in the county (*see* Literary Lakeland, p.28), feared the 'influx of strangers' would destroy the area's tranquillity and threaten the morals of local people. His protests, and those of other conservationists and local landowners, didn't stop the Kendal and Windermere Railway from penetrating the Lake District proper, although it didn't reach the lake itself; the line was terminated at Birthwaite, soon renamed **Windermere**, almost a mile from the lakeshore. The artist and social critic **John Ruskin**, another wealthy resident of the district, continued in that inimitably patronizing tone of the Victorian middle classes when, in the 1870s, there was an attempt to extend the railway line from Windermere to **Keswick**. Speaking of the potential tourists and fearing their moral character, he said: 'I do not wish them to see Helvellyn when they are drunk'.

But see Helvellyn they did, whether drunk or sober, and they saw it in ever-increasing numbers; numbers that continued to rise with the advent of the motor car in the 20th century and are still rising today.

Conservation – Preserving our Heritage or Creating an Anachronism?

The **National Trust**, now one of the largest conservation charities in Europe, was founded in 1895, and much of its early work was centred on the Lake District (*see* p.143). Worried about the effects of industrial and urban development on the country's heritage, the founders, Octavia Hill, Sir Robert Hunter and Canon Hardwicke Rawnsley, began setting up fundraising campaigns to purchase historic buildings, important tracts of land and even chunks of the coastline to protect them, in perpetuity, for the nation. Today, the National Trust protects about a quarter of the total area covered by the National Park.

In the early 20th century, with public demand for access to the countryside growing, groups such as the Ramblers Association, the Youth Hostels Association and the Council for the Preservation for Rural England began to urge the Government to set up National Parks.

Following the passing of the National Parks and Access to the Countryside Act 1949, the **Lake District National Park** was established on August 15, 1951. The National Park Authority is an independent body funded by central government. Its job is to 'conserve and enhance the natural beauty, wildlife and cultural heritage; and promote opportunities for the understanding and enjoyment of the special qualities of the National Park by the public'. Where there is a conflict between these two roles, the first takes priority.

With its strict planning and building regulations, the authority comes in for a lot of criticism. Some residents deplore the stifling of development and take a philosophical stand on the issues of conservation and preservation; others, although they might agree with the broad aims of the National Park, resent the interference when, for example, they want to install double glazing in their homes.

Perhaps the 19th-century writer Harriet Martineau should be allowed to have the last word on this subject:

'It is a desirable thing for every country that it should have within its borders a mountainous district... The wilder the mountain-region, the more certain it is to be the conservator of the antiquities of that country. When invaders come, the inhabitants retreat to the fastnesses where they cannot be pursued; and in places cut off from communication do ancient ideas and customs linger the longest. Every mountain-chain or cluster is a piece of the old world preserved in the midst of the new; and the value of this peculiarity far transcends that of any profitable quality which belongs to territory of another kind.'

Tourism and the Economy – the Modern Picture

With millions of people visiting the Lake District every year and other parts of the county seeing more and more visitors too, tourism plays a huge role in the economy of modern-day Cumbria. Employing around 30 per cent of the total workforce (that's about 35,000 people), it contributes almost £1.2 billion to the county's coffers every year. The value of tourism has grown by 32 per cent since 1992 (£812 million) and is forecast to grow to £1.5 billion in real terms by 2018.

Manufacturing employs 17 per cent of the county's workforce, compared with 11 per cent nationally – a surprising statistic in an area best known for its rural nature. This includes the defence industry in Barrow-in-Furness (mostly BAE Systems); food processing, largely in Carlisle; and the nuclear industry. Outside of the public sector, the latter, centred on the Sellafield reprocessing plant in west Cumbria, is the county's single biggest employer. And, with tentative plans to build nuclear power stations in the county in the not-so-distant future, the numbers involved are set to grow.

Although it employs less than 1.5 per cent of the workforce, and even that figure is declining, agriculture remains an important element of all things Cumbrian. The Borderway mart in Carlisle is one of the busiest livestock sales centres in the UK, and the county's dairy sector is one of the largest in the country. With a vast proportion of Cumbria's landmass given over to agriculture, no visitor can fail to be aware of its influence.

Topics

03

Literary Lakeland

'I wandered lonely as a cloud
That floats on high o'er vales and hills,
When all at once I saw a crowd,
A host, of golden daffodils...'

These are probably the best-known opening lines in English poetry – definitely the most famous lines ever written about the Lake District – but the area's literary heritage encompasses so much more than just William Wordsworth.

The Early Travel Writers

We have already seen how that intrepid traveller Celia Fiennes felt about the Lake District (*see* p.25). **Daniel Defoe**, the author of *Robinson Crusoe*, was even less impressed. Writing in his *A Tour Thro' the Whole Island of Great Britain* in 1724, he described the Westmorland landscape as 'the wildest, most barren and frightful of any that I have passed over in England, or even Wales itself; the west side, which borders on Cumberland, is indeed bounded by a chain of almost unpassable mountains which, in the language of the country, are called fells.' This seems a million miles away from the pastoral idyll and the awesome scenery that the Romantic writers later made famous.

It was only much later in the 18th century that writers began to look at those wild mountains and lakes in a more 'romantic' light, delighting in the human response to Mother Nature's magnificence. **Thomas Gray**, in his *Journal In The Lakes*, written in 1769, describes the view from beneath **Walla Crag** as 'the most delicious view that my eyes ever beheld'. He writes of the 'green and smiling fields embosomed in the dark cliffs', the 'turbulent chaos of mountain behind mountain, rolled in confusion' and the 'shining purity of the lake'.

The first travel guide, as such, was Thomas West's *A Guide To The Lakes*, published in 1778. This is a more practical piece of writing, intended to help would-be visitors. 'From Ambleside to Keswick,' he wrote, 'sixteen miles of excellent mountain road, furnishes much amusement to the traveller. If the season be rainy, or immediately after rain, all the possible variety of cascades, waterfalls, and cataracts, are seen in this ride; some precipitating themselves from immense heights...'

The Romantic Era

The Romantic movement of the late 18th and early 19th centuries really put the Lake District on the map with several writers and artists clearly moved by what they saw.

The most famous and influential of the Lakeland poets of this era was undoubtedly **William Wordsworth**, the only one to have actually been born in the county (*see* p.164). His *Lyrical Ballads*, written in 1798, convey to the reader his preoccupation with the powers and mysteries of the natural world, what he could see all around him in his native county, as well as his love of rural life.

It was Wordsworth who introduced his friend **Samuel Taylor Coleridge** to the area, via a walking tour starting at Temple Sowerby in the east and finishing at **Wasdale Head** in the west. Coleridge fell in love with the place and, although he wrote relatively little poetry about the Lake District, his letters and notebooks are full of impassioned descriptions of the scenery and his walks through it. His description of a climb on Scafell, in fact, is today regarded as a classic of climbing literature (*see* p.177).

Coleridge and his wife Sarah moved to the Lake District in 1800, living at first in Keswick's **Greta Hall** (*see* p.139). They were soon joined at Greta Hall by Sarah's sister, Edith, and her husband, **Robert Southey**, who was Poet Laureate from 1813 to 1843.

The influential trio – Wordsworth, Coleridge and Southey – received a host of visitors from the worlds of art and literature, thus passing on their love of the Lake District to the likes of Sir Walter Scott, Percy Bysshe Shelley, John Constable and John Keats.

Keats was clearly inspired. Following a walk along the shores of 'Winandermere' to Ambleside in 1818, he wrote, in a letter to his brother:

'What astonishes me more than anything is the tone, the colouring, the slate, the stone, the moss, the rockweed; or, if I may so say, the intellect, the countenance of such places. The space, the magnitude of mountains and waterfalls are well imagined before one sees them; but this countenance or intellectual tone must surpass every imagination and defy any remembrance. I shall learn poetry here and shall henceforth write, more than ever, for the abstract endeavour of being able to add a mite to that mass of beauty which is harvested from these grand materials, by the finest spirits, and put into ethereal existence for the relish of one's fellows.'

Writer and intellectual **Thomas De Quincey** was a friend of the Lake poets, and moved into **Dove Cottage** in Grasmere after the Wordsworths moved out. Best known for his work, *Confessions of an English Opium Eater*, first published in 1821, he said that Wordsworth's poetry consoled him during episodes of depression. His friendship with his hero was short-lived, however; the alterations he made to the garden at Dove Cottage angered Wordsworth.

Shelley too lived for a while in Cumbria. Having eloped to Scotland at the age of 19 with Harriet Westbrook, he took up residence with his new wife in **Keswick** in 1811. It was here that he wrote his first long serious work, *Queen Mab: A Philosophical Poem*, a revolutionary 'fairytale' presenting an image of a future utopian society. He didn't stay in the district long; by 1814, he had abandoned his pregnant wife and child and run away with Mary Wollstonecraft Godwin, later known as **Mary Shelley**, writer of the best-known of Gothic novels, *Frankenstein*.

The two great English landscape painters of the time, **Joseph Mallord William Turner** and **John Constable**, both spent formative stays in the Lake District. Turner's early work includes a dark and sombre view of Buttermere. Currently on display in the Turner Collection at London's Tate Britain, it was painted after a visit to Cumbria in 1797. A 30-year-old Constable spent nearly two months touring the Lake District in 1806. Although he told a friend that the solitude of the mountains oppressed his spirits, he managed to paint more than 100 scenes during the trip.

The Victorians and Beyond

The Lake District's literary tradition didn't end with the demise of Wordsworth in 1850; writers continued to be drawn to the area – as they are today. **John Ruskin**, born in London in 1819, first visited the Lake District when he was five years old. The poet-cum-artist-cum-social critic, made his home at **Brantwood** on the shores of Coniston Water in 1872 and lived there until he died in 1900 (*see* p.78). One of the great and most influential thinkers of his age, he wrote more than 250 works on subjects as diverse as art history, geology, mythology, ornithology, literary criticism and pollution. His ideas had a profound effect on the early development of the Labour Party in Britain and his many fans included

Leo Tolstoy, Marcel Proust and Mahatma Gandhi, who translated Ruskin's *Unto This Last*, a damning critique of capitalist economics, into Gujarati.

Moving, some might say, from the sublime to the ridiculous, another important Lake District literary figure is the children's book writer and illustrator **Beatrix Potter** (*see* p.73). Tourists from all over the world, particularly Japan, where Potter's books are used to teach English, flock to the National Park to join the Potter pilgrimage, visiting her home, her farms and the locations that inspired her work. Although born in London, Potter's love of the countryside stemmed from her childhood holidays in the Lakes. She eventually moved to the area and used the royalties from her books to buy farms. Although she is remembered mostly for books such as *The Tale of Peter Rabbit* and *The Tale of Mrs Tiggy-Winkle*, she spent most of her adult life as a farmer and conservationist. In particular, she became passionate about Herdwicks, the hardy sheep that graze the high fells. It is partly down to her and the efforts of her friend Canon Hardwicke Rawnsley (*see* p.143), co-founder of the National Trust, that the breed still exists today.

Another children's writer who made his home in the Lake District was **Arthur Ransome**, best known for *Swallows and Amazons*, published in 1930. The first in a series of books about childhood adventures, it tells the story of the Walker children, who have a dinghy called *Swallow*, and the Blackett youngsters, who sail *Amazon*. It is the school holidays and the Walkers are staying on a farm near a lake, while the Blacketts live on the opposite shore. The children meet on an island in the middle of the lake, and have a series of adventures. The settings used by the writer combine elements of both **Coniston Water** and **Windermere**. There is much debate among Ramsome aficionados as to whether Wildcat Island is Blake Holme on Windermere or Peel Island on Coniston Water.

Peel Island also features in **William Gershom Collingwood**'s *Thorstein of the Mere: A Saga of the Northmen in Lakeland*, first published in 1895. This was one of Ransome's favourite childhood books, and the two men later became friends. Collingwood, who moved to the Lake District after a brilliant academic career at Oxford, was a pupil of Ruskin, and became his secretary in 1881.

New Zealand-born **Hugh Walpole** wrote the *Herries Chronicle* while he was living near Derwent Water. The four novels, set in north Cumbria, tell the story of the Herries family from the 18th century to the Depression of the 1930s. Walpole lived in Cumbria from 1924 until his death in 1941. His home, **Brackenburn**, received many literary visitors including J. B. Priestley, Arthur Ransome and W .H. Auden.

The Last 60 Years

The Lake District continues to attract large numbers of writers, and it would be impossible to name them all here, but here are a few of the best known from the second half of the 20th century and the first decade of the 21st.

Apart from several years spent in a tubercolosis sanatorium as a teenager, poet **Norman Nicholson** (1914–1987) hardly ever left his home town of **Millom** in southwest Cumbria. His poems powerfully convey the passion he felt for his home county, and he often explored the relationship between man and landscape.

Although he no longer resides permanently in Cumbria, Wigton-born writer and broadcaster **Lord Melvyn Bragg** (1939–) is regarded as one of the unofficial ambassadors for the county. Many of his books are set in Cumbria, including *The Hired Man* and *The Maid of Buttermere*, based on the life of Mary Robinson (*see* p.169), and he often speaks out on local issues.

Hunter Davies (1936–) and his wife **Margaret Forster** (1938–) both went to school in Carlisle and now divide their time between London and their home at **Loweswater**. The prolific Davies is probably best known as The Beatles' biographer, but he has written dozens of other biographies, travelogues and children's books. Forster's *Georgy Girl* was made into a successful film starring Lynn Redgrave and Charlotte Rampling.

Cumbrian-born **Sarah Hall** (1974–) won the Commonwealth Writers Prize for 'best first book' in 2003 (*Haweswater*) and was short-listed for the Man Booker Prize in 2004 (*The Electric Michelangelo*). She grew up in the Haweswater area and now lives in Carlisle. As with so many local writers, Cumbria figures highly in her work, and it is this depiction of place that often wins her so much praise.

Another name to watch out for in the coming years is **Jacob Polley** (1975–). Best known as a poet, his 2009 debut novel *Talk of the Town*, set in and around his home city of Carlisle, was well received by the critics.

Natural History

Quaint villages, remote farmhouses and cultural heritage will always form a key element of any visit to the Lake District, but it is the mountains and lakes that are the essence of the area – the tourist industry's *raison d'être*, the inspiration for poets and painters, the spiritual home for so many outdoor enthusiasts.

Geology and Bedrock

Broadly speaking, the Lake District is made up of three bands of rock running roughly southwest to northeast and sitting on top of a 'raft' of low-density granite. The three bands are the Skiddaw slates, the Borrowdale volcanics and the Silurian slates of the Windermere Group.

Laid down by sedimentary processes more than 450 million years ago, the Skiddaw Slates in the north are the oldest rocks. They started life as a mush of black mud on the sea bed and were then hardened and compressed as the North American and European tectonic plates converged. The resulting landscape tends to be one of steep, smooth, rounded mountains such as those found in the Northern Fells, although there are also some more rugged areas – most visible on **Blencathra**'s southern arêtes.

The rough, angular, craggy landscape of the central fells is attributed to the Borrowdale volcanic series, made up of lava and ash that has been hardened. A volcanic episode occurred about 450 million years ago as the plate bearing the Iapetus Ocean moved under the plate on which England would one day form. Today, these rocks form the heart of the Lake District – extending from Wasdale in the west to High Street and Haweswater in the east, taking in the mighty **Scafell** and **Helvellyn** ranges along the way.

Further south, the smaller fells are made up of Silurian slates, not dissimilar to the rocks of the northern Lakes, but much younger. These slates, siltstones and sandstones were formed in the sea about 420 million years ago. Less resistant than the Borrowdale volcanics, they form a belt of foothills stretching from the Duddon estuary to Kendal.

The Lake District's underlying granite can also occasionally be seen at the surface – where it protrudes in **Eskdale** and **Ennerdale**, on **Skiddaw** and at **Shap**.

Mountain Building

About 400 million years ago, as the Iapetus Ocean finally closed, the collision of the continents created a period of mountain building known as the Caledonian Orogeny. Folding and faulting all the while, the rocks referred to above were pushed up to form a very high range of mountains. Back then, the Lake District would have looked more like today's Himalayas. Later in the Devonian period, these mighty ranges were eroded to low hills – so low, in fact, that, about 350 million years ago, they became covered by a tropical sea that was teeming with life.

As generation after generation of these sea creatures died, their shells formed a thick layer of sediment on the sea bed. This became the pale grey Carboniferous limestone that can be seen in the south and east of Cumbria – at places such as **Whitbarrow** and near **Crosby Ravensworth**. Later in the Carboniferous period, the sea became filled with mud and sand. The resulting swampy forests eventually formed the coal deposits that were once mined in the far east (e.g. **Alston Moor**) and west (e.g. **Whitehaven**) of the county.

As the tectonic plates carrying Euramerica (Laurussia) and Gondwana collided to form the supercontinent of Pangaea about 280 million years ago – and another important period of mountain-building took place – the Carboniferous rocks were lifted and folded into a broad dome.

By about this time, the section of the Earth's crust carrying what we now know as the Lake District had drifted north and crossed the equator. About 250 million years ago, it reached the latitude of today's Sahara Desert. Sand dunes (evident today in the red sandstone found in the **Eden Valley**) and salt lakes formed, and flash floods brought huge amounts of debris down from the hills (evident in the **St Bees** sandstone). These processes continued until about 190 million years ago. Slowly, but surely, the Lake District drifted ever further north until it reached the latitude it occupies today.

Glaciation

If the bedrock formed the raw material of the Lake District – the potter's clay or the sculptor's stone, so to speak – and the mountain-building periods associated with plate movement roughly moulded it into shape, it was the glaciers that put the finishing touches, that carved and sculpted the land into what we know and love today.

About 2.6 million years ago, the Earth began to cool, and glaciers formed, covering huge areas of land with massive ice sheets. People tend to refer to this, in very general terms, as the 'Ice Age', but within this 'Ice Age', there were cold periods (glacials) and warmer periods (inter-glacials) when forests thrived. There may have been as many as 11 cold phases, but it is the last one, which ended about 10,000 years ago, that had the most profound effect on the Lake District's landscape. Glaciers formed in the central part of the Lake District and produced the radial drainage pattern – like the spokes of a wheel – present today.

The glaciers gouged out deep, u-shaped valleys and created arêtes, waterfalls in hanging valleys and long, narrow lakes held back by terminal moraine – a pile of clay and stone abandoned by the retreating ice. High in the mountains, the ice plucked out corries, which are now home to bodies of water known as tarns.

Glaciation also played a key role in the limestone landscapes that we see in south and east Cumbria. The formation of limestone pavement began when thick, heavy glaciers scoured the rock and fractured it along existing horizontal lines of weakness known as bedding planes. As the ice sheets retreated, they left a layer of boulder clay on the

Landscape Terms

Arête: A narrow mountain ridge or spur formed by glaciation
Beck: Local word for a river or stream, from the Norse 'bekkr'
Corrie: A steep-walled, amphitheatre-like hollow carved out of the mountain by a glacier. Also known as a cirque, cwm or coombe
Drumlin: A small, elongated hill or ridge formed from glacial deposits
Erratics: Large boulders dragged by glaciers and then dumped miles from where they were first picked up
Fell: Local word for a hill or mountain, from the Norse 'fjall' or 'fjell'
Force: Local word for a waterfall, from the Norse 'foss'
Ghyll or **gill:** Local word for a ravine, from the Norse 'gil'
Hause: Local word for a pass or col, from the Norse 'hals'
Holm: Local word for an island, from the Norse 'holmr'
Moraine: Piles of boulders, stones and other debris deposited by a receding glacier
Scree: Loose piles of broken rock on mountain slopes
Tarn: A small body of water usually found in a corrie, from the Norse 'tjorn'

limestone, and, on top of this, soil formed. Since the end of the last glacial period, water has been exploiting the bedding planes as well as other cracks in the limestone. Over time, it has created the pattern of blocks (clints) and fissures (grikes) that we see at places such as **Great Asby** near Orton and on **Whitbarrow** today. These features became visible only after the soil on the top of the limestone platform was eroded, a process that increased with human activities such as forest clearance and grazing.

Wildlife and Habitats

Had man not cleared the forests for wood, and to make way for livestock, the Lake District mountains would today be mantled in a thick cloak of oak, birch and pine above which only the highest peaks would be visible. The valley bottoms would be impenetrable swamps dotted with alder and dense sedges. Instead, we have exposed rock slopes and expansive moor and pasture, all partitioned by drystone walls.

Patches of sessile oak remain on dry ground, while the damp still has some stands of birch and alder. There are also holly, cherry, crab apple, rowan, witch hazel, yew and occasional remnants of the huge juniper forests that once existed. Many of these produce gorgeous blossoms in the spring. There have been attempts in recent years to rid the landscape of some of the grimly regimented conifer plantations that were planted in the last century when reverence for the picturesque yielded to more pressing economic imperatives. In Ennerdale, for instance, a partnership of the National Trust, Forestry Commission and United Utilities is felling many of the sitka spruce trees planted in the 1920s in the hope that native broad-leaf trees will return (see p.173)

The fell-tops may seem to be covered in nothing more than heathers, bilberry, lichen and mosses, but there are wildflowers too – one can see wood anemone, asphodels, red campion, lady's mantle, bog myrtle, spotted orchids, stonecrop, saw-worth and thrift – and, of course, the odd daffodil. The bright blue Alpine gentian, one of Britain's rarest flowers, can be found only in Cumbria and parts of Perth and Kinross. Other examples of arctic-alpine flora such as roseroot, mountain sorrel and the dainty purple saxifrage still bloom, among other places, on the eastern slopes of **Helvellyn**.

The limestone grasslands, in particular, are a delight for amateur botanists. Hoary rockrose, wood sorrel and many rare orchids can be found on the limestone pavement. In the early summer, these areas are full of colour – not only thanks to the vast array of flora but also because of the butterflies that breed here: brimstones, dark green fritillaries, graylings and common blues as well as some of Britain's rarest species, including the high brown and pearl-bordered fritillaries.

Despite centuries of human interference, the Lake District remains relatively rich in birdlife. The fell-tops are home all year round to ravens, buzzards, peregrines and, in the eastern fells, England's last surviving golden eagle (*see* p.134). Spring migrants include the wheatear and ring ouzel (mountain blackbird). Lower down, in the spring, you'll encounter a range of migratory species, including redstart, pied flycatcher, wood warbler and tree pipit among the year-round residents such as chaffinch, green and great-spotted woodpeckers, nuthatch and sparrowhawk. On the lakes themselves, you can find good numbers of waterfowl, goosander, goldeneye and tufted duck, while rivers and streams are home to dippers, grey wagtails and common sandpipers. A pair of ospreys recently made the Lake District their summer home, returning from wintering in Africa to their nest in Dodd Wood on the shores of **Bassenthwaite Lake** every April (*see* p.154).

The Pennine moors of eastern Cumbria are home to a lot of species that have abandoned the Lake District over the years. These include curlew, red grouse, lapwing, visiting dotterel, the elusive but magnificent black grouse (*see* p.212) and the even rarer hen harrier, still one of the most persecuted birds in Britain.

Mammals of the high fells include foxes, hares and stoats. Herds of red deer can also be seen above the tree line, especially in the **Martindale** area of the eastern Lake District (*see* p.124). The autumn rut is one of the most exciting wildlife events in the fells. Its start is signalled by the deep roaring of the huge stags, which means they have abandoned the single-sex herds in which they congregate for much of the year and are now gathering their individual harems for the mating season. The deep bellow of the stag performs two functions. Firstly, females are attracted to the loudest, most frequent roar. Secondly, it forms part of the posturing used by a male to achieve dominance over other stags. Another element of this is the antler fight, during which the animals lock antlers and attempt to push each other away. The strongest secures a harem for mating. Some stags could have as many as 40 hinds in their harem.

Cumbria's woods are home to badgers, roe deer, voles, shrews, the occasional otter and, of course, red squirrels (*see* p.152). There have even been some unconfirmed sightings of pine marten in **Grizedale** and **Ennerdale** in recent years.

There are some interesting inhabitants to be found in Cumbria's lakes and becks too. The Lake District is the southern limit of the Arctic char, a slender fish that has been here since the last ice sheets disappeared; vendace, found in **Bassenthwaite Lake** and **Derwent Water,** is one of only three freshwater white fish native to Britain; and the native white-clawed crayfish, threatened with extinction, is found only in the rivers Kent and Eden.

Often overlooked by tourists, Cumbria also has a long and varied coastline. **St Bees Head**, with its large colonies of sea birds, is the only significant area of cliff (*see* p.186), but there is plenty of life to be found in the dunes, mud flats, salt marshes and other fragile habitats that can be found from **Morecambe Bay** in the south right up to the Scottish border in the north. The Solway Coast Area of Outstanding Natural Beauty (*see* p.191) is particularly fascinating – with wildflowers such as wild thyme, lady's bedstraw, restharrow, bird's-foot trefoil and harebell. You may also see curlews, oystercatchers, little terns, bartailed godwits and little plovers, some of which nest in the strandline vegetation, and, if you are extremely lucky, the natterjack toad, one of Britain's rarest amphibians.

Food and Drink

04

Cumbria's breathtakingly beautiful scenery may look like Mother Nature's proudest handiwork, but it is far from totally natural; it is the result of the ancient interplay between man and the environment – in particular, farming and the environment. It is hardly surprising then that the produce of that agricultural landscape is becoming an increasingly important part of any trip to the county, as chefs source more and more of their ingredients locally, and both farmers and artisan businesses market their delicious wares direct to the public.

Regional Produce

The county's reputation for quality food has been growing for some time now. The turning point came in 2001 with the outbreak of foot-and-mouth disease. Cumbria was one of the worst-hit regions, with thousands of head of cattle and sheep culled and the tourism industry devastated by the closure of the fells. Suddenly, the inter-relationship between farming and tourism made itself felt like never before and, as the region slowly recovered, businesses began to pull together to rebuild – and maybe even capitalize on the unprecedented publicity that the region had received during the crisis. At the same time, consumers became increasingly concerned about where their food was coming from – animal welfare, traceability, provenance and, later, food miles, started slipping off foodies' tongues just as easily as medium-rare, fine-dining and confit of duck.

Farmers, aware of the need for change, sought to develop new markets, closer to home; hoteliers and chefs could see the potential of using more locally-sourced produce; artisan bakers, jam-makers and smokehouses diversified and looked for new outlets as the tourists returned and business boomed.

Local stores, such as the Lancashire-based Booths chain of supermarkets and the family-owned Cranstons butcher shops, were suddenly stocking as much local produce as possible, proud to let the world know about The Village Bakery's tasty breads and cakes, the rich flavour of fell-bred Herdwick lamb and the delicious cheeses of the Thornby Moor Dairy. Smaller shops selling local produce also sprang up, including two farm shops at the Westmorland Services on the M6, opened by Prince Charles in 2003. An unusual development for a British motorway, the shops had 12 Cumbrian suppliers when they opened, but now receive regular deliveries from more than 40 producers.

The award-winning Plumgarths, in Kendal, is another good example of how local businesses are working together to promote the area. Run by livestock farmer John Geldard, it brings together small suppliers to help them market their produce both locally and to large supermarket chains, such as Asda.

Farmers' markets too are pushing Cumbrian produce. Kendal, Carlisle, Cockermouth and other towns host stalls where local producers can sell their wares, but probably the best known in the county is the Orton Farmers' Market (*www.ortonfarmers.co.uk*) where more than 40 businesses come together on the second Saturday of every month.

Local Specialities

You don't need to be especially observant to notice that there are a lot of sheep and cattle in Cumbria, so it won't come as a surprise to any visitor that there's plenty of meat here – and it's of a very high quality. Fell-bred lamb crops up on just about every menu you come across, but some very tasty and tender salt-marsh lamb is also produced in the county. Visitors can also expect to find good quality cuts of beef from the stocky Galloway breed, organic venison and rare-breed pork.

If it's meaty, spicy sausages you're after, they don't come any better than **Richard Woodall's Cumberland sausages** (*www.richardwoodall.com*). Using a family recipe that dates back to the 1820s, this Waberthwaite-based business is the proud holder of a royal warrant – bangers made by appointment to HM Queen Elizabeth II. Other top sausage producers include **Lakes Speciality Foods Ltd** of Staveley (*www.lakesspecialityfoods.co.uk*), **Cranstons** of Penrith (*www.cranstons.net*) and **Peter Gott** at Sillfield Farm, near Kendal (*www.sillfield.co.uk*).

As well as being a major meat producer, Cumbria has one of the UK's largest dairy farming sectors – and that means there's a lot of cheese being produced in the county. Some of the top producers include the award-winning **Lake District Cheese Company** (*www.lakedistrictcheesecompany.co.uk*), run by a farmer-owned co-operative; the **Thornby Moor Dairy** at Crofton Hall near Wigton; **Wardhall Dairy** (*www.wardhalldairy.co.uk*), which makes both goats' and cows' cheese; and **Holker Farm** with its delicious ewe's milk cheese.

And if you're wondering who ate all the pies, it was probably the customers of the Hodge family, who run the Threlkeld-based **Piemill** (*www.piemill.co.uk*). When the family began selling home-made pies at their pub in Mungrisdale, demand was so high that they had to move into larger premises. With business booming, they eventually sold the pub to concentrate on the pies. Award-winners include the Blencathra beef steak and ale pie and the gorgeous Galloway beef, black pudding and caramelized mushroom pie.

The Lyth Valley is damson country. The orchards and hedgerows surrounding the valley's many small farmsteads are where you'll find the unusually small Westmorland damson, which is sold from roadside stalls and in local shops in September. It is also used to make jams and chutneys. **Strawberry Bank Liqueurs**, of Crosthwaite, near Kendal, uses the local fruit to make the rather unusual damson gin and beer (*www.strawberrybank liqueurs.co.uk*). Damson Day is celebrated every April, when the valley is filled with the fruit's white blossom.

Many people forget that Cumbria also has access to the fruits of the sea – from Morecambe Bay in the south to the Solway Firth in the north. The **Morecambe Bay Potted Shrimp Company** (*www.morecambebayshrimps.com*) uses shrimps caught by fishermen going out on to the Cartmel Sands from Flookburgh and Bardsea, boils them in butter with a secret combination of spices and then packs them into pots with semi-melted butter. The delicate-tasting end result can be found in Booths supermarkets and in other stores under the brand name Marine Gourmet.

The award-winning **Hawkshead Relish Company** (*www.hawksheadrelish.com*) is one of the success stories to come out of the disaster that was the 2001 foot-and-mouth outbreak. Mark and Maria Whitehead were selling their home-made preserves in their busy café, but when disease descended, the day-trippers disappeared. Forced to diversify, the couple began to make more of their tasty chutneys and now their products can be found in shops all over the country, including Harrods. Other chutney and preserve producers worthy of note include **Staveley's Friendly Food and Drink** (*www.friendlyfood anddrink.co.uk*), which won several awards in the 2009 NW Food Awards, and the Wigton-based **Wild and Fruitful** (*www.wildandfruitful.co.uk*). The **World's Original Marmalade Festival** (*www.marmaladefestival.com*), where you can sample some wonderful preserves, is held every February at Dalemain. For those who collect celebrity autographs, Paddington Bear sometimes puts in an appearance.

For the sweet-toothed, Cumbria is seventh heaven. Not only is it the home of Kendal mint-cake, famously taken up Everest by Chris Bonington in 1975, and the supposed birthplace of that most mouth-watering of desserts, the sticky toffee pudding (*see* p.91), but it is also where you will find the world's best gingerbread (*see* p.109), the most sumptuous fudge – at the 100-year-old **Toffee Shop** in Penrith (*www.thetoffeeshop.co.uk*) – and a range of lovely cakes and teabreads. With rum and sugar once imported in large quantities through the port at Whitehaven, the county is also the place from where rum butter is said to have originated in the 18th century. Another by-product of the trade with the West Indies was Cumberland rum nicky, a rich and sticky pie made with ginger, brown sugar, dates and rum.

While we're on the subject of alcohol, we mustn't forget that Cumbria has a blossoming micro brewery scene. At last count, there were 23 producers of cask-conditioned beer. These range from the highly successful **Hawkshead Brewery** (*www.hawksheadbrewery.co.uk*), which recently moved into £500,000, purpose-built premises in Staveley, to the tiny **Great Gable Brewing Company** (*www.greatgable brewing.com*), which sells almost all its ales in the adjoining Wasdale Head Inn.

Eating Out

Cumbria's hotels, restaurants, pubs and cafés are among the best in the country. At the time of writing, there were three Michelin-starred restaurants – **L'Enclume** in Cartmel, the **Sharrow Bay** on Ullswater and **Holbeck Ghyll Country House Hotel**, near Ambleside – and a host of eateries sporting two or three AA rosettes (the only restaurant with four AA rosettes was Simon Rogan's L'Enclume). Many of these venues specialize in using local ingredients, but that doesn't mean you'll find nothing but Cumberland sausage and fell-bred rack of lamb on the menu (although they're likely to be superb when you do); you're just as likely to come across terrine of pheasant, partridge and grouse with toasted brioche and Cumberland sauce, or pan-fried duck breast and stir-fried vegetables topped with plum and thyme ice-cream.

The county's pubs, in particular, have experienced something of a revolution in recent years, shedding the traditional pie-and-pint image and donning much more sophisticated garb. The most renowned of the local 'gastropubs' include **The Drunken Duck** near Hawkshead, **The Wheatsheaf** at Brigsteer, **The Gate Inn** at Yanwath, the **Brown Horse** at Winster and the rather upmarket **Punch Bowl** at Crosthwaite, which won the coveted title of Michelin Pub of the Year in 2009.

If you're looking for something quick and simple to eat in the middle of the day and you want somewhere a little less formal than a restaurant or a 'posh pub', there are dozens of good cafés and tearooms from which to choose. To name them all would be impossible, but some of the most popular include **Wilf's Café** in Staveley, **Lucy's On a Plate** in Ambleside, **Siskins Café** in the Whinlatter Forest Park, the **Greenhouse** at Melkinthorpe near Penrith and **Hazelmere Café** in Grange-over-Sands, a past winner of the Tea Guild's Top Tea Place award.

Planning Your Trip

05

When to Go

Climate

If you thought the English climate was fickle, just wait until you get to Cumbria. The unpredictability of the UK's maritime climate is accentuated in the west, which bears the brunt of just about anything that's coming in from the Atlantic. Combine that with the presence of mountains, and you've got a recipe for something 'interesting'.

Yes, Cumbria is wet – Seathwaite in Borrowdale is the wettest inhabited place in England – but it is also part of a windy, fast-moving scenario, which means that the rain doesn't normally hang around for long. If you spend a week in the Lake District, you'd be unlucky if you had more than one day of constant rainfall; more likely, you'll get a few days of sunshine and showers and maybe one or two days of brilliant blue skies. And that applies whatever the time of year. Of course there are some months that tend to be drier than others – early spring and late autumn often hold some pleasant surprises – but don't expect August to be drier than November; it just doesn't work like that in Cumbria.

The wonderful thing about the Cumbrian climate is that the sky and the quality of the light are ever-changing entities. You can stand on a fell-top and see curtains of showers coming in from the west; look to the north and Skiddaw will be bathed in sunshine under a cloudless sky; turn round and there are bruised purple storm clouds gathering over the Pennines. It's never boring.

As far as temperatures go, Cumbria tends to be cooler than the south of England, but the warming effect of the Gulf Stream keeps the mercury above the levels experienced on the eastern side of the Pennines.

Cumbria receives regular snowfall, particularly in January and February. This tends to be confined to the high fells, but road passes such as Kirkstone, Wrynose and Hardknott can become blocked. The east of the county, particularly the Pennines, gets the most snow, and it isn't unknown for the top of Helvellyn to be covered from December until April.

The weather is an important consideration for people intending to head out on to the high fells, so outdoor enthusiasts are advised to get an accurate, mountain-specific weather forecast before setting out and ensure they are prepared for all eventualities (*see* p.50).

Holidays and Festivals

School holidays tend to be the busiest time of the year in Cumbria, particularly Easter, summer and Christmas. Accommodation fills up fast in the honeypots of Keswick, Grasmere, Ambleside and Hawkshead at these times, especially on the Bank Holiday weekends. Many of the more popular hotels and guest-houses take Christmas, New Year and August bookings up to 18 months in advance.

As soon as the children go back to school, the Lake District prepares for an influx of older families and retired visitors keen to see the region in its glorious autumn colours. September and October are, in fact, fast becoming just as busy as the main school holidays.

Having said all that, there is no 'off season' as such in the National Park. A few attractions and tourist information centres may close or run a reduced service during January and February – a few may even start winding down at the beginning of November – but in the main towns and the central Lakes, it's business as usual all year round.

Festivals and shows reach a crescendo of activity from July until the end of September. A list of some of the main events is given below, but this is far from comprehensive.

January to April

Keswick Film Festival, (Feb, *see* p.146); **The World's Original Marmalade Festival** at Dalemain, near Pooley Bridge (Feb, *see* p.123); **Words by the Water Festival,** Keswick – workshops, book launches and lectures (March, *see* p.146); **International Music Festival,** Ulverston (Apr, *see* p.90) and **Damson Day,** Lyth Valley (Apr, *see* p.59).

May

Keswick Jazz Festival (*see* p.146); **The Cumberland Ale Keswick Mountain Festival** – outdoor activities and lectures (*see* p.146); **Doodleshire May Fair,** Kendal (*see* p.60).

June

Dent Folk Festival, near Sedbergh – music, dance, workshops, guided walks, story-telling and street theatre (*see* p.217); **Keswick Beer Festival** (*see* p.146); **Whitehaven Maritime Festival** – every two years.

July

Brampton Live – folk music (*see* p.202); **Maryport Blues Festival** (*see* p.194); **rush-bearing ceremony** at St Mary the Virgin Church, Ambleside (*see* p.98); **Ambleside**

Sports, Rydal Park (see p.99); **Cumberland Show**, Carlisle Racecourse, Carlisle – agricultural show (see p.202); **Appleby Horse Fair** – huge gathering of travellers (see p.210); **Coniston Water Festival** – canoe racing, special cruises, sailing lessons for beginners and more fun on the lake (see p.80); **Cumbria Steam Gathering**, Flookburgh – show of traction engines and vintage vehicles (see p.86); **Potfest in the Park**, Hutton-in-the-Forest, near Penrith – pottery exhibition (see p.121).

August

Potfest in the Pens, Penrith – oldest potters' market in the UK (see p.121); **rush-bearing ceremony** at St Oswald's Church, Grasmere (see p.113); **Grasmere Sports and Show** (see p.109); **Rydal Sheepdog Trials and Hound Show** (see p.107); **Kendal Calling** – music festival (see p.60); **Mintfest**, Kendal - international street art (see p.60); **Solfest**, near Silloth – music festival (see p.194).

September

Ullswater Outdoor Festival – guided walks, kayaking, sailing, mountain-biking and climbing (see p.131); **Coniston Walking Festival** (see p.80); **Sedbergh's festival of 'books and drama'** (see p.215); **Borrowdale Shepherds' Meet and Show**; **Loweswater Show** (see p.170); **Eskdale Show**; **Egremont Crab Fair**, including The World Gurning Championships (see p.173); **Lantern Festival**, Ulverston (see p.90).

October to December

Wasdale Head Shepherds' Meet and Show (Oct); **Kendal Festival of Food** (Oct, see p.60); **Kendal Mountain Festival** – lectures, films and books, including the announcement of the winner of the Boardman-Tasker Prize (Nov, see p.60); **Dickensian Christmas Festival**, Ulverston (see p.90); **Victorian Christmas Fayre**, Keswick (Dec, see p.146).

Tourist Information

Tourist information centres, often staffed by knowledgeable, enthusiastic assistants, are a superb resource. They provide up-to-date information on places to visit, events, where to stay and eat, and local transport. They also sell maps, guides and entertainment tickets, and can book your accommodation on arrival or in advance. They are located in the main towns and some of the more popular villages. National Park information centres give specific advice on walking and other outdoor pursuits.

The official website of Cumbria Tourism can be viewed at www.golakes.co.uk. It includes information on accommodation and attractions, interactive maps and a few suggestions for walks and bike rides. (For other useful websites, see **Practical A–Z**, p.52.)

Embassies and Consulates

Australian High Commission, Australia House, Strand, London WC2B 4LA, t (020) 7379 4334, www.australia.org.uk

Canadian High Commission, 1 Grosvenor Square, London W1K 4AA, t (020) 7258 6600, www.canada.org.uk

Republic of Ireland Embassy, 17 Grosvenor Place, London SW1X 7HR, t (020) 7245 9033

New Zealand High Commission, New Zealand House, Haymarket, London SW1Y 4TQ, t (020) 7930 8422, www.nzembassy.com

US Embassy, 24 Grosvenor Square, London W1A 1AE, t (020) 7499 9000, www.usembassy.org.uk

UK Entry Formalities

Passports and Visas

Citizens of the EU need passports or identity cards, but not a visa. They can still expect to breeze through immigration in a separate queue though. Citizens of the USA, Canada, Australia and NZ must have a valid passport, but don't need visas. Other nationalities may need visas; check with your nearest travel agent or British embassy.

Customs

Coming into the UK from another EU country, you won't have to pay tax or duty on any quantity of tobacco or alcohol if it is for your own consumption but you are likely to face questions if you have more than: 3,200 cigarettes, 200 cigars, 400 cigarillos, 3kg tobacco, 110 litres of beer, 90 litres of wine, 10 litres of spirits or 20 litres of fortified wine.

The restrictions are tighter if you are arriving from outside the EU: 200 cigarettes or 100 cigarillos or 50 cigars or 250g of tobacco; 4 litres of still wine; 16 litres of beer; 1 litre of spirits or strong liqueurs or 2 litres of fortified wine; and £340 worth of other goods including perfume and souvenirs.

VAT Refunds

Value Added Tax (VAT) is included in the price of most things you buy in the UK. You can claim this back if you are travelling from outside the European Community and leave the UK within three months of your purchase. Unfortunately, not all retailers are part of the VAT Retail Export Scheme, so you need to check before you buy anything. If they are part of the scheme, you will need to complete a tax refund document from the retailer and present it to Customs at the air/ferry port on your departure. Do it before checking in your suitcases, because you need all the goods and receipts for inspection.

Disabled Travellers

Thanks to recent legislation and changing attitudes, travellers with disabilities are better catered for nowadays, but difficulties do still arise because of the age of Cumbria's tourism infrastructure, including hotels, attractions and transport. Modern developments are legally required to provide wheelchair access, and many older hotels and attractions are making concerted efforts to make life easier for disabled visitors, but some buildings – centuries-old coaching inns, for example – simply cannot be converted. For help and advice contact **RADAR** (*www.radar.org.uk*), which is a mine of information. It publishes an annual guide, *Holidays in Britain & Ireland – A Guide for Disabled People*, with advice on transport and accommodation. The websites *www.disabledtraveladvice.co.uk* and *www.tourismforall.org.uk* also contain useful advice, and decent directories of wheelchair-accessible accommodation in Cumbria can be found on *www.lakedistrict-stay.co.uk* and *www.iknow-lakedistrict.co.uk*.

The Lake District National Park Authority has published a set of 39 route cards, complete with a handy, see-through, waterproof holder, that provides details of easy-access paths suitable for people with limited mobility. These routes are the result of rangers replacing stiles, kissing-gates and other barriers with wide, easy-to-open gates. There is now even a wheelchair route right to the 1,204ft top of Latrigg, near Keswick. *Miles Without Stiles* is available across Cumbria, priced £6.99.

Health, Insurance and EHIC Cards

If you injure yourself, you will be seen for free in a hospital Accident and Emergency department, but prepare for a long wait. If it's not urgent, ask your hotel about finding a doctor.

European nationals are eligible for free medical treatment upon presentation of a European Health Insurance Card (EHIC), and Australians and New Zealanders may also benefit from reciprocal arrangements. To find out more, go to *www.dh.gov.uk*.

All travellers are advised to take out travel insurance. Keep two copies of your policy in separate places, in case your luggage disappears, and hang on to any receipts.

Money and Costs

Currency

While much of Europe now uses the euro, Britain's currency remains the pound (sterling).

There are 100 pennies to one pound. Coins come in 1, 2, 5, 10, 20 and 50 pence pieces, and £1 and £2 pieces. Notes are divided into £50, £20, £10 and £5 denominations. A pint of milk will cost you about 50p, a pint of beer about £2.70, an off-peak return train ticket from London to Carlisle about £92. At the time of writing, one dollar will buy you 61p and one euro will buy you 88p; put the other way around, one pound is worth about 1.63 dollars and 1.14 euros, but, of course, foreign exchange rates fluctuate wildly. Shop around: the worst rates tend to be at hotels, followed by bureaux de change in tourist areas. Banks and the Post Offices usually offer a slightly better rate. Always check the commission fee.

Cash and Credit Cards

If you are travelling from abroad, bring enough cash to get you to your first stop. Traveller's cheques remain the most secure means of carrying money around, but you will need to get to a bank to cash them. You can use credit and debit cards almost everywhere. ATMs abound in airports, towns and cities. Even some shops in small Lakeland villages now have cash machines, but these are only available during opening hours. If you are paying with a debit card, some supermarkets now offer a 'cash-back' service at the checkout.

Visa and MasterCard are widely accepted in hotels, restaurants and shops throughout Cumbria; American Express and Diners Club slightly less so.

Banks

Opening hours are usually Mon–Fri 9am–4.30pm, although larger banks may stay open until 5pm and small-town banks may close at 3.30pm. Some banks open on Saturday mornings.

Tipping

Diners usually tip about 10 percent of the price of the meal in a restaurant where there is table service, 15 per cent if your waiter or waitress has been especially attentive. Taxi drivers, porters, hairdressers and tour guides might expect a little something, but don't feel obliged if they have given you poor service.

Getting There

By Air

Cumbria does not have an international airport, although, over the years, there has been much talk of developing Carlisle Airport. Plans come and go, as do developers, so don't hold your breath. The nearest airports with a range of international and domestic arrivals and departures are at Newcastle, Glasgow, Edinburgh, Manchester and Liverpool.

By Train

If you are travelling to England from mainland Europe, the Eurostar trains run from Paris, Lille and Brussels through the Channel Tunnel to Ebbsfleet and Ashford international stations in Kent and to London St Pancras. The journey time from Paris to London can be as little as two hours and 15 minutes.

Eurostar: t 08705 186 186, *www.eurostar com.*

The reasonably fast West Coast Main Line, run by Virgin Trains, then links London (Euston) with Oxenholme, Penrith and Carlisle in Cumbria, before continuing on to Glasgow and Edinburgh. The journey time to Carlisle from London is about three hours and 30 minutes; one hour and 15 minutes from Glasgow; or one hour and 20 minutes from Edinburgh. If you're heading for the southern Lakes, it is best to get off at Oxenholme and then use the branch line to Windermere. Trains run approximately every hour and the journey takes 20 minutes. Penrith or Carlisle are the best stops for towns and villages in the north of the Lake District.

Much slower lines provide links between Carlisle and Newcastle (roughly every hour; journey time: one hour and 25 minutes) and between Carlisle and Leeds (about six trains a day; journey time: two hours and 45 minutes).

By Ferry

The main ports for ferry services from mainland Europe to England are Dover (Calais and Boulogne), Newhaven (Dieppe), Portsmouth (Bilbao, Cherbourg, Caen), Plymouth (Santander), Hull (Zeebrügge and Rotterdam), Harwich (Hook of Holland and Esbjerg) and Newcastle (Amsterdam). From Ireland you can come into Fishguard, Pembroke or Holyhead in Wales, or Liverpool; alternatively, travel to Northern Ireland and get the ferry to Stranraer or Cairnryan in Dumfries & Galloway, a two-hour road journey from north Cumbria.

By Coach

National Express (*www.nationalexpress.com*) operates a number of services between London and Cumbria. The daily 570 from London and Birmingham to Whitehaven calls at Kendal, Windermere, Ambleside, Grasmere, Keswick and Cockermouth. The total journey time is nine-and-a-half hours. The 590, another daily service, takes about seven hours to reach Carlisle from London, stopping along the way at Penrith. There are also at least six coaches (service 334) every day linking Carlisle with Glasgow (journey time: two hours), Manchester (four hours) and Birmingham International Airport (seven hours).

Arriva and Stagecoach jointly operate an hourly service (the 685) between Newcastle and Carlisle (journey time: two hours, 10 mins).

Getting Around

By Train

The West Coast Main Line runs up the eastern side of the county, covering Oxenholme, Penrith and Carlisle, although not all the trains stop at all these stations. The branch line from Oxenholme to Windermere (journey time: 20 minutes) also stops in Kendal, Burneside and Staveley.

The Eden Valley is well served by trains shunting backwards and forwards between Carlisle and Leeds using the scenic Carlisle-to-Settle railway line. Services stop at Armathwaite, Lazonby, Langwathby, Appleby, Kirkby Stephen, Garsdale and Dent. Even if you don't get off anywhere en route and you have no great desire to see either Carlisle or Settle, it is worth making the journey just for the lovely countryside that you'll see through the train window (*see* p.198)

The Cumbria Coast and Furness lines link Carlisle in the north of the county with Barrow-in-Furness in the south before going on to Lancaster. Other stations served include Arnside, Grange-over-Sands, Cark, Ulverston, Dalton, Barrow-in-Furness, Millom, Ravenglass, Seascale, St Bees, Whitehaven, Workington, Maryport, Aspatria and Wigton.

The county is also home to three narrow-gauge railways – the Lakeside and Haverthwaite Railway (see p.72), the Ravenglass and Eskdale Railway or La'al Ratty (see p.183) and the South Tynedale Railway (see p.212).

By Bus

The county's internal bus network has improved dramatically in recent years, but there are still some valleys that are not served by public transport and others that see their bus links with the outside world totally severed during the winter. Summer visitors to the Lake District should have little problem reaching the main attractions.

Information about area-specific services is included in each of the regional chapters, but one of the most popular buses is the 554/555/556 Lakeslink, providing a regular service between Carlisle and Lancaster via Keswick, Grasmere, Ambleside, Windermere and Kendal. This is particularly useful for walkers intent on doing any of the ridge routes accessed from the A591. Other tourist-friendly routes, most of which operate only during the summer, are the Osprey Bus (74) from Keswick to Whinlatter, Bassenthwaite and Dodd Wood; the Honister Rambler (77/77A) serving Keswick, Borrowdale, Buttermere and Whinlatter; the Borrowdale Rambler (78) from Keswick to Seatoller; the Coniston Rambler (505), which takes in Kendal, Windermere, Ambleside, Hawkshead and Coniston; the Langdale Rambler (516) from Ambleside to the Old Dungeon Ghyll Hotel; and the Kirkstone Rambler (517) from Bowness to Glenridding via Troutbeck and Kirkstone Pass. The Cross Lakes Experience links Bowness, Hawkshead, Grizedale Forest and Coniston via a series of carefully coordinated buses and boats.

Cumbria County Council and Stagecoach jointly publish a free booklet detailing most of the key services, but sadly there is no longer a comprehensive timetable covering the whole of Cumbria. This was abolished during budget cuts a few years ago. There are also several free leaflets providing visitors with a detailed description of what they can see and do along some of the most popular bus routes. These From A to B to See guides are available from bus stations and tourist information centres.

If you're going to be using a lot of buses, it might be worth buying an Explorer ticket. This gives you unlimited travel on Stagecoach buses throughout Lancashire and Cumbria. At the time of writing, a daily Explorer cost £9.75 for adults, £6.50 for children, £5.90 for elderly or disabled passengers and £19.50 for a group. Four-day and weekly Explorers are also available. Tickets can be purchased from drivers.

For more information on public transport: t 0871 200 2233; www.traveline.info .

By Boat

The largest of the lakes – Coniston Water, Derwent Water, Ullswater and Windermere – have boat services which can be used simply as a relaxing way of seeing the National Park from the water or as a way of getting from A to B. More information on these services is given in the relevant regional chapters.

In addition, there is one vehicle ferry across Windermere – from Ferry Nab near Bowness to Ferry House at Far Sawrey. This runs approximately every 20 minutes.

By Car

There have been concerted efforts in recent years to discourage visitors from bringing their cars to the National Park, but it seems to remain the preferred method of travel. If you are going to drive, remember that many of the county's roads are winding and narrow; a few, most notably Hardknott Pass, are also exceptionally steep. Be especially careful in the winter as few minor roads are gritted. Traffic jams can be a problem – and not just in the towns; long lines of traffic often build up in the most popular valleys at Bank Holiday weekends. Parking is a nuisance too – not only is it horrendously expensive (expect to pay up to £8 to park all day), but some car parks will fill up very early in the day.

The Lake District National Park Authority is rolling out a park-by-phone scheme at its 16 pay-and-display car parks. Once users have registered, they can enter their location and length of time they need via their mobile phone. And, if you find you are at the top of Coniston Old Man, or out shopping, and you need a bit more time, you simply call the number again to extend the limit.

On-street parking in towns and villages is often limited to one or two hours. Drivers have to display their arrival time on a disc that is placed on the car dashboard. The discs are free and can be picked up at most shops.

If you are coming from abroad note that the British drive on the left-hand side of the road, and speed limits are in miles per hour: generally 30mph in built-up areas; 60mph on main roads; 70mph on motorways. Familiarize yourself with the British Highway Code (available in newsagents) and take note of the strict drink-drive laws and the total ban on using hand-held mobile phones. If you are stopped by the police, you can be asked to present your driving papers at a police station within five days.

By Bike

Arm yourself with an Ordnance Survey (OS) map and a puncture repair kit and head out on to the county's network of bridleways, disused railway lines, forest tracks and country lanes.

Travelling with a bike can be a problem if you do not have a car as well. There are only a few bus routes in Cumbria on which bikes can be carried. The Cross Lakes Experience can take up to five bikes between Bowness and Grizedale and between Hawkshead and Coniston, call t (015394) 44451 or (01229) 860369 for more information. The 505 Windermere to Coniston service has room for two bikes, but you are advised to book in advance – and bikes can be loaded/unloaded only at a few major stops. The AD122 Hadrian's Wall Bus can also take two bikes. Bikes travel free of charge on all these services.

As far as taking your bike on the trains goes, it is always best to check with the rail company before setting out. There is always a limit on the number of bikes that can be carried, and reservations will be needed for some services.

Where to Stay

Cumbrians have been welcoming visitors for centuries, so the hospitality industry has it down to a fine art these days. The hotels, guesthouses and many other accommodation options are not simply a place to rest your head after a day of sightseeing or fell-walking; they are part of the Cumbrian experience, something to be savoured almost as much as the lakes and mountains.

Of those approved by Visit Britain, standards range from functional – 'here's your key, break-fast's at 8' – to gorgeous and/or luxurious. Visit Britain, in common with the AA and RAC, uses a one to five rating scheme and gives gold and silver awards to anywhere outstanding. The rating system works well for hotels, hostels, camping and caravan sites, but less well for guesthouses and B&Bs because it rewards facilities to the detriment of charm. This is one of the reasons why not all properties put themselves up for inspection.

Each section of this book lists places to stay. They all offer something special: a warm

Accommodation Price Categories

Luxury: more than £200
Expensive: £120-£200
Moderate: £55-£120
Budget: less than £55

welcome, interesting architecture, character, proximity to tourist attractions or value for money. Anonymous chain hotels and grim B&Bs have been avoided. Friendly is the first prerequisite for this book.

Booking

The Lake District's popularity is increasing year on year, so the better accommodation providers fill up their reservation books early. Always book in advance to avoid hassle or disappointment. If you exhaust the lists in this book, contact the tourist information centres, who will give you another clutch of phone numbers and often make a reservation for you for a small fee. Most accommodation providers now have their own website.

Prices

Prices in this book have been divided into five categories, from budget to luxury (see box).

These prices are for a full-price double room with bathroom, where there is one. If you think that things such as accommodation and eating out get cheaper the further north you go, banish this idea from your head immediately – it just doesn't apply in the Lake District. Prices here may not be as high as they are in London and the southeast, but they are on a par with many other parts of southern England. However, many hotels do midweek deals outside of the peak periods or will give discounts if you book multiple nights. Few places fall into the 'budget' bracket, but where they do, visitors can expect simple but clean and friendly accommodation.

Hotels and Inns

There are some fabulous hotels in the Lake District – almost all of them in charming old buildings with plenty of character. Castles, stately homes, 17th-century coaching inns with exposed beams and open fireplaces, rambling Victorian houses and mock-Gothic mansions. Renovation and refurbishment seem to have been the buzz words over the past few years so, although the building may be old, the facilities and furnishings won't be.

Guesthouses and B&Bs

Top-end guesthouses are often at least as good, if not better, than some of the cheaper hotels. Owners have really got their act together in recent years. Most rooms are en suite and, where they're not, private bathrooms are provided.

The main Lake District towns are full of large Victorian terraces and Edwardian town houses that often offer a surprisingly high standard of accommodation. Beyond the towns, take your pick from friendly working farmhouses with hearty breakfasts, country homes whose warm, welcoming owners have done up a couple of bedrooms for guests, and rambling houses with quirky, individual rooms.

Self-catering Accommodation

It is beyond the scope of this book to look in detail at the many houses, cottages, converted barns and wooden cabins that are available to rent, but it is a good option if you want the luxury of space and don't want to have to get up early for breakfast. They also give you a chance to enjoy the slower-paced domestic side of places: eating locally reared lamb or cooking vegetables from the farmers' market, putting together picnics, reading the odd selection of books on the shelves and playing board games into the night.

Budget Accommodation

Hostels and campsites are only mentioned where they offer something exceptional, such as yurts or a particularly remote location, as in the case of Skiddaw House. Having said that, the YHA runs quite a few hostels in the Lake District, some of which have undergone major redevelopment in the last few years. Many, like the Ambleside hostel, are in stunning spots. There are also several independent hostels.

If you're planning to camp, choose your site carefully. While there are many superb private sites all over Cumbria – quiet, friendly, with spotless facilities and dry, level pitches – there are also some horribly noisy, crowded sites. A good website, where fellow campers can post their reviews, is *www.ukcampsite.co.uk*.

The National Trust (*www.ntlakescampsites. org.uk*) runs three campsites, all of which are well run and in magnificent locations – Low Wray beside Windermere, Great Langdale and Wasdale. The Camping and Caravanning Club (*www.campingandcaravanningclub.co.uk*) sites also tend to be good. Several of them, including Eskdale, now have 'pods' –secure and

Cottage Rental Companies

Cottage Holidays, Drefach Felindre, Llandysul, Carmarthenshire SA44 5HW, **t** 0845 123 2782, *www.cottageholidays.co.uk*. Around 30 cottages in Cumbria, many in small Lakeland villages.

Cumbrian Cottages, Atlantic House, Fletcher Way, Parkhouse, Carlisle CA3 0LJ, **t** (01228) 599960, *www.cumbrian-cottages.co.uk*. One of the biggest local holiday cottage companies; more than 600 properties.

Heart of the Lakes, Fisherbeck Mill, Old Lake Rd, Ambleside, Cumbria LA22 0DH, **t** (015394) 32321, *www.heartofthelakes.co.uk*. More than 300 quality cottages, apartments and houses within the National Park.

Lakeland Cottage Company, Woodside, Charney Rd, Grange-over-Sands, Cumbria LA11 6BP, **t** (015395) 38180, *www.lakeland-cottage-company.co.uk*. Sixty properties, mostly in the southern part of the county.

Lakelovers, Belmont House, Lake Rd, Bowness-on-Windermere, Cumbria LA23 3BJ, **t** (015394) 88855, *www.lakelovers.co.uk*. More than 400 properties throughout the southern and central Lake District

Lakes Breaks, Cumbria and Lakeland Self Catering Association, Milburn Grange, Knock, Appleby-in-Westmorland Cumbria CA16 6DR, **t** (017683) 61867, *www.lakesbreaks.co.uk*. A collection of more than 100 well-equipped holiday cottages, apartments and log cabins.

National Trust, Holiday Cottage Booking Office, PO Box 536, Melksham, Wiltshire SN12 8SX, **t** 0844 800 2072, *www.nationaltrustcottages. co.uk*. The National Trust has about 20 holiday cottages in the Lake District, most of which are period properties with lots of character.

Rural Retreats, Retreat House, Draycott Business Park, Draycott, Moreton-in-Marsh, Gloucestershire GL56 9JY, **t** (01386) 701177, *www.ruralretreats.co.uk*. A national company with a good selection of cottages ranging from small, isolated properties to country houses.

Welcome Cottages, Spring Mill, Earby, Barnoldswick, Lancashire BB94 0AA, **t** 0845 268 0819, *www.welcomecottages.com*. One of the leading national companies, with more than 300 cottages in Cumbria.

insulated timber structures that will sleep a family of four; a good compromise for those who can't face a night under canvas. Others might like to consider a camping barn – usually converted farm buildings with sleeping platforms, running water and a toilet, although the level of facilities provided does differ.

Practical A-Z

06

Children

Travelling with children in the UK is still not as easy as it is in, say, North America, and things are only very slowly improving. The British still seem to believe in the Victorian maxim that children should be 'seen and not heard', and they definitely don't want to hear them while they're trying to relax on holiday. Some restaurants and hotels in the Lake District will provide facilities such as cots, high chairs and even organized activities, but many more don't.

That's not to say that there are no attractions suitable for children – there are dozens of them: from aquariums and wildlife parks to child-size badger setts, mazes and interactive museum displays. Older children will also love some of the more exciting outdoor activities on offer – such as Go Ape!, ghyll scrambling or quad-biking. Children pay less almost everywhere, and you can often get family deals – but bring proof of age if your teenagers look older than they are.

Countryside Code

• Guard against the risk of fire
• Leave gates as you find them
• Keep dogs under close control
• Keep to public footpaths across farmland, using gates and stiles to cross fences, hedges and walls
• Leave livestock, crops and machinery alone
• Take your litter home
• Don't remove any wildlife, plants or trees
• Don't make unnecessary noise
• Don't leave valuables in your car
• Don't take souvenirs of ancient monuments

Crime

In terms of crime, Cumbria is one of the safest places in England, but visitors should still take common-sense precautions such as not carrying excessive amounts of cash and taking extra care in town centres after dark, especially the towns outside of the National Park.

Car crime is a problem and drivers should not leave valuables in their vehicles. If you must leave luggage in your car, make sure it is locked away out of sight in the boot.

Restaurant Price Categories

Very expensive: cost no object
Expensive: £35-60
Moderate: £18-35
Budget: less than £18

Eating Out

For general information on food and drink, see p.35–38. This book divides meal prices into categories (see above) based on a two-course meal for two people, excluding drinks.

Most restaurants open for lunch and dinner. The former tends to be served between midday and 2.30pm. Dinner is usually between 6.30pm and 9pm. Some establishments stay open all day, especially at weekends. Hotel restaurants will open seven days a week, but others may close for one or two days – often Monday and/or Tuesday.

Electricity

The current is 240 volts AC, so US visitors will need a converter. Wall sockets take uniquely British three-pin (square) fused plugs, so you will need a plug adaptor too. You can pick them up quite cheaply at airports, department stores and some chemists.

Emergencies

The UK emergency telephone number is 999; an emergency operator will put you through to police, fire, ambulance, coastguard, mountain rescue or cave rescue (the last two via the police).

Maps

Ordnance Survey (OS) produces superbly accurate and detailed maps of the whole of England, Wales and Scotland. It's been making them since the Napoleonic Wars, when it was necessary to know the south coast like the back of an Englishman's hand to defend it from invasion, but now the emphasis is on leisure. The excellent Explorer 1:25,000 series (4cm to 1km or 2.5 inches to 1 mile) is the most detailed for walkers, mountain-bikers and and horse-riders. It shows contours, places of interest, rights of way, campsites, even field boundaries. The Lake District is covered by sheets OL4, OL5, OL6 and OL7; other parts of

Cumbria are covered by OL315 (Carlisle), OL43 (Hadrian's Wall), OL31 (North Pennines), OL19 (Howgill Fells and Upper Eden Valley) and OL2 (Yorkshire Dales). The Landranger 1:50,000 series is also good, but lacks the detail of the Explorer series. OS maps can be bought locally from tourist information offices, bookshops, newsagents and some supermarkets.

The OS sheets are the most commonly used maps, but there are others available. Harvey waterproof maps (*www.harveymaps.co.uk*) are always winning design awards, but are a little harder to get hold of than the OS ones. The Lake District is covered by six 1:25,000 sheets. There is also a single 1:40,000 map of the central Lakes which is produced in conjunction with the British Mountaineering Council.

Media

Local newspapers range from the archaic to the best in the country. The biggest media group in the county is the Carlisle-based CN Group, one of the UK's last independent newspaper publishers. It owns two evening titles – the *North-West Evening Mail* (Barrow) and Carlisle's *News & Star* (UK Daily Newspaper of The Year 2009) – and five paid-for weeklies, including *The Whitehaven News*, the *Times & Star* (Workington) and *The Cumberland News*, which has won such accolades as UK Weekly Newspaper of the Year in recent times. As well as publishing some smaller newspaper titles, CN Group is also behind several quality lifestyle magazines, including the highly regarded monthly *Cumbria Life*.

Also once fiercely independent and with a history dating back to 1818, *The Westmorland Gazette* is now owned by Newsquest, part of the US media conglomerate Gannett. Based in Kendal, it covers much of the South Lakes. Other local papers include the *Cumberland and Westmorland Herald*, established in 1860 and covering Penrith, Appleby, Kirkby Stephen, Keswick and Alston, and the *Keswick Reminder*. Both of these are independent.

As in other parts of England, the BBC runs a local radio station – Radio Cumbria, which is based in Carlisle. There is only one countywide commercial radio station – CFM.

Opening Hours

Shops tend to keep standard UK opening hours: 9am–5.30pm Mon–Sat and 10am–4pm on Sundays, although most towns will have at least one or two grocery stores that stay open until late in the evening during the week. Some shops will shut early on Saturdays; and Monday is a common day for some businesses, such as restaurants, to shut completely.

Most pubs will open around midday (earlier if they serve morning coffee) and close again at 3pm, before reopening for the evening at 6pm. Despite the existence of round-the-clock licences, most boozers stick with the traditional 11pm closing.

Pets

You can bring a dog or cat into Britain from the USA, Canada and some European countries under the Pet Travel Scheme (PETS) without quarantine on certain approved airlines, sea and rail crossings, providing they have been microchipped and vaccinated, and had a blood test at least six months before travelling. For more information contact the **Pet Travel Scheme Helpline** (t 0870 241 1710, *www.defra.gov.uk*). Ask your airline about the specifics of pet transport. The majority of city hotels don't welcome pets, but attitudes are often more animal-tolerant in the countryside where some B&Bs and most pubs do accommodate well-behaved dogs.

Post Offices and Royal Mail

Main post offices provide a dizzying array of services on top of letter and parcel post, including currency exchange and travel insurance; sub-post offices, a dying breed, often sit at the back of a corner shop. At the time of writing, a standard first-class stamp cost 39p; second-class, which you'll want for postcards sent within the UK, was 30p. Special Delivery guarantees next working-day delivery, but someone has to be in to sign for the parcel or it will be left at a central depot.

Delivery of letters or parcels to the USA, Canada, Australia or New Zealand by air mail takes about five days. You can get mail sent Poste Restante to any post office in Cumbria and pick it up with some form of identity.

Main post offices are usually open Mon–Fri 9am–5.30pm, Sat 9am–12.30pm, but sub-post offices often close on Wed or Thurs at 1pm. For more details about the Post Office, call t 0845 722 3344 or go to *www.postoffice.co.uk*; for information specifically about postal services, phone t 0845 7740740 or go to: *www.royalmail.com*.

Public Holidays

January: New Year's Day (1st)

March/April: Good Friday and Easter Monday

May: May Day (first Mon); Spring Holiday (last Mon)

August: Late Summer Bank Holiday (last Mon)

December: Christmas Day (25th) and Boxing Day (26th)

Shopping

The Lake District has long been a magnet for artists and creative entrepreneurs, so it is hardly surprising that it's a great place to buy pottery, ceramics, handmade jewellery, woodcarvings, furniture and, of course, paintings. For a good directory of Cumbrian craftspeople and local producers, visit *www.madeincumbria.co.uk*.

William Acland and Oliver Waters produce some impressive contemporary furniture, all made from native timber, which can be seen at their gallery and workshop at the Mill Yard complex in Staveley, **t** (01539) 822852, *www.watersandacland.co.uk*. The Ram Workshop at Kirklinton near Carlisle specializes in more rustic, often intricately carved furniture, **t** (01228) 675641, *www.ramworkshop. co.uk*. Another popular woodworking company is Croglin Designs, which is best known for its handmade toys (The Old School, Main St, Lazonby, **t** (01768) 870100, *www.croglin designs.co.uk*).

If it's pottery and ceramics you're after, don't miss Potfest in the Pens, held every August at Skirsgill Auction Mart, Penrith (*see* p.121). Up to 150 potters display and sell their work here. Two of the best potteries in the county are Gosforth Pottery (Hardingill House, Gosforth, **t** (019467) 25296, *www.potterycourses.co.uk*), which also runs courses; and Kentmere Studio Pottery (Kentmere, near Kendal, **t** (01539) 821621, *www.kentmerepottery.com*). There are many more fine ceramicists whose work is on show at the galleries listed in this guide.

The galleries are, of course, also the place to go if you're looking for paintings and fine art. Some of the best are the Heaton Copper Studio in Grasmere (*see* p.112), the Upfront Gallery near Penrith (*see* p.121), the Thornthwaite Galleries near Keswick (*see* p.139) and the Castlegate House Gallery in Cockermouth (*see* p.163). The Craft Shop at Blackwell also sells a wide range of jewellery, textiles, ceramics, glassware, wood and metalwork for the home.

Basic Advice for the Fells

1. Always get an up-to-date weather forecast before setting out. The Met Office issues five-day fell forecasts for the Lake District. Visit *www.metoffice.gov.uk*. More detailed, three-day forecasts for the Cumbrian fells are available on *www.mwis.org.uk*. The Lake District National Park Authority also runs a Weatherline on 0844 846 2444.

2. Take waterproofs and warm clothing with you – even in the height of summer. The weather in the mountains is unpredictable.

3. Always carry a map and compass and make sure you know how to use them. GPS devices are not a substitute.

4. Carry emergency equipment, including extra food rations; a mobile phone in case of accidents; a whistle/torch in case there is no mobile coverage and you need to use the distress signal (six whistle-blasts/flashes repeated at one-minute intervals) to summon help; a survival bag or 'space blanket' to keep accident victims warm; and a basic first aid kit.

5. Know your limitations. Don't attempt an exposed ridge such as Sharp Edge if you're scared of heights, or go out on the high fells in the snow if you don't know how to use an ice axe and crampons.

6. If you have an accident or come across an accident victim, dial 999 and ask for mountain rescue. But please remember that the mountain rescue service is staffed entirely by volunteers; only call them out if it is a genuine emergency.

Lake District slate is famous for its durability and its colours. Each of the quarries and mines still operating produces its own unique slate – sea green or silvery green from Kirkstone, dark blues from Brathay, the famous green slate of Honister, and the black and green products from the quarries around Coniston. The slate is beautifully crafted into decorative items, kitchen worktops, fireplaces, garden water features and tiles for both floors and roofs. Honister (*see* p.150) has a busy shop and visitor centre at the top of Honister Pass, and Kirkstone operates a showroom on Stramongate in Kendal: **t** (015394) 30810, *www.kirkstone.com*.

Wool is no longer the cornerstone of the Cumbrian economy it once was, but there are still a few producers. The Wool Clip is a co-operative of 15 farmers, textile and fibre artists, spinners, weavers, knitters and dyers producing yarns, rugs, bags, cushions, wall-hangings and clothing. It is based at Priest's Mill in Caldbeck, t (016974) 78707, *www.woolclip.com*.

Sport and Outdoor Activities

Cricket

Despite having Yorkshire and Lancashire for neighbours, Cumbria does not have a good record as far as cricket is concerned. It doesn't have a first-class team, but for details of town clubs' fixtures, etc. visit *cumbriacb.play-cricket.com*.

Cumberland and Westmorland Wrestling

A traditional sport that is thought to date back to the Vikings. It involves men grappling with each other while wearing their under-pants over their long-johns, but that is something of an oversimplification. For a more detailed description of what goes on in a Cumberland and Westmorland wrestling bout, *see p.170*.

Fell-running

Why would anyone want to run up and down steep, windswept, rain-soaked mountains? The answers are, apparently, many. Runners talk of the addictive buzz they get from pounding up and down the hills, the exhilaration they feel when they get to the top of a climb and the immense satisfaction they experience at the end of a race. They also wax lyrical about the wonderful sense of freedom they have while running in the hills and the great camaraderie that exists among this relatively small bunch of like-minded folk. Highlights of the fell-running calendar are the races in Borrowdale, Wasdale and Ennerdale. Participants also enjoy the occasional challenge run, the most famous of which is probably the Bob Graham Round. This involves running up 42 Lakeland peaks in 24 hours, a 70-mile route with about 27,000ft of ascent. To date, about 1,200 people have completed the round in less than 24 hours. The record is held by Billy Bland, who, in 1982, managed it in 13 hours and 53 minutes.

Fell-walking

Fell-walking is by far the most popular activity in the Lakes, with surveys showing that most visitors will don their boots at some point in their trip. There are about 800 square miles of access land in Cumbria – almost one-third of the entire county. That's in addition to the almost 5,000 miles of footpaths, bridle-ways and byways that criss-cross the countryside. That means there is plenty of choice; literally something for everyone – from gentle lakeside and woodland strolls to challenging fell walks. There is even a path to the top of Latrigg specially constructed for wheelchair users (*see* p.145).

Football

The main team in the county is Carlisle United, who, at the time of writing, were playing in League One, the third tier of the English football divisions. They are based at Brunton Park in the border city. Visit *www.carlisleunited.co.uk* for more information. Other popular teams include the non-league Workington Reds and Barrow AFC.

Golf

There are dozens of golf courses all over Cumbria. They range from the fell setting of Alston Moor to the magnificent links course at Silloth (*www.sillothgolfclub.co.uk*), which is consistently voted as being one of the top 50 courses in the country by the leading golfing magazines. Other premier courses include Carlisle and Penrith.

Horse-racing

Cumbria has two busy racecourses – one at either end of the county. Carlisle Racecourse (*www.carlisle-races.co.uk*) in the far north is home to the iconic Cumberland Plate and Carlisle Bell races which date back to the 17th century; Cartmel (*www.cartmel-racecourse. co.uk*) in the far south regularly sees race-day crowds of up to 30,000.

Hound Trailing

A Cumbrian tradition dating back to the early years of the 19th century. Lanky hounds follow a trail of paraffin and aniseed oil over moorland, fields and fells. The sport is particularly popular in the west of the county. The season lasts from April 1 to the end of October.

Kayaking and Canoeing

If you tire of the land-based outdoor activities, there are plenty of places throughout the Lake District where you can hire kayaks or canoes. The most popular lakes are Derwent Water, Windermere, Coniston Water and Ullswater. If you are bringing your own boat, bear in mind that not all the lakes and rivers have public access. A good starting point for information on access is *www.lakestay. co.uk/kayak*.

Mountain Biking

The Lake District is becoming a mecca for mountain-bikers. With purpose-built trails in the Whinlatter and Grizedale forests (see p.76) as well as many miles of bridleways crossing the open fells, there is plenty of variety out there. See the regional chapters for information on where to hire bikes.

Orienteering

If you spend a lot of time walking or mountain-biking in the Lake District, there's a good chance you may come across the red and white control points of an orienteering event. According to British Orienteering, the sport's governing body in the UK, the aim of orienteering is 'to navigate in sequence between control points marked on a unique orienteer ing map and decide the best route to complete the course in the quickest time'. There are permanent orienteering courses set up at Whinlatter and Tarn Hows. Maps are available from the Whinlatter Visitor Centre or the National Trust Land Rover at Tarn Hows.

Rock Climbing

Coleridge's blood-curdling descent of Broad Stand aside (see p.177), the Lake District played a major role in the early development of rock-climbing as a sport in its own right from the late 19th century onwards. One of the pivotal moments in the history of the sport came in 1886 when Walter Parry Haskett Smith, regarded by many as the father of modern climbing, completed the first ascent of Napes Needle on Great Gable. The area's many crags and buttresses continue to attract climbers today, and visitors should have no problem finding instructors if they want to give it a go. There are also several indoor climbing walls throughout the county. The pick of these are the Keswick Climbing Wall at Goosewell Farm near Castlerigg Stone Circle (www.keswickclimbingwall.co.uk) and the Lakeland Climbing Centre in Kendal (www.kendalwall.co.uk). The latter includes an 18-metre wall and two bouldering rooms with thick matting on the floors.

Rugby League

Rugby league is taken very seriously in west Cumbria, more so than football. Whitehaven (www.whitehavenrl.co.uk), who play at the Recreation Ground, known locally as the Recre, have been knocking on the door of the Super League for a few years.

Telephone and Internet

Most places in Cumbria have fast broadband connections. There are internet cafés in most towns, and many hotels and guesthouses have a computer available for guests to use. An increasing number have Wi-Fi.

If you are bringing a mobile phone from abroad, see if you can replace your SIM card with a British pay-as-you-go card for your stay (or you could end up paying extortionate roaming charges). Mobile phone coverage is pretty poor in some Lakeland valleys. Conversely, coverage on the fell tops tends to be surprisingly good.

Payphone calls cost a minimum of 40p. Some payphones do not accept coins; they will take only British Telecom charge cards and credit/debit cards. Calls from hotel phones are expensive. Dial 100 for the operator; 118 500 for BT directory enquiries (www.bt.com).

Time

The UK is all on one time zone: Greenwich Mean Time (GMT), the local time of the prime meridian or zero degrees longitude, which passes through Greenwich in London. British Summer Time (BST) runs from the end of March to the end of October; clocks are put forward one hour ahead of GMT to make the most of daylight hours.

Because Cumbria is several hundred miles north of London, it sees fewer hours of daylight during the winter than the capital. The happy flip side of this coin is that there can still be light in the sky at 11pm on a bright June day.

Websites

Useful websites include:

www.visitcumbria.com

www.cumbria-the-lake-district.co.uk

www.golakes.co.uk

www.lake-district.gov.uk

www.lakedistrictletsgo.co.uk

www.sugarvine.com

www.cumberlandnews.co.uk

www.thewestmorlandgazette.co.uk

www.walkingworld.com

www.lakedistrictoutdoors.co.uk

www.leaney.org

www.cyclingcumbria.co.uk

www.thecumbriadirectory.com

The South Lakes

The South Lakes provide a gentle but fascinating introduction to Cumbria and the Lake District. There is something positively soothing about being on or close to serene Windermere, the region's glimmering centrepiece. Lazily rolling hills and peaceful woodland reach down to its endless shores, while man's impact can be seen in the area's majestic monastic ruins and its quaint towns and pretty villages. The tranquillity of the area is echoed in its rich literary and artistic associations, which welcome the visitor like a childhood friend. The far south is made up of little-visited peninsulas tentatively reaching out into the notorious shifting sands of Morecambe Bay, while in the north the land begins to rise in anticipation of the mountains of central Lakeland.

07

Don't miss

⭐ **Cruise on England's largest natural lake**
Windermere p.62

⭐ **Visit Beatrix Potter's first farm**
Hill Top p.73

⭐ **Enjoy traffic-free forest bike trails**
Grizedale Forest p.76

⭐ **Conquer the Old Man for views of the coast**
Coniston Old Man p.77

⭐ **Wander around a charming historic village**
Cartmel p.84

See map overleaf

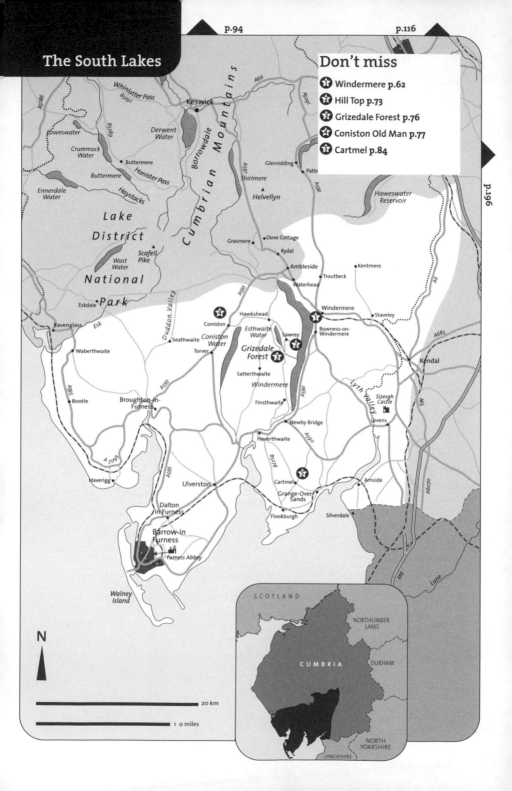

The southern part of the Lake District is dominated by Windermere – both the glorious lake and the town that was named after it. No visit to this area would be complete without spending some time on or near England's largest natural lake. For those seeking culture, Kendal is the place to be, with its galleries, museums and arts centre. There are also several interesting old houses nearby, including Levens Hall and Sizergh Castle. Many visitors miss out the coastal peninsulas south of the A590, but these are home to some true gems – Cartmel is a must and, if you get as far as Barrow-in-Furness, the red sandstone Furness Abbey (see p.88) is one of the grandest monastic ruins in the north of England. Troutbeck (see p.64) and Hawkshead (see p.74) are two of the prettiest villages within the National Park, and each contains a fascinating array of vernacular architecture. The latter is located in the heart of Beatrix Potter country and, although there are historic links to the children's writer all over the county, it is to Hawkshead and Near Sawrey (see p.73) that the Potter pilgrims flock in their thousands. There are plenty of relatively easy walks throughout this region, but serious fell-walkers will want to head for the hills to the north of Kendal or, better still, the more challenging mountains above Coniston. Mountain-bikers, meanwhile, will find plenty of challenges among the specially constructed trails in Grizedale Forest.

Kendal and Around

If you're approaching the Lake District from the south, Kendal will be your 'gateway' to the National Park. Many visitors will rush through it, but it is well worth taking some time to enjoy the Auld Grey Town, one of the most culturally 'happening' places in the whole of Cumbria.

Built from a combination of local grey limestone and slate, hence its nickname, Kendal stands on the banks of the River Kent, one of England's fastest flowing rivers. As in so many other Cumbrian settlements, the Romans were here and they built a fort, Alauna, to the south of the modern-day town – at Watercrook. Little can be seen of the fort today, but it was probably occupied from about AD 80 to the 4th century, and would have defended the roads to Lancaster, Ambleside and Brougham.

The town really took off in the 14th century when it became the centre of the woollen trade. Its motto, in fact is 'pannus mihi panis', which means 'wool is my bread'. Fulling mills in villages as far away as Grasmere and Hawkshead dressed and finished the wool for the markets in Kendal. Lakeland was an ideal place for the industry, not only because of the local sheep and the proximity of fast-flowing becks to operate the mills, but also because a number of plants growing on the fells could be used to dye the material. The famous 'Kendal green' cloth even gets a mention in Shakespeare's Henry IV.

In more modern times, Kendal has become renowned for its mintcake, a sweet concoction of glucose and peppermint that gives a much-needed sugar rush to weary walkers and mountaineers.

Getting to and around Kendal

By Train and Bus

Kendal is on the Oxenholme to Windermere branch line of the West Coast Main Line. From Oxenholme, passengers can board direct **trains** to Glasgow, Crewe, Manchester, Birmingham and London.

National Express runs a daily service (**570**) between Whitehaven and London that stops in Kendal (journey time to London, eight hours).

Kendal is well served by **buses**. There are regular services between the town and Carlisle, Keswick, Grasmere, Windermere, Arnside, Hawes, Barrow-in-Furness and Lancaster. Some local buses do not run on Sundays.

By Taxi

Ace Taxis, t (01539) 733430; Castle Taxis, t (01539) 726233; Blue Star Taxis, t (01539) 723670; and Crown Taxis, t (01539) 732181 – all in Kendal.

By Bicycle

To hire bikes, try Wheelbase, Mill Yard, Staveley, t (01539) 821443, *www.wheelbase.co.uk*.

The town also became the adopted home of Alfred Wainwright, probably the most famous of walking-guide writers. Although born in Blackburn, Lancashire, he lived in Kendal from 1941 until his death in 1991. An accountant by trade, he was the borough treasurer, but is best known for his books. As well as being a home to all the usual fascinating collections relating to local archaeology, geology and natural history that you would expect to find in a town museum, **Kendal Museum** also houses a reconstruction of Wainwright's office, some of his original pen-and-ink drawings, maps drawn when he was a child, his original map of Westmorland and personal items such as his walking jacket, rucksack, heavily-darned socks and famous pipe. Wainwright was honorary clerk and curator to the museum from 1945 to 1974.

Kendal Museum
Station Rd, Kendal,
t (01539) 721374,
www.kendalmuseum.org.
uk; open Thurs–Sat
12–5pm, closed for a week
at Christmas; adm

The award-winning **Quaker Tapestry Exhibition and Tearooms** houses a huge, 77-panel modern work of embroidery telling the story of the Quaker movement (for more details on the area's close links with the birth of the Quaker movement, *see* p.xx and p.xx). Even if you have no interest in tapestry or the Religious Society of Friends, the intricate piece of work is an impressive construction recalling a fascinating history. The centre also runs two- and three-day embroidery workshops.

Quaker Tapestry Exhibition and Tearooms
Friends Meeting House,
Stramongate, t (01539)
722975; www.quaker-
tapestry.co.uk; open
Apr–Oct Mon–Fri
10am–5pm and some
Saturdays; adm

Holy Trinity Church, a mostly Victorian construction but on the site of an earlier church, is Cumbria's largest parish church, and has five aisles and an attractive western tower.

Beside the church is the **Abbot Hall Art Gallery**, which is housed in an attractive Grade I listed Georgian villa beside the river. As well as hosting temporary, visiting exhibitions, the gallery also has its own substantial collection, which includes work by the 18th-century portrait painter George Romney (*see* p.xx), landscape watercolours by Edward Lear and J. M. W. Turner, drawings by John Ruskin and several highly-acclaimed modern works of art. Probably the finest gallery of its kind in Cumbria, Abbot Hall is a must for art lovers. It also contains some delightful period furniture and *objets d'art*.

Abbot Hall Art Gallery,
Abbot Hall, Kendal,
t (01539) 722464 ,
www.abbothall.org.uk;
open April–Oct Mon–Sat
10.30am–5pm, Nov–Mar
Mon–Sat 10.30am–4pm;
adm

Museum of Lakeland Life

Abbot Hall, Kendal
t (01539) 722464,
www.lakelandmuseum.
org.uk; open April–Oct
Mon-Sat 10.30am–5pm,
Nov-Mar Mon–Sat
10.30am–4pm; adm

The **Museum of Lakeland Life** is located in Abbot Hall's converted stable block. It has a number of 'period rooms' that show different aspects of Cumbrian life through the ages. Its most interesting collections include Arthur Ransome's original sketches for his popular series of children's books, *Swallows and Amazons*, a display tracing the development of the Arts and Crafts movement locally and nostalgic photographs of the Lake District in the 1940s and 1950s.

Just outside the town are the atmospheric 12th-century ruins of **Kendal Castle**. The castle was the home of various baronial families, including the Parrs who had a big influence on the development of the town. Katherine Parr, the last wife of Henry VIII – the one who 'survived' – was born in the castle in 1512. The castle walls are still standing, as is one of the towers. Parts of the manor hall also remain. Located on a hill overlooking the town and with views across to the fells, the castle grounds make an ideal spot for a picnic. The castle is open at all times and several public rights of way run through its grounds.

The town's first castle, dating from about 1092, is a motte-and-bailey affair known as **Castle Howe**. All that remains are the substantial earthworks. The mound is crowned by an obelisk erected in 1788 to celebrate the centenary of the so-called 'Glorious Revolution' of 1688, in which King James II was overthrown by William of Orange.

Take a stroll along the pretty riverside paths and through the ginnels and yards that characterize the town centre and you'll come across a host of other interesting buildings. These include the medieval **Sandes Hospital** in Highgate, built as a school and almshouses for poor widows by cloth merchant and former mayor Thomas Sandes; the 14th-century **Castle Dairy**, the town's oldest inhabited building; and **Stricklandgate**, which was built in 1690 and was slept in by Bonnie Prince Charlie both during his advance of 1745 and during his retreat when his pursuer, the Duke of Cumberland, slept in the same bed on the following night.

Just south of Kendal is a popular summer-only attraction – the **Lakeland Maize Farm Park** at Raines Hall Farm near Sedgwick. Here, a nine-acre field of crops has been cut into a maze in the shape of farm animals. There is also a mini maize maze for toddlers and, in September, an extra element of fun is added as torch-bearing visitors tackle the confusing route in the dark.

Lakeland Maize Farm Park

Raines Hall Farm,
Sedgwick,
t (015395) 61760,
www.lakelandmaze.co.uk;
open daily mid July–end
Sept 10am–6pm, then
weekends until end Sept;
adm

Sizergh Castle

Sizergh,
t (015395) 60951,
www.nationaltrust.org.uk;
open Mar–Nov Sun–Thurs
12pm–5pm; adm

Sizergh Castle is located about three miles south of Kendal town centre, just off the A591. Now in the care of the National Trust, this imposing medieval house has been the home of the Strickland family for 750 years. The main feature of the building, and its oldest surviving structure, is the impressive 14th-century peel tower. Many of the grey limestone buildings surrounding it were added during Elizabethan times. The landscaped gardens prove very popular with visitors, and there are various walks around the estate.

The interior of the house is renowned for its beautiful oak panelling, the highlight coming after visitors have climbed the four flights of

07 The South Lakes | Kendal and Around

stairs to reach the Inlaid Chamber. Here, the panels, recently returned to their original location after having been sold to the Victoria and Albert Museum in London, have an almost three-dimensional effect.

Walter Strickland was made a Knight of the Bath in 1306 for his loyal support of the Crown against the Scots. He was also granted a charter of free warren, which meant he had the exclusive right to kill game on his land, a privilege normally reserved for the king. Family members served in Parliament in almost every generation until the end of the 17th century.

Levens Hall

Levens Hall
t (015395) 60321,
www.levenshall.co.uk;
open Apr–Oct
Sun–Thurs 10am–5pm;
adm

Just a couple of miles south of Sizergh, on the banks of the River Kent, is **Levens Hall**, another of Cumbria's grandest stately homes. Like Sizergh up the road, this magnificent Elizabethan house was built around an earlier peel tower and also contains some marvellous examples of oak panelling. The house is the private home of the Bagot family, who have lived here for two centuries, but visitors can wander through many of the elegant rooms, viewing fine furniture, paintings, an excellent Spanish leather wall covering, the earliest English patchwork and an assortment of clocks and miniatures.

The Grade I listed garden is worth a visit by itself. Dating from 1694, it was designed by Guillaume Beaumont, one of the top gardeners of his time. Surprisingly, little has changed in 300-plus years. The immaculate yew topiary, which really has to be seen to be believed, is some of the oldest in the world.

The surrounding parkland is home to a small herd of Norwegian black fallow deer. Legend has it that whenever a white fawn is born, there will be a change in the fortunes of the family residing at Levens. On one occasion, the lord ordered the shooting of a newly-born white fawn. Within months, gambling debts forced the then owners to sell the hall and it changed hands twice in quick succession.

Like so many other old houses, Levens Hall also has a number of ghost stories associated with it. There's a phantom black dog, a pink lady and all sorts of strange goings-on in the Bellingham bedroom. One of the best stories relates to a gypsy woman who came knocking at the door of the house one bitterly cold winter's night, begging for food. The family ignored her pleas and she died on their doorstep – but not before she had cursed them. She told them that no son would inherit the hall until the River Kent stopped flowing and a white fawn was born in the park. The estate did pass through the female line for several generations after the curse until, in fact, the particularly harsh winter of 1896 when the river froze over and a white fawn was born. At the same time, Mrs Bagot finally gave birth to a male heir, Alan Desmond.

Kendal to Windermere

North of Kendal are two of the prettiest and least commercial of Lakeland valleys – Longsleddale and the Kentmere valley. **Longsleddale,** which was the inspiration for Greendale, the village where Postman Pat delivers his mail, starts at Garnett Bridge and continues for more than six miles. The pleasant, lightly wooded slopes and fields gradually give way to wilder country as the valley narrows. The road ends after less than five miles, at the tiny hamlet of Sadgill, and from here a rough track, formerly a drove road, continues up to Gatescarth Pass and then over to the Haweswater reservoir.

Kentmere is slightly more popular because it marks the start of the Kentmere Round, one of the Lake District's classic horseshoe routes – and one of its toughest. Visiting Yoke (2,316ft), Ill Bell (2,483ft), Froswick (2,362ft), Mardale Ill Bell (2,496ft), Harter Fell (2,551ft), Kentmere Pike (2,394ft) and Shipman Knotts (1,926ft), it gives walkers a long day of spectacular ridge walking in wild, remote country.

Kentmere Hall, located about a third-of-a-mile from the church of St Cuthbert's, is the valley's oldest building and includes a 14th-century peel tower with five-foot-thick walls. The rest of the hall dates from the 16th century. It is not open to the public, but several footpaths pass near to it. The Baron of Kendal gave the land here to Richard de Gilpin in the 13th century after he hunted down and killed a ferocious wild boar that had been plaguing the villagers between Kendal and Windermere. The hall was the birthplace, in 1517, of Bernard Gilpin, a leading churchman in Tudor times who became known as the 'Apostle of the North'. It is said that the hall's main beam, measuring 30ft, was lifted into place by the valley's legendary strongman Hugh Hird.

The River Kent has its source at the head of the valley. Because of its significant drop in height over a relatively short distance, the river is one of the fastest flowing in the country, making it ideal for powering mills. There are records of fulling mills in Staveley as far back as the 12th century, and the last watermill along the Kent – the snuff mill at Helsington – closed as recently as 1991.

Staveley, just off the busy A591, is a pleasant stop on the way to Windermere, if only to visit the church and have a look around the businesses in Staveley Mill Yard. The church of St James's was built in 1864 and contains some delicate stained glass designed by Burne-Jones. The tower of St Margaret's, standing next to the Duke William pub, is all that remains of the former church, founded in 1388.

Staveley Mill Yard is a more modern development. It comprises a collection of shops and businesses on the site of a mill constructed in about 1825 by local businessman Thomas Taylor. Here, visitors can taste beers in **Hawkshead Brewery's Beer Hall**. This looks down on to the busy brew house and has a connecting door with Wilf's Café next door, so that food can be brought to your table in the bar. Nearby is **Organico**, the UK's largest organic wine shop, which runs tasting events and has a bistro upstairs. **Lucy Cooks** is a cookery school run by the same people who run Lucy's On a Plate in Ambleside.

To the south of the A591 is the pretty **Lyth Valley**, an area of rolling hills and quiet hamlets. Visit in the spring when the damson trees are in blossom, turning the valley sides into a sea of snow-white flowers. Every April, the local people celebrate and help promote this small, flavoursome plum with a special Damson Day. The fruit itself can be

Hawkshead Brewery's Beer Hall
www.hawkshead
brewery.co.uk

Organico
www.organi.co.uk

Lucy Cooks
www.lucycooks.co.uk

07 The South Lakes | Kendal to Windermere

found on roadside stalls and in local shops usually in the second half of September.

For walkers, there are several low-lying limestone hills bordering the Lyth valley that provide great views of both the Lake District fells and the Yorkshire Dales to the east. Cunswick Scar and Scout Scar are both within walking distance of Kendal town centre. Further west, **Whitbarrow**, meaning 'white hill' is a Site of Special Scientific Interest and a National Nature Reserve. Take a walk through the pretty woods and on the limestone pavement on a sunny summer's day and you're likely to see some of Britain's rarest butterflies, including the high brown and pearl-bordered fritillaries. A lot of work has gone into improving the unusual habitats in this area. Felling and coppicing of the woodland encourages plants such as violet, primrose and hairy dog violet. These, in turn, provide nectar for adult butterflies, and their leaves provide food for the caterpillars. Cattle and sheep have been introduced to the grasslands to prevent the spread of woodland and bracken. Wildflowers such as dark red helleborine – a rare orchid – are beginning to thrive as a result.

Festivals and Events in Kendal

(i) **Kendal Tourist Information Centre**
Town Hall, Lowther St, t (01539) 725758; open March–Oct Mon–Sat 10am–5pm, Nov–Feb Mon–Sat 10am–4pm

The annual **Doodleshire May Fair** on Gooseholme celebrates the legend of Dickie Doodle, a messenger of King Richard I who was sent to Kendal, possibly to deliver its market charter, in the late 12th century. His first stop in the town was the Cock and Dolphin inn, where he got thoroughly drunk, caused a nuisance of himself and was chased off by locals. He fled across the river to the east bank where, because of rivalries which existed in the town, he received a much warmer welcome. Liking what he saw, he named this area Doodleshire and became its first mayor. Today, the area is known as Far Cross, but Dickie Doodle is remembered at the May fair, when the local people elect a mayor of Doodleshire. His name also lives on in one of the bitters of the Cumbrian Legendary Ales brewery.

One of the UK's biggest celebrations of all things mountainous takes place in Kendal every November. Originally known as the Kendal Mountain Film Festival, the event eventually became so big, encompassing lectures by some of the greatest climbers on the planet, art and book festivals, as well as films that it changed its name to the **Kendal Mountain Festival** (*www.mountainfest.co.uk*). One of the

highlights is the announcement of the winner of the Boardman-Tasker Prize, one of the world's top awards for mountain literature.

The first **Kendal Festival of Food** was held in October 2009. This included farm tours, tastings, a farmers' market, a beer festival, live music and special deals at local cafés and restaurants.

Kendal Calling (*www.kendalcalling. co.uk*) is another relatively new addition, held at Lowther Deer Park. In 2009 the main stage was graced by the likes of The Streets, The Zutons and Ash. There are also stages devoted to folk music and to comedy.

Mintfest, part of the Lakes Alive (*www.lakesalive.org*) programme of arts and performance events, is the biggest festival of international street art outside of London. Usually held at the end of August, it includes modern circus acts, fire sculptures, street performers and live music. Most of the events are free.

Where to Stay in Kendal

Riverside Hotel, Stramongate Bridge, Kendal, t (01539) 734861, *www.riversidekendal.co.uk* (*expensive–moderate*). This converted 17th-century tannery beside the River Kent is Kendal's best hotel. As well as smart rooms, it has great leisure facilities.

Beech House, Greenside, Kendal, t (01539) 720385, *www.beechhouse-kendal.co.uk* (*moderate*). A little more stylish than your average B&B, this smart, modern establishment has Wi-Fi, DVD players, roll-top baths and plush velvet sofas. Children and pets not allowed.

⭐ Eagle and Child >

Eagle and Child, Kendal Rd, Staveley, t (01539) 821320, *www.eaglechildinn.co.uk* (*moderate*). Decent views from most of the good, clean rooms in this welcoming inn. Superb breakfasts.

Heaves Country House Hotel, near Kendal, t (01539) 560396, *www.heaveshotel.com* (*moderate*). Four-poster beds, a grand piano, a billiard table and corniced hallways all contribute to the charm and elegance of this stately mansion close to Sizergh Castle.

Watermill Inn, Ings, t (01539) 821309, *www.watermillinn.co.uk* (*moderate*). Small, simply-furnished but comfortable rooms in a popular venue. Dogs are positively welcomed. Named CAMRA's Cumbria Pub of the Year in 2009. Microbrewery on site.

Balcony House, Shap Rd, Kendal, t (01539) 731402, *www.balconyhouse.co.uk* (*moderate–budget*). Pleasant B&B run by an equally pleasant couple. Nice touches in the rooms include fluffy bathrobes and DVD players. Parking can be a problem.

Highgate Hotel, Highgate, t (01539) 724229, *www.highgatehotel.co.uk* (*moderate–budget*). Handsome Georgian house that once belonged to a wealthy 18th-century chemist. Original staircase and fireplaces. Nice homely feel, although it could do with a lick of paint.

Hillside, Beast Banks, Kendal, t (01539) 722836, *www.hillside-kendal.co.uk* (*moderate–budget*). Comfortable and cosy B&B that is just a few minutes' stroll from the town centre.

Where to Eat in Kendal

The Punchbowl Inn, Crosthwaite, t (015395) 68237, *www.the-punchbowl.co.uk* (*expensive*). This is a seriously posh pub – winner, in fact, of

Michelin's Pub of the Year award in 2009. Leather chairs, polished oak floorboards and a beautiful bar made from local slate all add to the upmarket feel. Expect to find pot-roasted woodpigeon and confit of belly pork on the superb menu. The inn also has eight elegantly furnished bedrooms (*luxury–expensive*).

The Wheatsheaf, Brigsteer, t (015395) 68254, *www.thewheatsheafbrigsteer.co.uk* (*expensive*). Another of the Lyth Valley's excellent gastro-pubs. Again, they've gone for that slightly rustic feel with wooden floors and furniture, but the food is anything but rustic. Highlights include pan-fried seabass fillets served with fennel boulangere, buttered samphire and a caper and herb dressing. Regional produce and traceability are the pub's hallmarks. Comfortable rooms (*moderate*) are also available.

New Moon, Highgate, Kendal, t (01539) 729254, *www.newmoon restaurant.co.uk* (*expensive–moderate*). Good, modern British cuisine served up in stylish, contemporary surroundings. The early evening supper menu is particularly good value for money. *Closed Sun and Mon.*

The Brown Horse Inn, Winster, t (01539) 443443, *www.thebrown horseinn.co.uk*, (*expensive–moderate*). The Brown Horse has its own estate, which supplies all of its game as well as its lamb, and beef from a herd of Highland cattle. Children's menu also available. Upstairs are nine very comfortable en suite rooms (*moderate*).

The Watermill Inn, Ings, t (01539) 821309, *www.watermillinn.co.uk* (*moderate*). Particularly popular with families, this inn serves good bar meals and, if you're concerned about food miles, go for the steak – it comes from the pub's very own herd of Limousin cattle that live up the road.

The Famous 1657 Chocolate House, Branthwaite Brow, Kendal, t (01539) 740702, *www.chocolatehouse1657.co.uk* (*budget*). Step back in time in this delightful 17th-century building with exposed beams and ladies in starched bonnets, and enjoy one of the 18 speciality chocolate drinks or 14

⭐ The Wheatsheaf

>>

handmade chocolate gateaux. Heaven! *Closed Sun.*

Waterside Wholefood, Kent View, Kendal, **t** (01539) 733252, *www.watersidewholefood.co.uk* (*budget*). Lovely riverside location for this popular vegetarian and vegan café. Organic and fair-trade ingredients.

Wilf's Café, Mill Yard, Staveley, **t** (01539) 822329, *www.wilfs-cafe.co.uk* (*budget*). A bright and lively café that is much loved by people who enjoy the outdoors.

Entertainment in Kendal

Brewery Arts Centre, Highgate, Kendal, **t** (01539) 795090, *www.breweryarts.co.uk*. There's always plenty going on at this bustling arts centre – films, theatre, dance, comedy, live music, visual arts, lectures, festivals... There are also several cafés, bars and restaurants.

East of Windermere
Windermere and Bowness

Less than a mile short of the shores of Windermere, visitors reach Birthwaite which, together with adjoining Bowness-on-Windermere, forms the largest settlement in the National Park. Birthwaite? Never heard of it? Well, that's because, when the Oxenholme to Windermere branch line was opened in 1847, the marketing people decided that 'Birthwaite Station' wasn't going to attract the tourists, so they called it

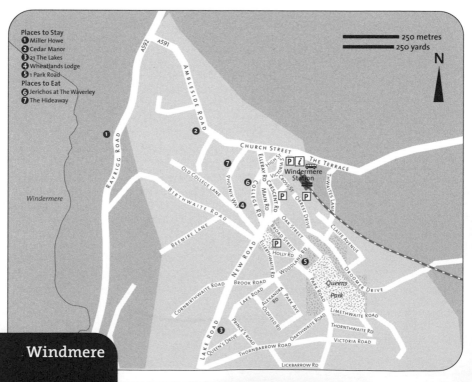

Windmere

Getting to and around Windermere

By Train

A branch line links Windermere with Oxenholme, which is on the West Coast Main Line, where passengers can board direct trains to Glasgow, Crewe, Manchester, Birmingham and London.

By Bus

National Express runs a daily service (570) between Whitehaven and London that stops in Windermere (journey time to London, 8 hours and 25 minutes). On Saturdays between April and October, the X8 from Keswick to Chorley in Lancashire stops at Windermere (journey time to Chorley, one hour and 40 minutes). During the school summer holidays, the bus runs on Sundays, Wednesdays and Fridays as well.

Windermere and Bowness-on-Windermere are fairly well served by **local buses**. There are regular services between the town and Carlisle, Keswick, Grasmere, Kendal, Lancaster, Glenridding, Newby Bridge, Ulverston and Barrow-in-Furness. Some local buses do not run on Sundays.

By Taxi

Abacus Taxis, t (015394) 88285; Bowness Taxis, t (015394) 46664; Lakes Taxis, t (015394) 44055; and Windermere Taxis, t (015394) 42355 – all in Windermere or Bowness-on-Windermere.

By Boat

The Windermere passenger and vehicle ferry connects Ferry Nab, just south of Bowness, with Ferry House, near Far Sawrey. Weather and water conditions permitting, the service runs all year. Ferries every 20 minutes, t (01228) 227653.

Windermere Lake Cruises operates boats from Bowness to Ambleside and various other points on the lake, *see* p.62.

By Bicycle

To hire bikes, try Country Lanes at Windermere railway station, t (01539) 444544, *www.countrylaneslake district.co.uk*; or Windermere Canoe Kayak near Ferry Nab, t (01539) 444451, *www.windermerecanoekayak.com*.

'Windermere' instead. What had been a gathering of cottages and a farm a few years before, soon grew into a Victorian resort.

Windermere, the town, has little of interest, although the short walk up to Orrest Head, just to the north of the railway station, provides some magnificent views of Windermere, the lake (*see* walk description below).

Heading south, it is hard to know when you are leaving Windermere and when you are entering Bowness – the two now merge into each other. But it hasn't always been so: before the railway opened, Bowness was just a small cluster of cottages and fishermen's huts. As in neighbouring Windermere, the trains brought commuters and tourists in unprecedented numbers. If you want a sense of what the village may have looked like before the railway came, head for the oldest part, Lowside, the area of narrow streets behind St Martin's Church.

Bowness occupies a fabulous location on the lake, but sadly suffers from a certain amount of tackiness. The lakeside area, in particular, is home to a row of cheap shops and the smell of hot dogs. And, most annoyingly, the shops get in the way of the lake view.

 Windermere Lake Cruises
Bowness,
t (015394) 43360,
www.windermere-lakecruises.co.uk;
sailings daily except Christmas Day; adm

The best thing about Bowness is that it houses the landing stages for the **Windermere Lake Cruises**, a superb way to see England's largest natural lake – and to escape from the vulgarities of the town. There are a variety of cruises on offer – from 45 minutes in length to a three-hour trip. A Freedom of the Lake ticket allows you to jump on and off as

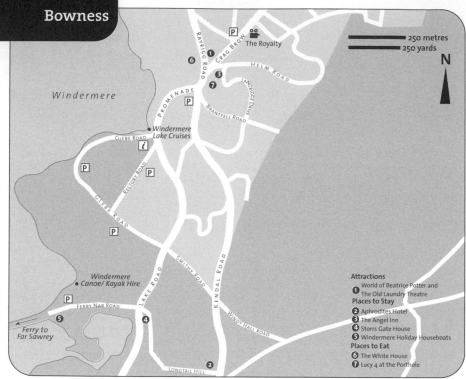

Bowness

The Royalty

250 metres
250 yards

N

Windermere

Windermere
Lake Cruises

Windermere
Canoe/ Kayak Hire

Ferry to
Far Sawrey

Attractions

1 World of Beatrice Potter and The Old Laundry Theatre
Places to Stay
2 Aphrodites Hotel
3 The Angel Inn
4 Storrs Gate House
5 Windermere Holiday Houseboats
Places to Eat
6 The White House
7 Lucy 4 at the Porthole

Windermere Canoe Kayak

Bowness, Ferry Nab Rd, t (015394) 44451; www.windermerecanoe kayak.com; open daily 9–5.30

World of Beatrix Potter

Bowness, t (015394) 88444, www.hop-skip-jump.com; open daily summer 10–5.30, winter 10–4.30; adm

Quayside Kids

The Quays, Glebe Rd, t (015394) 88444, www.quaysidekids.co.u k; open Mon–Fri 9–6, Sat–Sun 9.30–6, winter 9–5; adm

many boats as you want within a 24-hour period. During the summer, there is a jazz band and buffet on the evening cruises; and, in December, a proper Christmas lunch is served on some sailings.

Windermere Lake Cruises also has motor boats and rowing boats available. These can be hired from the wooden huts to the right of Bowness promenade.

Kayaks and canoes can also be hired from **Windermere Canoe Kayak** at Ferry Nab, just south of Bowness. Guides and instructors are available should you want to do something a little more adventurous than just paddle around Belle Isle and go back again.

Back on dry land, fans of Peter Rabbit and families with young children should head for the **World of Beatrix Potter**. This indoor attraction recreates scenes from all 23 of the popular writer's tales. So, as well as seeing a short film and exhibits about Potter's life, visitors can meet Jemima Puddle-Duck in the woodland glade and drop in on Mrs Tiggy-Winkle in her kitchen.

Another one for the youngsters, **Quayside Kids** is a good place to go when it's raining. Slides, look-out tunnels and soft balls are all part of the large indoor play area aimed at children up to the age of 11. Adults can enjoy a cup of Illy coffee in the relaxing lounge area.

Brockhole Lake District Visitor Centre

Brockhole
Windermere,
t (015394) 46601,
www.lake-district.gov.uk; open
Feb–Nov daily 10–5,
gardens and grounds
open all year; parking
fee

Don't go along to **Brockhole** expecting a simple Tourist Information Centre; this lovely lakeside spot north of Windermere town has peaceful landscaped gardens, an adventure playground, house, café and shop. Kids can enjoy rope walks, scramble nets, slides and zip wires while the grown-ups watch from nearby picnic tables. The 30-acre Arts and Crafts garden, with its magnificent views across the lake to the Langdales, was designed by Thomas Mawson and includes, among other things, fragrant displays of magnolias, rhododendrons and camellias. The grounds also include an arts trail – lines of poetry and unusual sculptures are among the pieces of public art on display.

Inside the house, there are two floors of interactive displays explaining the geology and history of the Lake District.

07 The South Lakes | East of Windermere: Troutbeck

Troutbeck

A world away from the commercialism of downtown Bowness, Troutbeck consists mostly of 17th- and 18th-century homes spread out along a 1.5 mile-long stretch of narrow road just above the valley bottom – following the ancient drovers' routes and linking together a series of natural springs. People searching for the Lake District idyll need go no further than this. Drystone walls snake up and down the western side of the verdant valley, dissecting the rolling farmland into small enclosures, and the area is dotted with pretty cottages. On the eastern side is a line of rugged fells, part of the Kentmere Horseshoe. There is nowhere more perfect on a sunny day when the sound of birdsong fills the trees.

At the southern end of the valley, before you reach the elongated village, you will find **Holehird Gardens** – 10 acres of enchanting Victorian walled gardens, extensive rock and heather gardens, alpine houses and herbaceous borders, all with fabulous fell and lake views. Home of the Lakeland Horticultural Society, the gardens also hold three important national collections – hydrangea, polystichum ferns and the hardy herbaceous astilbe, with its large plumes of flowers. Don't be put off by the deer gate – if you stop by the white line a few feet short of the entrance, it should open automatically.

Holehird Gardens
Patterdale Rd,
t (015394) 46008,
www.holehirdgardens.
org.uk; gardens open
daily dawn–dusk,
reception desk Apr–Oct
10–5

One of the most interesting properties in Troutbeck is **Townend**, a 17th-century stone and slate house that belonged to a wealthy 'statesman' farming family. It contains carved woodwork, papers, furniture and old domestic implements collected by the Browne family, who lived here from 1626 to 1943. The cylindrical chimneys are typical of the buildings in this area of the Lake District. Full of fascinating nooks and crannies, Townend is now owned by the National Trust and is open to the public, providing a fascinating insight into the life of yeoman farmers.

Townend
Troutbeck,
t (015394) 32628,
www.nationaltrust.org.
uk; open Feb–Mar
Sat–Sun 11am–3pm
Apr–Nov Wed–Sun
11am–5pm; adm

Other interesting properties include **Hoggart's House**, near Nanny Lane, named after playwright Thomas Hogarth, who lived here in the 17th century. 'Auld Hoggart', as he was known, was the uncle of 18th-century painter and cartoonist William Hogarth. He achieved some notoriety locally for his bawdy poems.

Herdwick Sheep

There are a lot of sheep in Cumbria, but only one captures the hearts of both locals and visitors – the Herdwick. Why does everyone love them? Maybe it is because of their tough lives – this is the hardiest of British breeds, grazing the high, exposed Lake District fells all year round. Maybe it is because of their appearance – although the lambs are jet black, adults have an attractive coat of slate grey that lightens with age, and seem to have permanent, fixed 'smiles' on their faces. Or maybe it's because, despite the odds, this relatively rare breed somehow managed to survive the foot-and-mouth culls of 2001.

The breed is thought to have come over with the Norsemen in the 10th century. The name comes from the Norse, 'herdvyck', meaning sheep pasture.

The lambs graze with their mothers on the 'heaf' belonging to a farm, which gives them a life-long knowledge of where they should be grazing, a knowledge that they will then pass on to their own lambs. This 'hefting' is crucial for farmers because a sheep that strays just a few miles over the fell-tops from Borrowdale to Eskdale will mean a 100-mile round trip by road for the farmer to collect it.

Herdwicks don't make much money for farmers these days, but their rough, scratchy wool is still used to make rugs, carpets and insulation materials. The slow-matured meat is like a combination of lamb and mutton – a tender meat with a slightly more gamey flavour than conventional lamb.

Down in the valley bottom, you will find **Jesus Church**. There has been a church on this site since the 16th century, but the whole building was dismantled and rebuilt in 1736 with further, major alterations in 1861. The large east window is the combined work of Edward Burne-Jones, William Morris and Ford Madox Brown. The local story is that Morris and Brown were in Troutbeck on a fishing holiday when Burne-Jones was working on the window, and they stayed to help him.

Further up the valley is **Troutbeck Park**. Beatrix Potter bought this 1,900-acre sheep farm in 1923. She decided to run the farm herself and enlisted the help of shepherd Tom Storey. The pair established a celebrated flock of Herdwick sheep, and Potter was eventually made president of the Herdwick Sheepbreeders' Association. She used Troutbeck Park as a setting in *The Fairy Caravan* and several other pieces. When she died in 1943, she left this and 13 other farms to the National Trust – a total of 4,000 acres of land (*see* p.143).

South of Bowness

As you leave Bowness and head south, but before you reach the ferry, you will see Windermere's largest island, **Belle Isle**, formerly known as Longholme. Its rather impressive 'pepper-pot' house, so hated by Wordsworth, was built in 1774 by Nottingham merchant Thomas English. Clearly inspired by Italian architecture, it has a dome and a four-column portico. But Mr English wasn't the first to build on the island. Roman remains, possibly of a villa, have been found; and, during the Civil War, the Royalist Philipson family had a fortified house here. They were besieged for eight months by Roundheads under the command of Colonel Briggs, who is said to have fired cannon at the island from Cockshott Point. After the siege, one of the enraged Philipsons, 'Robin the Devil', rode off to Kendal in search of revenge. Sword in hand, he rode into Kendal Parish Church, seeking Briggs. What happened next is uncertain. Some say he couldn't find his man, so left via a low door, which knocked him off his horse; others says he was dragged from his horse by the angry congregation. Either way, he left behind his sword and helmet, both of which can still be seen in the church today. The story was used by Sir Walter Scott in his epic poem, *Rokeby*:

'The outmost crowd have heard a sound,
Like horse's hoof on harden'd ground;
Nearer it came, and yet more near.
The very deaths-men paused to hear
'Tis in the churchyard now – the tread
Hath waked the dwelling of the dead!
Fresh sod, and old sepulchral stone,
Return the tramp in varied tone.
All eyes upon the gateway hung,
When through the Gothic arch there sprung,
A horseman arm'd, at headlong speed,
Sable his cloak, his plume, his steed.
Fire from the flinty floor was spurn'd,
The vaults unwonted clang return'd...'

There are two major visitor attractions south of Bowness on the eastern side of the lake. These are Blackwell and Fell Foot.

Blackwell
Newby Bridge Rd,
t (015394) 46139,
www.blackwell.org.uk;
open daily 10.30am–5pm
(4pm Nov–Mar); adm

Blackwell is a shrine to the Arts and Crafts movement, a bastion of calm and good taste that is overflowing with period furniture, *objets d'art* and some wonderful architectural detail. The Arts and Crafts movement was led chiefly by John Ruskin and William Morris, who, in the face of increasing mechanization during the Industrial Revolution, wanted to see designer-craftsmen valued more and a return to more authentic work.

The house was built in 1900 by the acclaimed architect Mackay Hugh Baillie Scott as a holiday home for the Manchester brewery owner, Sir Edward Holt and his family. The Lakeland Arts Trust bought it in 1999 and, thanks to lottery money, was able to undertake a huge restoration, finally opening the house to the public in 2001.

Blackwell hosts regular exhibitions of contemporary crafts and also has a café with a terrace overlooking Windermere.

Fell Foot
Newby Bridge,
t (015395) 31273,
www.nationaltrust.org.uk;
park open daily
9am–5pm, tearoom and
shop mid Feb–Nov daily
11am–5pm

Continuing south along the eastern shore of Windermere for several miles, you eventually come to **Fell Foot**, a National Trust-owned country park at the far, southern end of the lake. On a sunny summer's day, the handsome Victorian lawns that run right down to the water's edge are popular with picnicking families. It's an opportunity to relax and enjoy the simple pleasures – feed the ducks or take a rowing boat out on the lake. The 19th-century boathouses have been converted into a tearoom and shop.

Close to Fell Foot is **Gummer's How**, a popular little hill that provides superb views of Windermere and the Coniston fells. From Fell Foot, take the minor road heading north-east off the A592 and, in about three-quarters-of-a-mile you will see a small car park. The walk to the top, which shouldn't take much more than half-an-hour, is signposted from here.

Walk: Orrest Head and Dubbs Road

Start and finish:
Windermere Railway Station
Distance:
7 miles/11.3km
Total ascent:
1,036ft/316m

In brief:
Little Orrest Head (781ft) provides some magnificent views of Windermere, and for relatively little effort. But why stop there? This route takes walkers up to the popular summit and then out along the lonely Dubbs Road. Having left busy Windermere behind, you get a surprising sense of remoteness as you gaze into the beautiful Trout Beck valley from the old drovers' routes.

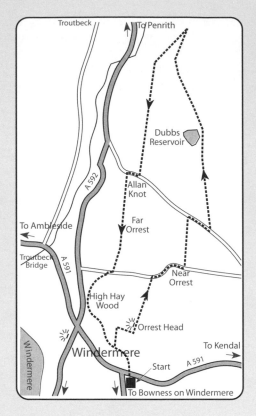

Route description:
Leaving the railway station, turn left and then, at the complicated junction where the station driveway meets the A591, carefully cross to the north side of the busy main road, to the pavement in front of **The Windermere Hotel**. Turn left along the A591 for a few yards until, just after you draw level with the bank on the other side of the road, you see a lane heading up to the right, clearly signposted to Orrest Head. Follow this, ignoring a path off to the left early on.

The lane winds gently uphill through the trees. Soon after the asphalt ends, bear right at a fork near a bench. Continue uphill and go through a metal kissing-gate to gain the steps that lead to the summit of **Orrest Head**.

It was on Orrest Head that guidebook writer Wainwright first fell in love with the Lake District. Fresh from his native Blackburn, he stood and looked out over the Coniston fells, Crinkle Crags, Bow Fell and Scafell Pike and declared that what he saw was a 'fascinating paradise'. There are some superb views of the surrounding fells from here.

From the top, pick up the grassy path heading NNE. Don't go through the next gate; instead, cross the stone stile in the wall to the right of it and then continue in a NE direction along a faint, grassy trail. Keeping to the right of the wall at all times, you eventually reach a minor road. Turn right and walk along the road for about 400m, ignoring the first footpath on the left, close to the buildings at **Near Orrest**. Keep going for another 120m and then cross the stile in the wall on your left – towards Moor Howe.

There is no path on the ground across the next couple of fields. Head NNE, straight towards the pole in the middle of the field and then continue up to and over a ladder stile. Maintaining the same NNE line, cross this field to exit it via a wooden gate – the left of two gates in the top wall. Now cross to the ladder stile over to your right. Beyond this, turn left to walk with the wall on your left.

Turn right along **Moorhowe Road** and follow it until you reach a clear, wide track on the left. This is **Dubbs Road**, which you now follow for just over a mile-and-a-half, passing **Dubbs Reservoir** on the way. The reservoir was originally constructed to supply Windermere, but then became an adjunct to the Thirlmere Aqueduct, serving Manchester. The reservoir and beck downstream provide important habitats for rare pearl mussels and crayfish.

On reaching a junction with another track, the **old Garburn Road**, turn sharp left, reluctantly turning your back on the lovely view up the Troutbeck valley. When the track forks, bear left to head gently uphill. As the track begins to drop, the views are dominated by Windermere stretching into the distance.

The track ends at a road, where you turn right. Then, in 110m, turn left through a gate – towards Far Orrest. Follow the grassy track south and then, as it approaches some trees, go through the left of two gates. Walk with a wall on your right until you reach a kissing-gate, which gives you access to a grassy lane between two drystone walls.

Approaching the buildings at **Far Orrest**, go through the gate on your right. A weathered sign indicates this is the path to Crosses Farm and Windermere. It heads west and drops to a ladder stile. Cross straight over the two tracks in front of you and over a step stile, signposted Windermere via Crosses.

The track goes through a gate and heads up to and over a ladder stile. Head SSW towards a gap in the wall, but don't go through the gap; instead, bear left to walk with the wall on your right. Cross one stone stile, followed soon after by a ladder stile. Go through the next large metal gate and on to a track to the left of a pretty white cottage.

When you reach the road, turn right. At the **junction with the A592**, go through the old metal gate to your left. When the gravel track swings left, bear right along a narrower path that soon reaches a vehicle track. Go straight over – towards Windermere and Orrest Head.

You now go through a rusty gate before crossing a footbridge and then climbing. When you reach **Elleray Bank**'s surfaced driveway, go straight across. Pass to the left of some buildings belonging to **St Anne's School** and ignore a turning on your left.

Eventually, you will come out on the lane that you took up to Orrest Head at the start of the walk. Turn right and then left along the main road to retrace your steps to the **railway station**.

Where to Stay East of Windermere

(i) Windermere
Tourist
Information
Centre
*Victoria St,
t (015394) 46499; open
March–Oct Mon–Sat
9.30–5, Sun 10–5;
Nov–Feb closed Thurs*

(★) Cedar Manor
>>

(i) Bowness Bay
Lake District
National Park
Information
Centre
*Glebe Rd,
t (015394) 42895; open
Apr–Oct daily
9.30–5.30; Nov–March
daily 9.30–4.30*

Luxury

Gilpin Lodge, Crook Rd, Windermere, t (015394) 88818, *www.gilpinlodge.co. uk*. Small, family-run country house hotel with a relaxed atmosphere. Peaceful location, fresh flowers and open fires in the winter. Spa treatments available in your room. The **restaurant** has a deservedly good reputation for its food.

Linthwaite House Hotel, Crook Rd, Windermere, t (015394) 88600, *www.linthwaite.com*. An award-winning establishment in glorious surroundings ideal for a romantic getaway or a special treat. Stylish, intimate **restaurant** (*expensive*) serves up rib of beef, red mullet and a good choice of vegetarian dishes.

Miller Howe, Rayrigg Rd, Windermere t (015394) 42536, *www.millerhowe .com*. One of the few hotels that have grounds running right down to the shores of Windermere, the Miller Howe is a great place to escape from it all. Go for a lake-view room with its own balcony.

The Samling, Ambleside Rd, Windermere, t (015394) 31922, *www.thesamlinghotel.co.uk*. There's an air of exclusivity surrounding this sumptuous luxury hotel. Hidden away at the top of a private driveway, it sits in a 67-acre estate with magnificent views across Windermere. The excellent **restaurant** has three AA rosettes and offers a nine-course gourmand menu.

Expensive

21 The Lakes, Lake Rd, Windermere, t (015394) 44165, *www.21thelakes. co.uk*. There is an eclectic, slightly humorous mixture of rooms in this rather unusual boutique hotel. Styles range from the regal to the minimalist. One of the rooms has a suspended bed that appears to 'float' above the floor and includes a huge spa bath in the room.

Aphrodites Hotel, Longtail Hill, Bowness, t (015394) 45052, *www.aphroditeslodge.co.uk*. The humour apparent at 21 The Lakes is even more noticeable at its sister hotel. Fun, themed rooms include the funky Austin Powers suite with its bold, bright 1960s colour scheme; and the Flintstone Suite, complete with imitation furs and made to look like a cave...albeit a luxurious cave. All the food is organic.

Cedar Manor, Ambleside Rd, Windermere, t (015394) 43192, *www.cedarmanor.co.uk*. It's easy to forget you're on a main road once you're behind Cedar Manor's high walls and hedges. This lovely, secluded hotel has a feeling of peace and tranquillity. Most rooms have king-size or superking-size beds. TVs are subtly hidden away in cabinets. Staff are friendly but unobtrusive. It also has a good **restaurant** (*expensive– moderate*), overlooking the garden, which is open to non-residents. *Booking is recommended.*

Moderate

Storrs Gate House, Longtail Hill, Bowness, t (015394) 43272, *www.storrsgatehouse.co.uk*. This place is far enough from Bowness for guests to feel that they've escaped from the excesses of the town, but close enough to walk in and benefit from its facilities. Winner of Cumbria Tourism's Bed and Breakfast of the Year award in 2009. Surprisingly good value for money.

The Angel Inn, Helm Rd, Bowness, t (015394) 44080, *www.the-angel inn.com*. Polished wooden floors and unfussy furniture give this smart hotel a fresh, airy feel. In the summer, the outside terrace is a pleasant place to sit and watch the world go by, or at least Bowness go by.

Wheatlands Lodge, Old College Lane, Windermere, t (015394) 43789, *www. wheatlandslodge-windermere.co.uk*. An elegant house that has recently been refurbished to a very high standard. Spacious rooms and superb bathrooms.

Self Catering

Heaning Barn Cottages, Heaning, near Windermere, t (01539) 766107, *www.heaningbarncottages.com*. Three quality cottages sleeping between four and six people in a barn conversion just to the east of

Windermere town. Each has a new kitchen, equipped to a very high standard.

Windermere Holiday Houseboats, Ferry Nab, Bowness, t (015394) 43415, *www.lakewindermere.net*. For something a bit different, why not rent a houseboat for the week? These two boats are well kitted-out and more spacious than you'd expect. Each is four berth, with two separate sleeping areas. Available all year round.

 White House >>

Where to Eat East of Windermere

Jerichos at The Waverley, College Rd, Windermere, t (015394) 42522, *www.jerichos.co.uk* (*expensive*). Imaginative dishes with the emphasis on flavour and simplicity are the hallmark of chef-proprietor Chris Blaydes, former head chef at the Miller Howe. A favourite among visitors and locals alike – and the holder of two AA rosettes – you will need to book. *Closed Thurs*.

Queen's Head Hotel >

Queen's Head Hotel, Townhead, Troutbeck, near Windermere, t (015394) 32174, *www.queenshead hotel.com* (*expensive*). There are lots of cosy pubs serving up good food all over the Lake District, but this centuries-old coaching inn has to be one of the cosiest of them all. What could be better on a cold winter's evening than indulging yourself in a huge plate of roast belly of pork with creamed potatoes, garden pea puree, crispy *pancetta* and wholegrain mustard sauce? There is also room at the inn – as well as in the barn conversion next door (*expensive–moderate*).

Lucy 4 at the Porthole, Ash St, Bowness, t (015394) 42793, *www.lucysofambleside.co.uk* (*moderate*). Another member of the ever-growing family of 'Lucy' businesses, this one specializes in tapas-style dishes to share.

The Hideaway, Phoenix Way, Windermere, t (015394) 43070, *www.thehideawayatwindermere.co.uk* (*moderate*). The Hideaway is, well, hidden away from the bustle of

Windermere town centre. Recently awarded an AA rosette, the restaurant specializes in uncomplicated fare such as lamb shank with rosemary and garlic, and pan-fried fillet of red snapper. Upstairs are 11 airy rooms, some traditional, some contemporary, but all en suite (*expensive–moderate*). *Restaurant closed Mon and Tues*.

White House, Robinson Place, Lowside, Bowness, t (015394) 44803, *www.whitehouse-lakedistrict.co.uk* (*moderate*). This smart but unpretentious establishment has a contemporary take on traditional favourites. Crispy, seared salmon cooked to perfection on the inside, perfectly pink duck and seriously indulgent desserts. Also has six well-equipped bedrooms (*moderate*).

Lighthouse, Main Rd, Windermere, t (015394) 88260 (*moderate–budget*). A light, airy and modern café-bar with a spacious upstairs seating area.

Purple Chilli, Windermere Bank, Bowness, t (015394) 45657, *www.purplechilli-bowness.co.uk* (*moderate–budget*). This lively, funky internet café uses mostly organic and fair-trade products. Great coffee and home-made cakes as well as light lunches.

Entertainment East of Windermere

The Old Laundry Theatre, Crag Brow, Bowness, t (015394) 88444 ext 223, *www.oldlaundrytheatre.co.uk*. Sponsored by the World of Beatrix Potter, with which it shares a building, the Old Laundry's short but busy season of drama, comedy and music runs from the end of August until the end of November. It is based on Alan Ayckbourn's original theatre in Scarborough and, as such, is one of only six 'in-the-round' in England.

The Royalty, Lake Rd, Bowness t (015394) 43364, *www.nm-cinemas. co.uk*. A good, old-fashioned cinema with three screens showing the latest releases as well as a few less commercial films.

West of Windermere

As travellers continue past the southern end of Windermere on the A592, the first place they come to is Newby Bridge, which represents their only chance of crossing to the western side of the lake by road since Ambleside, more than 13 miles to the north. The five-arched stone bridge spanning the River Leven, which issues from Windermere, was built in 1651.

Lakeside and Haverthwaite Railway
Haverthwaite Station, t (015395) 31594 www.lakesiderailway.co. uk; open daily Apr–Nov; adm

On the western side of the river is the **Lakeside and Haverthwaite Railway**, a short but delightful section of track featuring classic steam engines. It was once a branch line of the Furness Railway, carrying ore, timber and passengers between Lakeside and Barrow, but it was closed in the 1960s. All that remains today is a 3.5-mile length of standard gauge track between Haverthwaite and Lakeside via Newby Bridge. This popular attraction chuffs up and down the line five to seven times a day, and the trains are timed to coincide with boat arrivals and departures.

Lakes Aquarium
Lakeside, Newby Bridge, t (015395) 30153, www.lakesaquarium.co. uk; open daily 9am–5pm; adm

Right next door to the railway's northern terminus at Lakeside is the **Lakes Aquarium** which allows visitors to explore the exotic underwater worlds of Africa, Asia and the tropical rainforests, and there is also a chance to walk through an underwater tunnel that mimics a trip through the depths of Windermere. Carp, perch and the creepy 6ft-long wels catfish are among the local delights.

Stott Park Bobbin Mill
Newby Bridge, t (015395) 31087, www.english-heritage.org.uk; open Apr–Nov Mon–Fri 11am–5pm; adm

To escape from the bustle of Lakeside, there are plenty of lovely walks in the woods fringing the river and the lake. Nearby too is **Stott Park**, an old bobbin mill in a pretty woodland setting that has been restored by English Heritage. There used to be dozens of mills in the county producing bobbins for the textile industry of Lancashire and Yorkshire, but this one, built in 1835, is the only one that has been restored. The complicated mass of belts and Victorian machinery, first powered by water and then by steam, is in working order again, and visitors can watch bobbins being made and take one home as a souvenir. The informed guides give 45-minute tours and fascinating demonstrations.

Once upon a time, there would have been about 250 men and boys working here in often difficult conditions to produce 250,000 bobbins each week. Bobbin-turning was a dangerous and unpleasant job with long hours. Children would have been used for jobs such as log-peeling – hand-stripping the bark from logs for 12 hours a day, six days a week. They received no pay or education, just shelter and two meals a day. It was partly this dependence on child labour – as well as competition from abroad – that led to the decline of the industry after the 1867 Factory Act.

Graythwaite Hall Gardens
Graythwaite, t (015395) 31333, www.graythwaitehall.c o.uk; open daily Apr–Aug 10am–6pm; adm

Continuing north, that gardening genius Thomas Mawson strikes again as you reach **Graythwaite Hall Gardens**. In 1896, he was commissioned to create a garden combining both the formal and the informal. Surrounded by woodland, the result is 12 attractive acres that are particularly well known for their springtime displays of rhodo-dendrons and azaleas. There are also yew hedges, sundials, elegant gates, a rose garden and even a dog cemetery. Sadly, the attractive 17th-century hall is not open to the public.

At Near Sawrey, you will encounter the crowds again – this is the heart of Beatrix Potter country. In fact, the tiny village, with its limited

Getting to and around West of Windermere

By Bus

There are several local buses serving the western side of Windermere as far as Coniston. The **505** runs between Ambleside, Hawkshead and Coniston, roughly every hour, although there is a reduced service on Sundays and in the winter (total journey time, 33 minutes). The Grizedale/Hawkshead to Newby Bridge and Haverthwaite **X30** bus operates just a few services each day and only from April to November (journey time Hawkshead to Haverthwaite, 25 minutes). Another summer-only service, the **X31** visits Hawkshead, Coniston and Tarn Hows. The **Cross Lakes Experience** links Bowness, Hawkshead, Grizedale Forest and Coniston via a series of carefully co-ordinated buses and boats (*www.mountain-goat.com*). The **X12** links Coniston with Ulverston (journey time, 40 minutes).

By Taxi

Hawkshead Private Hire, **t** (015394) 36946.

By Boat

The Windermere passenger and vehicle **ferry** connects Ferry Nab, just south of Bowness, with Ferry House, near Far Sawrey. Weather and water conditions permitting, the service runs all year. Ferries every 20 minutes, **t** (01228) 227653.

Windermere Lake Cruises operates boats from Lakeside to Bowness and, from there, on to various other points on the lake, *see* p.62.

Weather permitting, the **Coniston Launch** operates regular services between Coniston, Waterhead, Torver, Brantwood and various other points, **t** (01768) 775753, *www.conistonlaunch.co.uk*. Except for the two weeks around Christmas and New Year, there are no weekday sailings between Dec and mid-Feb.

By Bicycle

To hire bikes, try Grizedale Mountain Bikes, **t** (01229) 860369, *www.grizedalemountainbikes.co.uk*; Bike Hire Hawkshead, **t** (015394) 36946; or Country Lanes at Lakeside, **t** 07748 512 286, *www.countrylaneslakedistrict. co.uk*, closed Nov to March.

 Hill Top
Near Sawrey,
t (015394) 36269,
www.nationaltrust.org.
uk; house open
Feb–Mar Sat–Thur
11am–3.30pm, Mar–Nov
Sat–Thur
10.30am–4.30pm,
gardens daily Mar–Dec;
adm

car parking, gets hellishly busy, so it is best approached by bus, either from Bowness (using the bus/ferry combination) or from Hawkshead. The main attraction here is **Hill Top**, Potter's first farm, which she bought in 1905 with the royalties from some of her books. Over the next eight years, she drew inspiration from the area and at least seven of her books are set on the farm or in the countryside surrounding it. Now owned by the National Trust, to which Beatrix bequeathed 14 farms and about 4,000 acres on her death in 1943, Hill Top is open to the public. Timed entry tickets avoid serious overcrowding, but you will still be tripping over your fellow tourists as you slowly shuffle around the lovely 17th-century farmhouse, admiring Potter's furniture and some of her most prized possessions, including books, pottery and china. Fans will be able to spot items in the farmhouse and in the village that featured in her illustrations. The local pub, the Tower Bank Arms, for example, was in *The Tale of Jemima Puddle-Duck*.

East of Near Sawrey you reach its equally pretty sister village, Far Sawrey, before dropping down to the Ferry House. If woods, gently rolling hills and hidden tarns are your thing, **Claife Heights** to the north will be like heaven on earth. There are dozens of paths criss-crossing this area, which runs right down to the shores of Windermere. Take a stroll up to Moss Eccles Tarn from Near Sawrey. Potter bought this pretty body of water in 1913. She and her husband William Heelis kept a boat on the tarn and spent many happy summer evenings here. If you

Potter's pigs

Just beyond the High Tilberthwaite turning on the A593 is Yew Tree Farm, built in 1693 and still sporting its ancient spinning gallery. If this picturesque farm looks familiar, that's because it was used as a setting in *Miss Potter*, the 2006 Beatrix Potter biopic starring Renée Zellwegger. The farm was one of many owned in the Lake District by Potter, but in the film it becomes Hill Top. The National Trust had invited the director to use the real Hill Top, but on visiting the Near Sawrey property, the designer, Martin Childs, realized that it would be too restrictive. He then had to convince the National Trust that Yew Tree Farm would be much better. He later confessed that, on the concept drawing that he showed to the charity, he drew what he described as a 'monster pig' with loads of piglets wandering around freely. His plan was to scare the National Trust into believing that the pigs, an essential part of any 'Hill Top' scenes, would destroy the real Hill Top's beautiful heritage garden.

are heading up to Claife Heights though, bear in mind that it is haunted...

One stormy night, a long, long time ago, the ferrymen of Windermere heard an eerie voice summoning them from the western shores. Most chose to ignore the call, but one young oarsman set off to collect his fare. He returned several hours later, ashen-faced and struck dumb. What had happened to him out there on the lake? What had he seen? His colleagues never found out for he soon developed a fever and, within days, was dead.

The voice continued to call out from the Claife Heights on wild nights, but the ferrymen ignored it. Finally, a priest was called and the spirit was silenced.

There have been several theories to explain the origins of the so-called Claife Crier. In the book, *Ghosts and Legends of the Lake District*, J. A. Brooks suggests it may have been 'an echo of one of the tragedies that occurred here in the 17th century'. In 1635 and again in 1681, two boats sank, drowning all on board. In the first accident, 47 wedding guests were killed on their way home from the ceremony. Perhaps it was one of these long-lost revellers that the young ferrymen saw.

Local legend has it that the calls came from the ghost of a monk from Furness Abbey who was prevented from marrying the woman he loved by his monastic vows. Tormented, he retreated to the forests of Claife where he died of grief. Walkers beware – for a hooded figure has been seen wandering the forest tracks after dark.

If you're not put off by stories of heartbroken monks, there is also a track that runs right along the western lake shore of Windermere, all the way up to Wray Castle. This huge, Gothic-style house was built in the 1840s by a retired Liverpool surgeon, using his wife's inheritance. It is said that she took one look at it when it was finished and refused to live there. The building itself isn't open to the public, but the grounds are managed by the National Trust, so you can wander right up to it.

Hawkshead

Despite its popularity – and it can get very crowded at the height of the summer – Hawkshead is a lovely, quaint little place to wander round. Visitors have to leave their vehicles in a sprawling, edge-of-the-

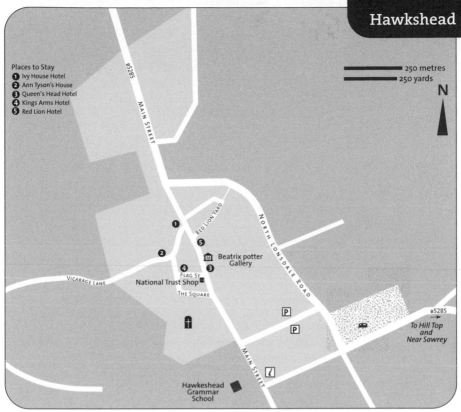

village car park, so the historic centre is refreshingly car-free. With a history going back to Norman times, Hawkshead is a jumbled muddle of narrow alleyways, low archways, timber-framed buildings over-hanging cobbled pavements and, of course, a market square. The market, which was initially an important centre for the wool trade, was first established by the wealthy monks of Furness Abbey.

Hawkshead Grammar School, a free school, was established in 1585 by Edwin Sandys, of nearby Esthwaite Hall, who spent some time in the Tower of London under Mary Tudor but then became Archbishop of York under Elizabeth I. Closed in 1909, the school's most famous pupil was William Wordsworth (see p.25, p.28, p.98). As well as seeing the schoolroom and the upstairs galleries, visitors can also see where the budding poet, clearly bored during one of his lessons, carved his initials into his desk.

While he was at the school, the young Wordsworth boarded with Ann Tyson, first in a beautiful 16th-century cottage in the village centre and then out at Colthouse. The former, known as Ann Tyson's Cottage, is now a B&B. Having lost his mother a few years earlier, he adored the kind, maternal Mrs Tyson. He writes about her in *The Prelude*, recalling a return to Hawkshead during a summer vacation from Cambridge:

'Glad greetings had I, and some tears, perhaps,

Hawkshead Grammar School
Hawkshead,
t (015394) 36735,
www.hawksheadgram
mar.org.uk; open
Apr–Sept Mon–Sat
10am–5pm, Sun
1pm–5pm; Oct Mon–Sat
10am–3.30pm, Sun
1pm–3.30pm; adm

From my old Dame, so motherly and good;
While she perus'd me with a Parent's pride.
The thoughts of gratitude shall fall like dew
Upon thy grave, good Creature! While my heart
Can beat I never will forget thy name.'

But, unusually in the Lake District, it isn't Wordsworth who is the main crowd puller here; it is Beatrix Potter. The **Beatrix Pottery Gallery**, housed in an attractive 17th-century building, contains a vast collection of her original illustrations. The collection includes not only the famous watercolours for her books, but also some of her detailed and perceptive sketches of plants and fungi. Potter herself used to visit this building because it housed the offices of her solicitor, W. H. Heelis and Son. When the royalties from her books started coming in, she began snapping up farmland in the area, and relied on William Heelis, youngest son of the firm's founder, for advice. Romance blossomed and the pair married in 1913.

Beatrix Potter Gallery
Main St,
t (015394) 36355,
www.nationaltrust.org.uk; open Feb–mid-Mar Sat–Thurs 11am–3.30pm, mid Mar–Nov Sat–Thurs 10.30am–4.30pm; adm

The village's oldest building is the **Old Courthouse**, which dates from the 15th century, although parts of it go back another 200 years. Situated on the northern outskirts of Hawkshead and now in the care of the National Trust, it was once a gatehouse to the grand manor, which has since disappeared. The villagers would come here to pay their rents and tithes, and wrongdoers would be tried and punished. Entry is free, but a £5 deposit is required for the key, which can be borrowed from the National Trust shop in the village centre.

The hilltop church of **St Michael and All Angels** is also worth a visit, if only for the impressive views over the village rooftops and to the fells beyond. The building is 15th century with later improvements.

Another church worthy of note is the pretty, white-washed Baptist chapel in nearby Hawkshead Hill. Baptists have been worshipping here since 1709, although a plaque outside mistakenly suggests the chapel dates back to 1678. In fact, this earlier date relates to the time when a group of Torver miners made a covenant to defy the law and worship in a style that wasn't accepted by the established church at that time. The Hawkshead Hill chapel was only used after the law had been relaxed. Just beyond the small graveyard is an outdoor baptistry, one of only two in Cumbria. It was last used in 1991.

Esthwaite Water Trout Fishery
The Boat House,
Ridding Wood,
t (015394) 36541
www.hawksheadtrout.com; open daily

South of Hawkshead is **Esthwaite Water**, a relatively shallow lake that is about 1.5 miles long. It is home to the largest trout fishery in the northwest of England and, as such, is one of the most popular fishing spots in the area. The fishery organizes day-long fly-fishing courses or you can simply take your own gear, buy a permit and settle down for the day. Boats are available to hire and there is also a large, on-site tackle shop.

🟢 Grizedale Forest Park
Visitor Centre, near Hawkhead,
t (01229) 860010,
www.forestry.gov.uk;
open daily 10am–5pm,
closes 4.30pm in winter

Grizedale

The Forestry Commission's immense **Grizedale Forest Park** stretches from Hawkshead in the north to Satterthwaite and beyond in the south, an area of 2,447 hectares. Tortuously narrow roads lead from Hawkshead to the smart new visitor centre. If you're driving a campervan you may want to consider approaching from the south instead.

The area has become a huge outdoor playground in recent years – for walkers, mountain-bikers, fans of orienteering, art lovers... The forest is criss-crossed by miles of paths and tracks. A popular destination for walkers is Carron Crag – at 1,030ft, the highest point in the forest. It may be pretty small compared with the fells further north, but the views are grand. The visitor centre has a map showing eight waymarked trails, including a route to Carron Crag. These range in length from 1 mile to 9.5 miles, visiting impressive waterfalls, ancient iron-smelting bloomeries, sites associated with Arthur Ransome's *Swallows and Amazons* books, and dozens and dozens of sculptures.

There are 80 sculptures scattered throughout Grizedale, some of which can be played, some of which can be used as hiding places, but all of which are meant to be fun and inspire. One of the most famous works is internationally-renowned artist Andy Goldsworthy's *Taking a Wall for a Walk*. This was created in the 1980s and the original intention, as with many of the other pieces, was for it eventually to be absorbed by the living forest. However, the area around it has since been felled and some restoration of the 'wall' has taken place.

Grizedale is also home to a whole load of mountain-biking trails. These range from the wide, gravel forest roads to the purpose-built 10-mile North Face trail.

And, as if a forest full of sculptures, paths and biking trails wasn't enough, the **Go Ape!** high-wire forest obstacle course is open to anyone – as long as they're over 10 years of age, taller than 4ft 7ins and weigh no more than 20.5 stone. You'll also need to be reasonably fit and have a head for heights to cope with the wobbly rope bridges and exhilarating zip slides. Everyone taking part wears a harness and uses a system of pulleys and karabiners to keep them safe from harm.

Go Ape! Grizedale Forest Park
near Hawkshead, t 0845 643 9086, www.goape.co.uk; open end March–end Oct daily 9.30am–3.30pm (last entry), Nov Sat and Sun only; booking in advance essential; adm

Coniston

It is only as you approach Coniston that the soft, rolling countryside associated with the Silurian slates suddenly yields to the more dramatic, craggy scenery of the Borrowdale volcanics. The humble little collection of houses and inns sits at the foot of some mighty mountains, the most famous and highest of which is the Old Man (2,635ft). To the south is Coniston Water, more than five miles long.

Coniston's growth was based on the copper-mining industry, which has left its seemingly indelible mark on **Coniston Old Man**, often compared to a holey cheese because of the lumps and chunks that the miners have ripped out of it over the years. The Romans are thought to have been the first to work the mineral veins here, and mining was definitely going on in Norman times, but it was only in the 16th century, when the German miners (*see* p.142) arrived, that things really began to take off. The most prosperous period was the middle of the 19th century, when the men were working at depths of up to 1,100ft beneath the surface – that's about 500ft below sea level. At one time, there were as many as 600 people working at the mines.

A railway linking Coniston with the Furness line at Broughton was opened in 1859, a great relief for the Coniston Mining Company, which

 Coniston Old Man

had previously had to shift ore and slate by barge down the lake or by horse and cart to the Ulverston canal. The mining industry began its inevitable decline after World War One and finally ceased operations in the late 1940s. The railway, which was meanwhile bringing tourists into the area, managed to hang on a little longer.

The story of the mines, the area's geology and just about everything to do with Coniston is told in the **Ruskin Museum**. Set up in 1901 by W. G. Collingwood, who had been Ruskin's secretary, it is intended partly as a memorial to Coniston's most famous resident, who died in 1900, and a celebration of all things Coniston.

Ruskin Museum
Coniston,
t (015394) 41164,
www.ruskinmuseum.
com; open Mar–Nov
daily 10–5, Nov–Mar
Wed–Sun 10.30–3.30;
adm

Some of the most popular exhibits relate to Donald Campbell's ill-fated attempt to break the world water-speed record on Coniston Water in 1967. In 2006, Gina Campbell, the daughter of the late speed ace, donated his boat, *Bluebird*, to the museum. It is expected to go on display following a major restoration in 2010 or 2011. There are also plans to take the boat for a run on Coniston Water again, taking her up to 100mph. The Lake District National Park Authority recently decided to temporarily lift the lake's 10mph speed limit to allow this to happen.

Donald Campbell came to grief on Coniston Water on January 4, 1967. While attempting to break the 300mph barrier, Bluebird K7 slowly lifted out of the water, did a backward somersault in the air and then plummeted into the lake nose first, killing Campbell instantly. Said to be travelling at 328mph at the time of the accident, Campbell shouted over his radio link: 'I'm going, I'm on my back... I'm gone.' His last words. A later trawl of the lake failed to find his body, but, in 2001, a team of divers brought the wreck of Bluebird to the surface. The same team went back a few months later and recovered Campbell's remains. He has since been buried in the village cemetery.

Also buried in the village, in the old churchyard of St Andrew's, is John Ruskin. He declined the prospect of a burial in Westminster Abbey and chose to remain in his beloved Lake District. His grave is marked by a large carved cross made from green Tilberthwaite slate and decorated with symbols depicting important aspects of Ruskin's life.

Brantwood
Coniston,
t (015394) 41396,
www.brantwood.org.uk;
open daily Mar–Nov
11am–5pm, winter
Wed–Sun 11am–4.30pm

Ruskin lived at **Brantwood** on the eastern shore of Coniston Water. The great Victorian intellectual was born in London in 1819, and first visited the Lake District when he was five years old. He once said that the 'first thing I remember as an event in life was being taken by my nurse to the brow of Friar's Crag on Derwentwater'. It was, he continued, 'the creation of the world for me'. It was clearly a moment that he never forgot, and he never forgot the Lake District either, choosing to set up home on the shores of Coniston Water in 1872.

Ruskin did a lot of work to Brantwood, renovating and expanding the 18th-century house. One of the most noticeable of his additions is the southwest turret, which gave him spectacular views over the lake and the surrounding countryside. He filled his home with works of art and items that he had brought back from his travels. There were Pre-Raphaelite paintings, watercolours by Turner, medieval manuscripts and a large collection of minerals. Visitors can still see many of these, as well as much of Ruskin's original furniture, as they walk around Brantwood's atmospheric rooms today. The eight gardens, which are maintained in a way of which Ruskin would probably have approved, are also open to the public. The 'Zig-Zaggy', for example, is based on an 1870s sketch by Ruskin that is said to represent the 'purgatorial mount' in Dante's *Inferno*.

A pleasant way to get to Brantwood from Coniston is via the National Trust's restored steam yacht, **Gondola**. As you serenely approach the house in the Victorian splendour of the boat's opulently upholstered saloon, it is easy to believe, for just a split second, that you are about to take tea with Professor Ruskin himself.

Steam Yacht Gondola
Coniston Water,
t (015394) 41288,
www.nationaltrust.org.
uk; cruises April–Oct
daily 10.30am–4.15pm;
adm

The original Gondola was first launched in 1859 by Sir James Ramsden, a director of the Furness Railway Company. She carried tourists up and down the length of the lake until 1936, when she was decommissioned. She then became a houseboat until a storm ripped her from her moorings and beached her in the early 1960s. She was finally restored and relaunched in 1980. Today, Gondola carries passengers between Coniston Pier and the Brantwood and Monk Coniston jetties, a round trip of about 45 minutes. Every Monday and Thursday, there is also a 90-minute cruise along the full length of Coniston Water, during which time visitors learn about some of the most famous people associated with Coniston – Ruskin, Campbell, Ransome et al.

07 **The South Lakes | West of Windermere: Coniston**

Coniston Launch
Coniston Water,
t (017687) 75753,
www.conistonlaunch.co
.uk; Mar–Oct daily
10.15am–4.55pm; Nov, 21
Dec–3 Jan, 14
Feb–March daily
10.25am–2.25pm; 1
Dec–20 Dec and 4
Jan–14 Feb Sat and Sun
10.25am–2.25pm; adm

Another great way to get around on the lake is via the **Coniston Launch**, which operates regular services covering two circular routes. The southern service takes almost two hours, and passengers can get off at any of the seven jetties. There are also two special, themed cruises – celebrating the work of Arthur Ransome and visiting some of the sites that inspired his writing; and remembering the Campbells and their many speed records.

The Lake District National Park runs the **Coniston Boating Centre**, just half-a-mile from the village. Here, visitors can hire rowing boats, sailing dinghies, sit-on kayaks, Canadian canoes and small motorboats. Qualified staff also run sailing and powerboat courses, all recognized by the Royal Yachting Association.

Coniston Boating Centre
Coniston Water,
t (015394) 41366,
conistonbc@lake-
district.gov.uk; daily
10am–4.30pm; adm

In terms of walking, there's something for everyone. Aside from the beautiful lakeshore paths, there are woodland walks, bridleways across low moorland and well-trodden routes on mountain tops and along high ridges. Some of the best, and most popular, fell routes are in the Coniston range. The **Old Man** – which, incidentally, was the basis for Ransome's fictional Kanchenjunga – can be climbed by the steep, stony tourist route up its east face. Better still, head up the Walna Scar Road and round the back of the mountain to approach it via the long, broad ridge connecting Brown Pike, Buck Pike and Dow Crag. You can then return to Coniston via the tourist route or stride out along the superb, high-level ridge as far as Swirl How. A scrambly descent along Prison Band leads to Swirls Hawse before you drop down to Levers Water reservoir and the Coppermines Valley. Craggy Wetherlam (2,503ft) also makes for a superb day out. Ascend via rocky Wetherlam Edge to add a bit of excitement to the outing – it's not too tricky, but you will need your hands from time to time.

Tilberthwaite Gill and its disused quarries provide interesting walking. Drive north along the A593 from Coniston for about 1.5 miles and then take the minor road on the left to High Tilberthwaite. The gill can be easily accessed from a car park just before the road end.

Also nearby is **Tarn Hows**, one of the most popular of Lake District beauty spots. It is a little strange that in a county endowed with so much natural magnificence, one of the biggest crowd pullers of them all is actually a Victorian creation. Tarn Hows was originally three tiny tarns, but the landowner, James Garth Marshall, dammed one of them to create the single tarn that exists today. He also planted the conifer plantations that surround it, intending both to frame and reveal views of his new creation. His plans were based on the ideas of the 'picturesque' that were prevalent at the time.

Tarn Hows and the nearby **Monk Coniston** estate, is now owned by the National Trust, which has carried out a tremendous amount of improvement work in the area in recent years. This has included woodland management, new public toilets at Tarn Hows, the restoration of the gardens at Monk Coniston and improved paths and access around the entire estate. A new permissive path through the grounds of Monk Coniston Hall links Monk Coniston, at the northern tip of Coniston Water, with Tarn Hows and allows visitors to enjoy the unusual tree collection and restored walled garden in the grounds. There is parking at Tarn Hows, but it does get unbelievably busy, particularly at weekends, so visitors do better to park at Coniston Water and then use the new trails. The round walk, including a circuit of Tarn Hows, is about five miles.

Festivals and Events West of Windermere

(i) **Hawkshead Tourist Office**
Main St, Hawkshead,
t (015394) 36946,
www.hawksheadtourist
info.org.uk. Open
March–Oct Mon–Sat
9am–5.30pm, Sun
9am–5pm, Nov–Feb
daily 10am–5pm.

(i) **Coniston Tourist Information Centre**
Ruskin Ave, Coniston,
t (015394) 41533,
www.conistontic.org.
Open March–Oct daily
9.30am–5pm, Nov–Feb
daily 10am–4pm.

(★) **Randy Pike >>**

The annual **Hawkshead Show** (*www.hawksheadshow.co.uk*), a mostly agricultural and equine show but with some horticultural and homecraft sections, normally takes place at Hawkshead Hall Farm in August. Keen walkers will also be interested to know that Coniston hosts a three-day **walking festival** *(www. coniston walkingfestival.org)* every September. One of the highlights of the weekend is the sunrise walk up the Old Man. Walkers set off at 5am and begin their climb by torchlight, reaching the summit in time to watch the sun rise. This is followed by a well-earned cooked breakfast back in the village.

The **Coniston Water Festival** (*www.conistonwaterfestival.org.uk*), which takes place in July, includes a duck race, canoe racing, special cruises, sailing sessions for beginners and It's A Lake Knockout.

Where to Stay West of Windermere

Luxury
Lakeside Hotel, Newby Bridge, t (015395) 30001, *www.lakeside hotel.co.uk*. The rooms are a tad on the expensive side, but you do get plush designer fabrics and smart bathrooms decked out in Italian marble. Some rooms also have access to their own private gardens. Many look out directly onto the shores of Windermere. Also has an indoor pool and good leisure facilities. The **Lakeview Restaurant** (*very expensive*), which has two AA rosettes, serves up first-class cuisine in beautiful surroundings.

Expensive
Randy Pike, Low Wray, t (015394) 36088, *www.randypike.co.uk*. The friendly owners have put their hearts and souls into restoring this Gothic-Revival hunting lodge. The result is a daring, original and stylish B&B that oozes luxury and wonderful little

flashes of opulence. Breakfast is brought to your sumptuous room. Throw open the double doors and watch the roe deer in the garden while you enjoy a pampered, leisurely start to the day.

The Knoll, Lakeside, near Newby Bridge, **t** (015395) 31347, *www.theknoll-lakeside.co.uk*. A perfect, get-away-from-it-all-type retreat in a tranquil woodland setting close to Windermere. Bold décor, iPod docking stations, a king-size sleigh bed, good cuisine and lovely lawns are all part of the experience.

The Swan Hotel, Newby Bridge, **t** (015395) 31681, *www.swanhotel.com*. Olde worlde charm on the outside, but all mod cons indoors. Nice rooms, indoor pool, gym, sauna, spa – you name it, they've got it. The **River Room** restaurant serves tasty, imaginative meals (*expensive–moderate*).

Yew Tree Farm, near Coniston, **t** (015394) 41433, *www.yewtree-farm.com*. The idyllic, 17th-century farmhouse that featured in the film *Miss Potter*. Upstairs, extraordinary oak-wood panelling separates the bedrooms. Simple things such as fresh coffee, real milk and home-made cakes in your room every afternoon make any stay in this lovely spot that extra bit special.

Moderate

Ann Tyson's House, Wordsworth St, Hawkshead, **t** (015394) 36405, *www.anntysons.co.uk*. A homely, traditional and slightly chintzy B&B where William Wordsworth is said to have lodged when he was at the local grammar school. Very reasonably priced for the location.

Beechmount Country House, Near Sawrey, **t** (015394) 36356, *www.beech mountcountryhouse.co.uk*. Great views over Esthwaite Water. Go for the Esthwaite Suite which has large bay windows in both the bedroom and the separate lounge area. As with so many properties in the area, it has its literary links – apparently, in 1915, Beatrix Potter leased the house for her mother.

Force Mill Guest House, Satterthwaite, **t** (01229) 860205, *www.forcemillfarm. co.uk*. The rooms may be a little spartan, but they are clean and comfortable and you'd be hard pushed to find anything this cheap nearby. Lovely old building in a peaceful setting in Grizedale Forest.

Ivy House Hotel, Hawkshead, **t** (015394) 36204, *www.ivyhouse hotel.com*. This top-notch Grade II listed Georgian house in the middle of Hawkshead is full of period furniture and elegant décor. Also has a good, fully-licensed **restaurant** (*expensive–moderate*) that is open to non-residents.

Lakes End, Newby Bridge, **t** (015395) 31260, *www.lakes-end.co.uk*. Good value accommodation in a bright, clean and friendly guesthouse.

Summer Hill Country House, Hawkshead Hill, **t** (015394) 36180, *www.summerhillcountryhouse.com*. Laura Ashley furnishings, soothing colour schemes and a computer in each room are just some of the features of this spick-and-span guesthouse between Coniston and Hawkshead. Comfortable communal areas in which to unwind, including a guest lounge and large gardens.

Walker Ground Manor, Hawkshead, **t** (015394) 36219, *www.walker ground.co.uk*. A beautiful 16th-century house, full of character and charm, that retains many interesting features, including exposed beams, wooden floors and panelling and a rare barley-twist oak staircase. The front bedroom has a four-poster bed and roll-top bath. Pretty woodland garden is a bonus in the summer.

Waterhead Hotel, Coniston **t** (015394) 41244, *www.waterhead-hotel.co.uk*. Perfect, peaceful location at the head of the lake, but just a few minutes' walk from the village.

Yewfield, Hawkshead Hill, **t** (015394) 36765, *www.yewfield.co.uk*. A splendid, Gothic-style building set in 30 lovely acres. Stylish rooms have oak panelling. Vegetarian breakfasts. Also hosts free classical music concerts. Luxury, self-catering cottages available.

Budget

Four Winds Lakeland Tipis, Low Wray Campsite, **t** (01539) 821227, *www. 4windslakelandtipis.co.uk*. These brightly coloured native American-style dwellings each come with futon

 Yewfield >>

bed, portable gas heater and outdoor picnic table and bench. Currently located at Low Wray campsite, but they are nomadic...

Self Catering

Bank Ground Farm, Coniston, t (015394) 41264, *www.bank ground.com*. Five beautifully restored cottages, sleeping between two and 16 people, just above the lake. Each of the cottages has stunning views and shares a picnic terrace. The farm is said to be one of the settings for *Swallows and Amazons*.

Shepherds Cottage, Howe Farm, Hawkshead, t (015394) 36345, *www.howefarm.co.uk*. Single-storey barn conversion on a working farm about half-a-mile outside Hawkshead. Spacious kitchen and good views from both bedrooms.

Where to Eat West of Windermere

Barngates

> **Drunken Duck**, Barngates, t (015394) 36347, *www.drunkenduckinn.co.uk* (*expensive*). Smart gastro-pub serving up some of the best food you'll find outside of the top hotels. Expect ale-braised belly of pork, butternut squash mille-feuille or breast of duck, salsify and baby onions with mashed potato and star anise jus. *Book well in advance.*

Coniston

The Crown Inn, t (015394) 41243; **The Sun, t** (015394) 41248 and the **Black Bull Inn, t** (015394) 41335 all serve standard pub food at *moderate* prices with little to tell them apart. For fans of real ale, the Bull Inn does have the added advantage of having its own microbrewery, which produces, among others, the award-winning Bluebird bitter.

 Church House Inn >>

Harry's Bar, Yewdale Rd, Coniston, t (015394) 41389, *www.harrys-coniston.co.uk* (*moderate–budget*). Surprisingly trendy-looking place for down-to-earth Coniston, but the food remains relatively simple. Great coffee, extensive wine list and a superb big breakfast.

The Bluebird Café, Lake Rd, Coniston, t (015394) 41649, *www.thebluebird cafe.co.uk* (*budget*). Great lakeside location provides a top spot to enjoy a light summer lunch or afternoon tea. Soups, salads, sandwiches and baked spuds. Terrace area gets understandably busy on a hot day. *Closed weekdays Dec–Feb.*

Grizedale Forest

The Café in the Forest, Grizedale Forest Park, t (01229) 860011 (*budget*). Smart café run in partnership with Kendal's Brewery Arts Centre. Parents can enjoy a coffee on the sunny terrace while the children enjoy the adventure playground next door.

Hawkshead

Queen's Head Hotel, Main St, Hawkshead, t (015394) 36271, *www.queensheadhotel.co.uk* (*expensive*). Good quality posh nosh in a quaint old inn with a roaring open fire and a family-friendly environment. Ingredients are sourced from local producers, including Winster valley pork, Esthwaite Water trout and fellbred lamb and beef.

Kings Arms Hotel, Hawkshead, t (015394) 36372, *www.kingsarms hawkshead.co.uk* (*moderate*). If you choose your pub according to the number of locals who eat there, the Kings Arms is the place to go in Hawkshead. Good list of daily specials.

Red Lion Hotel, Hawkshead, t (015394) 36213, *www.redlionhawkshead.co.uk* (*moderate–budget*). The new managers here are working hard to bring a fresh, lively feel to Hawkshead's oldest pub. Good, filling bar meals in a friendly atmosphere.

Torver

Church House Inn, Torver, t (015394) 41282, *www.churchhouseinn torver.com* (*expensive–moderate*). If you're looking for something a bit better than standard pub grub, this cosy old inn is worth the drive from Coniston. It prides itself on serving good-quality, local produce including Morecambe Bay brown shrimps and Cumberland tattie hotpot, using Herdwick meat from nearby Yew Tree Farm.

South Coast

Cumbria's south coast consists of a series of peninsulas jutting out into Morecambe Bay, separated by the treacherous sands of three river estuaries. Largely lying beyond the National Park boundary, they receive fewer visitors than areas to the north – and fewer visitors than they deserve.

Arnside to Haverthwaite

Working east to west, we start our coastal journey at **Arnside**, close to the border with Lancashire. The town stands on the mouth of the River Kent, once navigable at high tide. As recently as the early 19th century, ships would sail past Arnside on their way to Milnthorpe, laden with saltpetre and sulphur for Cumbria's gunpower industry. And the tiny town itself had a boatyard, making small fishing boats, up until 1938. In fact, Arthur Ransome's boat *Swallow*, the inspiration behind his *Swallows and Amazons* series, was made at the yard. Today, Arnside is quieter, but it still receives a few tourists and is also a popular retirement spot.

Above the town is the small limestone hill of **Arnside Knott**, a popular destination for walkers, providing amazing views across the sands to the Lake District fells. On the southern side of the hill are the romantic ruins of **Arnside Tower**, built as a stronghold against Scots raiders in the 15th century.

The attractive Edwardian resort of **Grange-over-Sands** is just over three miles from Arnside by rail or nearly 14 miles by road. The railway crosses the River Kent via an 170-yard viaduct that was built in 1857, effectively closing the River Kent to shipping forever, although silt was already contributing greatly to this. It was the railway managers who first tried to bring tourists into Grange, luring them with the promise of a mild climate, good air and spa waters (at nearby Humphrey Head). They even built a hotel and brought in the first gas supply.

It remains a charming spot today, although people walking along the lovely promenade can no longer enjoy watching the pleasure boats on the Kent. The river's channel changed course a while ago and the view now is of sheep grazing on the salt marshes. So, don't expect a seaside resort; instead, go for the atmosphere, the surprisingly dense and exotic trees and the ornamental gardens and duck pond, built in 1865.

From the town, an easy walk up through the woods brings you to the limestone grasslands of **Hampsfell**, and some breathtaking views. Squatting in the middle of the limestone pavement on the top of the fell is an unusual feature – the **Hampsfell Hospice**. This rather entertaining Victorian shelter was built in 1846 by the vicar of Cartmel, and panels inside invite the weary traveller to rest, enjoy the views and 'not by acts of wanton mischief and destruction show that they possess more muscle than brain'. A set of steps up the side of the building leads to a roof with an interesting viewfinder on it. Visitors can line up the arrow on the top with the angles given on a board to identify what they are

Getting to and around the South Coast

By Train

Arnside, Grange-over-Sands, Kents Bank, Cark, Ulverston, Dalton and Barrow-in-Furness are all served by trains running between Barrow-in-Furness and Lancaster/Manchester. It takes about an hour to get to Barrow from Lancaster, and there are roughly 16 trains a day, fewer on a Sunday. Barrow, Askam, Kirkby-in-Furness, Foxfield, Millom, Silecroft and Bootle are all on the **Cumbrian Coast Line**, which runs regular services from Barrow to Carlisle via Ravenglass, St Bees, Whitehaven, Workington, Maryport, Aspatria and Wigton, a total journey time of about two hours, 20 minutes.

By Local Bus

The hourly **X35** links Barrow with Kendal via Ulverston, Newby Bridge and Grange-over-Sands (total journey time, one hour, 40 minutes). The **618** runs six services a day (four on Sundays) between Barrow and Ambleside via Newby Bridge, Bowness and Windermere (one hour, 15 minutes). The **X12** runs between Coniston and Ulverston (journey time, 40 minutes). In addition, there are buses linking Kendal, Levens and Arnside (service **552/553**); Kendal, Grange and Cartmel (**530**); and more localized buses such as the **532**, which covers the Grange area, and the **6, 10** and **11**, which cover the Furness peninsula.

On Sundays only, there is also a bus (the **X6**) linking Barrow with Whitehaven via Muncaster Castle, Ravenglass, Gosforth and St Bees.

By Taxi

A–Z Cars, **t** (01229) 877277 and Coastline Taxis, **t** (01229) 430430 in Barrow. Geoff Taxi, **t** (01229) 586666, Acclaim Taxis, **t** (01229) 582779 and A 2 B Taxis, **t** (01229) 587030 in Ulverston. Road Runner, **t** (015395) 33792 in Grange-over-Sands. Arnside Private Hire, **t** (01524) 761938 in Arnside.

By Bicycle

To hire bikes (summer only), try Gill Cycles, The Gill, Ulverston **t** (01229) 581116, *www.gillcycles.co.uk*. Closed Sun.

---

looking at. The amazing panorama includes Blackpool Tower, the Isle of Man, Coniston Old Man, Scafell and Skiddaw.

Cartmel

 Cartmel

On the other side of the fell is Cartmel. If you have time to visit only one place in Cumbria's far south, make it Cartmel. In a county that is full to overflowing with gorgeous villages, this one does well to stand out head and shoulders above the rest. Its olde worlde atmosphere comes from the ancient monastic buildings that brush shoulders with pretty 17th- and 18th-century cottages, cobbled yards and traditional inns. The gently babbling River Eea, partly hidden by weeping willows, adds to the charm.

St Cuthbert first established a monastery here in the 7th century, although nothing remains of that early building. The priory church of **St Mary and St Michael** was built in 1190 by the Baron of Cartmel, William Marshall, and was originally part of an Augustinian priory. The church was saved from the ravages of Henry VIII's Dissolution of the Monasteries in the 16th century because Marshall had decreed that it was to serve the people of the village; Henry's commissioners were not authorized to destroy parish churches. Sadly, they did a thorough job of destroying much of the rest of the priory – aside from parts of the church, all that remains today is the 14th-century **gatehouse** close to the village's market cross.

The gatehouse is in the care of the National Trust, but is mostly a private residence now. The doors of the Great Room are opened to the public on just a few half-days every summer.

Cartmel Priory Gatehouse
The Square, Cartmel, **t** *(01524) 701178, www.nationaltrust.org. uk; open designated days only; donations*

The Shifting Sands

As you travel around the peninsulas, you will come across old signposts indicating the distance to a particular town 'over sands'. This isn't part of the place name, it indicates the quickest route to that place via the sands of the bay and the tidal river estuaries. Look at any OS map of the area and you will still see rights of way crossing the sands – together with the warning: 'Public rights of way across Morecambe Bay can be dangerous. Seek local guidance.'

Those dangers were brought home on the evening of 5 February 2004 when 23 Chinese cockle-pickers were killed while working the sands. They fell foul of the incoming tide, which moves notoriously rapidly, but there are other dangers too – ever-changing weather conditions, hidden deep-water channels, and, most sinister of all, terrifying quicksands that regularly shift as the river channels shift and are capable of swallowing tractors.

People have been using the bay as a public highway for centuries, millennia even. Tacitus was the first to record the crossing, claiming that he and his Roman soldiers were guided across the sands by native tribesmen. Local people trying to get from one village to another had no other option than to use the sands, and many of them perished on the crossing. The king appointed the first guides to the sands in the 16th century – a direct result of a petition by the local people.

The current Queen's Guide to the Sands is Cedric Robinson, who is now in his mid-70s. He was appointed to the post in 1963, becoming the 25th person to hold the position since 1536. The former Flookburgh fisherman gets paid a 'salary' of £15 per year to guide walkers across the treacherous sands each summer. His diary is booked up for months in advance by people hoping to make the crossing for charity, as part of a personal challenge or simply because they want to experience the famous sands for themselves. Cedric normally starts his walk at Arnside and finishes at Kents Bank, but the route can change according to the river conditions. Anyone who wishes to book a place on a walk should phone the **Grange-over-Sands Tourist Information Centre** on (015395) 34026.

The beautiful priory church, on the other hand, is open every day. A mixture of many different architectural styles, highlights inside the building include the huge stained-glass east window, dating back to the middle of the 15th century, beautifully carved oak choir stalls and a 750-year-old tomb. Look out for the southwest door, known as Cromwell's Door. The holes in it are said to be the bullet holes made by local parishioners firing at Cromwell's soldiers. Guided tours take place at 11am and 2pm every Wednesday, between April and October, but visitors are free to enjoy the church at other times too.

South of the village, **Humphrey Head** is one of Cumbria's two sea cliffs, the other being the higher and more dramatic St Bees Head (*see* p.186). Victorian tourists used to come here to partake of the spa waters that issued from Holy Well, but a modern sign warns that the water is no longer fit for drinking. The limestone cliff, now a nature reserve, is still worth visiting though – both for its views over the bay and for the unusual orchids that grow along the cliff.

Holker Hall and Gardens
Cark-in-Cartmel, ***t*** *(015395) 58328, www.holker.co.uk; house open Mar–Nov Sun–Fri 11–4, gardens open Mar–Nov Sun–Fri 10.30–5.30, gift shop, food hall and café open all year 10.30–5.30 (4pm in winter); adm*

Holker Hall

Holker Hall is one of the most magnificent of Cumbria's stately homes, surrounded by some of the most glorious of country gardens. The house dates back to the 16th century, although the areas open to the public today are 19th century, the building having undergone a major rebuild after a devastating fire in 1871. The Cavendish family, who have owned the estate since 1756, still live in one of the older wings of the house.

86

Among the highlights is the Long Gallery, an elegant Victorian interpretation of the original Elizabethan gallery complete with plasterwork ceiling and several fine desks and tables. The library, with its 3,500 leather-bound books – some of which survived the 1871 fire – is also worth a look. But probably most impressive of all is the magnificent carved-oak, cantilevered staircase reached through a grand archway of polished limestone.

Outside are 25 acres of superb gardens, part formal, part woodland. Visitors can enjoy a beautiful springtime display of rhododendrons as well as an arboretum and a large walled kitchen garden. Deer roam the parkland and worth visiting is a 400-year-old lime tree, with a girth of about 26ft.

A Food Hall sells produce from the estate and other local producers, and there is also a gift shop and courtyard café.

Attached to the hall is the **Lakeland Motor Museum**, home to more than 30,000 exhibits, including some wonderful old cars and motorcycles. There are also full-size replicas of some of Sir Malcolm and Donald Campbell's record-breaking Bluebird machines. The museum is expected to move to a new, purpose-built site at Backbarrow, near Newby Bridge in 2010.

Lakeland Motor Museum
Holker Hall, Cark-in-Cartmel, Grange-over-Sands, t (015395) 58328, www.holker-hall.co.uk; open Feb–Nov daily 10.30am–4.45pm; adm

The Furness Peninsula

Haverthwaite marks the southern terminus of the Lakeside and Haverthwaite Railway (*see* p.72). West of here, after you have crossed the River Crake, is the Furness Peninsula. The first settlement of note is **Ulverston**, a quiet, friendly town that becomes a little less quiet on market days – Thursdays and Saturdays. It has a fair few independent shops, some rather quirky, as well as an indoor market hall, making it a pleasant place to find an unusual bargain or two.

It seems hard to believe it now, but Ulverston was something of a boom town in the early 19th century. Busy iron furnaces and the construction of a canal, giving Furness its first port, pushed the population up to 50,000. But just as the growth of Ulverston had resulted in the slow demise of Hawkshead, Broughton-in-Furness and Cartmel, so the coming of the railways and the subsequent development of Barrow-in-Furness resulted in Ulverston's furnaces being closed down and the population seeking work elsewhere.

Motorists can't fail to notice the town's land-locked 'lighthouse', sitting up on Hoad Hill, as they drive into the town from the north. This 100ft-high model of Eddystone Lighthouse is a monument to one of the town's most famous sons, Sir John Barrow (*www.sirjohnbarrow monument.co.uk*). Born in 1764, he was the only son of a journeyman tanner. He became an explorer and writer, and was second secretary to the Admiralty for 40 years, a period that coincided with much of the Napoleonic Wars. There are several routes up to the monument from St Mary's Church, and if there is a flag flying, it means the monument is open for visitors to climb the 112 narrow steps up to the lantern chamber. As with so many of the viewpoints in this area, the vista from the top is pretty special.

Laurel and Hardy Museum
Brogden Street,
t (01229) 582292,
www.laurel-and-hardy.co.uk; open Feb–Dec daily (except Christmas Day), 10am –4.30pm; adm

Swarthmoor Hall
Ulverston,
t (01229) 583204,
www.swarthmoorhall.co.uk; tours mid-Mar–mid-Oct Tues–Fri, 2.30pm; adm

Conishead Priory
Ulverston,
t (01229) 584029,
www.conisheadpriory.org; grounds open daily dawn to dusk, temple and gift shop open Mar–Dec Mon–Fri 2–5pm; Sat and Sun 12–5pm, Dec–Feb daily 2–4pm. Guided tours of house Mar–Dec Sat, Sun and Bank Holidays 2.15pm and 3.30pm; adm

Gleaston Water Mill
Gleaston,
t (01229) 869244,
www.watermill.co.uk; open Tues–Sun 11am–4.30pm; adm

Stan Laurel, born in 1890 and one half of the famous Laurel and Hardy comedy double act, is another of Ulverston's famous sons. A bronze statue of the pair was unveiled in the middle of Ulverston in 2009, and the town's Roxy cinema is also home to the **Laurel and Hardy Museum**. This weird and wonderful collection of memorabilia includes letters, photographs, personal items, trademark bowler hats, and even some old curtains from a former home of Stan Laurel. A small cinema shows films and documentaries.

Just to the southwest of Ulverston is **Swarthmoor Hall**, a key location in the birth of the Quaker movement. Having preached to the 'great multitude' on Firbank Fell in the Howgills (*see* p.215) in 1652, George Fox, the founder of the Quakers, travelled to Ulverston to seek an audience with Judge Thomas Fell, the owner of Swarthmoor Hall. He was unable to convince Fell of the validity of his religious arguments, but he did manage to convince Fell's wife Margaret and much of the rest of the household. Consequently, Swarthmoor Hall became a meeting place for the Quakers and a powerhouse for the movement in its early years – even more so when George Fox married Margaret Fell after Judge Fell's death. The hall offers guided tours as well as B&B and self-catering accommodation.

Another important religious site is **Conishead Priory**, right on the edge of the estuary's sandbanks. Two huge octagonal towers dominate the building, a magnificent example of early Victorian Gothic architecture. No sign remains of the 12th-century Augustinian priory. During much of the 20th century, the house was a convalescent home for Durham miners – except for during World War Two, when it became the largest military hospital in the northwest. Today, it is home to the Manjushri Kadampa Buddhist meditation centre. The centre, including the new temple, gift shop and 70 acres of gardens, is open to the public daily, but the house is open on a guided-tour basis only, limited to weekends and bank holidays.

A little way off the main road from Ulverston to Barrow, the **church of St Mary and St Michael** at Great Urswick is well worth a visit. The building dates from the 13th century, but there has been Christian worship on the site for 1,000 years. Evidence includes a section of Viking cross with a runic inscription on it. The main reason visitors come to the church though is not for its ancient roots, but to see the excellent woodcarvings created by the Camden Guild in 1910. A colourful rush-bearing ceremony (*see* p.41) is held in the church at the end of September each year.

The village is surrounded by evidence of prehistoric settlement, including several burial mounds and traces of Iron Age or Romano-British settlement. Excavation of two stone rings on nearby **Birkrigg Common** revealed cremated remains on what is thought to be the site of a Druidic temple.

Just below the romantic ruins of the 14th-century Gleaston Castle, which can be viewed only from the road, is the restored **Gleaston Mill**, which is open to the public. This water-powered corn mill dates back to 1770, although there are records of a mill on the site since at least 1608.

Visitors can see the 18ft water wheel operating, find out how flour was made and then enjoy lunch in the adjacent Dusty Miller's tea and coffee shop.

The small town of **Dalton-in-Furness** was once the peninsula's principal town and, for more than 400 years, the monks of Furness Abbey held their courts here. The 14th-century peel tower at the top end of town, near the market cross, was built by the abbot as a prison. Today, it contains a local history exhibition organized by the Friends of

Dalton Castle
Market Place, Dalton-in-Furness,
t (01524) 701178,
www.nationaltrust.org.
uk; Apr–Sept Sat 2–5pm;
donations

Dalton Castle as well as a display about painter George Romney (see below).

Just behind the castle is a large Victorian church, St Mary's, built by the famous Lancastrian architects Paley and Austin, who were also responsible for the rebuilding of Holker Hall and the rather quaint little railway station that still stands at Grange-over-Sands. In the graveyard lies Dalton's most famous son, the celebrated 18th-century portrait painter George Romney. The son of a cabinet-maker, to whom he was apprenticed at the age of 11, Romney painted the rich and the famous. Some of his best-known works are of Emma Hart, who later became Lady Hamilton, Nelson's mistress.

South Lakes Wild Animal Park
Broughton Rd, Dalton-in-Furness,
t (01229) 466086,
www.wildanimalpark.
co.uk; open Easter–Oct
daily 10am–5pm,
Nov–Easter daily
10am–4.30pm; adm

The **South Lakes Wild Animal Park** is on the edge of Dalton, always a favourite with families. It is home to lions, tigers, white rhinos, giraffes, kangaroos, lemurs and all sorts of monkeys. Feeding events take place throughout the day, and visitors can join in with some of them, feeding the penguins and giraffes by hand, for instance. The park also has a café, gift shop and toy train.

Barrow

The Victorian planned town of Barrow isn't the most attractive of places. The industrialists of the Furness Railway Company and the Barrow Haematite Steel Company, who planned and controlled Barrow, built a practical town – a place that could produce huge quantities of steel and build massive ships, and a place where tens of thousands of workers and their families could live in decent conditions. Of course, much of the heavy industry has gone now – although BAE Systems operates a busy shipyard making submarines for the Royal Navy.

The Dock Museum
North Rd, Barrow-in-Furness,
t (01229) 876400,
www.dockmuseum.org.
uk; Easter–Oct Tues–Fri
10am–5pm, Sat and Sun
11am–5pm; Nov–Easter
Wed–Fri 10.30am–4pm,
Sat and Sun
11am–4.30pm

The story of Barrow's development from a tiny fishing port to an industrial powerhouse is told in the town's excellent **Dock Museum**. Built over a disused dry dock, the museum contains detailed models of some of the ships built in Barrow over the years – destroyers, aircraft carriers, submarines and massive passenger liners. There are also archaeological artefacts, objets d'art and geological samples.

Furness Abbey
Barrow-in-Furness,
t (01229) 823420,
www.english-
heritage.org.uk; open
Apr–June Thurs–Sun
10am–5pm, July and Aug
daily 10am–5pm, Sept
Thurs–Mon 10am–5pm,
Oct–March Sat and Sun
10am–4pm; adm

The striking red sandstone ruins of **Furness Abbey**, painted by Turner and written about by Wordsworth, stand in a peaceful valley on the edge of Barrow. The walls of the transept and choir still stand tall, and, with the help of an informative audio tour, it doesn't take much imagination to conjure up a picture of what this majestic building would have looked like before Henry VIII got his hands on it. The Cistercian monks of Furness arrived here in the first half of the 12th century and soon became one of the richest and most powerful monastic houses in the whole of northern England. They lived simple lives and would not accept any gifts except land – a policy that paid off as they eventually controlled huge tracts of Cumbria.

The trails in the adjoining narrow stretch of mixed woodland, known as **Abbotswood**, make for a pleasant stroll after a visit to the abbey ruins. Information panels explain the history, both natural and human.

There are several islands just off the coast of Barrow, the largest of which is **Walney Island**, reached from the town by a road bridge. Not many visitors get this far, although the island does have some large, sandy beaches – secluded enough to be popular with naturists. The beach at Earnse is also becoming well known among kite-surfers.

Piel Castle
open at all times; free

The most interesting of the islands is **Piel Island**, home to the ruins of 14th-century **Piel Castle** and the famous Ship Inn. The castle, standing guard over the mouth of Barrow's deep-water harbour, was built by the monks of Furness Abbey as a fortified warehouse. It is now in the care of English Heritage. In 1487, the forces of 10-year-old imposter to the throne, Lionel Simnel, landed on Piel Island as part of an attempt to overthrow Henry VII. Backed by the Yorkists and the Irish, and with an Oxford-trained priest pulling his strings, Simnel failed but was pardoned by the king and given a job in the royal kitchen as a spit-turner. This unusual episode in English history is thought to be behind the slightly mocking tradition of the 'King of Piel'. Each new landlord of the Ship Inn is crowned king in a ceremony which involves them sitting on a 'throne', wearing a helmet and holding a sword while alcohol is poured over their head.

Murphy's Miles
t (01229) 473746

To reach Piel Island, there are two ferries that operate during the summer from Roa Island, which in turn is connected to Rampside by a causeway. Contact the king of Piel Island Steve Chattaway on 07516 453784 or Alan Cleasby on 07798 794550. A local guiding company, **Murphy's Miles**, will take groups of walkers across the sands at low tide.

Millom and the Far Southwest

It takes quite a bit of effort to get to Millom; the M6 is almost 40 winding miles away, and the nearest of the main Lake District villages, Coniston, is a long 15 miles to the northeast. This is an isolated spot, but it is probably that which gives the area a certain attractive bleakness. The long curve of sandy beach at Haverigg is a bracing place for kite-flying and dog-walking on a windy autumn day. The impressive sculpture here, *Escape to the Light*, by the artist Josefina de Vasconcellos is dedicated to the inshore rescue teams. Silecroft, just a couple of miles further north, is one of the few places in England where you can ride a horse on the beach. The **Murthwaite Green Trekking Centre** organizes rides from one hour to a full day for all abilities along this wild stretch of coast, but visitors are advised to book well in advance. **Cumbrian Heavy Horses** also offers rides along the dunes and beaches of the Duddon estuary on the back of massive Clydesdales and shire horses.

Murthwaite Green Trekking Centre
t (01229) 770876, www.murthwaitegreen. co.uk

Cumbrian Heavy Horses
t (01229) 777764, www.cumbrianheavy horses.com

Millom Folk Museum
Old Station Building, Station Rd, Millom, t (01229) 772555, www.millomfolk museum.com; Apr–Oct daily 11am–4pm; adm

Millom itself is home to the **Millom Folk Museum** where shops and a miner's cottage have been recreated to tell the story of this once thriving industrial town. There is also an interesting display on the life and work of Millom's most famous son, the poet Norman Nicholson (*see* p.30).

Nearby, there is also a small **museum** dedicated to the aviation history and military heritage of the region.

RAF Millom Aviation and Military Museum
Unit 2, Devonshire Road Industrial Estate, Millom, t (01229) 777446, www.rafmillom.co.uk; daily (362 days a year) 10.30am–5pm; adm

Looming over the town and the surrounding beaches is the dark, brooding expanse of Black Combe, the Lake District's most south-westerly fell, largely neglected by walkers from outside the area. On the other side of neighbouring White Combe is the **Swinside** or **Sunkenkirk** **stone circle**, consisting of 55 stones set in a tight circle, an impressive sight and one of the Lake District's best-kept secrets. The circle is behind a drystone wall on private ground, but it can be viewed from a public footpath that passes very close by. It's a half-hour walk from the nearest parking area.

To the north of Millom is another Lake District secret – the **Duddon Valley**. In terms of visitor attractions and infrastructure, there's not a lot here – just a pub at Seathwaite (not to be confused with Borrowdale's Seathwaite), a post office and small shop at Ulpha and a wonderfully-located, but fairly basic campsite at friendly Turner Hall Farm. Stretching for 10 miles from Duddon Bridge in the south to Cockley Beck, between the Wrynose and Hardknott passes, in the north, visitors come here to escape the crowds and enjoy some great walking. Wallowbarrow Crag and the dark gorge formed by the Duddon below it make for interesting walking, as does Harter Fell. The more intrepid might want to head up the Walna Scar Road to access the high fells of Dow Crag, Swirl How and Grey Friar before descending via Seathwaite Tarn.

Festivals and Events on the South Coast

(★) **Number 43 >>**

Ulverston hosts several lively festivals throughout the year, the most popular and atmospheric of which is probably the **Dickensian Christmas Festival,** usually on the last weekend in November (*www.dickens ianfestival.co.uk,* t (01229) 580640). Stallholders don their Victorian best, brass bands come out to play and the streets are full of all sorts of entertainment. Other festivals include the **International Music Festival** (*www.ulverstonmusicfestival.co.uk*), a week-long feast of classical music held in the spring, and September's **Lantern Festival**, which culminates in a fireworks display.

Where to Stay and Eat on the South Coast

Arnside

Number 43, The Promenade, Arnside, t (01524) 762761, *www.no43.org.uk* (*expensive–moderate*). It looks like a pleasant Victorian house from the outside, but inside you'll find a real des res – designer chic and modern luxuries coupled with the intimacy of a homely B&B. Breathtaking sunsets over the Kent estuary are an added bonus.

Ye Olde Fighting Cocks, The Promenade, Arnside, t (01524) 761203, *www.fighting-cocks.co.uk* (*moderate*). Good rooms and a terraced garden with river views.

(i) **Barrow-in-Furness Tourist Information Centre**
Forum 28, Duke St,
t (01229) 876505. Open
Mon–Fri 9am–5pm,
Sat 9am–4pm

Barrow-in-Furness

Duke of Edinburgh Hotel, Abbey Rd, Barrow-in-Furness, t (01229) 821039, *www.dukeofedinburghhotel.co.uk* (*moderate*). It may have a touch of the corporate about it, but you can't fault the comfortable, well-equipped rooms here. This town centre hotel also has a very good bistro (*expensive–moderate*).

Broughton-in-Furness

Old King's Head, Church St, Broughton-in-Furness, t (01229) 716293, *www.oldkingshead.co.uk* (*expensive–moderate*). Classy food in the relaxed setting of a traditional village inn.

The Blacksmiths Arms, Broughton Mills, Broughton-in-Furness, t (01229) 716824, *www.theblacksmithsarms.com* (*moderate*). Good, old-fashioned pub grub in a good, old-fashioned country pub with a warm welcome. The lovely building dates back to the 16th century and contains a lot of historical features such as an oak-panelled corridor and a large black farmhouse range.

Cartmel

(★) **L'Enclume** >

L'Enclume, Cavendish St, Cartmel, t (015395) 36362, *www.lenclume.co.uk* (*very expensive*). Don't go along to Simon Rogan's Michelin-starred restaurant expecting anything ordinary. This is cutting-edge stuff – food that really challenges the diner and an experience you won't forget in a hurry. Choose from eight, 13 or 17 courses of the weird and wonderful. Pork cheeks and chocolate, seabass served with a reduction of oak bark and Kentish truffles and, for dessert, stiffy tacky pudding, a deconstruction of Cartmel's more famous dessert. The restaurant also has nine smart rooms, each of which is tastefully and individually furnished (*expensive*).

Rogan and Company, The Square, Cartmel, t (015395) 35917, *www.roganandcompany.co.uk*, (*expensive*). L'Enclume's sister restaurant is more conventional, serving up delicious main courses such as roast fillet of salmon, roast courgettes, spinach and curry oil in a more casual setting.

(i) **Grange-over-Sands**
Victoria Hall, Main St,
t (015395) 34026; open
daily 10–4, reduced
hours Nov–March.

The Cavendish Arms, Cartmel, t (015395) 36240, *www.thecavendisharms.co.uk* (*expensive*). Everything you'd expect of a 450-year-old coaching inn, including low ceilings, antique furniture and a blazing log fire.

Priors Yeat, Aynsome Rd, Cartmel, t (015395) 35178, *www.priorsyeat.co.uk* (*moderate*). Crisp white bedlinen and fluffy duvets more than make up for the flowery wallpaper in this friendly, relaxed guesthouse.

Dalton-in-Furness

Clarence House Country Hotel, Skelgate, near Dalton-in-Furness, t (01229) 462508, *www.clarencehouse-hotel.co.uk* (*expensive–moderate*). You'll be aching to sink into the lounge's warm red upholstery as soon as you step into this luxurious hotel. Upstairs, the sense of self-indulgence continues as you are greeted by elegantly furnished rooms and feather-top mattresses. Dining is a classy experience too – with excellent service in a lovely orangery.

Gleaston

Lile Cottage, Gleaston, t (01229) 869244, *www.watermill.co.uk* (*self-catering*). Small but cosy, this converted Grade II listed farm building (a former pigsty) has its own lovely garden.

Grange-over-Sands

Graythwaite Manor Hotel, Fernhill Rd, Grange-over-Sands, t (015395) 32001, *www.graythwaitemanor.co.uk* (*expensive*). Step back in time to a world of wood panelling, large fireplaces, sumptuous armchairs, heavy drapes and flowery bedspreads all surrounded by 10 acres of splendid, tranquil gardens with lots of secret nooks and crannies.

Lymehurst Hotel, Kents Bank Rd, Grange-over-Sands, t (015395) 33076, *www.lymehurst.co.uk* (*moderate*). Spacious rooms with a clean, modern feel to them in a bright, cheery hotel. The **Lymestone restaurant** (*expensive*) on the lower ground floor is well worth a visit.

Hazlemere Café, Yewbarrow Terrace, Grange-Over-Sands, t (015395) 32972, *www.hazelmerecafe.co.uk* (*budget*). This wonderful, award-winning café serves up a staggering array of teas as well as superb cakes and light meals. A good children's menu is also available.

Millom

Underwood House, The Hill, Millom, t (01229) 771116, *www.underwood house.co.uk* (*expensive–moderate*). A beautifully restored Victorian vicarage in eight acres of picturesque grounds. Very far from the madding crowds of the Lake District.

Ulverston

ⓘ **Ulverston Tourist Information Centre** *Coronation Hall, County Square, t (01229) 587120. Open Mon–Sat 10–4*

Rustique, Brogden St, Ulverston, t (01229) 587373, *www.eatatrustique. co.uk* (*expensive*). An adventurous menu that includes dishes such as roast duck breast with a cassoulet of white bean chorizo and rosemary. Chocolate lovers must leave room for the out-of-this-world chocolate tasting plate. *Closed Sun and Mon.*

The Bay Horse, Canal Foot, Ulverston t (01229) 583972, *www.thebayhorse hotel.co.uk* (*expensive–moderate*). An atmospheric, 18th-century inn at the very edge of the Leven estuary. Six bedrooms have French windows leading on to a terrace with panoramic views across the sands of Morecambe Bay. Both the bar and the **restaurant** (*expensive*) have a good reputation for fine food.

St Mary's Mount, Ulverston, t (01229) 583372, *www.stmarysmount.co.uk* (*moderate*). Lovely brass beds are a feature of the clean, comfortable rooms in this pleasant B&B just below Hoad Hill.

World Peace Café, 5 Cavendish St, Ulverston, t (01229) 587793, *www. worldpeacecafe.org* (*moderate– budget*). The Kadampa Buddhists of nearby Conishead Priory provide excellent and very filling vegetarian lunches as well as good coffee in this calm and quiet town-centre establishment.

Entertainment on the South Coast

Apollo Cinema, Hindpool Rd, Barrow-in-Furness t 0871 220 6000, *www.apollocinemas.com*. Modern, six-screen multiplex showing all the latest blockbusters.

Coronation Hall, County Square, Ulverston, t (01229) 588994, *www.corohall.co.uk*. Built to commemorate the coronation of George V, this attractive 20th-century theatre hosts dance, drama and live music events.

Forum 28, Duke St, Barrow-in-Furness t (01229) 876557, *www.forumtwenty eight.co.uk*. This recently refurbished arts complex hosts drama, dance, comedy, live music, lectures and exhibitions.

The Heron Theatre, Stanley St, Beetham, near Milnthorpe, t (01524) 761140, *www.theherontheatre.com*. A small, 80-seat theatre that puts on a fortnightly programme of plays, films, lectures and musical events between September and May.

The Roxy, Brogden Street, Ulverston, t (01229) 582340, *www.roxyulverston. co.uk*. Showing mostly Hollywood films, but there also is a film club that meets once a month to see less mainstream titles.

Ambleside and Grasmere

Say goodbye to the genial south and welcome the iconic peaks of central Lakeland with outstretched arms. The busy but pleasant market town of Ambleside is the southern gateway to a spectacular area of high, craggy fells and mirror-like lakes and tarns. Park up anywhere and you're never more than a few minutes from the start of a wonderful day's walking. To the west, narrow roads wind their way into Little Langdale and the magnificent Great Langdale, a steep-sided valley that is a mecca for climbers and scramblers. Head north and you reach Grasmere, the physical and cultural heart of the Lake District and a shrine to the father of Lakeland Romanticism, William Wordsworth.

08

Don't miss

⭐ **Rocky ridge hiking and scrambling**
Crinkle Crags p.103

⭐ **Stunning landscaped gardens**
Rydal Mount p.107

⭐ **The tastiest of treats**
Sarah Nelson's Gingerbread Shop p.109

⭐ **Wordsworth's home**
Dove Cottage p.110

⭐ **A stroll past waterfalls to a beautiful tarn**
Easedale Tarn p.111

See map overleaf

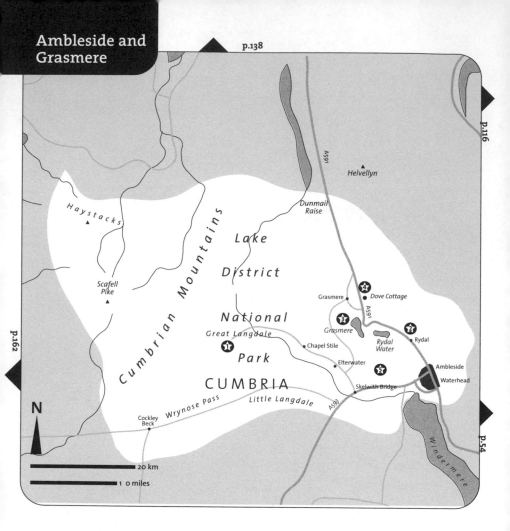

p.138

p.116

p.162

p.54

Helvellyn

A591

Haystacks

Dunmail Raise

Lake

District

Scafell Pike

National

Cumbrian Mountains

Great Langdale

Park

CUMBRIA

Grasmere

Dove Cottage

Grasmere

Rydal Water

Rydal

Chapel Stile

Elterwater

Skelwith Bridge

A593

Little Langdale

Wrynose Pass

Cockley Beck

Ambleside

Waterhead

Windermere

N

20 km

1 0 miles

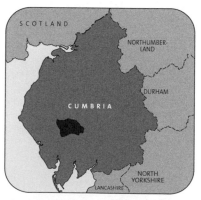

SCOTLAND

NORTHUMBER-LAND

DURHAM

CUMBRIA

NORTH YORKSHIRE

LANCASHIRE

Don't miss

⭐ Crinkle Crags **p.103**

⭐ Rydal Mount **p.107**

⭐ Sarah Nelson's Gingerbread Shop **p.109**

⭐ Dove Cottage **p.110**

⭐ Easedale Tarn **p.111**

Ambleside

Ambleside makes a great base from which to explore the central Lakes. It's a busy spot, packed with guesthouses and restaurants, but fortunately lacks the tacky commercialism of the lakeside at Bowness. You are now entering true fell country, the land of walkers and climbers – as is evidenced by the proliferation of outdoor gear shops that line the two main streets of this traditional, slate-built town.

The southern part of the town is known as Waterhead and it is here that boat passengers, on the half-hour cruise from Bowness, will get their first taste of the central Lakes. There's not much to see here, although several of the more top-end hotels and restaurants are located here, as is the YHA hostel with its perfect lakeside location, the envy, no doubt, of many of the more expensive joints.

The Romans made their mark on this area of the town – as they have on so many parts of the county. During the 1st century AD, they built a fort, Galava, on what is today known as **Borrans Field**. It was an important link in a chain of forts that included Ravenglass on the Irish Sea coast (*see* p.186), Hardknott (*see* p.181) and modern-day Brougham (*see* p.119). The Romans may even have built a pier here, using the lake as a major highway. The original fort was probably built from wood and earth, but it would later have been replaced by a stone-built structure. The land is owned by the National Trust today and visitors are free to wander round whenever they want (no admission fee). You can just make out the foundations of the fort gates, officer's home and the granary, but most of the stones were carted off to build Ambleside. There are also signs, buried beneath housing now, that a civilian settlement existed to the northeast of the fort. The Romans were probably here until at least the second half of the 4th century AD.

As you enter Ambleside proper, you will begin to notice that it isn't a town at all, just a large village – but it received its market charter in 1650, so the 'town' monicker remains, as does the market, held every Wednesday on King Street car park.

The oldest part of the modern town lies to the north – above Stock Ghyll, the beck that divides the town. **How Head**, on the edge of the settled area, is the oldest inhabited building, dating back to the early part of the 16th century. Another interesting building is the much photographed **Bridge House**, a tiny construction spanning the beck, not far from the large Rydal Road car park. It was probably built as a folly in the grounds of the long-gone Ambleside Hall, but what it was subsequently used for is a matter of debate – and probably conjecture. Some say it was a cobbler's, others an apple store, there is even a claim that it once housed a family of six. Today, it is home to a cramped National Trust shop.

The area around Stock Ghyll was once noisy with the sound of mills – wool fulling mills, later replaced by paper mills and bobbin-turning mills. Little of this heritage remains today, although there is a restored wheel at the Glass House restaurant just beyond Bridge House.

In Victorian times, travellers were attracted to the waterfalls of Stock Ghyll. They passed through a turnstile, paying a penny for the privilege

Getting to and around Ambleside

By Train and Bus

There are several buses linking Ambleside with Windermere, which has a railway station. Ambleside is fairly well served by **local buses**. There are regular services between the town and Carlisle, Keswick, Grasmere, Great Langdale, Hawkshead, Coniston, Windermere, Newby Bridge, Kendal, Barrow-in-Furness and Lancaster. Some local buses do not run on Sundays.

National Express runs a daily service **(570)** between Whitehaven and London that stops in Ambleside (journey time to London, nine hours).

By Taxi

Ambleside Taxis, **t** (015394) 33842; Billy's Taxi Service, **t** (015394) 31287; Browns Private Hire, **t** (015394) 33263; Kevin's Taxis, **t** (015394) 32371.

By Bicycle

To hire bikes, try Bike Treks, Rydal Rd, **t** (015394) 31245, *www.biketreks.net*; or Ghyllside Cycles, The Slack, **t** (015394) 33592, *www.ghyllside.co.uk*, closed Wed.

By Boat

Windermere Lake Cruises operates boats from Ambleside to Bowness and, summer only, Wray Castle, **t** (015394) 43360.

of seeing the falls from the well-maintained bridges and benches. Bathing was permitted beneath the falls. The falls can still be seen today, in an attractive, tree-lined gorge that can be accessed from near Barclays Bank. A turnstile is still there – at the top end of the path – but you no longer have to pay. Walkers with their sights set on popular Wansfell Pike can access the bottom of the fell via the ghyll path.

One particularly outspoken Victorian made her home in Ambleside and became one of its most famous residents. Harriet Martineau (1802–1876) was a journalist and campaigner who intelligently questioned all she saw in the world. A feminist and advocate of giving working men the vote, she also wrote passionately about abolishing the slave trade and reforming the Poor Laws. She moved to Ambleside in 1845, where she built a home and small farm, The Knoll. Visitors to the house included her friend Charlotte Brontë and, of course, her ageing neighbour William Wordsworth. Her many travelogues include her *Complete Guide to the Lakes* and the *Description of the English Lakes*, refreshingly lacking much of the romantic leanings of earlier writers. Today, The Knoll, a Grade II listed building, is a holiday cottage.

Not all Victorians loved Ambleside. Charles Dickens had this to say of the town in *Household Words* during the 1850s:

'Round Ambleside you will indeed find hills and waterfalls – decked with greasy sandwich papers and porter bottles, and the hills echo with the whistles of the Windermere steamers... brass bands play under your hotel windows, char-a-bancs, wagonettes and breaks of all colours rattle about with cargoes of tourists who have been 'doing' some favourite round. Touts pester you in the streets and in the hotel coffee room you overhear a gentleman ask angrily "Why don't they build an 'ut on 'elvellyn – they've got one on Snowdon".'

Thankfully, things are a lot quieter today.

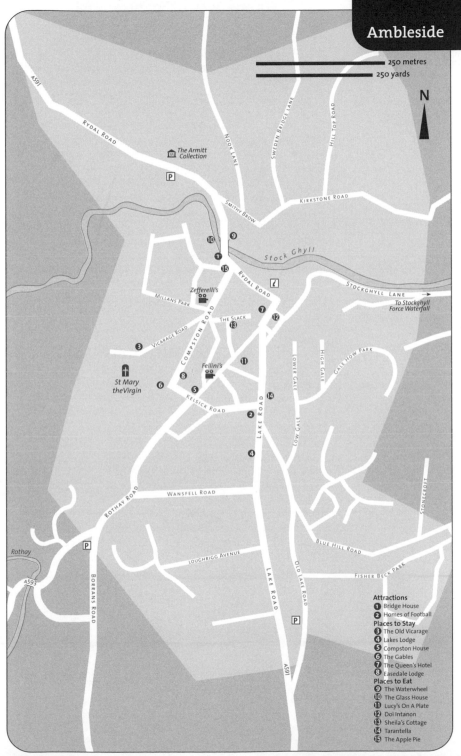

250 metres
250 yards

N

A591

RYDAL ROAD

The Armitt Collection

P

NOOK LANE

SWEDEN BRIDGE LANE

HILL TOP ROAD

SMITHY BROW

KIRKSTONE ROAD

Stock Ghyll

STOCKGHYLL LANE

To Stockghyll
Force Waterfall

RYDAL ROAD

Zefferelli's

MILLANS PARK

VICARAGE ROAD

COMPSTON ROAD

THE SLACK

St Mary
theVirgin

Fellini's

KELSICK ROAD

LAKE ROAD

LOWER GATE

HIGH GATE

GALE HOW PARK

ROTHAY ROAD

WANSFELL ROAD

LOW GATE

Rothay

P

A593

BORRANS ROAD

LOUGHRIGG AVENUE

LAKE ROAD

OLD LAKE ROAD

BLUE HILL ROAD

FISHER BECK PARK

STONECROFT

P

A591

Attractions
1 Bridge House
2 Homes of Football
Places to Stay
3 The Old Vicarage
4 Lakes Lodge
5 Compston House
6 The Gables
7 The Queen's Hotel
8 Easedale Lodge
Places to Eat
9 The Waterwheel
10 The Glass House
11 Lucy's On A Plate
12 Doi Intanon
13 Sheila's Cottage
14 Tarantella
15 The Apple Pie

The Armitt Collection
Rydal Rd, t (015394) 31212, www.armitt.com; museum open daily 10am-5pm, library Tues and Fri 10am-4pm; adm

The town's history is told in **The Armitt museum**, gallery and reference library on Rydal Road, just inside the entrance to the university campus. The purpose-built library was established in 1912 as part of the will of local historian Mary Armitt. It contains numerous books and manuscripts contributed by many famous authors including Charlotte Mason, Harriet Martineau, Arthur Ransome and Beatrix Potter. In 1943 Beatrix Potter bequeathed her collection of more than 450 watercolours of fungi, natural history and archaeology to The Armitt. There are also works by the German artist Kurt Schwitters, who lived in Ambleside from 1945 to 1948, the last three years of his life. He was forced to flee Germany in 1938 after he discovered that he was wanted for 'interview' by the Gestapo. Like all his compatriots, when he eventually arrived in England – via Norway – during the Second World War, he was interned.

The **Old Stamp House**, where Wordsworth worked as Distributor of Stamps for Westmorland at a salary of £400 a year, is at the top of Church Street. He held the position, in effect a tax collector, from 1813 to 1843.

Homes of Football
Lake Rd, t (015394) 34440, www.homesoffootball. co.uk; open daily 10am–5pm.

Nearby is a slightly more prosaic attraction – the **Homes of Football** – which is a gallery devoted to the work of local sports photographer Stuart Clarke. Collections of festival images and pictures of Cumbria are also on display, and available to purchase.

Every year in July, the parish church of St Mary the Virgin, easily identified throughout the town by its enormous spire, hosts a **rush-bearing ceremony**. The custom dates from the time when the church floor was mud and had to be strewn with rushes. (This also helped mask the smell of any shallow burials beneath the church.) Every year, the old rushes were removed and replaced with fresh ones. Of course, the earthen floor disappeared many decades ago, but the tradition lives on in Ambleside as well as in four other Cumbrian villages – Grasmere, Urswick, Great Musgrave and Warcop.

A huge variety of walks start from Ambleside. One of the most popular routes, Wansfell Pike, has already been mentioned, and **Loughrigg Fell** sees a lot of visitors. If you don't fancy climbing to the top of this relatively low-lying peak, which is criss-crossed by a maze of paths, you can follow paths around the base of the fell for wonderful views that change with every turn on the circuit. As you climb to the southeast of the fell, it is Fairfield which dominates the scene. The top of the ascent provides a stunning view of Windermere to the south. Then, as you round Ivy Crag at the far southern tip of Loughrigg and drop down to gorgeous **Loughrigg Tarn**, the Langdale Pikes suddenly appear in all their splendour. As if that wasn't enough, the return route on the northern side uses a terrace path high above the serene lake of Grasmere.

Seasoned fell-walkers will undoubtedly want to 'do' the **Fairfield Horseshoe**, one of the most famous Lake District rounds. This classic, high ridge walk is 10.5 miles long and includes almost 3,500ft of ascent, but it's worth every drop of sweat and every gasp for breath.

For a great view down Windermere and a pleasant picnic spot, walk to **Jenkyn's Crag** from the Low Fold car park at Waterhead. A path

Stagshaw Gardens
Ambleside,
t (015394) 46027,
www.nationaltrust.org.uk;
open daily Apr–June
10–6.30; adm

continues past here to Troutbeck from where you can return to Ambleside via Wansfell Pike.

Just below Jenkyn's Crag are the National Trust's **Stagshaw Gardens**. Noted for their collection of rhododendrons, azaleas and camellias, the gardens cling to a steep, wooded slope just above the lake.

To take to the water, the **Low Wood Watersports and Activity Centre** at the Low Wood Hotel just south of Ambleside hires out rowing boats, Canadian canoes, sit-on kayaks and 16ft motorboats. Experts are also on hand to give instruction in water-skiing, kayaking and sailing, although some of these are multi-day courses.

Low Wood Watersports and Activity Centre
Low Wood, Windermere,
t (015394) 39441,
www.elh.co.uk; open daily
Easter–Oct, winter sessions
can be arranged; adm

(i) **Ambleside Tourist Information Centre**
Central Buildings,
Market Cross,
t (015394) 32582,
www.amblesidetic@southl
akeland.gov.uk. Open
Mon–Sat 9am–5.30pm,
Sun 9am–5pm. Closed
Christmas Day and Boxing
Day.

Festivals and Events in Ambleside

Ambleside's **Rush-bearing Ceremony** (*see* p.98) normally takes place on the first Saturday in July. Aside from replacing the church rushes, the Ambleside celebrations also incorporate an afternoon of children's sports, including a junior fell race.

Adults in the town also enjoy their races and the annual **Ambleside Sports** is held on the last Thursday in July at Rydal Park, half a mile north of the town on the A591 (*www.ambleside sports.co.uk*). Events include hound trails, Cumberland and Westmorland wrestling (*see* p.170), cycle races, craft displays, stalls and, if you're masochistically inclined, a fell race.

Where to Stay in Ambleside

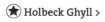

(★) **Holbeck Ghyll >**

(★) **Easedale Lodge >>**

Holbeck Ghyll, Holbeck Lane, near Ambleside t (015394) 32375, *www.holbeckghyll.com* (*luxury*). Famed for its superb restaurant (*see* below), high-class hospitality and stunning views, this multi-award-winning luxury hotel occupies a hillside location overlooking Windermere. Sherry, fresh flowers and fluffy bathrobes await guests in the spacious, exquisitely decorated rooms, many of which have lake views.

Lakes Lodge, Lake Rd, Ambleside, t (015394) 33240, *www.lakeslodge. co.uk* (*expensive–moderate*). Part guesthouse and part hotel, this smart, but slightly over-priced establishment has 12 clean and spacious rooms. The friendly staff will serve drinks in your room all day and evening.

The Old Vicarage, Vicarage Rd, t (015394) 33364, *www.oldvicarage ambleside.co.uk* (*expensive–moderate*). Gorgeous slate-brick Victorian vicarage with pointed gables and church-style windows, tucked away near St Mary's Church. Elegant and spacious inside. Also has a heated indoor pool, sauna and hot tub.

Waterhead Hotel, Ambleside, t (015394) 32566, *www.elh.co.uk* (*expensive–moderate*). You'll receive first-class service in this snazzy lakeside hotel. Uncluttered rooms and large quantities of slate and chrome everywhere give it a smart, contemporary feel. Guests also get complimentary membership of Low Wood's leisure complex, which is about a mile down the road.

Compston House Hotel, Compston Rd, t (015394) 32305, *www.compston house.co.uk* (*moderate*). Bright and cheerful rooms, each themed around an American state. The hotel is run by a couple from New York, so expect good pancakes for breakfast.

Easedale Lodge, Compston Rd, Ambleside, t (015394) 32112, *www.easedaleambleside.co.uk* (*moderate*). Spotless rooms, quality décor and furnishings, tasteful ornaments and art – all are indicative of the effort and pride that the owners put into this popular guesthouse. Superb value for money means that visitors come back time and time again.

Queen's Hotel, Market Place, t (015394) 32206, *www.queenshotel ambleside.com* (*moderate*). Popular town-centre Victorian coaching inn with 26 decent rooms, and the occasional clash of flowery wallpaper.

Riverside Hotel, Under Loughrigg, Ambleside, **t** (015394) 32395, *www.riverside-at-ambleside.co.uk* (*moderate*). Warm, friendly guesthouse in a quiet, riverside location on the edge of Ambleside. Light and airy rooms. The superb breakfasts use mostly local produce.

The Gables, Church Walk **t** (015394) 33272, *www.thegables-ambleside.co.uk* (*moderate*). With its mock-Tudor frontage, The Gables looks a little imposing from the outside, but the interior of this 14-bedroom guesthouse is bright and airy.

 **Lucy's On A Plate** >>

The Waterwheel Guesthouse, Bridge St, Ambleside, **t** (015394) 33286, *www.waterwheelambleside.co.uk* (*moderate*). A small but charming cottage on a cobbled lane in the middle of the town. Luxuriously deep clawfoot baths in two of the three rooms.

Grove Cottages, Grove Farm, Stockghyll Lane, Ambleside, **t** (015394) 33074, *www.grovecottages.com* (*self-catering*). Five well-appointed and spotless cottages on a secluded farm close to Kirkstone Pass.

Where to Eat in Ambleside

Holbeck Ghyll >

Holbeck Ghyll Holbeck Lane, near Ambleside **t** (015394) 32375, *www.holbeckghyll.com* (*very expensive*), has held on to its Michelin star for 10 consecutive years, and it's hardly surprising. Top-class dishes are served up by thoughtful staff in beautiful surroundings. If you're looking for a real treat, this is fine dining at its very finest. And for that extra special occasion, why not splash out on the seven-course gourmet menu (£72.50): hand-dived scallops; fricassee of boneless frogs' legs with ceps and artichoke *velouté*; and boudin blanc with sautéed langoustine.

Log House, Lake Rd, Ambleside, **t** (015394) 31077, *www.loghouse.co.uk* (*expensive*). If this unusual building looks like it's straight out of the fjords, that's because it is – landscape painter Alfred Heaton Cooper had it imported from Norway, log by log, in the early 20th century. Today, it houses a contemporary restaurant that makes for a quality, but relaxed dining experience. *Closed Mon.*

Fellinis, Church St, Ambleside, **t** (015394) 33845, *www.fellinis ambleside.com* (*moderate*). Ambleside's new vegetarian restaurant has a distinctly Mediterranean flavour – rocket and ricotta ravioli; thyme-roasted butternut squash risotto. *Closed Mon in winter.*

Lucy's On A Plate, Church St, Ambleside, **t** (015394) 31191, *www.lucysofambleside.co.uk* (*moderate*). You might have to queue, especially at lunchtime in the summer, but it'll be worth it. Hearty, imaginative dishes come with a sense of humour – try Lamb Rumpy Pumpy, fell-bred lamb served with sweet potato mash and Jerusalem artichokes.

Sheila's Cottage, The Slack, Ambleside, **t** (015394) 33079 (*moderate*). Good-quality meals in a cosy, side-street restaurant that is more tearoom than evening venue.

Tarantella, 10 Lake Rd, Ambleside **t** (015394) 31338, *www.tarantella restaurant.co.uk* (*moderate*). Smart, modern Italian restaurant serving up pizzas and pastas as well as a few more adventurous concoctions such as crab and chilli linguini. *Closed Tues and Wed.*

The Glass House, Rydal Rd, Ambleside, **t** (015394) 32137, *www.theglasshouse restaurant.co.uk* (*moderate*). Wooden floors and simple, but tasteful furniture help give this popular spot a relaxed, easy-going feel. Menu includes many classic dishes with a subtle modern twist, such as fillet steak with pea and mushroom noodles.

The Apple Pie, Rydal Rd, Ambleside **t** (015394) 33679, *www.applepie ambleside.co.uk* (*budget*). If you haven't got time to wait around for a table in this popular baker's shop-cum-café, at least grab yourself a takeaway. The traybakes and carrot cake are delicious, but it's the pies that people queue for.

Entertainment in Ambleside

Fellinis, Church St, Ambleside, **t** (015394) 33845, *www.fellinis ambleside.com*. Zeffirelli's (*see* below) new sister act is a smaller cinema showing mostly arthouse films. It also has a vegetarian restaurant (*see* above).

Zeffirelli's, Compston Rd, Ambleside, **t** (015394) 33845, *www.zeffirellis.com*. Ambleside's original independent cinema has four screens (showing mostly mainstream films), a jazz bar and a pizzeria.

Langdale

Heading west from Ambleside, the valley road gets increasingly narrow until it hugs the foot of the mountains. This is walking country par excellence; dozens of paths climb the steep fellsides. Tarns glitter like jewels in breathtaking passes or lurk, cold and dark, in mountain cirques. Waterfalls plunge through deep, forbidding chasms. And, all along the valley floor, ancient drystone walls carve up the farmland before snaking up into the hills.

There's an increasing sense of more down-to-earth living as you head further into the heart of Cumbria – not the gritty realism of the grim-up-North towns of Lancashire and Yorkshire, but a growing realization that the Lake District isn't just a playground for tourists, it is a working environment, a place where people live all year round. The landscape, although carved millennia ago by glaciers, has subsequently been shaped by human activity – mining, quarrying and farming, in particular. And, in places such as Langdale, much of this activity still continues – not independent of tourism, but co-existing, often forming complicated relationships.

The A593 crosses the River Brathay at Skelwith Bridge, heading for Coniston. It is here that visitors turn off, along the B5343, for the Langdales. Skelwith Bridge itself is a pleasant spot with a riverside path to **Skelwith Force** – not a high waterfall, but impressive because of the sheer volume of water. Beautiful **Loughrigg Tarn**, with the Langdale Pikes forming the perfect backdrop for photographers intent on capturing picture-postcard scenes, can be easily reached on foot from here too. There is hardly any parking near the tarn itself and all the roads up to it are extremely narrow, so the short, easy walk from Skelwith Bridge is the best option.

The first village you reach in Langdale is **Elterwater**, just west of the reedy lake with which it shares a name. The village developed as an industrial settlement based on quarrying and the manufacture of gunpowder. The gunpowder works were built beside the fast-flowing beck in 1824. The powder had to be very finely ground, so it was passed between a series of millstones along the beck, each separate from its neighbour to avoid accidents. Charcoal was supp-lied by the local alder and juniper coppices. The gunpowder works were closed in 1928, but the quarrying of slate continues today.

Getting to and around Langdale

By Local Bus

The **516 Langdale Rambler** runs between Ambleside and the road end at the Old Dungeon Ghyll Hotel. There are six buses in each direction every day (five on Sundays).

By Taxi

Ambleside Taxis, t (015394) 33842; Billy's Taxi Service, t (015394) 31287; Kevin's Taxis, t (015394) 32371 – all are based in Ambleside.

By Bicycle

If you want to hire bikes, try one of the Ambleside outfits – Bike Treks, Rydal Rd, t (015394) 31245, *www.biketreks.net*; or Ghyllside Cycles, The Slack, t (015394) 33592, *www.ghyllside.co.uk*, closed Wed.

The name Elterwater is said to come from the Norse for 'Swan Lake' and whooper swans from Scandinavia do sometimes grace the lake during the winter.

Elterwater is a good base for climbing **Lingmoor Fell**, which stands between Great Langdale and Little Langdale (*see* below). From the top, a path continues northwest on to Side Pike and its infamous 'Squeeze', a narrow gap between the rocks through which walkers must pass. People carrying large packs may struggle!

Continuing deeper into Great Langdale, **Chapel Stile** is the valley's main village. The picturesque Holy Trinity church was built in 1857 of green slate from the nearby quarry. Chapel Stile is also home to **Copt Howe**, an important prehistoric rock art site. Rediscovered in 1999, the large boulders boast a series of cup and ring markings believed to have been created between 4,000 and 6,000 years ago. The site is difficult to find – ask in the village for directions.

"No mountain profile in Lakeland arrests and excites the attention more than that of the Langdale Pikes ... That steep ladder to heaven stirs the imagination, and even the emotions..."

Alfred Wainwright, 1958

Beyond Chapel Stile there is little in the way of settlement – just a handful of farms and the hotels – until the road's westward progression is halted by the high wall of rock thrown up by the ridge comprising Crinkle Crags and Bow Fell. But visitors don't come here seeking idyllic villages, they come to explore those rocks and ridges, and especially those icons of the Lake District, the **Langdale Pikes**.

The adventure starts in one of two places – the New Dungeon Ghyll Hotel, which is the first you come to if approaching from the east; or the Old Dungeon Ghyll Hotel, where the B5343 ends and a minor road begins its ascent towards Blea Tarn. But more about that later!

From the New Dungeon Ghyll, a pitched path leads steeply to **Stickle Tarn**. Pounded by thousands and thousands of boots every year, this popular route experiences a lot of erosion and has recently been repaired by the Fix The Fells project, a partnership between the National Trust, Lake District National Park Authority, Natural England, Friends of the Lake District and other organizations.

For many, Stickle Tarn, 1,250ft above the valley floor, is as far as they will get, but for others, this is just the start of a great day out. From here, the Langdale Pikes can be accessed by a variety of different routes of varying difficulty. Probably one of the trickiest is **Jack's Rake**, a natural groove through the seemingly impenetrable, craggy face of

Pavey Ark. It can be clearly seen from the tarn, running from the bottom right-hand corner of the crag to the top left. As scrambles go, the sense of exposure is relatively low for most of the way, especially if you stay close to the cliff wall and deep within the channel. However, this is not a good route for those who do not have a head for heights and the last section, as you leave the relative safety of the rock groove and have to negotiate a large, potentially slippery rock slab, is particularly vertiginous. Many walkers have come a cropper here.

The Pikes themselves are Loft Crag, Harrison Stickle and Pike o' Stickle, also known as Stickle Pike (some people also regard Pavey Ark as one of the Pikes). The summits of the former two are easily reached once you have attained the ridge path, but there's an awkward clamber over rocks to reach the top of Pike o' Stickle.

One of Cumbria's most fascinating Neolithic sites is located on Pike o' Stickle's steep scree-covered slopes – the **Langdale stone axe factory**. High up on the mountainside, Neolithic workers would have quarried the exposed seam of 'greenstone', a flint-like volcanic rock, and roughed out axe heads from it. It is assumed the heads were then taken to the coast for sharpening and polishing. There was a significant trade in these tools and Langdale axes have been found as far away as Cornwall. The site of the axe factory is on horribly steep and unstable ground and a visit is not recommended. Content yourself with gazing up at it from Mickleden – and pondering how Neolithic man managed to discover the outcrop in the first place.

The Langdale Pikes can also be accessed from the **Old Dungeon Ghyll Hotel**, close to the head of the valley. This is also a good launch-pad for any assaults on Pike o' Blisco, **Crinkle Crags** and Bow Fell (*see* p.104). And, at the end of a tough day, you can enjoy a drink in the rather rustic Hikers Bar, a popular haunt of walkers and climbers for decades.

⭐ **Crinkle Crags**

The hotel was originally a farm and an inn, known as Middlefell Inn. At the end of the 19th century, in the days when horse-drawn coaches would bring visitors from Little Langdale over Blea Tarn Pass, the driver would stop at the top and blow his horn, a signal to get lunch or tea ready – the number of blasts informed the staff of the number of passengers requiring a meal. The hotel was sold to Professor G. Trevelyan in the early 1900s for £4,100. He gave it to the National Trust – the organization's first property in Langdale.

The B5343 might end at the Old Dungeon Ghyll Hotel, but a narrower road continues up to the left – to the **Blea Tarn Pass**. Like Loughrigg Tarn, this small but perfectly formed body of water is a great place from which to view the Langdale Pikes. There is a car park just beyond the pass and, from here, a wheelchair-accessible path leads to the tarn.

Beyond Blea Tarn, the road drops to a T-junction. To the right is Wrynose Pass and the **Three Shires Stone**, which marks the spot where the old counties of Cumberland, Westmorland and Lancashire used to meet. Cross the pass and you either head down into the Duddon Valley (*see* p.90) or across Hardknott Pass (*see* p.181).

To the left of the T-junction lies the quiet, less-visited valley of **Little Langdale**. Fell-walkers won't find much entertainment here, but there are plenty of low-level routes to enjoy – if you can find somewhere to

08 Ambleside and Grasmere | Langdale

Walk: Crinkle Crags

Start and finish:
National Trust car park at Old Dungeon Ghyll Hotel (grid reference NY286060)
Distance:
7.3 miles/11.8km
Total ascent
2,850ft/869m

In brief:
This is a classic route among some of the best mountain scenery the Lake District has to offer. Crinkle Crags (2,816ft) is made up of a series of dramatic buttresses, scree gullies and gnarled, rocky peaks that tower above the western end of Great Langdale. They make for great walking. This route takes the steep, constructed path up from Oxendale to Red Tarn and then curves around the top of Browney Gill to gain the magnificent ridge path. There are some sections of scrambling along the tops, but the most difficult can be easily avoided. The route then drops down to the beautiful Three Tarns before descending The Band, a mostly easy walk along a well-used grassy ridge. Avoid in poor visibility because the terrain on the tops can be confusing.

Route description:
Leave the car park and head back to the road, along which you turn right. In 100 yards, when the road bends sharp left, keep straight ahead along the surfaced farm track. As you approach **Stool End Farm**, follow the clear waymarkings, passing to the left of the white farmhouse.

The path rises briefly beyond the farm and then levels off. Ignore the clear path heading up the ridge to your right. The wide track now heads out across flat ground – straight towards Crinkle Crags at the head of the valley.

Almost half-a-mile beyond the farm, having passed through a series of gates, you turn left to cross **Oxendale Beck** via a narrow, gated footbridge. In just a few moments, the path begins to climb. It's a fairly tough pull up to **Red Tarn**, but there are no technical difficulties and there are plenty of opportunities to stop and admire the fantastic views back across the valley to the Langdales and, later in the climb, down into Browney Gill.

Eventually, you reach an obvious T-junction where you turn right. At least as far as the first Crinkle, the gradient is now quite a bit gentler than during the first part of the climb, although it can still feel like quite a slog. Don't worry – your rewards are just around the next corner.

Things get a lot more interesting when you have to clamber up on to the first Crinkle. The views, both near and distant, become more and more impressive. It is rocky in places, but as long as you stick to the main path, it shouldn't present the average fell-walker with any problems. The second Crinkle, on the other hand, is quite a different matter...

Having dropped down from the first top into a dramatic, stony saddle, you are faced with a choice. Straight ahead, at the top of a mess of scree, is the infamous '**bad step.**' This is a tricky little rock climb if you're not used to scrambling. Alternatively, by turning left at the base of the scree slope, you will find yourself on an easier, albeit very steep and loose, route on to the summit. If you choose this path, make sure that

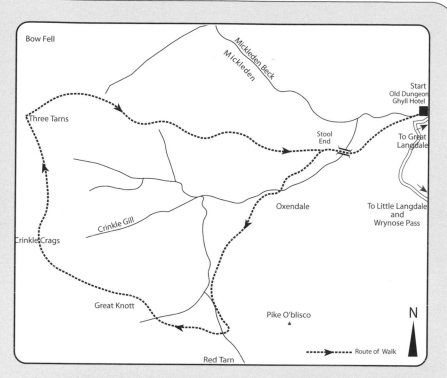

Bow Fell

Mickleden Beck

Mickleden

Three Tarns

Start
Old Dungeon
Ghyll Hotel

Stool
End

To Great
Langdale

Oxendale

To Little Langdale
and
Wrynose Pass

Crinkle Gill

Crinkle Crags

Great Knott

Pike O'blisco

N

Red Tarn

- - - ▶ - - - Route of Walk

you bear right as soon as the Scafells make their first, dramatic appearance at the top of the climb – this will ensure you get back on to the ridge route and don't miss the summit of the second, and highest of the Crinkles.

From the summit cairn, continue heading generally north along the ridge, made up of a line of rocky summits. The going is rough underfoot and there is some easy scrambling to do – nothing exposed or terrifying; just enough to give you a definite sense of being in the mountains.

Eventually, you descend from **Shelter Crags** to reach a stunning pass, home to **Three Tarns**. No doubt you'll want to rest a while here to enjoy the magnificent view across to Scafell Pike and Sca Fell and to gaze up at the dark, forbidding, but nevertheless impressive parallel gullies of Bowfell Links.

Those with both the time and energy may want to continue on to Bow Fell and possibly even Esk Pike from here. You could then descend via Rossett Gill.

But the main route heads east from the pass – to follow the mostly grassy ridge known as **The Band**. Cross a boggy area via stepping stones and the well-walked route bears right, soon becoming a constructed path. Do not be tempted by the less well-trodden path off to the right of the beck – this heads down to Hell Gill.

The descent down The Band is a little steep at first, but it eases off as it follows the south side of the ridge and then gets steeper again as you near Stool End Farm.

At a T-junction at the bottom of the ridge, turn left. Go through the farm gate and follow the waymarkers back through the yard. You are now retracing your steps from earlier in the walk. Continue down the farm track, out through the entrance gate and then straight down the road. Turn left at the Old Dungeon Ghyll signpost and the car park is just round to your right.

park your car. It's a little out of the way, but try parking at the old Hodge Close quarry, which can be reached via a minor road from the A593, 3.3 miles south of Skelwith Bridge. Parking here will enable you to visit the **Colwith Force** falls and the interesting old Slater Bridge at the eastern end of Little Langdale Tarn.

The quarry itself is also worth a look, although visitors should be careful because the edges are unfenced. This is no place for small children or uncontrolled dogs. This massive excavation has resulted in sheer sides that are popular with abseilers. Divers too find plenty of interest here – the quarry pool has a maximum depth of about 100ft and there is an underwater tunnel entrance that leads to three chambers and two interconnecting tunnels.

Even more interesting are The Cathedral quarries near Slater Bridge. Popular with climbers, this impressive network of interconnected chambers is managed by the National Trust. The largest and most famous of the chambers is known as The Cathedral and has walls that are 40ft high. The Cathedral can be reached via a relatively short tunnel, but if you decide to go deeper into the system, you will need a torch – one of the tunnels is about 400ft long. A National Trust sign at the entrance warns that 'private individuals enter at their own risk'.

If you're intending to stay in Langdale, be warned that you are likely to be paying for the location rather than for the accommodation. Rooms tend to be pricier than in many other parts of the Lake District, and facilities poorer.

Where to Stay in Langdale

The Langdale Hotel, The Langdale Estate, Great Langdale, t (015394) 37302, *www.langdale.co.uk* (*expensive*). Part of an award-winning country club, this is by far the classiest place to stay in the valley. Modern, luxurious rooms with good facilities, including bathrobes, free Wi-Fi and access to the laundry service. The spa has a 20m pool, gym, tennis courts, bike hire, bars and restaurants.

New Dungeon Ghyll Hotel, Great Langdale, t (015394) 37213, *www.dungeon-ghyll.com* (*expensive–moderate*). Fairly basic rooms, but it's the location you're paying for...at the very foot of the Langdales. Good views from just about every window in the hotel.

Skelwith Bridge Hotel, Skelwith Bridge, t (015394) 32115, *www.skelwithbridge hotel.co.uk* (*expensive– moderate*). Decent rooms in an interesting old building. Great location for touring – with Ambleside, Langdale and Coniston all within easy driving distance.

The Eltermere Inn, Elterwater, t (015394) 37207, *www.eltermere.co.uk* (*expensive–moderate*). Formerly the Eltermere Country House Hotel, this place has been given a refreshing new look since it changed hands in 2008. The slightly stuffy, old-fashioned atmosphere has been replaced by a more contemporary feel, and there's a rather nice bar and terrace too.

Old Dungeon Ghyll Hotel, Great Langdale, t (015394) 37272, *www. odg.co.uk* (*moderate*). Don't go along to the ODG expecting luxury and mod cons – there's no TV, no mobile reception and the rooms are fairly small, although comfortable. People come here for the location – to walk or climb in some of the best fell country in the Lake District. Some rooms have shared bathroom facilities.

The Britannia Inn, Elterwater, t (015394) 37210, *www.britinn.co.uk* (*moderate*). Slightly cramped, but immaculate rooms in a cosy, 500-year-old inn. Guests receive a pass for the leisure facilities at the nearby Langdale Estate Country Club.

The Three Shires Inn, Little Langdale, t (015394) 37215, *www.threeshires inn.co.uk* (*moderate*). A small, family-run inn in a peaceful spot close to the Wrynose Pass and surrounded by lovely scenery. Slightly lacking in atmosphere, but the staff are generally helpful.

 Fell Foot Farm
>

Fell Foot Farm, Little Langdale, t (015394) 37149, *www.fellfootfarm. co.uk* (*budget*). A beautifully located, 17th-century, working hill farm that is far from the madding crowds. After a restful night in one of the two clean, well-equipped guest rooms, tuck into a superb farmhouse breakfast and then head out on to the fells for the day. Stands out in the Langdale area for providing good value for money.

Where to Eat in Langdale

Decent pub food can be had at the **Skelwith Bridge Hotel** (*moderate*), the **New Dungeon Ghyll Hotel** (*moderate*) and the **Old Dungeon Ghyll Hotel**

(*moderate*). The **Britannia Inn** (*moderate*) and the **Three Shires Inn** (*moderate*) also serve meals, although the standard is variable. The **Eltermere Inn** (*expensive*) has a good restaurant with nice views over Elter Water. There are two restaurants within the grounds of the Langdale Estate: **Purdey's** (*expensive*) has been awarded an AA rosette for its imaginative menu, presented in a relaxed, oak-floored restaurant; the family-oriented **Terrace Restaurant** (*moderate*) specializes in Mediterranean dishes.

Chesters Café by the River, Skelwith Bridge, t (015394) 32553, *www.chesters-cafebytheriver.co.uk* (*moderate*). A cut above your usual paninis-and-baked-spuds type of café. Expect wild boar sausages or broccoli, stilton and walnut linguine in this modern riverside establishment. Or, if you can't manage a big lunch, crash out on one of the comfy sofas with coffee and a chunk of delicious, home-made cake.

08

Ambleside and Grasmere | Grasmere and Rydal: Rydal

Grasmere and Rydal

Rydal

Before you reach Grasmere from Ambleside, you will come to the small, but lovely lake of Rydal Water and the scattered buildings of Rydal itself. **Rydal Water** is one of the smallest and shallowest of the lakes and, as such, occasionally freezes over in especially cold winters. This was a more common occurrence in Wordsworth's time, and his entire family often used to skate on the lake. **Rydal Mount** was home to the great poet from 1813 until his death in 1850. The family continued to live in the house until the death of William's wife, Mary, in 1859. Today, it is back in the hands of the Wordsworth family, having been bought by the poet's great-great-grand-daughter Mary Henderson (née Wordsworth) in 1969.

This is a much larger house than pokey Dove Cottage (*see* below) and was, socially, a step up for the Wordsworths. The move was made possible by William's new position as Distributor of Stamps for Westmorland and the growing proceeds from his writing. Rydal Mount, packed with original furniture, manuscripts and interesting artefacts such as the poet's pen and inkstand, is open to the public. Although Dove Cottage is more famous, the larger, more elegant home, which dates from the 16th century, probably gives visitors a greater insight into Wordsworth and his family. Visitors can wander round three of the

 Rydal Mount and Gardens
Rydal,
t (015394) 33002,
www.rydalmount.co.uk;
open daily Mar–Oct
9.30am–4.30pm, winter
Wed–Sun 11am–4pm;
adm

Getting To and Around Grasmere

By Local Bus

The **554/555/556 Lakeslink** is a regular service between Carlisle and Lancaster via Keswick, Grasmere, Ambleside, Windermere and Kendal. Grasmere is also served by the open-top **599** that runs between the village and Bowness.

By Taxi

Grasmere Taxi Service, **t** (015394) 35506.

By Bicycle

If you want to hire bikes, try one of the Ambleside outfits – Bike Treks, Rydal Rd, **t** (015394) 31245, *www.biketreks.net*; or Ghyllside Cycles, The Slack, **t** (015394) 33592, *www.ghyllside.co.uk*, (closed Wed).

family bedrooms as well as Wordsworth's attic study, which contains the sword that belonged to the poet's younger brother, John, who was killed in the wreck of the *Earl of Abergavenny*. (He had been captain of the ship of which his cousin had previously been master, *see* p.118.)

An even bigger draw than the house itself are the graceful but informal gardens, laid out according to the poet's own designs. He built several terraces and, at the end of one of these is the summerhouse where he liked to write. He would then pace up and down along the Far Terrace, testing his latest verses by reading them out loud.

Wordsworth rented Rydal Mount from the le Fleming family, who lived in nearby **Rydal Hall**. Today, the latter building is a conference centre and Christian retreat owned by the Diocese of Carlisle. Its Victorian facade conceals a 17th century house. The recently restored Italianate gardens were the work of the great garden designer and landscape architect Thomas Hayton Mawson in 1911. Interesting features include an informal woodland garden with ponds, a restored summerhouse overlooking a waterfall, an orchard and a 19th-century ice house. The path to the Fairfield Horseshoe passes Rydal Hall's Old School Room Tea Shop, which is open every day except Christmas Day.

Rydal Hall
Rydal,
t (015394) 32050,
www.rydalhall.org;
open daily
10.30am–4.30pm;
donations

Below Rydal Hall and Rydal Mount, closer to the road, is **St Mary's Church**. Built in 1824, this too has a Wordsworth link – he played a role in its design and was church warden here for a while. The Wordsworth family pew was the one in front of the lectern.

Just behind the church is Dora's Field. Wordsworth bought the field in 1826, apparently planning to build a house for his daughter there – although this may merely have been a threat to deter Lady le Fleming from turning him out of Rydal Mount and giving the house to her aunt. Whatever his reasons for buying it, when Dora died from tuberculosis in 1847, Wordsworth and his wife planted it with daffodil bulbs in her memory. The poet's grandson, Gordon Wordsworth, gave the field to the National Trust in 1935, and, every spring, it is covered in a carpet of the yellow flowers.

Above the road, on the south side of Rydal Water, are the **Rydal Caves**, the remains of a disused slate quarry that was used as a setting in Ken Russell's horror film *The Lair of the White Worm*. Some of the caves can be reached only if you're prepared to do some scrambling, but the most popular is located right next to a footpath. This cave has been closed from time to time in recent years due to rock falls.

Part way between Rydal and Grasmere, on the A591, is another building with Romantic associations. The beautiful, 18th century **Nab Cottage**, now a language school, was once home to the writer and intellectual Thomas De Quincey, best known for his 1821 work *Confessions of an English Opium-Eater*. Whilst lodging here, he courted the owner's daughter, Margaret Simpson, who, in 1816, gave him a son – much to Dorothy Wordsworth's disgust. The pair got married four months after the boy's arrival – much to William Wordsworth's disgust; the poet felt that his young friend was marrying below his station, and the match was the final nail in the coffin of the two men's friendship.

Grasmere

Grasmere is the physical and spiritual heart of the Lake District. It is the place most closely associated with William Wordsworth – his home for many years and his final resting place. And, borrowing from Wordsworth's own description of the Lakeland valleys as being like 'spokes from the nave of a wheel', the fells above the village form the hub of that wheel. Stand on top of Sergeant Man and you will see what he means – mountains as far as the eye can see and valleys heading off in each direction.

At the centre of the village, on the banks of the River Rothay is **St Oswald's Church**, where William Wordsworth and his family are buried. At first sight, the grey, pebble-dashed building doesn't look that impressive, but closer inspection reveals that parts of it date from the 13th century. The site is thought to have been a place of worship since Saxon times, and St Oswald, a 7th-century Christian King of Northumbria, is said to have preached here. Inside, 19th-century oak pews, white-washed walls and exposed beams give the place an austere but tranquil feel, an atmosphere that is strengthened every August when the church floor is strewn with rushes during the annual rush-bearing festival (*see* p.41). Wordsworth's own prayer book is contained in a glass case near the organ – but it isn't the poet's prayer book that the tourists have come to see; it is his grave. Wordsworth, who died on April 23, 1880, and his wife Mary share a simple headstone in a quiet corner of the churchyard. His sister Dorothy is buried nearby as are his children – Dora, William, Thomas and Catherine – as well as Mary's sister Sara Hutchinson, and other members of the family. Coleridge's son Hartley is also buried here.

🟦 Sarah Nelson's Gingerbread Shop

Next door to the church is **Sarah Nelson's Gingerbread Shop**. This tiny shop, built in 1660, used to be the village school, and it was briefly attended by some of the Wordsworth children. Sarah Nelson moved into Gate Cottage, as it was then known, in about 1850. She soon began selling her gingerbread to Victorian tourists and, as word of it spread, she was forced to lock the secret recipe away in a bank vault. That same delicious, slightly spicy recipe is used to this day, and the shop remains little changed since Sarah Nelson's time – the school coat pegs are still in place, as is the cupboard used to house the school slates.

⭐ **Dove Cottage, The Wordsworth Museum and Art Gallery**
t (015394) 35544, www.wordsworth. org.uk; open summer daily 9.30–5.30, Nov–Feb daily 9.30–4.30, closed Jan 4–29; adm

Dove Cottage, on the edge of the village, close to the A591, was the Wordsworth family home from 1799 until 1808, although it has only been known as Dove Cottage since the Wordsworth Trust bought it in 1891. The tiny cottage is a perfect example of Lake District twee – with slate roof tiles, latticed windows and roses climbing the external walls, lime-washed to keep the damp out. Inside, the poky downstairs rooms all have flagstone floors. Upstairs, visitors can see the family bedrooms and the poet's study. Wordsworth was a keen gardener, and he spent many hours tending the vegetables and flowers that he planted at the back of the cottage. The half-wild garden, like the interior of the cottage, has been meticulously restored by the Wordsworth Trust.

The Dove Cottage years were an extremely good period in Wordsworth's life. He was writing some of his best work and, in 1802, he married his and Dorothy's life-long friend Mary Hutchinson.

The Wordsworths received many guests at Dove Cottage, including Sir Walter Scott, Robert Southey and, their most frequent visitor, the poet Coleridge. After the Wordsworths moved out, Dove Cottage became the home of the poet's young friend, Thomas De Quincey. He actually lived there for 22 years, much longer than the Wordsworths. As well as the many fascinating Wordsworthian artefacts on show in Dove Cottage, there is also a set of scales which is said to have been used by De Quincey to weigh his opium. Visitors are given a guided tour of the cottage and are then allowed to look around by themselves.

Next door to Dove Cottage is the **Wordsworth Museum and Art Gallery**, home to a huge collection of material relating to the Romantic movement in Britain. Manuscripts, paintings, portraits and odd artefacts such as Wordsworth's favourite Panama hat are all housed here. The museum hosts a number of temporary exhibitions every year and is also the venue for poetry workshops and readings by modern poets. Recent visiting poets have included a number of local poets as well as internationally renowned figures Simon Armitage and the poet laureate Carol Ann Duffy.

Pilgrims following in Wordsworth's footsteps may also want to see **Allan Bank**, the house to which the family moved in 1808, when Mary was expecting her fourth child. It can be seen from one of the footpaths up to Silver How, but it is now a private home. Canon Hardwicke Rawnsley (*see* p.143) bought the house in 1915 and then left it to the National Trust. Although still owned by the Trust, it is not open to the public. Wordsworth once described the building as the 'temple of abomination' because he felt it spoiled the view of Grasmere. The Wordsworths were at Allan Bank until 1811 when they moved to the Rectory – then known as the Parsonage – opposite St Oswald's Church. Clearly an unsettled time in the family's lives, they stayed in this damp, unhealthy house for only two years, before finally making Rydal Mount their permanent home in 1813.

One of the best ways to take in many of the key Wordsworth attractions is to walk the old Corpse Road from Grasmere as far as Rydal. Before St Mary's Church in Ambleside was consecrated, coffins had to be transported along this route from Ambleside to St Oswald's

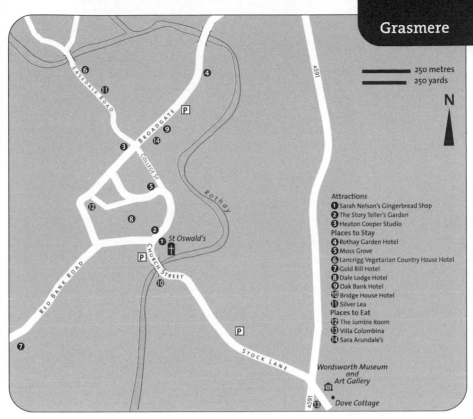

250 metres
250 yards

N

Attractions
1 Sarah Nelson's Gingerbread Shop
2 The Story Teller's Garden
3 Heaton Cooper Studio
Places to Stay
4 Rothay Garden Hotel
5 Moss Grove
6 Lancrigg Vegetarian Country House Hotel
7 Gold Rill Hotel
8 Dale Lodge Hotel
9 Oak Bank Hotel
10 Bridge House Hotel
11 Silver Lea
Places to Eat
12 The Jumble Room
13 Villa Colombina
14 Sara Arundale's

Wordsworth Museum
and
Art Gallery

Dove Cottage

Church in Grasmere for interment. Starting at St Oswald's, the route heads away from the village centre and past the Wordsworth Museum and Art Gallery as well as Dove Cottage. Passing the Coffin Stone or Resting Stone along the way – used to support the coffin while the bearers rested – it climbs slightly to follow a rough track that weaves in and out of the pretty woodland and across grazing land with views down to Rydal Water. Dropping into Rydal, you can then visit Rydal Mount, St Mary's Church and Dora's Field, before returning to Grasmere via beautiful lakeside paths.

⭐ Easedale Tarn

Grasmere is the starting point for many other great walks. One of the nicest is the walk up to **Easedale Tarn** via the dramatic waterfalls of **Sourmilk Gill**. Although a little steep in places, the walk is short and well within the capabilities of most people. In Victorian times, there used to be a refreshments hut beside the water here, serving light lunches and hot drinks to the tourists who hiked up to see the spectacularly located tarn. If you look just to the left of the path just before you reach the water, you will see a large, upright boulder. This used to form part of the wall of the hut. Some of the foundation stones are still visible nearby. Sadly, the hut had to be demolished in the 1960s after it was damaged by vandals.

There are superb views from the top of Silver How, a small fell to the west of the village, and Alcock Tarn, to the east, also makes for a pleasant morning's walk, but if you have time for only one hike, head up to **Helm Crag**, to the north. Its summit rocks inevitably attract the attention of motorists as they drive along the A591. The highest rocks, known as the Howitzer, are clearly identifiable as you come down from Dunmail Raise. The Lion and the Lamb, on the other hand, are best seen on the journey up from the south. When you reach the short summit ridge, you find an amazing collection of jagged pinnacles and shattered crags. The highest point, the infamous **Howitzer**, can be reached only by scrambling, but it is easily avoided. Helm Crag is just one of 214 Wainwrights – the fells listed in the guidebook writer's famous *Pictorial Guide to the Lakeland Fells* series. It is, however, the one peak which defeated him. In *The Central Fells*, the third volume of the series, he described the Howitzer as 'a pinnacle of rock airily thrust out above a dark abyss... not to be attained by walking... brought underfoot only by precarious manoeuvres of the body'. In his description of Helm Crag, he left a small space surrounded by dotted lines with a note saying: 'This corner was reserved for an announcement that the author had succeeded in surmounting the highest point. Up to the time of going to press, however, such an announcement cannot be made.' The space remained empty.

The Story Teller's Garden
Church Stile, Grasmere, **t** (015394) 35641, www.taffythomas. co.uk; scheduled events throughout the year; adm

The Story Teller's Garden, right in the middle of the village and behind one of its oldest cottages, is an enchanting place for children – and often proves pretty popular with adults too. Here, in a delightful National Trust garden, Taffy Thomas, storyteller extraordinaire (and the recipient of an MBE for his work), entertains his enthralled audiences with tall tales and 'story walks'. The Christmas event is particularly popular, with its torch-lit mixture of stories and songs with mince pies and wassail, a warm cider spiced with cinnamon, ginger, nutmeg and cloves.

The Heaton Cooper Studio
t (015394) 35280, www.heatoncooper. co. uk; open Mon–Sat 9–5

Grasmere village is also home to the **Heaton Cooper Studio**, a gallery and art shop established by landscape painter Alfred Heaton Cooper in 1905 and now managed by the fourth generation of artists in the family.

Dunmail Raise

North of Grasmere, the main road climbs to 781ft above sea level to cross Dunmail Raise, a gap in the mountains created by a geological fault. The pass, which marks the old boundary between Cumberland and Westmorland, is named after Dunmail, the last Celtic king of Cumbria. He was defeated by Edmund I, the Saxon king of England, in a battle at Dunmail Raise in AD 945. All of Dunmail's land north of the pass was ceded to Malcolm, king of Scotland.

Right in the middle of the busy road, where a grassy reservation has been left between the short section of dual carriageway, is an ancient cairn – the subject of many interesting local legends. Some say King Malcolm had it built to mark the southernmost point of his kingdom; others say it was erected by Edmund I to celebrate his victory. More romantic still is the idea that it marks the spot where Edmund personally killed Dunmail, telling his men to pile stones on the dead king's body. Dunmail's warriors, so the story goes, meanwhile retrieved the crown from their leader's head and threw it into Grisedale Tarn to prevent the Saxon king from flaunting it. Dunmail, it is said, will rise again from beneath that very cairn when his people need him. The one major flaw in this story is that Dunmail was almost definitely not killed by Edmund I; he fled to Rome after his defeat and died some time later.

Festivals and Events in Grasmere and Rydal

The annual **Grasmere Sports and Show** event (www.grasmeresportsand show.co.uk) is normally held on the Sunday of the late August Bank Holiday. This involves Cumberland and Westmorland wrestling competitions, fell races, a dog show, hound trails and, a recent addition, mountain-bike races.

Where to Stay in Grasmere and Rydal

(★) **Moss Grove** >

Moss Grove, Grasmere, t (015394) 35251, www.mossgrove.co.uk (luxury–expensive). Proof that organic and environmentally-friendly doesn't mean you have to scrimp on luxuries. This place really does have the 'wow' factor. Magnificent, imaginatively-designed rooms, some of which contain handmade wooden beds, Bose sound systems and heated slate bathroom floors. All water is filtered to remove chlorine and pesticides. In keeping with the relaxed atmosphere, guests simply go into the farmhouse kitchen, choose what they want and watch it being cooked by the chef.

Rothay Garden Hotel, Broadgate, Grasmere, t (015394) 35334, www.rothaygarden.com (luxury–expensive). This four-star hotel has just undergone a full refurbishment. The result is a beautiful conservatory **restaurant**, smart public areas and some of the classiest accommodation in the village. Half of the rooms have king-size beds, and the lovely loft suites have binoculars to help guests appreciate the views.

(★) **Cote How Organic Guest House** >

Cote How Organic Guest House, Rydal, t (015394) 32765, www.cotehow.co.uk (expensive). The owners have clearly put a lot of thought into turning this lovely, 16th-century home into a luxurious, welcoming guesthouse. Rooms are spacious with warm, rich furnishings. It is one of only three Soil Association-licensed organic guest houses in the UK. *Room rate reduction for those who arrive by public transport.*

Lancrigg Vegetarian Country House Hotel, Easedale Rd, Grasmere, t (015394) 35317, www.lancrigg.co.uk (expensive). Rambling bohemian house in a secluded woodland setting. The rooms are elegantly and individually furnished, and the lovely Georgian dining room serves up possibly the best vegetarian food in the whole of Cumbria.

The Gold Rill Hotel, Grasmere, t (015394) 35486, www.gold-rill.com (expensive). A bright and cheery place with an outdoor swimming pool and putting green. Appeals to an older clientele.

Dale Lodge Hotel, Grasmere, t (015394) 35300, www.dalelodgehotel.co.uk (expensive–moderate). This charming Georgian building has recently undergone a tasteful refurbishment. The result is a bright and upbeat hotel with a cosy, intimate **restaurant**.

Oak Bank Hotel, Broadgate, Grasmere, t (015394) 35217, www.lakedistricthotel. co.uk (expensive–moderate). Pleasant gardens and a light, airy conservatory **restaurant** that serves up a great four-course meal with good vegetarian options. First-class, friendly service.

Beck Allans, College St, Grasmere t (015394) 35563, www.beckallans.com (moderate). Cheerful and homely with five small, unexciting rooms. Also has some nice *self-catering* apartments. The owners are very friendly and a mine of useful information on local sights and activities.

Silver Lea, Easedale Rd, Grasmere t (015394) 35657, www.silverlea.com (moderate). Delightful cottage just a few minutes' walk from the village.

(★) **Lancrigg Vegetarian Country House Hotel** >>

White Moss House, Rydal, t (015394) 35295, *www.whitemoss.com* (*moderate*). The former home of Wordsworth's son is full of character.

 The Jumble Room>>

The Traveller's Rest Inn, Dunmail Raise, Grasmere, t 0500 600 725, *www.lakedistrictinns.co.uk* (*moderate–budget*). A 16th-century coaching inn on the busy A591, which skirts the edge of Grasmere. Eight simple rooms, all with fell views. No children allowed.

Rockwood, Grasmere, t (01344) 624896, *www.rockwood-lakedistrict.com* (*self-catering*). Spacious, six-bedroom cottage in a quiet location on the edge of Grasmere village.

Sara Arundale's >>

Rothay Lodge, Grasmere, t (01159) 232618, *www.rothay-lodge.co.uk* (*self-catering*). Five-bedroom cottage and two-bedroom apartment in a traditional Lakeland slate building. Decorated in a simple style.

Where to Eat in Grasmere and Rydal

Whether you are a vegetarian or not, **Lancrigg Vegetarian Country House Hotel** (*expensive*) is the best place to eat in Grasmere, but other good options among the hotels listed above include the **Oak Bank Hotel**, the **Dale Lodge Hotel** (*expensive*) and the elegant **Conservatory Restaurant** at the Rothay Garden Hotel (*expensive*), which has two AA rosettes.

The Jumble Room,Langdale Rd, Grasmere, t (015394) 35188, *www.thejumbleroom.co.uk* (*expensive–moderate*). Locals and visitors alike rave about this place. They just love the cosy, friendly, slightly bluesy feel of the place, the mad décor and, of course, the wonderfully eclectic menu. Hand-made sweet potato and coriander-filled ravioli with roast sweet potatoes and a delicate Thai green curry sauce sits alongside plain old fish and chips. Leave room for dessert. Also open for lunch. *Closed Tues.*

Sara Arundale's, Broadgate, Grasmere t (015394) 35266 (*moderate*). Good-quality, non-fussy food that is cheap by Grasmere standards. Also open for lunch.

Villa Colombina, Town End, Grasmere, t (015394) 35268, *www.howfoot.co.uk* (*moderate*). A sort of Jekyll and Hyde place – by day a simple tearoom popular with visitors to nearby Dove Cottage, by night a warm and inviting Italian restaurant. Booking recommended if you're coming in the evening.

Ullswater and the Northeast Lakes

Glorious Ullswater. Everyone has their favourite lake – Buttermere, Wastwater, Derwent Water...but no other lake winds for miles through the mountains like Ullswater does. From the low-lying hills and farmland around Pooley Bridge in the north to Glenridding and the very foot of the mighty Helvellyn range in the south, the lake stretches for more than seven wonderful miles. To the northeast is Penrith, an interesting and attractive market town with a fascinating history. It seems that everyone has played a role in shaping this area – Bronze Age peoples, the Celts, the Romans, the Norsemen, Anglo-Saxons, the Scots, Norman barons – and they've all left their mark in one way or another.

09

Don't miss

⭐ Atmospheric waterfall and arboretum
Aira Force p.124

⭐ Climb England's third-highest mountain
Helvellyn p.126

⭐ Cruise on an Ullswater steamer
Ullswater p.126

⭐ Traditional afternoon tea beside the lake
Sharrow Bay Hotel p.132

⭐ Spot England's only golden eagle
Riggindale p.134

See map overleaf

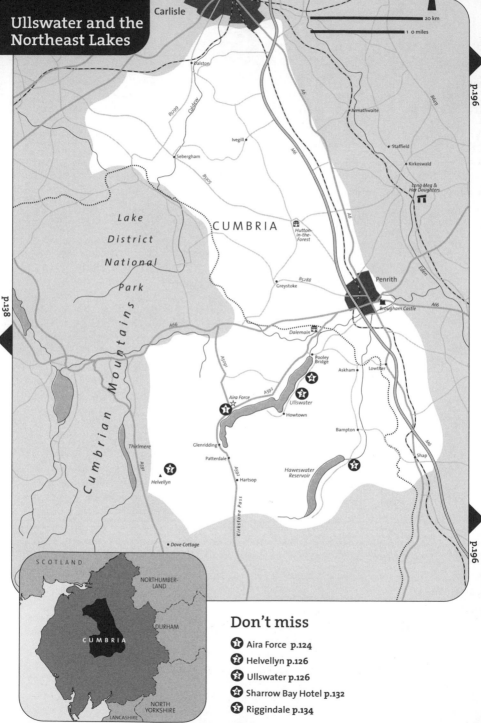

Carlisle

**Ullswater and the
Northeast Lakes**

20 km

1 0 miles

Dalston

B6299

Caldew

Armathwaite

A6

B6413

Ivegill

M6

Staffield

Sebergham

B5305

Kirkoswald

Long Meg &
Her Daughters

*Lake
District
National
Park*

C U M B R I A

Hutton-
in-the-
Forest

Cumbrian   Mountains

B5288

Greystoke

Penrith

Eden

Brougham Castle

A66

A66

Dalemain

A592

Fooley
Bridge

Askham

Lowther

Aira Force

A592

Ullswater

Howtown

M6

Thirlmere

A591

Glenridding

Bampton

Shap

Patterdale

A592

Helvellyn

Hartsop

A5091

Haweswater
Reservoir

Kirkstone Pass

Dove Cottage

SCOTLAND

NORTHUMBER-
LAND

DURHAM

CUMBRIA

NORTH
YORKSHIRE

LANCASHIRE

Don't miss

① Aira Force **p.124**

② Helvellyn **p.126**

③ Ullswater **p.126**

④ Sharrow Bay Hotel **p.132**

⑤ Riggindale **p.134**

Penrith

With a motorway junction at the edge of the town, several trunk roads converging here and a mainline railway station, it is only natural that Penrith has become something of a gateway for the northeastern corner of the Lake District. There is a temptation for travellers to rush through it, seeing it only as a stepping stone to somewhere else, but Penrith is worth some exploration.

One of the first things that strikes the visitor on arrival is the colour of the town – red. All the significant buildings and landmarks are constructed from the red sandstone found in the Eden Valley.

The name Penrith, in fact, is thought to mean the town under the 'red hill', probably refering to Beacon Hill, which overlooks the town. Another school of thought claims that Penrith comes from the Celtic for 'chief ford', but, as the nearest ford is more than a mile from the centre of town, this seems a little unlikely.

Travellers have been passing through what is now Penrith since the Bronze Age and the Romans built two forts nearby, but it was only in the 9th and 10th centuries that the town really gained stature. This is when it became the capital of the ancient kingdom of Cumbria, a semi-independent state that formed part of the kingdom of Strathclyde.

In medieval times, the town suffered greatly at the hands of the Scots and was burned down on at least three occasion during the 14th century. Finally, in 1382, licence was given to build a defensive tower. This was added to by the Neville family and then, in the 1470s, by the Duke of Gloucester. As lord warden of the Western Marches, the duke, who later became Richard III, stayed here on occasions as he carried out his role of defending the Scottish border. The castle's decline began after Richard was killed by Henry Tudor's Lancastrian forces at Bosworth Field, the penultimate battle of the Wars of the Roses.

Today, all that remains of the **castle** is the high south wall and the ruins of two towers. It is located in a public park opposite the railway station so there are no restrictions on visiting, or admission fees.

Like much of the town, **St Andrew's Church** has suffered for being so close to the Scottish border. Apart from the medieval tower, most of the building that visitors see today dates from the 18th century, but it is thought there may have been a chapel here since pre-Norman times, and an Augustinian priory was founded in the town in 1291.

Interesting features of the bright, colourful interior include a brass candelabra which was a gift from the Duke of Cumberland in 1745 as a reward for the town's loyalty during the Jacobite Uprising. A plaque at the head of the tower stairs commemorates more than 2,200 people who died of the plague in 1597. Older, more fascinating artefacts lie outside in the churchyard. Local legend has it that the Giant's Grave is the final resting place of Owen (or Ewan) Caesarius, a 10th-century king of all Cumbria. He was famed for being a formidable warrior and the four hogback stones that form the grave are said to represent the wild boar he killed in Inglewood forest. Despite the romantic appeal of the story, it is more likely that the 'grave' is simply a collection of Saxon or

Getting to and around Penrith

By Train and Bus

Penrith is on the West Coast Main Line, with direct **trains** to Glasgow, Crewe, Manchester, Birmingham and London Euston. **National Express** runs a daily service (**588**) between Inverness and London Victoria that stops in Glasgow and Penrith (journey time to London, six hours and 10 minutes).

Penrith is well served by **buses**. There are regular services between the town and Carlisle, Workington, Keswick, Cockermouth, Shap, Pooley Bridge, Patterdale, the Eden Valley villages, Kirkby Stephen and Appleby. Some local buses do not run on Sundays.

By Taxi

Ace Taxis, t (01768) 890731; Eden Taxis, t (01768) 865432; Penrith Taxis, t (01768) 899298.

By Bicycle

Arragon's Cycle Centre, Brunswick Rd, Penrith t (01768) 890344, *www.arragons.com*; Eden Cycle Centre, Brougham Hall, Brougham t (01768) 840400, *www.cycleactive.co.uk*.

Norse artefacts, including the two 11ft-high cross shafts at either end. Nearby in the churchyard is the **Giant's Thumb** – not the remains of Caesarius's body part, but a fine example of a Norse wheel cross.

A wander around Penrith will inevitably take you along narrow passageways that radiate out from the more open areas in the centre of town. This layout dates from the times of cross-border raids when the local people would herd their cattle into the centre while they defended the town gates. The gates have since gone, but the names remain – Castlegate, Middlegate, Sandgate, Burrowgate and Friargate.

Like so many Cumbrian towns, Penrith has Wordsworth connections. In fact, the poet spent much of his childhood here. He lived with the Cooksons, his mother's family, who ran a draper's shop next to the George Hotel. It was a miserable time for him; the Cooksons regarded the young Wordsworth as a burden and resented his social status.

William, his sister Dorothy and their friend Mary Hutchinson, who was to become William's wife, began their schooling at Dame Ann Birkett's school, which is now part of the Tudor Coffee Room overlooking St Andrew's churchyard.

Today's **Town Hall** was formerly two ornate sandstone houses designed in 1792 by Robert Adam. Wordworth's first cousin John, master of the East India Company's *Earl of Abergavenny*, lived in the left-hand house, which is now marked by a plaque.

Penrith Museum
Middlegate,
t (01768) 867466;
open April–Oct
Mon–Sat 9.30am–5pm
(6pm in school summer
holidays), Sun
10am–4pm; Nov–Mar
Mon–Sat 10am–4pm

Penrith Museum and the Tourist Information Centre are housed in the old Robinson's School, an Elizabethan structure that was altered in 1670. The museum contains displays of local history, geology and archaeology, including pottery from a nearby Roman fort and prehistoric 'cup and ring' stones from Little Meg Stone Circle. There is also an art gallery.

Just to the north of the town rises tree-covered Beacon Hill, once an important link in the country's communication chain and now a popular beauty spot with superb views in all directions – as befits a beacon. Take a stroll from the town centre and, on a clear day, you'll be able to see the Lake District mountains, the very highest of the Pennine moors, the beautiful Eden Valley and even the Scottish hills. It's about

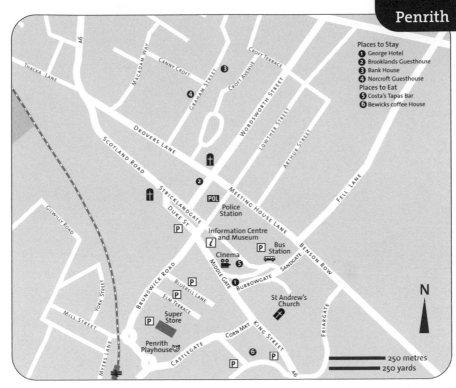

1.5 miles from the railway station, partly along wide streets of large, red-stone terraced houses and partly through woods.

The monument on the top of the hill was built in 1719 to mark the spot where beacons have been lit in times of emergency since the reign of Henry VIII. The last time the Penrith Beacon was fired to warn of the approach of the enemy was in 1804, during the Napoleonic Wars.

In 1767 Thomas Nicholson was hanged on Beacon Hill for the murder, on the same spot, of Langwathby butcher Thomas Parker. A few years later, a five-year-old William Wordsworth, having become separated from his servant James while out on a ride, stumbled across the site of the murder and subsequent execution. He fled the scene in terror and the memory stuck with him throughout his adult life. He recalled the incident in the *Prelude*, one of the few instances that Penrith gets a mention in poetry.

Around Penrith

Brougham Castle
Brougham t (01768) 862488, www.english-heritage.org.uk; open Apr–Oct daily 10am–5pm; adm

Beyond the town itself and scattered along the banks of the River Eamont are several interesting historical sites, all within walking distance of each other. The substantial ruins of picturesque **Brougham Castle** (pronounced 'Broom') are located on the banks of the river, near the site of Brocavum, the Roman fort that guarded the ford here. The impressive 13th-century keep survives as do many of the buildings later added by the powerful Clifford family. A dark, spiral stairway leads to the top of the keep, from where there are good views of Cross Fell, the very top of the long Pennine chain, and the Lake District fells. The property was one of many castles and churches restored by Lady Anne Clifford (*see* p.207) in the 17th century. An exhibition at the site tells the story of her life and includes carvings from the Roman fort.

Half a mile east of the castle is the ornate Countess Pillar, which Defoe described as 'the best and most beautiful piece of its kind in Britain'. The monument was erected by Lady Anne Clifford in 1656 to commemorate the place where she said goodbye to her mother 40 years before. Money used to be given to the poor here on the anniversary of their parting.

Heading west from Brougham Castle, you come to the remains of **Brougham Hall**. A fortified house has existed here since the 14th century, but the hall became famous in Victorian times when it was home to the Lord Chancellor. At this time, it was known as the 'Windsor of the north'; situated almost exactly halfway between Windsor and Balmoral, it played host to Edward VII and the future George V on several occasions. Today, it is home to craft workshops, a café and several other small businesses.

West again and you reach the village of Eamont Bridge where two prehistoric henges lie almost side by side. **Mayburgh Henge** is a large and impressive Neolithic circular bank built of stones taken from the river. It is 6.4 metres (21ft) high in places and contains a single standing stone, close to its centre. Sketches from the 18th century suggest the stone was one of a group of four. Nearby is **King Arthur's Round Table**, a circular enclosure with a surrounding ditch. Like Mayburgh, it dates from Neolithic times, but, sadly, this henge has been badly damaged by road-building. Legend has it that this was King Arthur's jousting arena. Access is free to both sites.

Heading south from Brougham and Eamont Bridge, the first village you come to on the A6 is **Clifton**. This was the site of the last military skirmish – battle is too grand a word – on English soil. It took place on 18 December 1745 when about 1,000 of Bonnie Prince Charlie's retreating Jacobite rebels clashed with the Duke of Cumberland's forces. Lord George Murray, one of the Jacobite's most competent officers, was leading the group and, by engaging the government troops, was acting against Prince Charlie's orders to withdraw and make for Carlisle. The dozen or so Highlanders who were killed are said to be buried under the Rebels' Oak, a large tree behind the George and Dragon pub. There is also a small monument – in St Cuthbert's churchyard, to the right of the entrance – to the dragoons who died.

Close to the church is a pele tower, all that remains of **Clifton Hall**. Probably built in the late 16th century, it stands alone in a farmyard and is in the care of English Heritage. Information panels help visitors understand the layout of the buildings to which it was once attached.

Slightly further afield, at Clifton Dykes, **Wetheriggs Pottery** is a thriving complex of artists' galleries, studios and shops where ironwork, ceramics, paintings, glassware and sculptures are created. Visitors can try their hand at just about anything in the Pots of Fun studio – throw your own pot, paint a vase or create a mosaic.

Wetheriggs Pottery
Clifton Dykes,
t *(01768) 892733,*
www.wetheriggs-
pottery.co.uk; open
daily, 10am–4.30pm

Red Barn Gallery
Melkinthorpe,
t *(01931) 7127670,*
www.redbarngallery.co.uk;
open Mar–Dec Thurs–Tues
10am–5pm

Artists clearly love this area of Cumbria and there are galleries and exhibition spaces dotted all over the place. **Red Barn**, located in a converted 18th-century barn and stables, features contemporary artists and sculptors working in a wide variety of media, and exhibitions change monthly.

Center Parcs
Whinfell Forest
near Penrith,
t *(01768) 893000,*
www.centerparcs.co.uk;
daily 10am–midnight; adm

Should the weather turn bad, there is plenty to keep families entertained at **Center Parcs Whinfell Forest**, which is open to day visitors and boasts one of the UK's longest falling rapids ride. Outside you can enjoy quad bikes, paintball and laser combat in the forest, archery, zip wires and abseiling.

Hutton-in-the-Forest
t *(017684) 84449,*
www.hutton-in-the-
forest.co.uk; gardens open
April–Oct Sun–Fri
11am–5pm; house open
April–Oct Wed, Thurs and
Sun 12.30–4pm; adm

To the north of Penrith, **Hutton-in-the-Forest** is a rambling old gem of a house, the home of Lord and Lady Inglewood. The house has been in the family since 1605, but some of it predates that, including a 14th-century peel tower. Outside, the wonderful walled garden contains a large collection of herbaceous plants and there is also an impressive topiary. Every summer, the grounds play host to Shakespearean productions as well as a number of other events.

Upfront Gallery
t *(017684) 84538,*
www.up-front.com; open
Tues–Sun and Bank
Holidays 10am– 5pm

The popular **Upfront Galler**y, located just west of Hutton-in-the-Forest on the B5305 holds about 18 exhibitions each year in four different spaces. The gallery, which is housed in a converted 17th-century farmhouse, also has a busy vegetarian café and is home to the Upfront Puppet Theatre, which stages superb productions during the school summer holidays.

High Head Sculpture
Valley
High Head Farm, Ivegill
t *(016974) 73552,*
www.highheadsculpture
valley.co.uk; open
Thurs–Tues, 10.30–5; adm

Further north still and you come to sculptor Jonathan Stamper's rather unusual gallery. His life-size creations, carved from wood, stone, iron and bronze are located in pretty meadows alongside the River Ive. Otters, herons, dippers and kingfishers make their home here too. Visitors can follow specially made trails through the **High Head Sculpture Valley** to view a number of interesting pieces.

09

Ullswater and the Northeast Lakes | Penrith

Festivals and Events in Penrith

(i) **Penrith Tourist**
Information Centre
Middlegate **t** *(01768)*
867466; open April–Oct
Mon–Sat 9.30am–5pm
(6pm in school summer
holidays), Sun 10am–4pm;
Nov–Mar Mon–Sat,
10am– 4pm

Potfest in the Pens (*www.potfest.co.uk*), the oldest potters' market in the UK, is held at the beginning of August at Skirsgill Auction Mart on the edge of Penrith. It's an open event, with up to 150 potters of all levels of experience showing off their abilities. The event is preceded by Potfest in the Park, an exhibition of selected potters' work in the grounds of nearby Hutton-in-the-Forest.

Where to Stay in Penrith

North Lakes Hotel and Spa, Ullswater Rd, **t** (01768) 868111, *www.north lakeshotel.com* (*expensive*). There is a bit of a corporate feel to this large hotel, but situated so close to junction 40 of the M6, it makes a convenient base from which to explore the area. Light, bright and airy rooms.

Roundthorn Country House, Beacon Edge, **t** (01768) 863952, *www.round thorn.co.uk* (*expensive*). Handsome, white-painted Georgian mansion in large, landscaped gardens at the end of a long drive, just beyond Penrith town centre. Good views over the

Eden Valley and Lakeland fells. Individually furnished rooms.

The George Hotel, Devonshire St, t (01768) 862696, *www.lakedistrict hotels.net/georgehotel/* (*expensive*). Handsome red-sandstone town centre hotel with lamp-lit, polished-wood interiors. The hotel has the hushed atmosphere of an old-fashioned country inn. Includes bar, **restaurant** and grand ballroom with balcony.

Bank House Bed and Breakfast, Graham St, t (01768) 868714, *www.bankhousepenrith.co.uk* (*moderate*). Cosy rooms in friendly, family-run B&B. Huge breakfasts, including imaginative vegetarian option. Nice touches include hand-made toiletries made from sustainably-sourced ingredients.

⭐ George and Dragon >>

⭐ Brooklands Guesthouse >

Brooklands Guesthouse, Portland Place, t (01768) 863395, *www.brooklandsguesthouse.com* (*moderate*). Beautifully refurbished, large Victorian terraced house with original timber fittings. Immaculate rooms decorated in rich, warm colours. Added extras include bathrobes, small fridges, hairdryers, and complimentary Wi-Fi. Superb value for money.

Hornby Hall, Brougham, t (01768) 891114, *www.hornbyhall.co.uk* (*moderate*). This 16th-century farmhouse is hidden away, reached by a long farm track. The rooms are fairly basic, but the house has a lot of interesting features, including a spiral staircase leading to two of the guest rooms.

Norcroft Guesthouse, Graham St, t (01768) 862 365, *www.norcroft-guesthouse.co.uk* (*moderate*). Large red-sandstone Victorian house, spacious and homely with clean, simple rooms on three floors.

⭐ The Greenhouse >>

Carrock Cottages, Carrock House, Hutton Roof, near Penrith, t (01768) 484111, *www.carrockcottages.co.uk* (*self-catering*). Five stone holiday cottages built around a cobbled courtyard. Home-cooked meals can be prepared and placed in your fridge with re-heating instructions.

Where to Eat in Penrith

Yanwath Gate Inn, Yanwath t (01768) 862386, *www.yanwathgate.com* (*expensive–moderate*). Award-winning, cosy gastro pub in a tiny village close to Penrith. Rotating selection of local ales from Cumbria's growing number of microbreweries, but the emphasis is firmly on food. Native oysters shucked to order; crab and sweetcorn chowder with sweet chilli dumplings; Herdwick lamb cutlets in smoked paprika and garlic marinade.

George and Dragon, Clifton, t (01768) 865381, *www.georgeanddragon clifton.co.uk* (*moderate*). Old coaching inn recently renovated to an exceptionally high standard by Charles Lowther, of the local land-owning family. A bright, lively atmosphere and friendly service. Classic British dishes cooked using produce that is sourced mostly from the Lowther estate. Seasonal game is regularly on the specials board. Good wine list with a wide selection available by the glass.

Grants of Castlegate, Castlegate t (01768) 895444 (*moderate*). This small but smart and modern wine bar-cum-bistro serves tasty food from around the world. Very busy at weekends. *Closed Mon and Tues.*

Costa's Tapas Bar, Queen St, t (01768) 895550, *www.costastapasbar.co.uk* (*moderate–budget*). Tacky, but hugely popular and the food can't be faulted. *Closed Mon.*

No 15 Café Bar and Gallery, Victoria Rd, t (01768) 867453 (*moderate–budget*). This arty café-bar is a popular lunchtime spot for locals. Good, filling sandwiches, salads, light meals and a scrumptious selection of home-made cakes.

The Greenhouse, Larch Cottage Nursery, Melkinthorpe, t (01931) 712404, *www.larchcottage.co.uk* (*moderate–budget*). Interesting pizzas such as smoked salmon and coriander with chilli oil, and delicious lunches with a Mediterranean emphasis make this friendly, jazzy venue a cut above. Make sure you get there early, in the summer, because the open-air balcony is very popular. The Italian coffee is just about the best you'll find in the east of the county.

Bewicks Coffee House, Princes Court, Rowcliffe Lane, t (01768) 864764 (*budget*). Traditional-looking coffee shop with a bistro-style menu. Roasted aubergine and feta fritters, roasted vegetable and goats' cheese salad. *Café open Mon–Sat, restaurant Fri and Sat eves.*

Entertainment in Penrith

Lonsdale Cinema, Middlegate, t (01768) 862400, *www.penrith-alhambra.co.uk*. Two screens that show blockbusters and devote Sunday evenings to foreign-language and independent films.

Penrith Playhouse, Auction Mart Lane, t (017680) 865557, *www.penrithplayers.co.uk*. Home of the Penrith Players, an amateur dramatic group that puts on about six productions each year.

Ullswater

Ullswater is the second largest lake in the National Park, curling from the eastern fells to within a stone's throw of Penrith. In the north, gentle green slopes run down to the lake; further south are the mountains, including craggy Helvellyn. Its accessibility from the northeast makes Ullswater popular, but without a lakeside town it has kept its romance. Approaching it from Penrith, visitors first reach the

Rheged Centre
Redhills, near Penrith, t (01768) 868000, www.rheged.com; open daily 10am–5.30pm

Rheged Centre, a vast warren of galleries, shops, restaurants and visitor attractions that blends carefully into its natural surroundings by having been built into the hillside. There are indoor and outdoor play areas for the kids as well as a huge cinema screen that shows 3D films.

Located on A592 between Rheged and Pooley Bridge is **Dalemain**, an

Dalemain
t (017684) 86450, www.dalemain.com; gardens open Mar–Oct daily 10.30am–5pm; Nov, Dec and Feb Sun–Thurs 11am–4pm; house open Mar–Oct daily 11.15am–4pm; adm

attractive mansion that is open to the public during the summer. It has been home to the same family since 1679 and behind its imposing facade, it has architectural features from the medieval, Tudor and early Georgian periods. The interior contains gems such as Tudor oak panelling and original hand-painted wallpaper. The 16th-century barn in the courtyard is one of the largest loft barns in the north of England. It houses a display of agricultural equipment and a small museum dedicated to the fell pony. The gardens and tearoom are open all year round. Visit in May to see the dazzling display of Himalayan blue poppies or in June and July to appreciate the Rose Walk.

Nearby **Dacre** has an interesting church that is thought to have once been the site of a Saxon monastery. The church itself is an attractive Norman construction with later additions and modifications, but more fascinating are the four carved stones in the churchyard depicting a bear eating a cat. The origin of the stones is unknown.

Pooley Bridge spans the start of the River Eamont as it issues from Ullswater. Aside from the lake itself, the village has little to recommend it. There are several places nearby where boats can be hired and it is also the northern terminus of the Ullswater Steamer (*see* p.126).

'upon the whole, the happiest combination of beauty and grandeur which any of the Lakes affords.'
William Wordsworth on Ullswater

The Pennine-like moorland above Pooley Bridge contains several ancient and often mysterious sites. The most interesting of these is probably **The Cockpit** (grid reference NY483222), a Bronze Age stone

Getting to and around Ullswater

By Bus

The **108** runs between Penrith and Patterdale via Pooley Bridge (journey time, 50 minutes), Mon–Sat; Sun, April–Aug. The **208** runs between Keswick and Patterdale via Aira Force (40 minutes), Sat, Sun and Bank Holidays, May–July; daily in summer holidays. The **517** runs between Bowness-on-Windermere and Glenridding via the Kirkstone Pass (55 minutes), Sat, Sun and Bank Holidays, May–July and Sept–Oct; daily in summer holidays.

By Boat

Ullswater Steamer, **t** (017684) 82229, *www.ullswater-steamers.co.uk*; operates all year daily, weather permitting.

By Taxi

Ullswater Taxis, **t** (017684) 82213

By Bicycle

Bicycles can be hired, summer only, from St Patrick's Landing **t** (01768) 482393, *www.stpatricksboatland ings.co.uk*; Park Foot Caravan and Camping site, **t** (017684) 86309, near Pooley Bridge; and Waterside House Camp Site, **t** (017684) 86332, also near Pooley Bridge.

circle, about 90ft in diameter, raised on the inside of a low bank. There are about 73 stones in the circle and a standing stone 300 metres to the southwest. It acquired its name in more recent history, when it was used for cockfighting. There are also several Bronze Age stone burial mounds and standing stones nearby. **The Cop Stone** (grid reference NY495216) is 4ft tall and about 3ft thick. It forms part of a man-made bank believed to be a ring cairn.

A narrow road heads southwest from Pooley Bridge, hugging the eastern shore of the lake before reaching **Howtown**. After a steep, zig-zagging ascent, the tortuous road ends in remote and tranquil **Martindale**. There are two churches here – the 'new' church of St Peter's (built in 1882) and the tiny, isolated church of St Martin's, which is lit by candle because it doesn't have any electricity. This plain, stone building with flagstone floors was constructed in 1634, but the enormous yew in the churchyard is about 1,300 years old. A storm destroyed the roof of St Martin's on the day that St Peter's was consecrated.

Keen fell-walkers will find Howtown and Martindale good launch-pads for some great hikes. Hallin Fell, Beda Fell, Steel Knotts and Swarth Fell can all be accessed from here, and there's a good chance of spotting England's oldest native herd of red deer as you explore these lonely, mostly grassy hills. In the autumn, listen out for the eerie noise of the males rutting.

🟊 **Aira Force** On the opposite side of Ullswater is **Aira Force**, a spectacular waterfall with a single, 70ft plunge. Using safe paths and stairways leading up from the National Trust car park on the A592, visitors can walk to the very base of the noisy cataract and, even in relatively dry conditions, feel the spray on their faces. The top of the drop has a stone humpback bridge spanning it – not a place for the faint-hearted. Most visitors do not continue upstream from here, but it is worth carrying on because there are higher, albeit less impressive falls further up the beck.

The gorge of the Aira Beck is cloaked in a delightful mixture of trees, an arboretum that was planted by the Howard family of Greystoke. They were lords of the manor here from the late Middle Ages until they sold the land to the National Trust in 1906. Some of the lovely specimens here include enormous Douglas firs, a collection of fine yews and a Chilean pine or 'Monkey Puzzle' tree.

Wordsworth was clearly a fan of the gorge and wrote several poems about it, including *Airey-Force Valley*:

Not a breath of air
Ruffles the bosom of this leafy glen.
From the brook's margin, wide around, the trees
Are stedfast as the rocks; the brook itself,
Old as the hills that feed it from afar,
Doth rather deepen than disturb the calm
Where all things else are still and motionless.
And yet, even now, a little breeze, perchance
Escaped from boisterous winds that rage without,
Has entered, by the sturdy oaks unfelt,
But to its gentle touch how sensitive
Is the light ash! that, pendent from the brow
Of yon dim cave, in seeming silence makes
A soft eye-music of slow-waving boughs,
Powerful almost as vocal harmony
To stay the wanderer's steps and soothe his thoughts.'

The nearby woodlands of **Gowbarrow Park** also made a lasting impression on him and his sister Dorothy. Having walked through the woods on 15 April 1802, Dorothy noted in her diary: 'I never saw daffodils so beautiful. They grew among the mossy stones about and about them, some rested their heads upon these stones as on a pillow for weariness and the rest tossed and reeled and danced and seemed as if they verily laughed with the wind that blew upon them over the lake; they looked so gay ever dancing ever changing.' Two years later, William used Dorothy's observations as the basis of the poem *Daffodils*, the first line of which is probably one of the most famous lines in English poetry... 'I wandered lonely as a cloud...'

Glenridding and Patterdale

Heading south along the A592, the lakeside scenery grows ever-more impressive. Towering crags and steep-sided mountains loom over the few settlements here, gradually crowding the grazing land between the fells and the water until the sheep disappear and the road is forced to hug a narrow shelf, with dark, wooded cliffs on one side and the lake on the other.

Finally, at the base of the Helvellyn range, is **Glenridding**, a former mining village that now exists almost solely to service the walkers, climbers, kayakers, scuba divers, mountain-bikers and even skiers who come here to enjoy the great outdoors.

Lead was discovered at Greenside in the middle of the 17th century, with Dutch adventurers driving the first level in the 1690s and then transporting the dressed ore to the Stoneycroft smelter near Keswick. Serious development didn't begin until 1822 when the Greenside Mining Company was formed. By 1849, there were 300 workers at Greenside, making it the largest lead mine in England.

It was the first mine in Britain to use electrical winding and underground haulage, generating its own electricity by means of water turbines. The water was supplied by the damming of nearby tarns. One of them, in Keppel Cove, burst its banks in October 1927, bringing devastation to Glenridding below. The promontory on which the steamer pier is situated is formed from the flood debris.

The mine operated until 1962. In its lifetime, it had produced about 2.4 million tons of lead ore and 2 million ounces of silver. Today, some of the converted mine buildings are used as outdoor education centres.

Glenridding itself is little more than a collections of small shops, hotels, guesthouses and cafés, but it makes a great base from which to explore the area. Many walkers approach **Helvellyn** from here. Tackled from this side instead of the Thirlmere side, the mountain takes on a radically different appearance, a much more rugged appearance. Above Glenridding, it's all crags, cliffs and glacial cirques. The best-known route on to the mountain is via **Striding Edge**, one of the two vertiginous arêtes that cradle Red Tarn. (The other arête is Swirral Edge, which forms an interesting descent route.) Come the summer, there is often a long queue of walkers strung out along the exposed, rocky ridge. Sadly, there have also been a lot of accidents on Striding Edge, many of them fatal, particularly in the winter.

🎇 Helvellyn

The exit from Striding Edge is marked by a plaque telling the story of Charles Gough, whose body was found in 1805 at the base of the crags beneath this spot. His rotting remains had been guarded for three months by his emaciated dog, a story that inspired William Wordsworth to pen *Fidelity* and Sir Walter Scott to write these poignant lines in *Climbed the Dark Brow of Mighty Helvellyn...*

'How long didst thou think that his silence was slumber?
When the wind waved his garment, how oft didst thou start?
How many long days and long weeks didst thou number,
Ere he faded before thee, the friend of thy heart?
And, oh, was it meet, that – no requiem read o'er him –
No mother to weep, and no friend to deplore him,
And thou, little guardian, alone stretch'd before him –
Unhonour'd the Pilgrim from life should depart?'

🎇 Ullswater Steamers
Glenridding,
t (017684) 82229,
www.ullswater-
steamers.co.uk; operate
all year daily, weather
permitting; adm

But Helvellyn isn't the only attraction for fell-walkers. Sheffield Pike makes for a grand half-day out and easier walks up to Keldas and Lanty's Tarn are suitable for children.

Back down in the valley again, Glenridding is home to the main pier of the **Ullswater Steamer**. The Ullswater Navigation and Transit Company Limited started operating services in 1859, carrying mail, provisions and passengers around the lake. Two 19th-century 'steamers' still operate on the lake – the *Raven* and the *Lady of The Lake*

– although both were converted to diesel in the 1930s. Another two boats were added to the fleet this century.

There really is no better way to experience this beautiful lake than from one of these boats, which run all year round, weather permitting. The other two piers are at Howtown and Pooley Bridge., A popular option is to take the boat from Glenridding to Howtown and then walk the seven miles back along the lakeshore.

Glenridding Sailing Centre
t (017684) 82541,
*www.glenriddingsailing
centre.co.uk*

Alternatively, to get a bit closer to the water, boats of all shapes and sizes can be hired on Ullswater from **Glenridding Sailing Centre**, which can be found down a dirt track opposite the entrance to the main car park.

St Patrick's Landing
t (01768) 482393,
*www.stpatricksboat
landings.co.uk*

Slightly closer to Patterdale, **St Patrick's Landing** has small, self-drive motor boats as well as rowing boats.

Eden Rivers Trust
t (01768) 866788.

For visitors with their own canoe or kayak, the **Eden Rivers Trust** has published a useful canoe trail leaflet for the lake. It helps paddlers to identify a number of potential routes. Copies can be found at Tourist Information Offices, canoe hire shops and direct from the Eden Rivers Trust.

Patterdale is just beyond the top end of the lake. The dale is named after St Patrick. Local legend has it that, when his ship foundered on Duddon Sands in AD 540, he walked across the mountains and ended up in this isolated valley. The settlement was known as Patrichesdale in the 12th century and became Patricdale in the 13th century. Like many parts of western Britain, Cumbria claims the patron saint of Ireland as her own son.

The church of St Patrick was built by Anthony Salvin in 1853. The interior contains embroideries by Ann Macbeth, who lived and worked in Patterdale in the first half of the 20th century and belonged to the influential Glasgow School, which included Charles Rennie Mackintosh. The largest panel depicts 'The Good Shepherd', but there are smaller panels showing the Nativity and the score of Parry's music for Blake's *Jerusalem*.

There are some superb walks from Patterdale. The **Deepdale Round** is a tough, 10-mile route with almost 3,400ft of ascent that takes in St Sunday Crag, Fairfield, Hart Crag and the lonely ridge of Hartsop Above How. Place Fell, looming over Patterdale on the eastern side of the lake, is a popular summit with good views across to the mighty Helvellyn range. Alternatively, follow the route of the *Coast to Coast* up to Boredale Hause and then on to Angletarn Pikes and the beautifully situated Angle Tarn.

Beyond Patterdale

Between Patterdale and the top of Kirkstone Pass, there are scattered farms and just one hamlet, **Hartsop**. This higgledy-piggledy cluster of unspoilt stone cottages lies just off the main road, so doesn't receive as many visitors as it deserves. It's a pretty spot and small, colourful, well-kept gardens add to its appeal. Once renowned for wool-spinning, several homes, some of which date from the 17th century, still have their external spinning galleries.

Walk: Aira Force and Gowbarrow

Start and finish:
National Trust car park at Aira Force (grid reference NY400200)
Distance:
 4 miles/6.4km
Total ascent:
1,158ft/353m

In brief:
It often seems that some of the best views in the Lakes are from the minor tops. Gowbarrow, at only 1,578ft, is a good example. Heading up through the gorgeous arboretum and past spectacular Aira Force at first, this route then does a circuit of the top of the fell. Visiting the summit and then coming round the eastern side of the fell, it's a generally pleasant excursion, but it's when you reach the southern edge that you stop in your tracks... The view down Ullswater towards the Helvellyn range is simply breathtaking.

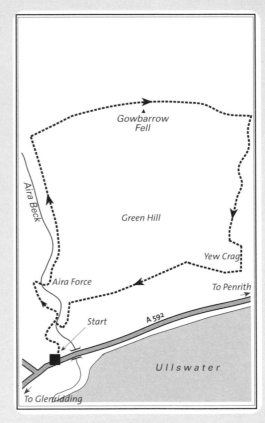

Route description:

Go through the gap in the National Trust stone construction at the far end of the car park and when you reach an area of yew trees, bear left away from the iron railings to ascend with the beck on your right. After about 10 minutes, turn right to head steeply down the stone staircase to the base of the powerful **Aira Force**. Cross the bridge and then turn left up another steep, stone stairway, joining a path coming in from the right.

There is quite a bit of clambering to be done as you wend your way upstream. In a couple of hundred yards, you will see a path branching off to the left to a wooden footbridge below. Ignore this, and continue with the beck on your left.

The woods start to thin out after you pass through gap in a wall and then disappear entirely after a gate in a fence. Just before you reach another gate – a small, wooden gate beside a larger farm gate – turn right to start climbing on a faint path. Cross the ladder stile and head steeply uphill with the wall on your left.

After about half-an-hour of uphill slog, the path finally levels off slightly and you will see the trig point just off to the right. Swinging round to the right on an obvious but sometimes boggy path, make a beeline for the summit. The views from here include Helvellyn (SW), Blencathra (NW) and your first glimpse of Ullswater.

Picking up a path running in a NE direction, drop down from the summit knoll. You now weave in and out of similar, small, heathery knobbles as the path starts to swing round to the SE. With the sparkling waters of Ullswater ahead, bear right at a ruined building, an old **shooting lodge**, to follow a narrow path around the eastern side of the fell.

Just over half-a-mile beyond the old lodge, keep left at a fork. Coming round the side of a crag, you are suddenly faced with one of the most magnificent panoramas in the eastern Lakes. The western expanse of **Ullswater** is revealed, blue and inviting, with the dark, craggy Helvellyn range in the background, providing a perfect counterpoint to the water's serenity. Just a few yards away is a perfectly placed bench, a chance to sit and admire.

Always with that sumptious view ahead, you continue on a level path for a few minutes and then begin descending gently. You should be able to see what looks like a medieval tower below. This is **Lyulph's Tower** and was actually built as a shooting lodge by the Duke of York in 1780.

Go through the gate at the bottom of the path and then turn left to descend through woodland to a bridge over **Aira Beck**. Having crossed, climb the steps on the other side and then bear left through a gap in the iron railings. It's now a five-minute woodland stroll back to the car park.

It's hard to believe it now, but sleepy Hartsop was once buzzing with industrial activity. There were two lead mines in the area as well as a large slate quarry on Caudale Moor. The scant remains of Low Hartsop mine are still visible, about half-a-mile east of the hamlet, at the confluence of Hayeswater Gill and Pasture Beck. Stone piers and a wheel pit are all that remain of a huge water wheel that was constructed to drain the mine, which suffered badly from flooding.

Hartsop makes a good starting point for some pretty wild fell-walking. The unremittingly steep slopes of Caudale Moor, Hartsop Dodd and Gray Crag see few hikers, but they can be used as routes on to High Street. Alternatively, an easier path takes you on to this well-known top via the lovely Hayeswater reservoir.

On the other side of the A592, the fells above lonely Dovedale include High Hartop Dodd, Dove Crag and Hart Crag, the latter two situated on the high, windswept ridge that forms part of the magnificent Fairfield Horseshoe. The cliffs on the eastern face of Dove Crag proper are home to one of the area's most famous and largest caves – **Priest's Hole**, a popular overnight bivvy spot for those who are brave enough to attempt the tricky scramble to get to it. The natural cave is about 15ft deep and a low wall has been built at the front to provide added protection from the elements. A small metal casket contains a log book and various items left by previous visitors.

'In some parts it is almost frightfully steep; for the road being only the original mountain track of shepherds, gradually widened and improved from age to age… is carried over ground which no engineer, even in alpine countries, would have viewed as practicable,'

Thomas De Quincey, 1807

Beyond Hartsop, the road begins its long, slow climb, passing Brothers Water on the way. Hardknott Pass may be the steepest, but, at almost 1,500ft, **Kirkstone Pass** is the highest Lakeland pass open to motor vehicles. It can be a taxing climb for motorists – more so for cyclists – but take heart from the fact that it is at least asphalted. Not so in that intrepid traveller, Celia Fiennes's day. She tackled the pass on horseback and found the landscape both beautiful and intimidating. 'I was walled on both sides by those inaccessible high rocky barren hills which hang over ones head in some places and appear very terrible.'

The pass and its pub have a number of ghost stories associated with them. In 2004, The *Westmorland Gazette* reported that a teenager living at the pub had captured the 'otherworldly outlines' of a young girl on his mobile phone while he was locked in a disused room there. A woman hanged for murdering her child is said to haunt the pass and ghosthunters believe that the apparition on the boy's mobile phone may have been the ghost of the murdered child.

The remote, centuries-old travellers' inn already had several ghost stories associated with it. There are tales of the spirit of a woman who died while trying to cross the pass in a snowstorm and of a lost hiker who worked at the hotel and now plays poltergeist tricks there. A coachman dressed in 17th-century clothing mysteriously appeared in a photograph taken in front of the inn in 1993.

Festivals and Events in Ullswater

ⓘ National Park
Information
Centre
Beckside Car Park,
Glenridding **t** *(017684)*
82414. Open Easter–Oct
daily 9.30am–5.30pm;
Nov–Easter Sat–Sun
9.30am–3.30pm

The **Ullswater Outdoor Festival** (*www.ullswater.com*) is a nine-day celebration, at the end of September, of the fantastic scenery that the area has to offer, . It includes guided walks and scrambles, instruction in kayaking and sailing, mountain-biking events and climbing sessions for beginners. And it's all free. It's not every day that you can get expert guides to introduce you to the scary delights of St Sunday Crag's exposed Pinnacle Ridge – one of the Lake District's classic scrambles – for nothing. All the gear you need is thrown in too – including harness, helmet, rucksack and lightweight waterproofs.

Where to Stay in Ullswater

(★) Sharrow Bay
Country House
Hotel >

Luxury
Sharrow Bay Country House Hotel, Ullswater, **t** (017684) 86301, *www.sharrowbay.co.uk*. The perfect place for a special occasion. Secluded, lakeside location with 12 acres of gardens and woodland, private jetty and boathouse. Large, luxurious rooms, some with spectacular views up the lake. Service is superb, but not pretentious.

Expensive
Cherry Holme, Glenridding, **t** (017684) 82512, *www.cherryholme.co.uk*. Mini-bars and hand-carved king-sized beds, make this B&B stand out from the crowd, but the rooms are slightly overpriced for their size. The sauna is a real treat.

Glenridding Hotel, Glenridding, **t** (017684) 82289, *www.bw-glenridding hotel.co.uk*. Plain but decent rooms, including several that sleep up to five. Very traditional public areas, including restaurant, bar with flagstone floor and library with billiards table.

Inn on the Lake, Glenridding, **t** (017684) 82444, *www.lakedistrict hotels.net/innonthelake*. Lovely, spacious rooms, many with great views of the lake and all furnished with large beds and soft chairs.

There's a children's play area, pitch-and-putt golf course and leisure suite.
Macdonald Leeming House, Watermillock on Ullswater, **t** 0844 879 9142, *www.macdonald hotels.co.uk/leeminghouse/*. Another superb lakeside, country house hotel, this time with 22 acres of gardens and woodland, direct access to Ullswater, a private fishing licence and, should you need it, a helipad.

The Rampsbeck Country House Hotel, Watermillock on Ullswater, **t** (017684) 86442, *www.rampsbeck.co.uk*. Elegant country house with gentle, laid-back ambience. Rooms individually furnished to a high standard, three with private balconies. Friendly, unobtrusive service. Lovely terrace for afternoon teas and Immaculately-kept grounds running right down to the lake.

Moderate
Deepdale Hall, Patterdale, **t** (017684) 82369, *www.deepdalehall.co.uk*. The floors are all wonky and the doors aren't always a perfect fit, but that's part of the charm of this warm and cosy 17th-century working farmhouse, located in a quiet side valley.

Gill Head Farm, Troutbeck, near Penrith **t** (017687) 79652, *www.gill headfarm.co.uk*. Homely rooms on a working farm that dates back to the 17th century. Wood-burning stoves and exposed oak beams give the place a lot of character. Evening meals and packed lunches also available.

Grisedale Lodge, Grisedale Bridge, Glenridding **t** (017684) 82155, *www.grisedalelodge.co.uk*. Friendly, small B&B in a peaceful location. The modern, comfortable residents' lounge, decorated in soothing neutral tones, has a balcony with great views across to Place Fell.

(★) Styan Bew >

Styan Bew, Hartsop **t** (017684) 82139, *www.styanbew-b-and-b.co.uk*. Just the one guest bedroom in this delightful stone cottage in the pretty, secluded hamlet of Hartsop. Wooden floors, exposed stonework and beams. Guests have use of a private dining and sitting room, complete with wood-burning stove.

The Ullswater View, Watermillock on Ullswater, **t** (017684) 86286, *www.theullswaterview.co.uk*. Recently refurbished. Good bathrooms.

Budget

Mosscrag, Glenridding, t (017684) 82500, *www.mosscrag.co.uk*. One of most popular and comfortable budget guesthouses in the area. Small, but clean and comfortable rooms. Small bar for guests; dinner also available. Welcomes dogs.

Old Water View, Patterdale t (017684) 82175, *www.oldwaterview.co.uk*. Cracking guesthouse with pine furniture, oak beams and Victorian fireplaces.

(★) **Fellbites Café Restaurant >>**

Stone Cottage, Grove Barn, Hartsop, Patterdale t (017684) 82647), *www.lakelandstonecottage.co.uk* (*self-catering*). Serious chic in a traditional and beautiful Lakeland setting, this superb cottage won Enjoy England's self-catering holiday of the year award in 2008.

Where to Eat in the Ullswater area

Several hotels in the area have good restaurants that are open to non-residents, notably **Sharrow Bay** (*see* below), the **Inn on The Lake** (*expensive–moderate*), the recently refurbished **Rampsbeck**, which has three AA rosettes (*expensive*) and the rather grand **Regency Restaurant at the Macdonald Leeming House** (*expensive*).

(4) **Sharrow Bay Country House Hotel**

Sharrow Bay Country House Hotel, Ullswater, t (017684) 86301, *www.sharrowbay.co.uk* (*very expensive*) has one of the finest restaurants in the county, one of only three to be awarded a Michelin star. Six courses will set you back £70. Afternoon tea, with a wonderful lakeside view and lots of tasty delicacies, is a special treat. If you can't manage it all, the waiter will package up what's left and let you

take it home. Some claim Sharrow Bay to be the birthplace of the sticky toffee pudding, but this is disputed.

Brackenrigg Inn, Watermillock on Ullswater, t (017684) 86206, *www.brackenrigginn.co.uk* (*moderate*). One menu, two venues – a smart, modern restaurant with high-backed chairs overlooking the lake and a cosy dark-wood bar. Outdoor seating front and back. The wild mushroom and tarragon risotto with rocket and Parmesan is delicious.

Fellbites Café Restaurant, Greenside Rd, Glenridding, t (017684) 82781, *www.fellbites.co.uk* (*moderate*). By day, a simple café, but come the evening, this simple venue with exposed stone walls and wooden floors serves up some of the best food around – cranberry, mushroom and brie wellington; perfectly pink duck breast. Superb value for money. *Lunch daily; dinner Thurs–Sat.*

The Royal, Dockray, t (017684) 82356, *www.the-royal-dockray.co.uk* (*moderate*). Adventurous and tasty menu includes dishes such as pan-fried duck breast on a bed of stir-fried vegetables in a deep-fried tortilla basket topped with home-made plum and thyme ice-cream. A little off the beaten track, the pub has one of the nicest and largest beer gardens in the area. Beers from a number of local microbreweries are featured.

Greystone House Farm Shop and Tearoom, Stainton, near Penrith, t (01768) 866952, *www.greystone housefarm.co.uk* (*budget*). Simple but great quiches, sandwiches and salads at reasonable prices.

Greystones Coffee House, Glenridding, t (01768) 82392, *www.greystones gallery.co.uk* (*budget*). Great espresso and wonderful cakes in the snazzy, yellow interior or on the popular front patio beside Glenridding Beck.

Haweswater and Shap Area

Askham

Approaching Haweswater from Pooley Bridge or Penrith, you pass through a number of villages, including Askham, close to the ruins of **Lowther Castle**. Looking like something out of a fairy tale – all turrets, towers and Gothic arches – this was once the home of the Lowther family. It was built between 1806 and 1811 by Robert Smirke who went on to design the British Museum. Distinguished visitors to the castle included Kaiser Wilhelm II and the Prince of Wales, later Edward VII, but the building proved too much for the Lowthers and they abandoned it in the 1930s. All that remains today is a shell, which can be seen from the road, but there are plans to turn the site into a visitor attraction.

The Lowthers are the largest private landowners in the Lake District. Much of their wealth came from the coalfields of west Cumbria and they are often credited with bringing the Industrial Revolution to Cumberland many years before it reached other northwestern counties, including Lancashire.

Probably the most famous of the Lowthers was the fifth Earl of Lonsdale, Hugh Cecil (1857–1944), who was passionate about sport. A celebrated horseman and yachtsman, he was also well-known in boxing circles where he initiated the presentation of the celebrated Lonsdale Belt to British champions. Because of his liking for yellow livery on his cars, horseboxes and coachmen, Hugh Lowther was dubbed the 'Yellow Earl', and his Lonsdale yellow was adopted by the Automobile Association when he became its president in 1907.

Haweswater

'What we see is not a dale with a lake in it, but a group of fells plunged up to the waist in cold water'

Norman Nicholson

As reservoirs go, Haweswater is not unattractive. It is located in a cul-de-sac that culminates in the wild crags and dark tarns that sit below the towering High Street range. On one side is a narrow road that ends at the Mardale Head car park; on the other is a public footpath that forms part of Wainwright's Coast to Coast route from St Bees to Robin Hood's Bay. But far below the dark waters lie the remains of a once tranquil settlement, a peaceful dale that was dotted with farms, a church, a school and a pub.

The reservoir was constructed to satisfy Manchester's growing thirst for water in the first half of the 20th century. Construction of the dam, roads and underground aqueduct began in 1929. Burnbanks was built to house the labourers. It was regarded as quite forward-thinking at the time; instead of the usual squalid navvy settlements, the men and their families lived in a model village. The bungalows had electricity, hot and cold running water and bathrooms. Manchester Corporation also paid for a policeman, a shopkeeper and a nurse. Eighteen of the 66 bungalows have recently been rebuilt and provide homes for people working within the National Park.

Getting to and around Haweswater and Shap

By Bus

The **106** runs between Penrith and Kendal via Shap roughly every two hours (journey time, 25 minutes to Penrith from Shap, 45 minutes to Kendal). No buses on Sun. Bampton and the northern end of Haweswater at Burnbanks is served by the **111** bus from Penrith, which runs on Tues and Sat only (Penrith to Burnbanks, 40 minutes).

By Taxi

Ace Taxis, **t** (01768) 890731; Eden Taxis, **t** (01768) 865432; Penrith Taxis, **t** (01768) 899298.

By Bicycle

For bike hire, try Slug and Hare Bicycle Company, Bampton CA10 2RQ, **t** (01931) 713386, *www.slugandhare.co.uk.*

The level of the natural lake was eventually raised by almost 100ft and water finally began to flow to Manchester in 1941. Lost forever were the Dun Bull pub, the farms and Holy Trinity Church. When the latter was demolished in 1936, 100 bodies had to be exhumed and reburied in Shap. In times of drought, the skeleton of **Mardale Green** becomes visible as the water recedes to reveal stone walls and the village bridge at the southern end of the reservoir. A fictional account of the drowning of the valley is told in Cumbrian writer Sarah Hall's 2002 award-winning novel *Haweswater.*

Despite the human interference, the valley retains a 'wild' character and nothing exemplifies this better than its most famous resident – England's last remaining golden eagle. Eagles have been nesting here since 1969, producing 16 young in that time. Sadly, the female bird went missing in 2004. She was the second female to occupy the Haweswater site and first arrived in 1981. It is believed that she would have been at least 28 years old when she went missing. The male bird, who is 13 years old, is still in the area, having arrived at the site in 2001.

viewpoint
t (01931) 713376; open Apr–Aug, 11am–4pm

 Riggindale

To reach the RSPB's **viewpoint,** park at Mardale Head and then take the right-hand path beyond the gate. After crossing the bridge over Mardale Beck, turn right again and then follow the main path as it swings left into the next valley, **Riggindale**. The viewing area is in the valley bottom, on the southern side of dale, just over a mile from the car park.

The head of the valley is dominated by the 2,716ft High Street, which can be tackled by walkers via at least four different routes from Mardale Head. Until the 19th century, shepherds from all over the eastern Lake District used to hold their annual meets on the top of High Street. Strictly speaking, it was a chance for stray animals to be claimed by their rightful owners, but it also became an excuse for revelries, including wrestling and even horse-racing. The flat summit area of the mountain is still known as Racecourse Hill.

Nearly 2,000 years ago, the Romans marched their legions across this fell-top on their way between the forts of Galava (Ambleside) and Brovacum (Brougham). It was the highest Roman road in the country and most of the 25-mile route is still used as a bridleway.

Shap

Shap consists of two rows of grey houses and pubs on either side of the A6. It's not an interesting destination in itself, although walkers on Wainwright's *Coast to Coast* route will inevitably stop here, having walked 15 miles from Patterdale and with some 20 miles to go before reaching the next stop, Kirkby Stephen.

The ruins of **Shap Abbey** are about one mile west of the village, on the banks of the River Lowther. The abbey was founded in 1199 in the place then known as 'Hepp', meaning 'heap' and probably referring to the stone circle nearby. (Over the years, the place name changed to 'Hiap' and then 'Shap'.) The monks were of the Premonstratensian order and were known as the White Canons because of the colour of their habits.

The last abbot surrendered the abbey to the Crown in 1540 and, in the centuries following, the stonework of the original church was looted and found its way into local farmhouses, drystone walls and even Lowther Castle. The foundation walls are all that can be seen of this early building today, but the huge west tower, built in the late 15th century, has stood the test of time. English Heritage now manages the site.

Keld 'Chapel', about half-a-mile's walk across the fields from the abbey, is thought to have been a 'chantry' owned by the White Canons, dating from about 1350. The custom of saying Mass for those who had died became very popular in the Middle Ages, some wealthy people even leaving money so that prayers could be said in perpetuity. Religious houses became overwhelmed by this practice, so 'chantries' dedicated entirely to this purpose were set up.

By the late 17th century, Keld Chapel had become a private home. It was repaired in the middle of the 19th century and used to house labourers working on the nearby railway. The tiny, charming chapel is today in the care of the National Trust and remains locked, but the key can be collected from a house opposite.

The fields around Shap are dotted with assorted Neolithic standing stones and a stone circle, much of which was damaged when the railway was built.

Shap also claims to be home to the highest open-air swimming pool in England.

About four miles south of the village is **Shap Wells Hotel**, where the Victorians used to partake of the medicinal spa waters. Owned by the Earl of Lonsdale, the hotel became the place to be seen in the area, and many members of the aristocracy, including Princess Mary, visited. During World War Two, it was requisitioned as a prisoner-of-war camp for senior Luftwaffe and German naval officers. The sulphurous well still exists in the hotel's grounds.

Also nearby is **Sleddale Hall**, which featured as the home of Uncle Monty in the cult comedy film *Withnail and I*. Made in 1987 starring Richard E. Grant and Paul McGann, the film used several locations in the area.

Where to Stay in Haweswater and Shap

Haweswater Hotel, Lakeside Road, Bampton, t (01931) 713235, *www. haweswaterhotel.com* (*expensive–moderate*). It may look a little drab from the outside, but the Haweswater Hotel, built in the 1930s to replace the Dun Bull which was demolished when the reservoir was built, is pleasant inside. It's also in a great location, right beside Haweswater. Suites have balconies overlooking the water.

Shap Wells Hotel, Shap t (01931) 716628, *www.shapwells.com* (*expensive–moderate*). The charms of this 19th-century spa hotel are a little faded now, but if you're looking for a remote location, the Shap Wells hits the target.

Beckfoot Country House, Helton, t (01931) 713241, *www.beckfoot.co.uk* (*moderate*). Large rooms in an old-fashioned country manor surrounded by paddocks and woods. Canine companions are given their own doggie bed, a water bowl and a welcome chew.

(★) Mardale Inn >

Mardale Inn, Bampton, t (017684) 713244, *www.mardaleinn.co.uk* (*moderate*). This cosy 18th-century inn has recently been carefully refurbished to give it a fresh, light and modern feel. Original wood fittings have been kept and the spacious guest rooms are decorated in a natural style. Free internet access.

The Greyhound Hotel, Main St, Shap, t (01931) 716474, *www.greyhoundshap. co.uk* (*moderate*). Dark floors and bare stone walls in some of the rooms give a bit of a gloomy feel, but the facilities are clean and comfortable. Good, filling breakfasts include enormous Cumberland sausages and delicious black pudding.

Whale Farm Cottage, Whale, near Penrith, t (01931) 712577, *www.lowther. co.uk* (*self-catering*). You're in for a treat if you stay at the Lowther Estate's classy Whale Farm Cottage – Farrow & Ball paints, sumptuous Colefax and Fowler curtains, free Wi-Fi and a Bose iPod dock are the order of the day. The main bedroom has a delectable bamboo, four-poster bed.

Where to Eat in Haweswater and Shap

Punchbowl Inn and Restaurant, Askham, t (01931) 712443, *www.punch bowlaskham.co.uk* (*moderate*). There's a high standard of food in this traditional pub on the village green. Large leather sofas and chairs provide snug corners for visitors to enjoy a drink or two after a meal of twiced-baked smoked-cheese-and-caramelized-onion soufflé or slow-roasted belly of pork.

Queen's Head Inn, Tirril, t (01768) 863219, *www.queensheadinn.co.uk* (*moderate*). Low beams, a crackling open fire, sandstone flags and a warm, cosy atmosphere – everything you'd expect of a 300-year-old inn in the 21st century. Good gastro-pub fare from steamed mussels poached in a white wine and garlic sauce to pork steak with black pudding mash. Annual beer and sausage festival in August.

Mango, Main St, Shap t (01931) 716343, *www.fellhouse.com* (*budget–moderate*). You don't expect to find a taste of the Caribbean beside the A6 in Cumbria, but that's exactly what Mango attempts to provide. Curried goat and jambalaya (spicy seafood and chicken) brush shoulders with Italian, Turkish and Mexican dishes. *Closed Mon–Wed.*

Keswick and the North Lakes

The looming bulk of Skiddaw, England's fourth highest mountain, towers over Keswick, the Lake District's single largest town, while Derwent Water, one of the most beautiful of the lakes, laps at its southern and western edges. To the south is gorgeous Borrowdale, an almost unbelievably idyllic valley of drystone walls and Herdwick sheep, where steep crags, beloved of the climbing fraternity, lead up to high, rocky peaks. The valley road winds ever deeper into the mountains, culminating in windswept Honister Pass. There's no getting away from the fact that this is a hugely popular area all year round, but it is possible to get away from the crowds – by heading north to the tiny, scattered villages and hamlets tucked in at the base of the lonely Northern Fells.

10

Don't miss

⭐ Experience enigmatic mystery
Castlerigg Stone Circle
p.140

⭐ Climb one of England's highest mountains
Skiddaw p.140

⭐ Glacial landscape and pretty hamlets
Borrowdale p.148

⭐ Mine tours and via ferrata
Honister Slate Mine p.150

⭐ Fish-eating birds of prey
Dodd Wood's ospreys
p.154

See map overleaf

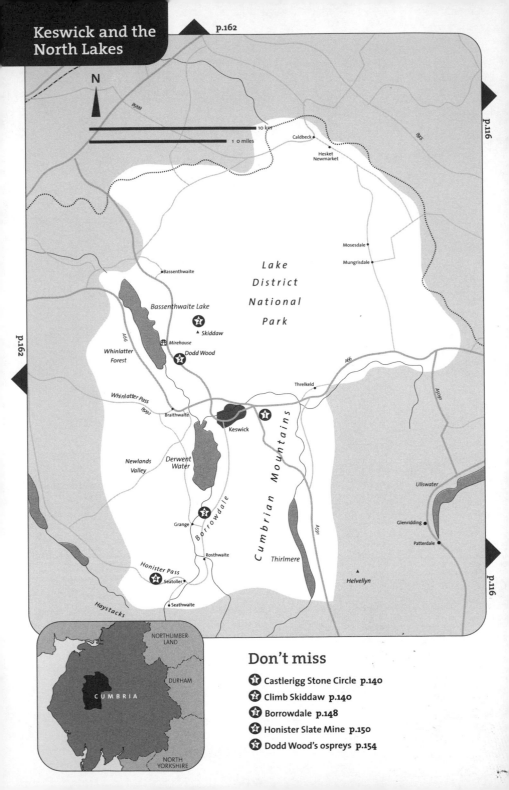

Keswick and the North Lakes

N

10 km

1 0 miles

Caldbeck

Hesket Newmarket

Mosesdale

Mungrisdale

Lake District National Park

Bassenthwaite

Bassenthwaite Lake

Skiddaw

Whinlatter Forest

Mirehouse

Dodd Wood

Whinlatter Pass

Threlkeld

Braithwaite

Keswick

Newlands Valley

Derwent Water

Cumbrian Mountains

Ullswater

Grange

Borrowdale

Glenridding

Patterdale

Rosthwaite

Thirlmere

Honister Pass

Seatoller

Helvellyn

Haystacks

Seathwaite

NORTHUMBER-LAND

DURHAM

CUMBRIA

NORTH YORKSHIRE

Don't miss

⭐ Castlerigg Stone Circle **p.140**

⭐ Climb Skiddaw **p.140**

⭐ Borrowdale **p.148**

⭐ Honister Slate Mine **p.150**

⭐ Dodd Wood's ospreys **p.154**

Keswick

The area's wealth has always come from its mountains: from copper-
and lead-mining in Elizabethan times; through the 19th century when
rivers and becks rushing down from the fells powered several bobbin
and textile mills; to the modern day, when tourism forms the backbone
to the economy. Thousands of people flock to this area every year to
enjoy the great outdoors – whether it is to hurtle down a hillside at
30mph on a mountain bike or simply to admire the views from the
relative comfort of a boat on the lake.

Assuming you book in advance, finding accommodation in this area
shouldn't be too difficult – there are quality guesthouses and hotels at
every turn. Be warned though, Borrowdale and Keswick get extremely
busy during the summer, September and at bank holidays. Things get a
little quieter the further north you go.

Keswick, the largest town in the Lake District, was made famous by
the likes of Coleridge, Keats, Southey, Scott, Gray, Tennyson and Ruskin –
the first poets and travellers to venture into the region. Coleridge and
his wife Sarah moved into the town's **Greta Hall** in 1800 to be near
Wordsworth in Grasmere, and Southey joined them there in 1801,
bringing his own wife (Sarah's sister) as well as a third Fricker sister, the
widowed Mrs Lovell. The Coleridges had three children (Hartley,
Derwent and Sarah), and the Southeys had eight (although two died
young) making the house a crowded place at times. Shelley visited
Greta Hall in the winter of 1811–12, and was astounded by the number
of books stashed in every conceivable space. Other visitors included
John Ruskin and Sir Walter Scott. Today, Greta Hall is a private home
that offers self-catering accommodation.

In the 21st century, Keswick is part old market town, part Victorian
resort (museum and public gardens) and part holiday town. At the top
of a broad, busy street of hotels, pubs and shops is the 17th-century
Moot Hall with its Bavarian hat roof and one-handed clock. This is
where you will find the Tourist Information Centre.

The **Museum and Art Gallery**, located next to the children's play area
in Lower Fitz Park, has a number of interesting, albeit disparate exhibits
including the original manuscript of *Goldilocks and the Three Bears*, a
665?-year-old cat, John Ruskin's shoes and Robert Southey's clogs. The
thing that most visitors seem to remember is the glockenspiel-like
Musical Stones of Skiddaw, made from lumps of rock. These were
played by royal command at Buckingham Palace in 1848; today, anyone
can have a go – and most people do. This is about as interactive as the
museum gets – there are no electronic gizmos or video screens; it's just
a good, old-fashioned collection of...well, fascinating bits and bobs.

The history of graphite and pencil-making is brought to life in a
fascinating way at the **Cumberland Pencil Museum**. Youngsters have
the chance to put their creativity to the test in the Drawing Zone,
where their work can be entered into regular competitions.

The **Cars of the Stars Motor Museum**, located close to the Bell Close
Car Park in the middle of Keswick, is home to Del Boy's original three-

Keswick Museum and Art Gallery
Fitz Park, Station Rd,
t (017687) 73263; open
Tues–Sat and Bank
Holidays 10am–4pm

Cumberland Pencil Museum
Southey Works,
t (017687) 73626,
www.pencilmuseum.co.uk;
open daily 9.30am–4pm;
adm

Cars of the Stars Museum
Standish St,
t (017687) 73757.
www.carsofthestars.com;
open Easter–Nov daily
10am–5pm; adm

Keswick and the North Lakes | Keswick

Getting to and around Keswick

By Long-Distance Bus

National Express runs a daily service (**570**) between Whitehaven and London that stops at Keswick (journey time, eight-and-a-half hours). Between April and October, the **X8** runs every Saturday between Keswick and Chorley in Lancashire, via Preston and Windermere. (Journey time, two hours and 50 minutes). During the school summer holidays, the bus runs on Sundays, Wednesdays and Fridays as well.

By Bus and Train

The **554/555/556** Lakeslink is a regular service between Carlisle and Lancaster via Keswick, Grasmere, Ambleside, Windermere and Kendal. Carlisle and Lancaster are both on the West Coast Main Line, with direct trains to Glasgow, Crewe, Manchester, Birmingham and London. Carlisle also has train services to other locations, including Newcastle and Leeds. The journey time to Carlisle is about 70 minutes; to Lancaster, more than two-and-a-half hours. The **X4** and **X5** buses provide a regular service between Keswick and Workington (via Cockermouth) to the west (journey time 50 minutes) and Penrith to the east (40 minutes). Both Workington and Penrith are on railway lines. The latter is on the West Coast Main Line.

The half-hourly **78** bus runs between Keswick and Seatoller in Borrowdale (30 minutes). A summer-only bus service (**77/77A, Honister Rambler**) links Keswick with Buttermere and Lorton via Borrowdale and Whinlatter. Other summer-only services include the **74/74A Osprey Bus**, which runs around the shores of Bassenthwaite Lake with a detour to Whinlatter; and the **208 Keswick to Patterdale bus.**

By Taxi

Davies Taxi, **t** (017687) 72676 and KLM Taxis, **t** (017687) 75337, both in Keswick.

By Boat

Keswick Launch, **t** (017687) 72263, *www.keswick-launch.co.uk*

By Bicycle

To hire bikes, try Keswick Mountain Bikes, **t** (017687) 75202/75752, *www.keswickmountainbikes.co.uk*, open daily 9am–5pm, or the Keswick Motor Company, Lake Road, **t** (017687) 72064, closed Sundays.

The Bond Museum
Southey Hill,
t (017687) 72090,
www.thebondmuseum.
com; open daily
10am–5pm; adm

wheeler van from *Only Fools and Horses*, the Batmobile, the magical car from *Chitty Chitty Bang Bang* and Herbie *The Love Bug* VW Beetle. Sister museum to the Cars of The Stars collection is the new **Bond Museum**, located behind the Pencil Museum. Former dentist and James Bond enthusiast Peter Nelson travelled the world buying up cars and props from the 007 films. He even learned how to drive a tank so that he was familiar with the workings of one of the museum's attractions – the 42-ton Russian tank which featured in *Goldeneye*.

 Castlerigg Stone Circle
Just off the A66, east of Keswick, **Castlerigg Stone Circle** is an enigmatic group of stones with Skiddaw and Blencathra forming a beautiful backdrop. It is thought to date from about 3000 BC, and Neolithic stone axes have been found within the circle, but its use remains a source of speculation. It is best seen at the beginning or end of the day when that special interplay of shadow and light creates a truly magical sight. There is no admission charge and the circle is accessed through a roadside gate that is always unlocked.

Skiddaw
Skiddaw itself can be climbed relatively easily from nearby. Beginning at the Latrigg car park at the end of Gale Road, which is almost 1,000ft above sea level, you get something of a head start on the climb. The constructed path from here is relentlessly steep, but it's decent underfoot with no difficulties in good weather conditions. Return via Sale How, remote Skiddaw House and the steep-sided Glenderaterra valley to add some interest to an otherwise unexciting day out. A

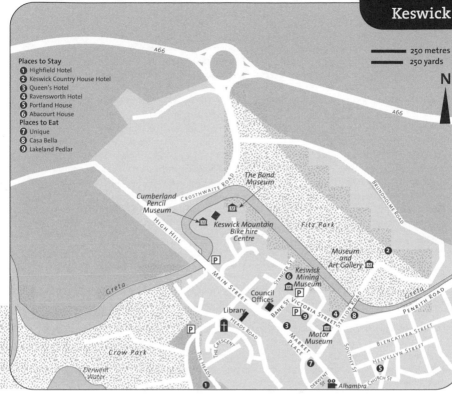

250 metres
250 yards

N

Places to Stay
1 Highfield Hotel
2 Keswick Country House Hotel
3 Queen's Hotel
4 Ravensworth Hotel
5 Portland House
6 Abacourt House
Places to Eat
7 Unique
8 Casa Bella
9 Lakeland Pedlar

The Bond Museum
Cumberland Pencil Museum
CROSTHWAITE ROAD
Keswick Mountain Bike hire Centre
HIGH HILL
Fitz Park
BRUNDHOLME ROAD
Museum and Art Gallery
2
Greta
MAIN STREET
STANGER ST
Keswick Mining Museum
6
Council Offices
Library
BANK ST
VICTORIA STREET
STATION ROAD
Greta
PENRITH ROAD
P
HEADS ROAD
9
4
8
BLENCATHRA STREET
Crow Park
THE HEADS
THE CRESCENT
Motor Museum
MARKET PLACE
SOUTHEY ST
HELVELLYN STREET
Derwent Water
7
5
1
DERWENT ST
Alhambra
CHURCH ST
A66
A66

better ascent by far starts from near the Ravenstone Hotel and then goes up via Ullock Pike and an airy ridge. The final part of the climb makes use of a loose path through the steep screes on the mountain's southwestern slopes. This is a much more interesting way on to Skiddaw and shouldn't present walkers of average fitness and experience with any serious challenges.

Theatre By The Lake

Theatre By The Lake

Lakeside, t (017687) 74411, www.theatrebythelake. com

You'd be hard pushed to find another theatre in the UK with a more dramatic setting than Keswick's **Theatre By The Lake**. Located just yards from the wooden piers of the Keswick Launch on Derwent Water, it is home to Cumbria's leading professional theatre company and puts on a popular summer season of plays. It also hosts visiting groups throughout the year and stages music, dance, talks and comedy events.

The only English regional producing theatre to have been built with National Lottery funding, it celebrated its tenth birthday in 2009. Before that, Keswick's theatre was a small blue box...literally. The portable Blue Box Theatre, the rather quirky former touring venue of Century Theatre, occupied the site of the current building from 1976 until 2006, when building work on the more substantial Theatre By The Lake began. Century Theatre had made its debut in 1952 and first visited Keswick in 1961. When changes to the Road Traffic Act brought Century Theatre touring to an end, the Blue Box settled in Keswick.

Mineral Wealth

Looking at those seemingly perfect fells that surround Keswick and form such a photogenic backdrop to Derwent Water's shores – Cat Bells, Maiden Moor, Grisedale Pike to name just a few – it is hard to believe that, for centuries, miners tore into the heart of them for their mineral wealth. Copper, graphite, lead, coal, slate, cobalt, zinc and even silver have all been mined here, some possibly since Roman times, but it was in the 16th century that the industry really took off.

German miners, at that time the best in Europe, were invited to England by Elizabeth I in 1564. Employed by the Company of Mines Royal, they established copper and lead mines throughout Cumbria, the centre of operations being Keswick. At first, there was some discord between the immigrants and the locals, and the miners were, at one time, forced to flee to Derwent Isle (see p.143) on Derwent Water after several of them were murdered. But they brought prosperity to the area, and were quickly accepted. By 1600, at least 60 miners had married local women, and their anglicized family names, including Stanger and Hindmarch, can still be found in the local phone book today.

The discovery of graphite in the early 1500s gave rise, several hundred years later, to Keswick's famous pencil industry. According to local legend, it all started with a violent storm in Borrowdale: trees were uprooted and an unknown black material was discovered beneath. Shepherds began using the mysterious substance to mark their sheep, creating the world's first pencils. That material, of course, turned out to be graphite, known locally as 'wad'.

The Cumberland Pencil Company, established in the mid-19th century to commercially exploit the graphite, was originally located in Braithwaite, two miles west of Keswick. The company moved to Keswick in 1898 after the Braithwaite factory was destroyed by fire. Although the museum remains in Keswick (see above), the factory has since moved to west Cumbria.

If you want to know more about the area's mining history, there are a couple of mining museums – the **Keswick Mining Museum** on Otley Road in the town (t (017687) 80055, www.keswickmining museum.co.uk; Tues–Sun 10am–5pm, adm) and the **Quarry and Mining Museum** in Threlkeld, about four miles east of Keswick (t (01768) 779747, www.threlkeldminingmuseum.co.uk; daily 10am–5pm Mar–Oct, adm). The National Trust also organizes occasional tours of the surface workings of the **Force Crag mine** in Coledale (www.nationaltrust.org.uk).

Derwent Water

'the most delicious view that my eyes ever beheld...'

Thomas Gray describing Derwent Water in his *Journal In The Lakes*,1769

There are many iconic images of the Lake District, but probably one of the most famous is the view from the landing stages of the Keswick Launch across Derwent Water to Cat Bells and its mighty neighbours in the Derwent Fells. If the water is still and the reflection of the mountains unbroken, then all the better.

Wordsworth devoted a whole section of his *Guide* to the best views of the lake; Ruskin's first memory was the view of Derwent Water from Friar's Crag; and one of Canon Rawnsley's reasons for setting up the National Trust was to preserve the lakeside from developers.

By far the easiest way to get around the lake is on the Keswick Launch, based close to the Theatre By The Lake. The boats stop at seven landing stages around the lake, so you can hop on and off wherever you want – or simply sit back and enjoy the 50-minute circuit.

Nichol End Marine
(017687) 73082,
www.nicholendmarine.
co.uk

Derwent Water Marina
(017687) 72912,
www.derwentwater
marina.co.uk

If you're reasonably confident on the water, the best way to enjoy this scenery is under your own steam – or, more accurately, your own paddle power. The lake has several marinas where you can hire canoes and kayaks. Sailing dinghies, rowing boats, windsurfers and small motorboats are also available. Two of the most reliable are in Portinscale, which is within walking distance of Keswick – **Nichol End Marine** and **Derwent Water Marina**.

The National Trust

The origins and early development of the National Trust, which is now one of the largest conservation charities in the whole of Europe, are rooted deeply in the Lake District and, in particular, the Keswick area. It was Wordsworth who first developed the idea of the Lake District belonging to the nation. In 1822, his bestselling *Guide to the Lakes*, describes the Lakes as 'a sort of national property, in which every man has a right and interest', anticipating the National Trust by about 70 years.

In 1872 John Ruskin moved to Coniston. A Wordsworthian, he preached in books and lectures about the moral development of working people through manual work, clean air and an appreciation of art and literature. In 1875, Ruskin played a key role in the formation of the National Trust by introducing Canon Hardwicke Rawnsley, vicar of Low Wray Church, and later Crosthwaite in Keswick, to his friend Octavia Hill, a social reformer. Together with lawyer Sir Robert Hunter, they crusaded passionately for a National Trust to be formed to preserve places of natural beauty and historic interest for the nation.

The first building purchased by the trust was Alfriston Clergy House in Sussex, bought for £10 in 1896, but it was in 1902, when the 108-acre Brandelhow estate on the western shore of Derwent Water came on the market that the trust set about its most ambitious scheme to date. A brilliant and inspirational speaker, Rawnsley led the campaign to raise funds for the purchase. The scheme's success was never in doubt with him at the helm, and Princess Louise, daughter of Queen Victoria and a supporter of the National Trust's work, performed Brandelhow's opening ceremony on October 6, 1902.

There are memorials to both Rawnsley and Ruskin at the National Trust-owned Friar's Crag, which is located about a third of a mile south of the Keswick Launch landing stages. The view across the lake from the handy bench at the end of the promontory is pretty special – Ruskin described it as one of the three most beautiful scenes in Europe.

Today, the National Trust protects a massive 123,500 acres of land in the Lake District – that's about a quarter of the total area covered by the National Park. The trust owns the bed of England's deepest lake – Wastwater – as well as the summit of England's highest mountain – Scafell Pike. Beatrix Potter (*see* p.66) left 14 farms and 4,000 acres of land to the National Trust when she died in 1943. She had been introduced to Rawnsley in 1882 while staying at Wray Castle. Moved by the natural beauty surrounding her family's holiday home, she was heavily influenced by his views on the need to preserve that landscape for future generations.

The largest and most northerly of the four islands on Derwent Water is **Derwent Isle**, which was owned by Fountains Abbey in medieval times. It became the refuge of German miners in the 16th century, and, in 1778, the island passed into the hands of Joseph Pocklington. Apart from building a villa, Pocklington also constructed a number of follies including Fort Joseph. This was used during the Derwent Water Regatta, the centrepiece of which was a mock battle where local teams would attempt to land boats on the island and storm the fort's supply of beef and beer while avoiding fire from Pocklington's cannon. The island is now the private home of tenants of the National Trust, although the organization does arrange occasional visits.

There is unrestricted public access to **St Herbert's Isle**, which sits almost in the middle of the lake, a pleasant paddle from Portinscale on a calm day. Long-time friend and disciple of St Cuthbert, the Bishop of Lindisfarne, St Herbert was a religious recluse who lived here in the seventh century. A chapel was consecrated on the island when the cult of St Herbert was revived in 1374. It is said that the remains of his chapel and cell may still be traced at the northern end of the island.

Lord's Island, close to the eastern shore, was once the home of the Earls of Derwentwater – until the Crown confiscated their lands. James Radcliffe, the third and last Earl of Derwentwater, was one of the many

Walk: Latrigg and the Railway Path

Start and finish:

Public parking around the back of the Keswick Country House Hotel (grid reference, NY272237)

Distance:

5.6 miles/9km

Total ascent:

1,174ft/358m

In brief:

Latrigg, with its magnificent views over Keswick, Derwent Water and the surrounding fells, is a grassy little hill crouching at the base of the mighty Skiddaw. The walk up from the outskirts of Keswick makes for a pleasant stroll on good paths with just one short climb. The return route is along the disused Cockermouth, Keswick and Penrith Railway.

Route description:

Starting with the platform buildings of the old Keswick Station, now part of the **Keswick Country House Hotel**, on your left, walk to the leisure centre's service road and turn right. You need to bear left at the small roundabout – along Brundholme Road – but don't head off yet; if you look just to the right of the roundabout, on the other side of the road, you will see a small footpath at the top of a few steps. This path provides a safer, more pleasant alternative to the road. It crosses straight over one minor road and then ends as you reach the houses at **Briar Rigg**. Now continue along the road in the same direction until you reach **Spooney Green Lane**, a wide lane heading NE. The start of the lane is marked by a fingerpost, which reads 'Public Bridleways Skiddaw 4 miles'. Turn right here, soon crossing the bridge over the busy A66.

Having passed through a gate near **Spooney Green B&B**, you start making your way uphill on a wide track, ignoring one turning off to the right signposted 'Circular walk Brundholm Woods'. Joining another track coming in from the right, the path crosses a tiny beck as it swings left. Ignoring a shortcut on the right, you then swing right with the main track to reach a fork. Bear left here.

The mixed woodlands of Latrigg contain a rich variety of birdlife, as well as red squirrels, roe deer and badgers. Foresters are encouraging natural regrowth of oak, ash, birch, hazel and other native species. Many non-native conifers are being felled, although some are allowed to remain because the red squirrels love the cones.

The climb eases considerably now and you soon find yourself walking with a fenced plantation on your left. As the trees begin to thin out, turn sharp right – almost heading back on yourself – to climb the northern slopes of Latrigg on a clear, zig-zagging path. Eventually, the zig-zags end and you join up with the wheelchair route coming up from the left.

Follow this mostly level path as it curves round the gully to a bench. This is a great spot to rest and admire the fantastic views – over Keswick and Derwent Water and across to the fells – before swinging left for the last, easy bit of the climb.

Latrigg was the scene of a mass trespass in the late 19th century, many years before the famous Kinder Scout trespass in Derbyshire in the 1930s. The dispute started when landowner Anthony Spedding locked gates and built wire fences on a popular path here. Everything came to a head when five youths were taken to court for a shilling's worth of damage. The local people had had enough. Two thousand of them

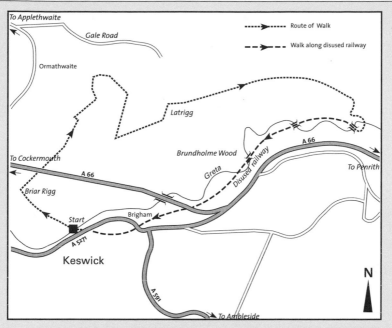

gathered, including MP Samuel Plimsoll, tore down the barriers that Spedding had put up and marched up the hill singing *Rule Britannia*. Some of the protesters were taken to court and charged with trespass, but the judge managed to bring the two sides to the negotiating table so that a compromise route on to Latrigg could be agreed.

The summit isn't marked. You only realise you've reached it when the path ahead starts to drop. Keep to this clear path along the southern edge of the fell and through a gate in a fence, beyond which it becomes grassier and a little more indistinct.

Having walked three-quarters of a mile from the bench, the path appears to make straight for a fence. Bear left here, still with a faint path on the ground, to head for a clear track near a gate in the fence. Turn right along this track and follow it until you reach another gate. Turn left beyond the gate and then right down a surfaced lane.

As you approach the **River Greta**, watch for a gate to your right. Go through this and then through another gate giving you access to the railway footpath close to a small shelter. Once on the old railway, turn right. It's hard to go wrong now – this clear, wide, level track takes you all the way back to Keswick. This track is part of the 31-mile Cockermouth, Keswick and Penrith Railway, built by Thomas Bouch in 1865. You pass the site of an old textile mill near **Low Briery**. This was known locally as the 'Fancy Bottoms Mill' because it made the intricate edgings for waistcoats. It closed in 1961.

Passing Low Briery and its caravan site, you reach the beginning of a boardwalk section as the track, temporarily abandoning the line of the railway, negotiates the increasingly steep-sided gorge. The track goes under the massive A66 road bridge, a hideous monstrosity that won the surprising accolade of Best Concrete Engineering Structure of the Century in 1999.

Having passed through the **Brigham** area of Keswick and crossed the river one last time, the track ends at the old station.

The top of Latrigg can also be reached by a 'limited mobility path' from the Gale Road parking area. The route is fairly steep, so it isn't recommended for people operating their own wheelchairs, but it is made of well-compacted stone.

members of prominent local families who had adhered to the Catholic faith and supported the Jacobites in the 1715 rebellion. The Highlanders, proclaiming James Stuart as king, under the title of James III, got as far as Preston, where they were forced to surrender to General Willis. Radcliffe admitted his involvement with the uprising when he appeared before the privy council on 10 January 1716, and begged for mercy, blaming his participation in the uprising on youth and inexperience. He was executed on Tower Hill

At the top of Cat Gill, close to the summit of Walla Crag, is a steep gully called Lady's Rake. This is reputedly the route by which Lady Derwentwater fled from Lord's Island on hearing of the impending execution of her husband.

Festivals and Events in Keswick

(i) **Keswick Information Centre**
Moot Hall, Market Square, Keswick
t (017687) 72645. Open April–Oct daily, 9.30am–5.30pm; Nov–March daily, 9.30am–4.30pm

(★) **Howe Keld >>**

Speakers from the worlds of literature, politics and the media descend on Keswick for 10 days in the late winter to share their love of the written word with Theatre By The Lake audiences. The **Words by the Water Festival** (*www.wayswithwords. co.uk*) features workshops, book launches and talks by illustrious speakers whose ranks over the past few years have included BBC journalist Kate Adie, political campaigner Tony Benn, Cumbria-born Lord Melvyn Bragg and the former poet laureate Andrew Motion.

The colourful and noisy **Keswick Jazz Festival** (*www.keswickjazzfestival. co.uk*) takes place in various venues around the town during May, bringing together some of world's finest exponents of mainstream and traditional jazz.

The Keswick Mountain Festival (*www.keswickmountainfestival.co.uk*) in May offers visitors a chance to try their hand at all sorts of exciting outdoor activities and hear some of the UK's top adventurers share their experiences.

June's **Keswick Beer Festival** (*www.keswickbeerfestival.co.uk*) attracts about 6,000 visitors and features 170 real ales plus bottled beers and ciders, making it the largest in the north of England.

Late summer is the time for the local agricultural shows including Keswick and Borrowdale. This is a good chance for visitors to get a taste of the real Cumbria and watch traditional sports such as Cumberland and Westmorland wrestling (*see* p.170). And as if all that wasn't enough, there's also the **Keswick Film Festival** (*www.keswick filmfestival.org*) in Feb, and the Victorian **Christmas Fayre** in Dec.

Where to Stay in Keswick

Expensive

Highfield Hotel, The Heads, t (017687) 72508, *www.highfieldkeswick.co.uk*. Victorian splendour in an attractive spot close to Derwent Water. Magnificent views from the gardens. Not as expensive as it looks.

Howe Keld, The Heads, t (017687) 72417, *www.howekeld.co.uk*. Refurbished to a very high standard in 2008. Rooms beautifully decorated using natural tones, some with solid wood floors. Award-winning breakfasts – as you'd expect from the owners' pedigree: David used to manage Cranks vegetarian restaurants and Valerie co-authored two of the Cranks cookery books.

Lairbeck Hotel, Vicarage Hill, t (017687) 73373, *www.lairbeckhotel-keswick. co.uk*. Fussy, Victorian-style décor doesn't detract from the fact that this is a friendly, pleasant place to stay. Peaceful location on the edge of town, but not far from the A66.

The Keswick Country House Hotel, Station Rd, t (017687) 72020, *www.choicehotels.co.uk*. Splendid Victorian hotel with turrets close to

⭐ **A Different Taste >>**

⭐ **Cafe-Bar 26 >>**

the foot of Skiddaw. Part of a small chain.

Moderate

Glendale Guest House, 7 Eskin St, t (017687) 73562, *www.glendalekes wick.co.uk*. Clean, comfortable guest house decked out in light wood furnishings, making the rooms bright and cheerful. Excellent value for money.

Portland House, 19 Leonards St, t (017687) 74230, *www.portlandhouse. net*. Victorian townhouse with five rooms. Popular with walkers. Quality accommodation and bright, airy breakfast room make it stand out among all the other Victorian guesthouses behind the town centre.

The Ravensworth Hotel, 29 Station St, t (017687) 72476, *www.ravensworth-hotel.co.uk*. Cheerful, peaceful hotel close to the centre of town. Nine individually and tastefully furnished rooms. Thoughtful touches include umbrellas in the rooms.

Budget

Abacourt House, 26 Stanger Street, t (017687) 72967, *www.abacourt.co.uk*. Quiet, cul-de-sac location on the edge of the town centre. Many original features, including a lovely wooden staircase.

Self Catering

Morrel's Apartments, 34 Lake Rd, Keswick t (017687) 72666, *www.morrels.co.uk*. Bright, modern, town-centre apartments with leather suites and widescreen TVs. Well-equipped kitchens include dishwasher, microwave and electric double oven.

Where to Eat in Keswick

Expensive

Highfield Hotel, The Heads, t (017687) 72508, *www.highfieldkeswick.co.uk*. The smart, high-ceilinged restaurant is open to non-residents and serves up some great food. Mesmerizing views and two AA rosette-winning food, including breast of corn-fed chicken wrapped in locally smoked pancetta on a wild mushroom risotto and Madeira cream sauce.

Moderate

A Different Taste, Station St, t (017687) 80007. The locals have been raving about this restaurant since it opened in 2008. Lots of chrome and wood give it a clean, contemporary feel. *Closed Mon.*

Cafe-Bar 26, Lake Road, t (017687) 80863, *www.cafebar26.co.uk*. This stylish but comfortable wine bar is the best place in town for a light lunch. Grilled halloumi, warm tomato, mozzarella and basil tart or, best of all, the mouth-watering lamb and mint burger in warm ciabatta and served with tomato and pepper relish, crispy wedges and salad. Superb coffee.

Morrel's, Lake Rd t (017687) 72666, *www.morrels.co.uk*. Modern, smart but casual restaurant that is popular with the theatre crowd. Meat-eaters will love the chorizo, peppered salami, smoked bacon and tomato risotto. *Closed Mon.*

Unique Fine Dining, St Johns St, t (017687) 73400. Good food at surprisingly good prices. Much of the produce is sourced locally including fell-bred lamb, Borrowdale trout and venison steak. Menu changes regularly. *Closed Wed.*

Budget

Casa Bella, Station St, t (017687) 75575, *www.casabellakeswick.co.uk*. Good, simple Italian food in pleasant surroundings.

Lakeland Pedlar Wholefood Cafe, Bell Close, t (017687) 74492, *www.lakeland pedlar.co.uk*. Tasty and filling vegetarian snacks including full breakfast, falafel, hummus and pitta bread, soups and sandwiches.

Entertainment in Keswick

The Theatre By The Lake (*see* p.141).

Alhambra Cinema, St John's St, t (017687) 72195, *www.keswick-alhambra.co.uk*. Shows latest releases and hosts the award-winning Keswick Film Club, which screens independent and foreign-language films.

10

Keswick and the North Lakes | Keswick

148

Borrowdale to Honister

Keswick lies on the edge of two different rock types. To the north is Skiddaw slate, the oldest rocks in the Lake District, giving rise to the smooth slopes of the gently rounded Northern Fells. To the south, as you enter **Borrowdale**, the steep, craggy mountains are made of much harder stuff, the Borrowdale Volcanics, formed about 450 million years ago. The valley itself was gouged out by a glacier more than 10,000 years ago, and there is evidence of that last Ice Age all around as you travel up Borrowdale – *roches moutonnées* (rock outcrops smoothed by the passing ice), hanging valleys and erratics (large boulders dumped by the retreating ice). Borrowdale itself is a typical example of a classic, U-shaped, glacial valley.

 Borrowdale

The valley road on the east side of Derwent Water and the River Derwent is scenic, with several beauty spots along the way and access to dramatic fells. The **Lodore Falls**, reached from behind the hotel of the same name at the southern tip of Derwent Water, are impressive – but only after very heavy rain. The rest of the time, they are a disappointment. Southey wrote a pleasantly un-Romantic poem about the falls 'thumping and plumping and bumping and jumping and hissing and whizzing'.

Further up the valley is a 400-million-year-old lump of rock with a sturdy wooden ladder up the side of it, a magnet for tourists since Victorian times. **The Bowder Stone** is more than 10 metres high, about 30 metres in circumference and balanced apparently precariously on one edge. It was probably left here by a passing glacier. There is no admission charge to the site, which is open at all times.

Millican Dalton

Have you ever felt the burning desire to abandon all the stress of modern life and go back to a more basic way of living? Ever wanted to leave all your material possessions behind and go and live in the woods? Well, that's almost exactly what Millican Dalton did in the early part of the 20th century – except that he made his home in a cave in the woods. Sick of commuting and dissatisfied with his comfortable career in the City, he went back to the county of his birth, Cumberland, when he was in his 30s to offer adventure holidays to would-be climbers in the Lake District. An intelligent and well-educated man, he called himself the Professor of Adventure and offered 'camping holidays, mountain rapid shooting, rafting and hair's breadth escapes'.

Desperate to get back to nature, Dalton lived at first in a tent at High Lodore in Borrowdale, then in a split-level quarried cave halfway up nearby Castle Crag, which is crowned by the remains of an Iron-Age hill fort. Despite having a waterfall pouring through his roof, he turned one cave into a living area and one into a bedroom, which he called 'The Attic'.

A strict vegetarian, he grew potatoes on the terrace outside his cave, baked his own bread, ate hazelnuts picked from the woods around his cave and made his own clothes. Dalton loved to pit himself against the elements. He climbed trees in winter to keep fit for climbing and, on his 50th ascent of Napes Needle, is said to have lit a fire on the airy summit and made a pot of coffee.

Normally, he would spend winters in the forest hut that he built for himself at Marlow Bottom in Buckinghamshire, but during the London Blitz of 1940/41, he braved snow, ice and sub-zero temperatures to remain all winter on Castle Crag.

Sadly, he didn't get to end his days on his beloved fells; he died in hospital in Amersham after contracting pneumonia in 1947 – at the age of 79.

Getting to and around Borrowdale

The half-hourly **78 bus** runs between Seatoller and Keswick (30 minutes). A summer-only service (**77/77A**, Honister Rambler) links Borrowdale with Buttermere and Keswick via Lorton and Whinlatter.
For **taxis**, try Davies Taxi, **t** (017687) 72676 and KLM Taxis, **t** (017687) 75337, both in Keswick.
By **boat**: Keswick Launch, **t** (017687) 72263, *www.keswick-launch.co.uk*

Grange, Rosthwaite, Stonethwaite, Seatoller and **Seathwaite** are the valley's main settlements, pretty little villages with popular teashops and traditional pubs. They also mark the starting point for many walkers' explorations of the high fells. One of the most popular routes on to **Scafell Pike** starts from Seathwaite before going up Grains Gill to Esk Hause. It then heads towards Great End and the start of a superb, high-level ridge path that ends at the highest point in England. The return is via a path known as the Corridor Route. **Glaramara** and **Allen Crags** are less well-known, but make for a wonderful day out. You can see practically all of the Lake District's major fell groupings from the top of Glaramara – it's a superb place to stand on a clear day – and Allen Crags is even better – a stone's throw from Bow Fell, Great End and Great Gable, it is dwarfed by its imposing neighbours.

Don't assume that you're missing out if you can't manage the high fells; lower down, there are some hidden gems that, rather surprisingly, attract only a few visitors. **Dock Tarn** is in a secluded setting surrounded by heather-clad hills above Stonethwaite; and **Grange Fell**, between Watendlath and Grange, is a maze of paths and rocky tops only a few hundred feet above the valley floor.

If you are out walking and want to know whether there's rain on the way, keep an eye on the Borrowdale Sop, a small cloud that sometimes develops at the head of Borrowdale near Styhead Tarn. Amateur weather forecasters watch its movements to predict the weather. It is said that if it heads towards St John's in the Vale, the weather will be fair; but if it moves towards Langdale, rain will follow within a day. It doesn't always move towards Langdale, although it may sometimes seem like it does – Seathwaite famously being the wettest inhabited place in Britain.

'Watendlath was an exceedingly remote little valley lying among the higher hills above Borrowdale... It was utterly remote, with some twenty dwellings, a dark tarn and Watendlath Beck'

From *Judith Paris* by Hugh Walpole

Watendlath and Sir Hugh Walpole

The pretty, unspoilt hamlet of Watendlath is hidden high above Borrowdale in one of the area's hanging valleys. 'Hanging' above the level of the glaciated valley floor, it was gouged out by a tributary to the main glacier, and so didn't erode as deeply.

Although it is no more than a cluster of whitewashed dwellings, there is a small car park and teashop in the hamlet. If you're driving up, it's worth stopping on the narrow road leading up from the B5289 to enjoy two of the area's best and most famous views of Derwent Water and its surrounding fells – **Ashness Bridge** and **Surprise View**. Bear in mind though, the road is extremely narrow. The best way to approach Watendlath is on foot – either via the woodland paths leading up from High Lodore or using the old Corpse Road from Rosthwaite.

The hamlet, which didn't get mains electricity until 1978, was the setting for Hugh Walpole's 1931 novel *Judith Paris*. It was the second of four novels belonging to the *Herries Chronicle*. Set in Keswick, Borrowdale, Watendlath, Uldale and Ireby, these books told the story of the Herries family from the 18th century to the depression of the 1930s. Foldhead Farm is generally thought to be the model for Rogue Herries Farm, the home of the eponymous heroine.

Hugh Walpole was born in New Zealand in 1884, but lived in Cumbria from 1924 until his death in 1941. He made his home on the lower slopes of Cat Bells on the western side of Derwent Water. Brackenburn, his 'little paradise on Cat Bells', received many literary visitors including J. B. Priestley, Arthur Ransome and W. H. Auden.

Honister Slate Mine

The B5289 winds its way slowly along the floor of Borrowdale before reaching Seatoller, where it begins its even slower climb to Honister Pass. The naked fellside stands in stark contrast to the leafy cloak of the valley below, and things get bleaker still when you reach the workings of England's last operating slate mine. Generations of miners and quarrymen, in search of the famous green slate, have left their indelible scars on the craggy landscape.

⭐ **Honister Slate Mine**
*Honister Pass,
t (017687) 77230,
www.honister.com; open
daily 9am–5pm; adm for
tours and via ferrata*

Today, **Honister Slate Mine** is a major visitor attraction. As long as you don't suffer from either claustrophobia or vertigo, you could find enough here to entertain for almost a whole day. Tours of the cathedral-like caverns and some of the 11 miles of tunnels hollowed out by almost three centuries of mining can't fail to impress. Visitors are kitted out with safety helmets, lamps and battery packs before being led deep inside the mountain.

For those who prefer the outdoors, the mine is also home to England's only **via ferrata**, an adventure climbing system that uses a permanently fixed cable to allow people to climb the old miners' route up the steep and craggy northern face of Fleetwith Pike. Terrifying or exhilarating, depending on your head for heights, the route includes scrambling on bare rock and culminates in an exciting zip wire 'flight' over a 200ft-deep ravine. Harnesses and helmets are provided and climbers are with a guide at all times.

Where to Stay and Eat in Borrowdale

Borrowdale Gates Hotel, Grange-in-Borrowdale **t** (017687) 77204, *www.borrowdale-gates.com* (*expensive*). Luxurious, country house hotel in a quiet location off main Borrowdale road. Spacious rooms. Also has a good restaurant (*expensive–moderate*) with an extensive wine menu.

Scafell Hotel, Rosthwaite, **t** (017687) 77208, *www.scafell.co.uk* (*expensive*). Traditional coaching inn on the outside, modern bedrooms on the inside. Deep, earthy tones, dark-wood furniture and leather armchairs. The hotel does bar lunches and has a restaurant (*moderate*) for evening meals. Dishes include griddled ostrich steak garnished with deep-fried, shredded leeks and served with a whisky and shallot sauce.

The Leathes Head, Borrowdale, **t** (017687) 77247, *www.leatheshead. co.uk* (*expensive*). The beautiful Leathes Head, surrounded by peaceful woodland, is a little more expensive than many of the other hotels in

⭐ **The Leathes Head >>**

Borrowdale, but it's worth every penny. Superb views from most rooms. Go for a double-aspect, superior room. Spacious, relaxing lounge areas, including a well-stocked bar. The **restaurant** (*expensive–moderate*) has a small, but perfectly formed menu that changes regularly.

Hazel Bank Country House, Rosthwaite, t (017687) 77248, *www.hazelbankhotel.co.uk* (*expensive–moderate*). The first thing you notice on entering this huge Victorian house are the many awards lining the hallway. And Hazel Bank lives up to its many accolades – the rooms, some with six-foot beds, are lovely; and the atmosphere is very laid-back.

Langstrath Country Inn, Stonethwaite, t (017687) 77239, *www.thelangstrath. com* (*expensive–moderate*). Lovely, family-run inn, far from the madding crowds and looking down the lonely dale known as Langstrath. Eight simple but contemporary rooms. The new **dining area** (*moderate*) offers good pub food with fantastic views. Food miles are kept to a minimum.

Royal Oak Hotel, Rosthwaite, t (017687) 77214, *www.royaloak hotel.co.uk* (*expensive–moderate*). Friendly, welcoming former farmhouse in the cosy village of Rosthwaite. Popular with walkers.

Yew Tree Farm, Rosthwaite, t (017687) 77675, *www.borrowdaleyewtreefarm. co.uk* (*moderate*). Chintzy guest rooms with stout furniture, low beams, uneven floors, no TV and no mobile reception are the order of the day on this working sheep farm. Hearty breakfasts feature landlady Hazel Relph's wonderful home-made marmalades and jams.

Seathwaite Farm, Seathwaite, t (017687) 77394 (*budget*). Wonderful farmhouse at the southern end of Borrowdale close to Sourmilk Gill.

The Flock-In, Rosthwaite, t (017687) 77675, *www.borrowdaleherdwick.co.uk* (*budget*). Most of the dishes in this tiny café are based on Yew Tree Farm's (*see* above) own Herdwick sheep, including hearty stews and the delicious Herdi-burger. Packaged meat is available for sale. *Closed Wed.*

Thirlmere

Heading southeast from Keswick, visitors quickly reach Thirlmere. There isn't much to keep you here, although the car parks at Swirls and Wythburn both make good starting points for an assault on Helvellyn, England's third highest mountain.

The **Thirlmere reservoir** was formed by the damming of two small, natural lakes in 1894. Victorian engineers devised a system, still in use today, which allows water to flow by gravity, without any pumps, all the way from the reservoir to Manchester, 100 miles away. The water flows at a speed of almost 4mph and takes just over a day to reach the city.

It was in 1874 that Manchester Corporation advisers realised that the city's ever-increasing demand for water, then averaging 18 million gallons per day, would soon exhaust the supply. They first recommended sourcing water from Ullswater, but it was later decided to create Thirlmere. Despite being stalled by the Thirlmere Defence Association, the project eventually received Royal Assent in 1879 and Manchester was granted the right to extract 25 gallons of water per head per day. The first water to arrive in Manchester from Thirlmere was marked with an official ceremony on October 13, 1894.

Probably the best thing about this area today is the drive itself. A survey of motorists recently found the A591 between Keswick and Grasmere to be Britain's 'best drive'. Since the survey, the journey has been made better still by the felling of conifers beside the road, making room for native trees and giving road users a better view of the

Getting to and around Thirlmere

The **554/555/556 Lakeslink** runs along the side of Thirlmere. This regular bus serves Carlisle and Lancaster via Keswick, Grasmere, Ambleside, Windermere and Kendal. Carlisle and Lancaster are both on the West Coast Main Line, with direct trains to Glasgow, Crewe, Manchester, Birmingham and London. Carlisle also has train services to other locations, including Newcastle and Leeds. The journey time to Carlisle is about 80 minutes; to Lancaster, two-and-a-half hours. For **taxis**, try Davies Taxi, **t** (017687) 72676 and KLM Taxis, **t** (017687) 75337, both in Keswick.

reservoir. And what a moody, magnificent view it is. If you don't fancy driving and just want to sit back and enjoy the scenery, take the 555 bus from Keswick, one of the Lake District's more regular services. Watch out for the South American alpacas near the King's Head Hotel. These llama-like animals are generally kept for their soft wool, but they also have excellent shepherding skills and will protect vulnerable newborn lambs from foxes, crows and birds of prey.

The A591 runs along the eastern side of Thirlmere, but there is also a narrow minor road on the western shore. Parking areas on this side provide walkers with access to the lonely, often boggy fells of Ullscarf, High Seat and Bleaberry Fell. **Watersports** enthusiasts can take canoes, kayaks and dinghies on to the reservoir, but fishing is subject to a charge. Details can be obtained from Windermere Ambleside and District Angling Association, **t** (015395) 35630.

Several years ago, United Utilities' Thirlmere estate became the country's first **red squirrel refuge**. Conservationists hope that careful management of the woodland, including the installation of rope bridges for the squirrels' safety and the provision of special food hoppers will save the native species from extinction. Cumbria is one of the last strongholds of the red squirrel, which has been replaced in most of England and Wales by the grey, introduced from North America in 1876. Partly because greys breed rapidly, with two litters a year, and are better able to survive a severe winter because of their extra body fat, they out-compete the reds, particularly in lowland deciduous woodland. They have been known to displace the much cuter native species completely within seven years of arrival in a wood. Red squirrels are also more susceptible to certain diseases and find it less easy to adapt when hedgerows and woodland are destroyed. Saving the reds by putting a stop to the steady incursion of the greys has become an emotive subject in Cumbria in recent years with normally placid animal lovers suddenly keen to see a bloody cull of the American species.

Where to Stay and Eat near Thirlmere

Dale Head Hall, Thirlmere, **t** (017687) 72478, *www.daleheadhall.co.uk* (*expensive*). Rather basic rooms are overpriced, but the views across Thirlmere are priceless. Quiet location.

King's Head Hotel, Thirlmere **t** (017687) 72393, *www.lakedistrictinns.co.uk* (*expensive–moderate*). Lots of character in this 17th-century coaching inn close to the foot of Helvellyn. Also good bar meals (*moderate*).

Stybeck Farm, Thirlmere, near Keswick, **t** (017687) 73232, *www.stybeckfarm. co.uk* (*moderate*). Clean, simple farmhouse accommodation in an area with few other places to stay.

> 'The lake is narrow, averaging less than a mile in breadth... its charm is in the opening out views from its foot, through radiating valleys, into the plain country which stretches to the sea and the Solway.'
>
> Harriet Martineau

Bassenthwaite Lake

To the north of Keswick is Bassenthwaite Lake, known locally as Bass Lake. It is flanked by the steep, grey slopes of Skiddaw to the east and the mountain biker's paradise of Whinlatter to the west. The further north you travel, the quieter things become. Hamlets and centuries-old inns lie scattered about; villages are few and far between here, the largest being Braithwaite at the foot of the Whinlatter Pass.

One of the more unusual features of the drive north along the A66 towards Cockermouth is the white rock that stands out like a sore thumb on the scree-covered slopes of Barf behind Thornthwaite. This is known as the **Bishop of Barf**. Legend has it that, in 1783, the foolhardy Bishop of Derry was staying at an inn in Thornthwaite when, after a few too many drinks, he had a wager with the locals. He claimed that he could ride up Barf's steep slopes. The next day, he and his horse headed up the steep, scree-covered fell. His wager – and his life – came to a sudden end when he slipped and plunged down the fellside. The white rock 700ft up the fell marks the place at which he fell.

Thornthwaite Galleries
Thornthwaite, t (017687) 78248, www.thornthwaite galleries.co.uk; open daily 10am–5pm

Thornthwaite is also home to the **Thornthwaite Galleries**, housed in a converted 18th-century barn, with displays of paintings, photographs, jewellery, sculpture, pottery and glassware by more than 130 exhibitors.

Trotters World of Animals
Coalbeck Farm, Bassenthwaite, t (017687) 76239, www.trottersworld.com; open daily 10am–5pm

Located at the northern end of the Bassenthwaite Lake, close to Armathwaite Hall Country House Hotel, is **Trotters World of Animals**, which is home to gibbons, zebras, the ferocious Asian fishing cat and the UK's only Canadian lynx. Audience participation events throughout the day enable visitors to handle some of the animals, and the birds of prey put on regular flying displays. The site also has play areas, picnic benches and an indoor soft-play climbing centre.

Whinlatter Forest Park

Terrifying downhill mountain-bike runs and an exciting obstacle course high up in the forest canopy brush shoulders with sedate walking trails and a fun children's playground at the Forestry Commission's Whinlatter Forest Park.

Mountain-bikers have been using the forest roads here for years, but it is only recently that the Forestry Commission has brought in experts to design and build trails with two wheels in mind. The results include the 19km red-grade Altura Trail, intended for experienced riders with good off-road skills and a high level of fitness and stamina, and a 7.5km blue-grade trail for intermediate riders. The less experienced can, of course, stick to the tried-and-tested forest roads, although even these are steep in places and riders have to share the trails with walkers.

Go Ape
Whinlatter Forest Park, t 0845 643 9215, www.goape.co.uk; open Mar–Oct daily 9am–5pm (closed Tues in term time), Nov weekends only; adm

Go Ape! styles itself as a 'high-wire forest adventure'. Ladders, walkways, bridges and tunnels all made of wood, rope and wire create a giant and rather wobbly obstacle course high up in the trees. Guaranteed to get your adrenalin pumping, this is not for the faint-hearted.

Getting to and around Bassenthwaite Lake

By Bus and Train

The **554/555/556 Lakeslink** runs along the side of Bassenthwaite Lake. This regular bus serves Carlisle and Lancaster via Keswick, Grasmere, Ambleside, Windermere and Kendal. Carlisle and Lancaster are both on the West Coast Main Line, with direct trains to Glasgow, Crewe, Manchester, Birmingham and London. Carlisle also has train services to other locations, including Newcastle and Leeds. The journey time to Carlisle is about 60 minutes; to Lancaster, almost three hours. The **X4** and **X5** between Workington (via Cockermouth) and Penrith (via Keswick) run along the side of Bassenthwaite Lake. Both Workington and Penrith are on railway lines. The latter is on the West Coast Main Line.

By Local Bus

A summer-only bus service (**74/74A Osprey Bus**) runs around the shores of Bassenthwaite Lake and also stops at Whinlatter and Keswick. It operates on weekends only outside of the school holidays. Another summer-only bus service (**77/77A, Honister Rambler**) links Braithwaite and Whinlatter with Keswick and Buttermere via Borrowdale and Lorton.

By Taxi

Davies Taxi, **t** (017687) 72676 and KLM Taxis, **t** (017687) 75337, both in Keswick.

Whinlatter Forest Visitor Centre
t (017687) 78469; open April–Oct daily 10am–5pm, Nov–Mar daily 10am–4pm

Lovers of less adventurous pastimes can take a stroll through the forest, watch the Dodd Wood ospreys on huge video screens in the **Visitor Centre** or crawl through the Amazing Badger Sett, a warren of low passageways built into a small earth mound.

The forest boundary climbs to more than 1,500ft above sea level and provides fell-walkers with access to Lord's Seat and, to the south, Grisedale Pike.

Dodd Wood and its Ospreys

🌟 **Dodd Wood**

Dodd Wood, home to the Lake District's only ospreys, is on the eastern side of the lake. There are walking trails here, a tearoom and two special viewing platforms where high-powered telescopes enable you to watch these magnificent fish-eating birds of prey. Optics in the higher viewing area are trained on the nest just 400 yards away, while the lower one provides views of them hunting. Razor sharp eyesight enables the osprey to spot a fish while hovering high above the lake.

Watch out for their white or slightly mottled underparts. The long wings have a distinctive black patch that contrasts with the white wing linings. At a distance, they could be mistaken for large gulls.

The Forestry Commission and Lake District National Park Authority spent years trying to encourage ospreys back to Cumbria after they were persecuted to extinction in the area in the middle of the 19th century. They built tree-top platforms for the birds, and, finally, in 2001, a passing pair took a fancy to one of these 'nests' and decided to set up home. The birds spend the summer in the county, arriving in April and returning to Africa in September, having reared a small family of chicks.

Dodd Wood is about 3.5 miles north of Keswick on the A591. The Osprey Bus links Keswick with a circular route of Bassenthwaite Lake that takes in both the Dodd Wood viewpoints and the exhibition in the Visitor Centre at Whinlatter.

In the 1860s, Dodd was home to a Scottish hermit called George Smith. He lived in a wigwam on a ledge on the fell, staying there in all weathers because he loved being close to nature. His shelter consisted of a low stone wall and a framework of branches and reeds as a roof. Known as the **Skiddaw Hermit**, he made ends meet by painting farmers and their wives, although his favourite subjects were said to be local pub landlords who paid his fees in whisky. He also did character assessments at local fairs by feeling the shape of people's heads. George's weakness for alcohol got him into trouble with the police on several occasions and he eventually returned to Scotland, where he died in a psychiatric home.

Mirehouse

Mirehouse
t (017687) 72287,
www.mirehouse.com;
gardens open Apr–Oct
daily 10am–5pm; house
open Apr–Oct Weds and
Sun 2pm–5pm;
adm

Opposite the Dodd Wood car park is the entrance to the elegant, 17th-century **Mirehouse**. The Earl of Derby built the house in 1666, and its many illustrious visitors over the years have included Alfred Lord Tennyson, William Wordsworth and Edward Fitzgerald, who translated Omar Khayyam's poetry.

The ground floor is open to the public and, besides an interesting collection of furniture and portraits, there is a fascinating display of manuscripts. These include letters from Wordsworth, Tennyson, Southey, Carlyle and John Constable – all friends of the Spedding family. The Speddings have owned and lived in the house since 1802, and it is probably this strong family influence and continuity that make the house a real home, more than merely a relic of the past.

On a dry day, visitors can take a stroll in the sprawling lakeside grounds or get lost in the heather maze. There is plenty here to keep children entertained. As well as four adventure playgrounds, regularly updated children's nature notes are provided to keep the youngsters occupied while the adults enjoy their walk.

Nearby **St Bega's Church** inspired Tennyson, during a sojourn at Mirehouse in 1835, to write the opening lines of his poem *Morte D'Arthur*:

'...to a chapel nigh the field,
A broken chancel with a broken cross,
That stood on a dark straight of barren land'

The Newlands Valley

Hidden between Derwent Water and the Whinlatter forests is a quiet valley that sees relatively few visitors. This is the Newlands Valley, an oasis of calm, green pastures and steep slopes leading on to some of the best ridges in the Lake District. There are no villages here, just a few farms and hamlets. The most notable of the latter is **Little Town**, with its delightful, whitewashed chapel, sitting all alone in a beckside meadow. The children's story writer Beatrix Potter used to holiday at Lingholm and Fawe Park, both on Derwent Water, and was a frequent visitor to Little Town. The location figures highly in *The Tale of Mrs Tiggy-Winkle*, and the character, Lucie of Little Town, was based on the

10
Keswick and the North Lakes | Bassenthwaite Lake: The Newlands Valley

daughter of the vicar of the church here. It was at Lingholm that Potter sketched the squirrels while working on *The Tale Of Squirrel Nutkin*. The view of Cat Bells was also used in the book, and St Herbert's Island in Derwent Water is renamed Owl Island, the destination of a convoy of squirrels who cross the lake on rafts. The Fawe Park gardens are said to have formed the basis for the gardens in *The Tale Of Benjamin Bunny*.

But the Newlands Valley hasn't always been a peaceful place; like much of this corner of the Lakes, the heart of these fells was once ripped open by mining. The spoil heaps of the Goldscope Mine are still clearly visible on the eastern side of Scope End, where the ridge of Hindscarth comes to an abrupt end. The copper ore vein here was a particularly rich one, and the mine also produced lead, silver and some traces of gold. It probably got its name from the German miners who were first brought over to Cumbria during the 16th century. They called it 'Gottesgab' or 'God's gift'. The veins were worked until the second half of the 19th century, when the high costs associated with pumping out water from the mine made it unprofitable.

The Newlands Valley holds other riches too – if ridge walking's your thing. The Newlands fells can be easily accessed from here, including Cat Bells, Maiden Moor, High Spy, Dale Head, Hindscarth and Robinson. On the other side of the valley, climbing knobbly Causey Pike provides an alternative start to the magnificent Coledale Round.

Where to Stay and Eat in the Bassenthwaite Lake Area

Armathwaite Hall Country House, Bassenthwaite Lake, Keswick, t (017687) 76551, *www.armathwaite-hall.com* (*expensive*). Constant upgrading of this off-the-beaten-track 17th-century hall means that you always get a good mix of both the traditional and the contemporary. Wood panelling, grand staircases, open fires and rich, deep colours are found alongside plasma screens in the bathrooms, iPod docking stations and activity clubs for the youngsters.

Lyzzick Hall, Underskiddaw, near Keswick, t (017687) 72277, *www.lyzzickhall.co.uk* (*expensive*). Amazing views of the fells from the pretty gardens and terrace. Rooms feature light oak furniture and are pleasant and airy. Modern, spacious bathrooms.

Ravenstone Hotel, Bassenthwaite, t 0800 163 983, *www.ravenstone-hotel.co.uk* (*expensive*). Sprawling Victorian house with 19 guest bedrooms, all with lovely, soft mattresses and crisp linen sheets.

Games room includes a full-sized snooker table.

The Pheasant, Bassenthwaite Lake, near Cockermouth, t (017687) 76234, *www.the-pheasant.co.uk* (*expensive*). Everything you'd expect of a good, old-fashioned inn, including open fires and exposed beams, and some things you wouldn't, including spacious rooms. King-size beds and soft chairs add a sense of self-indulgent luxury. The **restaurant** (*expensive–moderate*) is particularly popular with locals.

Underscar Manor, Applethwaite, near Keswick, t (017687) 75000, *www.underscarmanor.co.uk* (*expensive*). Some of its charm may be fading now, but it's still a treat to stay at the grand Underscar Manor. Quintessentially English with chintzy décor and solid-looking furniture. Also has a small health club with pool. The lace-bedecked conservatory **restaurant** (*expensive*) is superb – unless you're a vegetarian. The service is of a very high standard. Traditional dishes include venison casserole served with winter vegetables and potato dumpling with bacon and chives.

The Cottage in the Wood >

The Cottage in the Wood, Whinlatter Forest, near Keswick **t** (017687) 78409, *www.thecottageinthewood.co.uk* (*expensive–moderate*). Luxurious, comfortable, calm, tranquil, friendly, cosy, warm – there are so many lovely adjectives to describe this hotel that is in the middle of the forest. The owners Kath and Liam have turned this former inn into something that's a little bit special without being prohibitively expensive. They recently added a light and airy, conservatory-style **restaurant** (*moderate*) with an emphasis on high-quality, local produce. *Restaurant closed Sun/Mon.*

 Ellas Crag >

Ellas Crag, Stair, Newlands Valley, **t** (017687) 78217, *www.ellascrag.co.uk* (*moderate*). Bright, spotless and very reasonably priced rooms in a friendly guesthouse at the foot of the fells. Great location for walkers – and the red squirrels love it too. Hearty breakfasts include award-winning sausages and porridge cooked overnight and dressed with whisky and cream.

Uzzicar Farm, Newlands Valley, **t** (017687) 78026, *www.uzzicarfarm. co.uk* (*moderate*). Recently modernized farmhouse with good, simple accommodation in a quiet location.

Middle Ruddings, Braithwaite, **t** (017687) 78436, *www.middle-ruddings.co.uk* (*moderate–budget*). Better-than-average pub meals served in a choice of locations – the bar, the restaurant or the conservatory. A great place for real ale – there is a rotating selection of beers from almost two dozen Cumbrian microbreweries.

Siskins Café, Whinlatter Forest Park, Braithwaite, **t** (017687) 78410 (*budget*). This café adjoining the Whinlatter Forest visitor centre is hugely popular – and for good reason. The freshly made sandwiches and enormous salads are tasty and good value. And the home-made cakes are to-die-for.

Skiddaw House, Bassenthwaite, near Keswick, **t** 07747 174293, *www. skiddawhouse.co.uk* (*budget*). Isolated Skiddaw House YHA is 1,550ft above sea level and more than three miles from the nearest road. Don't expect luxury, but you're guaranteed a warm welcome from wardens Martin and Marie-Pierre.

Bassenthwaite Lakeside Lodges, Scarness, Bassenthwaite, **t** (017687) 76641 or 0845 456 5276, *www.bll.ac* (*self-catering*). A range of centrally-heated, double-glazed lodges sleeping up to six people. French doors lead to a private patio with gas barbecue. Pricier lodges have an uninterrupted views of the lake.

10

Keswick and the North Lakes | Northern Fells

Northern Fells

Further north still and Keswick's summer crowds are consigned to the past; and the traffic of Windermere and Ambleside become a dim and distant memory. Sheep and friendly fell ponies, unique to the area, are the order of the day on the quiet country lanes that wind in and out of tiny fellside settlements. Uldale, Caldbeck, Hesket Newmarket and Mungrisdale are some of the National Park's best-kept secrets – laid-back, pretty villages that seem almost untouched by tourism.

Expect peace and solitude if you head out on to the rolling, grassy fells here. The hiking experience on the Northern Fells, apart from Blencathra and Skiddaw, is very different from elsewhere in the Lakes; instead of bare rock, you'll feel grass under your boots, and you're unlikely to meet the crowds that you'll find on Cat Bells or Helvellyn, just the occasional fox or hare. Head up High Pike from Fell Side or haunted Souther Fell from Mungrisdale. A walk on **Carrock Fell**, which is topped by the substantial remains of what is thought to be an Iron-Age hill fort, will almost guarantee a close encounter with fell ponies (*see* p.159). For a perfect tarn, dark and moody below steep cliffs, take a

Getting to and around the Northern Fells

By Bus
There are no regular scheduled buses serving the communities of the Northern Fells.

By Taxi
Thomason Travel in Wigton, **t** (016973) 44116.

walk up to **Bowscale Tarn**, which occupies a secluded basin carved from the mountains by a corrie glacier. It can be reached easily via a track from the tiny settlement of Bowscale, about a mile north of Mungrisdale.

The tarn is often used as a field study destination by local geography teachers trying to explain the processes associated with glaciation. It was also a popular destination in the 19th century. Victorian ladies and gentlemen would make their way up hoping to catch sight of the two immortal giant carp – made famous in a Wordsworth poem – that were said to inhabit its dark waters.

Caldbeck

It is hard to believe it now as you walk around the pretty conservation village, but Caldbeck was once a hive of industrial activity, home to more than a dozen mills. Corn mills, bobbin mills, woollen mills, a paper mill and a brewery were all powered by the waters of Cald Beck as it came rushing down from the fells. Many of these buildings still exist today. Visitors can take an easy stroll from the free car park, past the duck pond and up to the picturesque ruins of the Howk, an old bobbin mill located in a stunning gorge.

The 12th-century **St Kentigern's Church** (*see* p.159) is the resting place of Mary Robinson, the Beauty of Buttermere (*see* p.169), the parents of John Dalton, the originator of atomic theory, and 19th-century huntsman, John Peel. Peel (1776–1854) is probably one of the most famous Cumbrians, having been immortalized in the verses of *D'ye ken John Peel*, written by his close friend John Woodcock Graves and based on a Scottish dance. Peel began hunting in earnest soon after marrying Mary White. She was from a relatively wealthy farming family and her parents gave the couple enough land to provide them with a comfortable income. Freed from having to farm full-time, Peel seems to have led a self-indulgent life. Even Graves admitted that hunting dominated his life: 'Business of any shape was utterly neglected...indeed this neglect extended to paternal duties of his family. I believe he would not have left the drag of a fox on the impending death of a child or any other earthly event.'

A two-mile walk alongside Cald Beck and the River Caldew leads to another lovely village – **Hesket Newmarket**. Every Christmas, the village green plays host to a Nativity scene and, come the spring, it is awash with daffodils.

St Kentigern/Mungo

The churches in Caldbeck and Mungrisdale are both dedicated to St Kentigern, as are many others throughout the county. St Kentigern, who is probably better known as St Mungo, the founder of the city of Glasgow, was an important religious figure in the sixth century. Unfortunately, the little that has been written about him dates from the 12th century – several hundred years after his death – so it is difficult to work out what is true and what is not.

His mother was Thenew, the daughter of King Llew or Loth, after whom Lothian is named. How she became pregnant is a source of debate – some say she had made a vow of chastity, but was raped by a local chieftain; others says she had an affair with her uncle, Urien, the Prince of Rheged. Either way, when her furious father found out, he sentenced her to a cruel death. She was bound to a wheel and driven down a steep hill. Miraculously, she survived, but her father wasn't going to stop there. He next had her cast adrift on the North Sea in an open coracle, but again she survived, finally landing at Culross, where she gave birth to Kentigern. Her boy was raised by St Serf, who ran a religious establishment in Fife.

Discrepancies again arise in Kentigern's story when he reaches adulthood. Some scholars have him becoming Bishop of Glasgow quite early in life; others say this title came only after he had returned from 'exile' in Wales. Whichever is correct, it is known that he was forced to flee what is now Scotland when some sort of dispute arose between him and Morken, who had murdered Urien and then incorporated Rheged into his own lands.

On his journey south to Wales, Kentigern stopped in Carlisle where he discovered that the local people were 'given to idolatry'. He decided on a short stay in the region to try to educate them.

Jocelyn of Furness had this to say of Kentigern's arrival in Karleolum (Carlisle) in his 1185 work *The Life of Kentigern*: 'Wherever the saint went at that time, virtue went out from him to restore many to health. And when Kentigern had arrived at Karleolum, he heard that many in the mountains had been given to idolatry or were ignorant of the divine laws. And so he turned aside to that place, and he converted to the Christian religion, with the aid of God and confirming this word with accompanying signs, many who were strangers to the faith and others who were erring in the faith.'

The village inn, the Old Crown, became Britain's first co-operative-owned pub a few years ago when 125 locals, including the mountaineer Sir Chris Bonington, clubbed together to stop it falling into the hands of a major brewery. The traditional bar serves beers produced at the Hesket Newmarket Brewery, also owned by a local co-operative.

Fell ponies

Explore the commons to the south of Caldbeck and Hesket and it won't be long before you encounter a group of fell ponies. These adorable animals, which have a habit of sticking their heads through car windows in search of tasty treats, have been wandering the fells for many hundreds of years, if not millennia. Their history can be traced back to the Romans, when indigenous ponies bred with the horses introduced by the occupiers and their foreign mercenaries. The result of this and subsequent crossbreeding with the Galloway breed and the Welsh cob is a sturdy, but lively little animal that has served many purposes over the years.

At one time, shepherds would have used fell ponies for rounding up their flocks. Before that, the Vikings used them for ploughing. It was only in the 13th century, with the rise of the wool trade, that they began to be used as pack animals on a large scale, carrying merchandise along old routes that still exist today. Come the Industrial Revolution and they began carrying lead and iron ore from the fells to the smelting works on the northeast coast. They would have travelled in 'trains' of up to 20, covering as much as 240 miles a week.

Although they may look wild, all of these ponies belong to someone, but they run free on hundreds of acres of common land. They are brought down from the fells only twice a year – in the late spring, when the mares are gathered for foaling; and in the autumn, when the colt foals are sold at auction.

The Queen keeps her own team of fell ponies, mostly for carriage-driving, and the Duke of Edinburgh has driven competitively with them at European and World Championship level.

Where to Stay and Eat in the Northern Fells

Overwater Hall, Ireby, t (017687) 76566, *www.overwaterhall.co.uk* (*expensive*). This hidden gem is tucked away in 18 acres of formal gardens and woodland at the base of the Northern Fells. As you'd expect of an 18th-century country house, the rooms are generally spacious. High ceilings with intricate cornices, log fires and a mahogany-panelled bar.

Boltongate Old Rectory, Boltongate, near Ireby, t (016973) 71647, *www.boltongateoldrectory.com* (*expensive–moderate*). A great place to just kick back and unwind in calm, elegant surroundings. Boltongate is close to the northern edge of the National Park and, as such, is far from the bustle of the honeypots.

High Houses, Snittlegarth, near Ireby, t (016973) 71549, *www.highhouses. co.uk* (*expensive–moderate*). The expression 'secluded location' doesn't do justice to High Houses. To get to this beautifully restored farmhouse you have to drive for miles along narrow, country lanes and farm tracks.

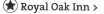 **Royal Oak Inn** >

Royal Oak Inn, Curthwaite, Wigton, t (01228) 710219, *www.royaloakinn curthwaite.co.uk* (*moderate*). This rather ordinary-looking pub has developed a reputation locally for its extraordinary food. The extensive menu includes dishes as diverse as moules mariniere; wild rice, spinach and honey-roast vegetable bake; Cajun-spiced chicken with sweet chilli and garlic dressing; and good, old steak and ale pie. *Booking highly recommended.*

The Snooty Fox, Uldale, t (016973) 71479, *www.snootyfox-uldale.co.uk* (*moderate*). Good choice of vegetarian dishes and a long list of specials in this traditional pub. *Closed Wed in winter.*

Brownrigg Farm, Caldbeck, t (016974) 78626, *sallyvaux@aol.com* (*budget*). One bright and spacious guest bedroom on this friendly, former hill farm just outside the village of Caldbeck.

The Old Crown, Hesket Newmarket t (016974) 78288, *www.theoldcrown pub.co.uk* (*budget*). Good-value pub food in a cosy, traditional bar, but the real reason for visiting is to try the rich-flavoured ales made at the neighbouring brewery, including the award-winning Doris's 90th Birthday Ale (ABV 4.3%) and the dark, malty Blencathra Bitter (ABV 3.2%).

Watermill Café, Priest's Mill, Caldbeck, t (016974) 78267, *www.watermillcafe. co.uk* (*budget*). Light, wholesome lunches made using mostly local produce and, wherever possible, Fairtrade goods. In warm weather, there is a lovely outdoor terrace overlooking the beck that once powered the 18th-century mill.

High Greenrigg House holiday cottages, Caldbeck t (016974) 78430, *www.highgreenrigghouse.co.uk* (*self-catering*). Three restored cottages in a tranquil spot above Caldbeck. Many original, 17th-century features as well as all the modern facilities you'd expect.

Western Lakes and the Coast

The wild, relatively inaccessible dales of west Cumbria – Eskdale, Wasdale, Ennerdale and the Buttermere valley – are guarded by the impossibly steep and exposed passes of Hardknott and Honister. Overcome these barriers and you enter a lonely, remote region where ancient traditions live on and thousands of years of human history are there for all to see – if you're prepared to make the effort. It is here, where England's highest and craggiest mountains meet the Irish Sea, that you are most likely to hear local dialects, possibly even the old shepherds' counting system, a remnant of one of the country's longest-surviving Celtic kingdoms. In the northwest, where visitors gaze out across the water to the Scottish hills, dunes and salt marshes hide the defences constructed by the Romans in their most far-flung outpost.

11

Don't miss

① Birthplace of the Romantic poet
Wordsworth House, Cockermouth **p.164**

② The wildest valley
Ennerdale **p.171**

③ The best view in Britain
Wastwater **p.174**

④ Spectacularly located Roman fort
Hardknott Castle **p.181**

⑤ Scenic railway through peaceful dale
The La'al Ratty **p.183**

See map overleaf

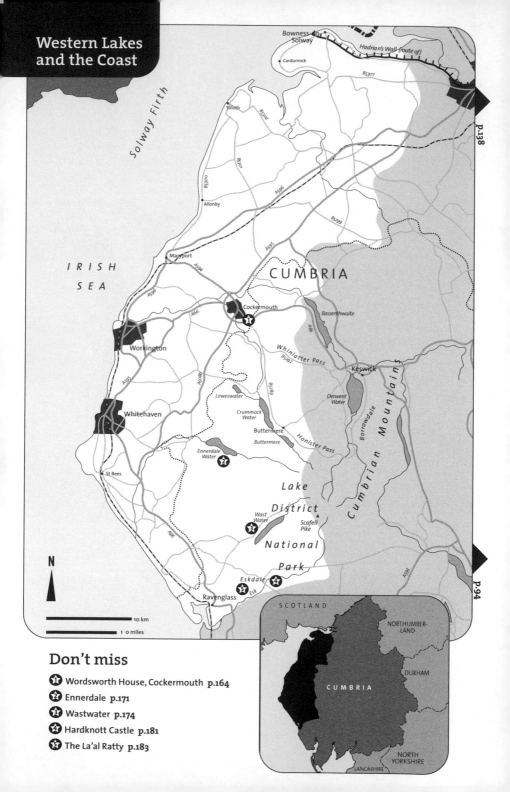

Solway Firth

Bowness-on-Solway

Cardurnock

Hadrian's Wall (route of)

B5307

Silloth

B5302

B5300

Allonby

A596

A595

B5299

IRISH
SEA

Maryport

CUMBRIA

A596

A594

Cockermouth

Bassenthwaite

A66

A66

Workington

Whinlatter Pass
B5292

Keswick

A595

A5086

Loweswater

B5289

Derwent
Water

Borrowdale

Cumbrian Mountains

Whitehaven

Crummock
Water

Buttermere
Buttermere

Honister Pass

Ennerdale
Water

St Bees

A595

Lake

District

Wast
Water

Scafell
Pike

National

A595

Park

A595

A595

Eskdale

Esk

Ravenglass

N

10 km

1 0 miles

SCOTLAND

NORTHUMBER-
LAND

DURHAM

CUMBRIA

NORTH
YORKSHIRE

LANCASHIRE

p.138

p.94

Don't miss

1. Wordsworth House, Cockermouth **p.164**
2. Ennerdale **p.171**
3. Wastwater **p.174**
4. Hardknott Castle **p.181**
5. The La'al Ratty **p.183**

Cockermouth

The pleasant town of Cockermouth, with its hidden courtyards and colourful Georgian buildings, is tucked away just beyond the northwest boundary of the National Park. Surrounded by rolling green countryside with the grey outlines of the high fells rising behind it to the south, it is named after the River Cocker, which flows down from the mountains to meet the River Derwent in the middle of the town.

Cockermouth owes its existence to its rivers. The Romans built a camp, Derventio, at a crossing of the River Derwent just on the outskirts of the modern town, where the village of Papcastle now stands. Derventio was probably a strategic cavalry base, supplying reinforcements for the border defences along the Solway coast and Hadrian's Wall. A medieval settlement then grew up around the confluence of the two rivers, and that has been added to over the centuries, resulting in what you see today. The rivers were the main stimulus for the growth of industry and, in the mid-19th century, there were more than 40 factories, tanneries and mills here.

Most visitors would probably not stray this far from the central Lake District if it wasn't for the fact that William Wordsworth was born here in 1770 (*see* below). But Cockermouth is worth a visit in its own right – there are plenty of pubs, several good restaurants and a surprising number of attractions. Simply wandering along the wide, tree-lined Main Street is a pleasure, or you can lose yourself in the complicated network of narrow alleyways and medieval courtyards. There is a **Town Trail** to help – small cast-iron, numbered plaques created by the pupils of Cockermouth School, act as a guide, along with a leaflet available from the tourist information centre.

Jennings began brewing in the nearby village of Lorton in 1828. It moved to Cockermouth in 1874, where it has been brewing traditional beers ever since. Visitors can enjoy a tour of the Victorian **brewery** and then sample some of the ales, including Cocker Hoop, Cumberland Ale and the strong Sneck Lifter.

The **Lakeland Sheep and Wool Centre**, located on the A66 roundabout on the edge of town, has a visitor centre where you can learn about Lakeland's famous woolly residents.

Also worth a visit is the **Castlegate House Gallery**, which exhibits contemporary paintings, ceramics and sculptures in a listed Georgian house opposite Cockermouth Castle. It specializes in the work of Cumbrian and Scottish artists, including Sheila Fell, Percy Kelly and Winifred Nicholson, with exhibitions changing regularly.

Cockermouth Castle, built from the stones of the Roman fort at modern-day Papcastle, is now the private residence of Lady Egremont, but it opens its doors to the public on a few days every year. The Normans are thought to have built the first castle here in 1134, but the Scots burned it down in 1387, so most of the current buildings date from the end of the 14th century. In 1568, Mary, Queen of Scots spent a night here on her way from Workington to temporary imprisonment at Carlisle. In 1648, it was besieged by Royalist forces during the Civil War.

Jennings Brewery
t 0845 129 7185, www.jenningsbrewery. co.uk; tours Jan, Feb, Nov and Dec Mon–Fri 2pm, Sat 11am and 2pm; Mar–June, Sep and Oct Mon–Sat 11am and 2pm; July and Aug daily 11am and 2pm; adm

The Lakeland Sheep and Wool Centre
Egremont Rd, t (01900) 822673, www.shepherdshotel. co.uk; open daily 9.30–5.30

Castlegate House Gallery
Castlegate House, t (01900) 822149, www.castlegatehouse. co.uk; open Mon, Fri, Sat 10.30am–5pm

Getting to and around Cockermouth

By Bus and Train

The hourly **600** bus service, which runs between Carlisle and Whitehaven, stops at Cockermouth. Both Carlisle and Whitehaven are on railway lines. The former is on the West Coast Main Line, with direct **trains** to Glasgow, Crewe, Manchester, Birmingham and London. Carlisle also has train services to other locations, including Newcastle and Leeds. The journey time to Carlisle is about one hour; to Whitehaven, about 45 minutes. The **X4** and **X5** buses provide a regular service between Cockermouth and Workington to the west (journey time, 25 minutes) and Penrith (via Keswick) to the east (85 minutes). Both Workington and Penrith are on railway lines. The latter is on the West Coast Main Line.

By Local Bus

The **58** bus to Maryport runs every two hours (journey time 45 minutes). The **217** runs five times a day to Lamplugh (35 minutes) and Cleator Moor (53 minutes). Many local buses do not run on Sundays.

By Taxi

Cockermouth Taxi Company, t (01900) 826649.

By Bicycle

Bike hire from 4 Play Cycles, Market Place, t (01900) 823377.

The large marble statue in the middle of Main Street is of Dublin-born Richard Southwell Bourke, the sixth earl of Mayo and MP for Cockermouth from 1857 to 1868. It was erected after he was assassinated in 1872, while visiting the Andaman Islands as Viceroy and Governor-General of India.

Wordsworth House

⓱ Wordsworth House
Main St, t (01900) 820884, www.wordsworthhouse.org.uk; open Apr–Nov Mon–Sat 11am–5pm; adm

This attractive Georgian townhouse on Main Street was the birthplace, on 7 April 1770, of the most famous of Lakeland's Romantic poets. The house was built in 1745, and was then owned by Sir James Lowther of Lowther Castle. William Wordsworth's father, John, was a lawyer who worked as an agent for the Lowthers – still one of the major landowners in Cumbria – and the Wordsworths lived there rent-free.

Four sons and a daughter were born here – Richard (1768), William (1770), Dorothy (1771), John (1771) and Christopher (1774). Their mother died in 1778 and their father passed away five years later. After his mother died, William spent much of his childhood with relatives in Penrith – relatives, sadly, who he didn't like. His favourite sibling, Dorothy, was sent away to other relatives in Yorkshire.

After John Wordsworth died, the Cockermouth house became a private residence until the 1930s. In 1937, a local bus company bought it, intending to knock it down and turn Wordsworth's birthplace into a bus station. There was a national outcry at this plan to desecrate such an important part of the nation's literary heritage, and a fundraising campaign ensued, allowing the town eventually to buy it back. Cockermouth then handed the house to the National Trust in 1938.

In 2003, after a long period of research and planning, the National Trust began an imaginative restoration of the house. Costing £1 million, the work returned the building to its 18th-century magnificence. The original staircase, fireplaces and panelling remain, as do effects and furniture that belonged to the Wordsworths. There are also some

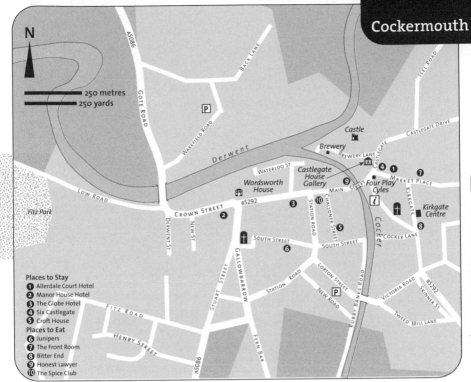

Places to Stay
1. Allerdale Court Hotel
2. Manor House Hotel
3. The Globe Hotel
4. Six Castlegate
5. Croft House

Places to Eat
6. Junipers
7. The Front Room
8. Bitter End
9. Honest Lawyer
10. The Spice Club

original manuscripts on display. Costumed interpreters bring the place to life for visitors – the maid gives interactive demonstrations and tastings in the working kitchen and the clerk in John Wordsworth's office might allow you to test your writing skills with quill pen and ink. Children can also play with the sorts of toys and games that would have kept the young Wordsworths entertained all those years ago.

The garden, once a favourite playground of William, has been attractively restored. The budding poet loved his childhood home, and refers to the views and the River Derwent, which runs along the back of the garden, in his poem *The Prelude*.

Opposite Wordsworth House is a bronze bust of the poet, unveiled on April 7, 1970, the bicentenary of his birth. As part of the same celebrations, 27,000 daffodils were planted on open spaces and approaches to the town, creating a dazzling spectacle every spring.

Other important Wordsworth sites in the town include **All Saints' Church**, which has a stained-glass window commemorating the poet. His father's grave is in the churchyard. Nearby, a hall stands on the site of the old grammar school that Wordsworth attended.

Around Cockermouth

Isel Hall

Isel, t (01900) 821778; open Mar–Oct Mon 2pm–4pm; adm

Isel Hall is a beautiful Elizabethan range with a fortified peel tower that is thought to have been built in about 1400. Situated on the banks of the River Derwent, about three miles northeast of Cockermouth, it commands some wonderful views of the surrounding countryside. From 1572 to 1986, the hall was the home of the Lawson family, whose interesting crest – the sun supported by the arms of the law – is a common motif throughout the hall and its attractive gardens. The last Lawson, Margaret Austen Leigh, died in 1986, leaving the estate to her friend and distant relative, Mary Burkett, the former director of Abbot Hall in Kendal. She still lives there, opening her home to the public for just a couple of hours every week during the summer.

Close to Isel Hall is a beautiful Norman chapel in an even more beautiful setting beside the River Derwent. In his *Guide to English Parish Churches*, Sir John Betjeman described Isel as 'a perfect English harmony of man and nature'.

Dominated by Skiddaw, **Elva Plain Stone Circle** is located on private farmland about four miles east of Cockermouth. Only 15 of the original 30 stones remain. The site is thought to date from the late Neolithic period, and has been linked with the axe trade.

Where to Stay in Cockermouth

ⓘ **Cockermouth Tourist Information Centre:** *Town Hall, Market Street, t (01900) 822634, www.cockermouth.org. uk; open July and August weekdays 9.30am–5pm, Sat 10am–4pm, Sun 10am–2pm; Sept–June weekdays 9.30am–4pm, Sat 10am–4pm, closed Sun*

⭐ **Junipers Restaurant and Café Bar >>**

⭐ **Six Castlegate >**

Manor House Hotel, Crown Street, t (01900) 828663, *www.manorcocker mouth.co.uk* (*expensive–moderate*). Grand old Georgian-style building with spiral staircase, mouldings and alcoves. Free Wi-Fi.

The Allerdale Court Hotel, Market Place, t (01900) 823654, *www.allerdale courthotel.co.uk* (*expensive–moderate*). Quaint, wood-panelled hotel dating from the 1740s. Lots of nooks and crannies, exposed beams and uneven floors. Superior rooms include four-poster beds and leather armchairs.

Croft House, Challoner Street, t (01900) 827533, *www.croft-guesthouse.com* (*moderate*). Georgian townhouse on the outside, modern guesthouse on the inside. Tastefully decorated with reclaimed timber floors.

Rose Cottage, Lorton Road, t (01900) 822189, *www.rosecottageguest.co.uk* (*moderate*). Clean, bright and comfortable rooms in this friendly bed and breakfast on the outskirts of town.

Six Castlegate, Castlegate, t (01900) 826786, *www.sixcastlegate.co.uk* (*moderate*). Large and characterful Georgian townhouse that has been lovingly and carefully refurbished by the current owners. Original staircase leads from the spacious entrance hallway to guest bedrooms. Huge attention to detail.

The Globe Hotel, Main Street, t (01900) 822126, *www.globe-hotel.co.uk* (*moderate*). Thirty simple but comfortable rooms off endless corridors. Robert Louis Stevenson stayed here in 1871.

Where to Eat in Cockermouth

Honest Lawyer, Main Street, t (01900) 827377 (*moderate*). Friendly riverside restaurant occupying a series of small rooms with exposed beams, beneath the Old Courthouse. Good, simple dishes, but slightly overpriced. *Closed Sun lunch and all day Mon.*

Junipers Restaurant and Café Bar, South Street, t (01900) 822892, *www.junipersrestaurant.co.uk* (*moderate*). Great food in great surroundings. The downstairs café serves lunches, and becomes tapas bar in evenings. The upstairs, a la carte restaurant is a cosy, intimate venue serving such dishes as fillet of pork on a bed of creamed leeks flavoured with mature blue stilton.

The Bitter End, Kirkgate, t (01900) 828993, *www.bitter end.co.uk* (*moderate*). Imaginative dishes served in a friendly pub that is popular with the locals. Poached cod wrapped in Chinese leaf with crab-and-ginger sauce. Also home to a microbrewery.

The Front Room, Market Place, **t** (01900) 826655 (*moderate*). In a town packed with good places to eat, this is one of the nicest. Bright, cheerful bistro with good-value, Mediterranean-style food.

The Old Stackyard Tearooms, Wellington Farm, near Cockermouth, **t** (01900) 822777, *www.wellington jerseys.co.uk* (*budget*). Popular spot for light lunches on a working farm on the edge of Cockermouth. Home-made cakes and award-winning Jersey ice cream. Also has a farm shop, farm trails and a display of work by local artists.

The Spice Club, Main Street, **t** (01900) 828288, *www.thespiceclub cockermouth.co.uk* (*budget*). Popular Indian restaurant that's a cut above the average. Friendly and modern. *Closed Mon to Wed.*

Entertainment in Cockermouth

Kirkgate Centre, Kirkgate, **t** (01900) 826448, *www.thekirkgate.com*. Small arts centre that acts as cinema, theatre, music venue and exhibition venue.

The Northwestern Lakes

Follow the River Cocker south from Cockermouth and you enter pretty **Lorton Vale**. The only settlement of note here is Lorton itself – made up of High and Low Lorton, a collection of attractive cottages and other traditional buildings. The village's 1,000-year-old yew tree was made famous by Wordsworth's lines:

There is a yew-tree, pride of Lorton Vale,
Which to this day stands single, in the midst
Of its own darkness, as it stood of yore...

George Fox, the founder of the Quaker faith, preached under its 'pillared shade' in the 17th century, as did John Wesley, the founder of Methodism, a century later. Although not as large as it was in Wordsworth's time – its girth was reduced from 27ft to a mere 13ft soon after the poem was written – the tree still exists. It is behind the village hall, which occupies the site of the original Jennings Brewery.

Lorton Hall, now occupied by the Winder Hall Hotel, is built around an attractive 15th-century peel tower. Charles II is said to have stayed here in 1653, when he was out rallying support during Cromwell's rule.

Beyond Lorton, the mountains begin to close in again. Visitors now have a choice. They can either head west – towards Loweswater and gentler surroundings – or east towards Crummock Water, Buttermere and an area of dark, craggy mountains.

Buttermere

Heading east from Lorton Vale, the first lake you reach is **Crummock Water**, a beautiful spot with brooding Melbreak on one side of it and the seemingly impenetrable slopes of Grasmoor on the other. (Impenetrable they aren't; scramblers with a head for heights and the sure-footedness of mountain goats, can find a way up through its steep, dark gullies and via a scrappy, exposed ridge. There are easier ways on to the mountain for lesser mortals.)

Getting to and around the North Western Lakes

By Bus

A summer-only bus service (**77/77A**) links Buttermere and Lorton with Borrowdale, Whinlatter and Keswick.

By Taxi

Cockermouth Taxi Company, **t** (01900) 826649; Davies Taxis in Keswick, **t** (017687) 72676; KLM Taxis in Keswick, **t** (017687) 75337.

'Long sweeps of orange and gray soil and stones descend to the water; and above, there are large hollows, like craters, filled now with deep blue shadows, and now with tumbling white mists, above which yellow or purple peaks change their hues with every hour of the day.'

Harriet Martineau on Crummock Water

Many travellers rush past Crummock Water in their hurry to get to Buttermere and its famous beauties, but it is worth pausing a while here to appreciate this delicious stretch of water. **Low Ling Crag** on the western shore makes a great place to stop and spread out a picnic. This little mound at the end of a grass-topped shingle spit sticking out into Crummock Water provides spellbinding views across the lake to Grasmoor. Sit on the shingle here and dip your feet in the beautiful blue lake.

Hidden behind the low crags of Rannerdale Knotts is **Rannerdale**, a tiny valley that becomes awash with blue during bluebell season. In 1930, Rannerdale became the setting for local historian Nicholas Size's novel *The Secret Valley*. Based partly on fact but using fictional characters and events, it tells of how the early Norse settlers resisted Saxon and, later, Norman attempts to conquer their mountain home. Size has Rannerdale as the site of a battle where Normans were ambushed and slaughtered by the Norsemen in the 12th century. He attributes the abundance of bluebells to the soil, enriched by the bones of the many warriors buried here.

Scale Force, with its 125ft fall, has the longest single drop of any Lakeland waterfall. Wordsworth accurately described it as '...a fine chasm, with a lofty, though but slender, fall of water'. Located between Crummock Water and Buttermere, it is most easily reached via Buttermere village, from where it is a two-mile walk. As with most waterfalls, it is best seen after heavy rain.

The village itself, if village isn't too grand a word, consists of a farm – which makes and sells its own delicious Ayrshire ice creams – a few cottages, two pubs and a tiny church huddled together between the valley's two lakes. Although the church is worth a visit (*see* opposite), it isn't the buildings that attract visitors to this remote area; it is the spectacular scenery, some of the best that the Lake District has to offer.

The peaks of Wandope and Robinson dominate to the north; to the south, the magnificent, craggy High Stile range of mountains rises steeply from the shores of Buttermere. The relatively easy four-mile walk around the lake, suitable for all the family, is the best way to appreciate this scenery, especially on a calm day when Fleetwith Pike's steep ridge is perfectly reflected in the still, dark waters. Park either in the National Park car park in the village or at Gatesgarth Farm at the opposite end of the lake. But, if you're claustrophobic, be warned – there is a short tunnel cut through the rock on the northern side of the lake, close to Hassness House.

The Maid of Buttermere

The Fish Hotel in Buttermere was home, 200 years ago, to Mary Robinson, the 'Beauty of Buttermere' made famous in Melvyn Bragg's novel *The Maid of Buttermere*. She first became a celebrity in 1792 when Captain J. Budworth wrote about her in his *Fortnight's Ramble to the Lakes*, saying: 'Her hair was thick and long, of a dark brown and, though unadorned with ringlets, did not seem to want them; her face was a fine oval, with full eyes and lips as red as vermilion...'

Consequently, she received many noteworthy visitors, including Wordsworth, who wrote about her in *The Prelude*. In 1802, an apparently prosperous tourist arrived in Keswick – Colonel the Honourable Alexander Augustus Hope, MP for Linlithgow and brother of Lord Hopetoun. He ingratiated himself with Mary's parents, wooed her and then married her at nearby Lorton.

When the newspapers reported the wedding, Scottish readers pointed out that the real Colonel Hope was in Vienna at the time. Mary had married an impostor – John Hatfield, a bankrupt linen draper's traveller who was wanted for forgery and bigamy. He had married two women previously, abandoning them when their money started running low.

He was arrested in Cumbria but escaped, eventually reaching Wales where he was caught. Although Mary refused to testify against him, he was tried in Carlisle and was hanged in 1803 for forgery. Mary later married a Caldbeck farmer.

> *'For a man trying to forget a persistent worry, the top of Hay Stacks is a complete cure.'*
> Alfred Wainwright

For the more adventurous, the high-level hike from Red Pike to **Hay Stacks**, taking in High Stile and High Crag along the way, is probably one of the best ridge walks in the National Park. With some of the Lake District's highest fells seemingly just a stone's throw away and nothing but unremitting rock underfoot for most of the time, there is a sense here of being totally immersed in the mountains. Having said that, there is nothing especially dangerous or frightening on this walk in good, non-winter conditions – just a bit of steep clambering on loose ground at times. Come strong wind or heavy snow though and, as with all the high fells, it's a different story.

The guidebook writer and illustrator Alfred Wainwright, whose name has become almost as synonymous with the Lake District as that of Wordsworth, loved this area of the fells, and Hay Stacks was his favourite of all Lakeland mountains. In fact, his ashes were scattered here after his death in 1991. So, what made him love this 'shaggy and undisciplined terrier' of a mountain? 'You have to climb to the top and wander about to understand,' he wrote. 'Above the wall of defending crags is a fascinating landscape, a confusing labyrinth of miniature peaks and tors, of serpentine tracks, of lovely tarns, of crags and screes, of marshes and streams, of surprises around every corner, with magnificent views all around'.

There is a stone tablet set into the sill of one of the windows in **St James's Church** in Buttermere as a memorial to Wainwright. The window looks out on his beloved Hay Stacks. Whether or not he would have approved of such a thing is debateable; he tended to shy away from all public attention, rarely giving interviews and never seeking self-publicity. When Kendal announced that it was to erect a statue to the famous fell-walker, his friend Percy Duff told *The Times*: 'He would not have liked it at all. He did not like all the publicity. He was a loner.'

Perched on a tiny knoll overlooking the village, St James's is a lovely church in an even lovelier setting. Wordsworth wrote of it: 'A man must be very insensible who would not be touched with pleasure at the sight of the chapel of Buttermere'.

Cumberland and Westmorland Wrestling

The embroidered felt 'underpants' form part of the 'uniform' of a Cumberland and Westmorland wrestler. The origins of this unusual sport are unknown, but some think the Vikings brought it to England; others say it may have developed out of a longer-standing Celtic tradition. The wrestlers stand chest to chest, grasping each other around the body with their chins on their opponent's right shoulder. Once the umpire has started the contest by telling the men to 'tekk hod', they attempt to unbalance each other, or make their opponent lose their hold, using any method other than kicking. If any part of a wrestler's body touches the ground aside from his feet then he loses. Matches are decided by the best of three falls.

The traditional costume worn by the wrestlers can make these usually strong men look anything but butch – vests, white long johns, socks and, of course, those 'underpants' worn on the outside. But don't go along expecting the prancing of modern American wrestling; this is a contest of skill, cunning and power, and it's taken very seriously.

One of the most outstanding wrestlers in the long history of the sport was George Steadman, who won the heavyweight contest at Grasmere no fewer than 17 times in the second half of the 19th century. This powerful but paunchy man, who came from the Appleby area, measured almost 52 inches around the chest.

There are two roads heading away from Buttermere towards the east: one goes up to Honister Pass via Gatesgarth Farm, a great drive through some increasingly wild countryside; the other, much quieter road, goes up steeply beside St James's to the Newlands Pass. A small parking area at the top provides access to Moss Force, another impressive waterfall. Walkers seeking an off-the-beaten-track route would be hard-pushed to find anything as good as Knott Rigg. Having already driven up to almost 1,100ft, it's a relatively easy climb on to the fells to the north of the pass and then, from Knott Rigg, a comfortably narrow but unfashionable ridge leads to Ard Crags.

Loweswater

To the west of Buttermere and Crummock Water are the scattered farms and cottages that make up Loweswater. The beautifully located church of **St Bartholomew** was built in 1827, although Christian worship is thought to have taken place on the site since the 12th century. Next door, always bursting at the seams with diners and drinkers, is the **Kirkstile Inn**, which has its own award-winning range of local beers. Near to the hamlet is the delightful lake that shares its name. Sadly, visitors do not have access to all of Loweswater's shoreline, but the woods to the southwest are full of tracks that make for lovely walking and an excellent chance of seeing red squirrels. A more ambitious hiking route goes straight up the front of Melbreak, the brooding fell standing aloof from its neighbours to the south of the hamlet.

As the mountains begin to give way to gentler-sloped hills, the bustle of the Lake District's tourism industry is all but forgotten; here, agriculture seems to be a bigger concern. The Loweswater Show, usually held in September, is one of a couple of dozen agricultural shows that take place throughout Cumbria in the summer and early autumn. By county standards, it is a fairly typical show and includes sheepdog trials, shows of livestock, horses and dogs, carriage-driving

Where to Stay and Eat in the North Western Lakes

Bridge Hotel, Buttermere, **t** (017687) 70252, *www.bridge-hotel.com* (*expensive*). Some four-posters in well-kept rooms within walking distance of the two lakes. This traditional pub is very busy in the summer and also serves better-than-average pub food.

Derwent Lodge

>

Derwent Lodge, Embleton, **t** (017687) 76606, *www.thederwentlodge.co.uk* (*expensive*). Beautifully-appointed, fully-serviced luxury apartments with leather suites and giant flat screen TVs. Each is individually furnished and decorated to a very high standard. Available on nightly basis. Also clean, modern en suite rooms. Large indoor pool. The Lodge also has an attractive **restaurant** (*moderate*) overlooking the fells, that is open to non-residents. Meat is sourced locally and herbs and vegetables are grown on the premises.

New House Farm, Lorton, **t** 07841 159 818, *www.newhouse-farm.co.uk* (*expensive*). Luxurious B&B accommodation in a beautiful 17th-century farmhouse. Spacious and spotless rooms in the main house have oak four-poster beds and spa baths. Two bedrooms in an annexe. Quiet location at the base of the fells.

Winder Hall Country House, Low Lorton, **t** (01900) 85107, *www.winder hall.co.uk* (*expensive*). Good-sized bedrooms with old metal bedsteads and mullioned windows in this grand old hall a few miles outside of Cockermouth. Pleasant gardens, hot tub and sauna. Wood-panelled **restaurant** is fully licensed and open to non-residents.

The Old Homestead at Byresteads, near Cockermouth, **t** (01900) 822223, *www.byresteads.co.uk* (*moderate*). Hidden away down a farm lane about two miles outside of Cockermouth, this interesting farm conversion has 10 rooms of many different shapes and sizes, all containing oak furniture, comfy leather chairs and solid oak or stone floors – with under floor heating.

The Kirkstile Inn, Loweswater, **t** (01900) 85219, *www.kirkstile.com* (*moderate–budget*). Popular place to eat with locals and visitors alike, this cosy pub is in the heart of beautiful countryside close to the western edge of the Lake District. Emphasis on local produce.

Southwaite Green Cottages, Lorton, **t** (01900) 821055, *www.southwaite green.co.uk* (*self-catering*). Four luxurious cottages in 10 acres of land. Look out of your window and you might spot badgers, red squirrels, deer and hares. Traditional buildings using energy-efficient technology.

The Lazy Fish, Embleton, **t** (017687) 76179, *www.thelazyfish.co.uk* (*self-catering*). All the luxuries of the 21st century but in as eco-friendly a manner as possible. This yummy barn conversion has an outdoor spa pool, wood-burning stove, under floor heating, mountain bikes and a computer with internet access.

displays, a fell race, hound trailing (a kind of fell race for hounds) and Cumberland and Westmorland wrestling (*see* box opposite). For anyone from outside the county, it might seem quite exotic with farmers communicating with their dogs via a series of whistles and shouts, apparently masochistic athletes tackling the toughest running terrain imaginable, and men grappling with each other while wearing their underpants over their long johns.

Ennerdale

Ennerdale

With little settlement to speak of, no major roads nearby and nothing but a rough track through the valley itself, Ennerdale is probably the loneliest of the major Lake District dales. It's fast becoming the wildest too, but we'll get to that later...

Getting to and around Ennerdale

By Bus

The 219F dial-a-ride service operates between Ennerdale Bridge and nearby Cleator Moor. To book, phone Ginger Taxis, t (01946) 815811 before 9.30am on the day of travel.

By Taxi

Ginger Taxis, Cleator Moor, t (01946) 815811; Bigrigg Cabs, Bigrigg, Egremont, t (01946) 810024; Geoff's Taxis, Egremont, t (01946) 824554.

By Bicycle

Ainfield Cycle Centre, Jacktrees Road, Cleator, t (01946) 812427 hires out bikes.

Whichever way you come at it, it's a fair journey to get to Ennerdale and there's little in the way of public transport. If you're coming from the north, you'll pass through a number of tiny settlements that hug the base of the grassy fells near Loweswater.

Mockerkin has a tiny, water lily-laden tarn surrounded by lush pastures. Legend has it that this was the site of the palace of a Celtic king of Cumbria called Morken, who was struck down and died from an acute form of gout after insulting St Mungo.

The next village down is **Lamplugh**, a peaceful but scattered collection of cottages and farmhouses. Nearby are the remains of the iron mines of Kelton and Knockmurton. Even though the mines were relatively inaccessible, the high quality of the local haematite meant that mining here in the mid-19th century was worth the costs involved. It wasn't until about 1880, when the Gilchrist process meant ores of a lesser quality could be used in the iron industry, that production began to decline. If you're interested in the history of the industry, there are plans to develop a **Florence Mine Cultural Centre** on the outskirts of **Egremont**. Florence Mine was Europe's last working deep iron-ore mine until it closed in 2008. As well as information on how the miners worked and lived, the centre will house displays of their clothes, their tools and even the clay pipes that they smoked.

Quiet, winding roads then lead to **Ennerdale Bridge**, the gateway to Ennerdale itself. Here, travellers will find a couple of very ordinary pubs, some bed and breakfasts and not much else. It's a suitable introduction to 'wild' Ennerdale.

The shores of Ennerdale Water can be found about a mile east of the village. Leaving the car park near Bleach Green and walking down to the water's edge, you can look up Ennerdale and get a teasing taste of the spectacular mountain scenery that lies further up the valley. The circuit of the lake is popular with walkers of all ages – following rough paths along the southern shore and then a good track along the north.

The other main car park is at Bowness Knott on the northern side of the lake. Motor vehicle access beyond here is restricted, although cyclists can continue for another six miles, as far as **Black Sail Hut**, one of the most isolated youth hostels in England. It is this restriction on cars that makes Ennerdale stand out from other Lake District valleys, and gives it its increased sense of remoteness. It's a great area for fell-

World Gurning Championships

Probably because it remained relatively isolated for so long, Cumbria has retained a lot of weird and wonderful traditions. Cumberland and Westmorland wrestling may look a little strange to visitors and the concept of an island king may be hard for some people to get their heads round, but none of these traditions is more unusual than the World Gurning Championships held every year in Egremont.

A gurn is a distorted facial expression, for example, projecting the lower jaw as far forward and up as possible, and covering the upper lip with the lower lip. So, basically, it's a competition to pull a silly face – while sticking your head through a horse's collar or 'braffin'.

It's taken very seriously in west Cumbria where competitors spend weeks training for the event and getting their facial muscles in shape. The best-known gurner was probably Peter Jackman, who won the world title at Egremont four times with his 'Bela Lugosi' face, and achieved national fame in 2000 when he had his teeth removed to make his features easier to manoeuvre.

The World Gurning Championships form part of the Crab Fair (*www.egremontcrabfair.com*), which has been held in Egremont since 1267. It all began when the Lord of Egremont started giving away crab apples at harvest time. The tradition continues today with the Parade of the Apple Cart, where apples are thrown to the crowds which fill Main Street. Other fair highlights include Cumberland and Westmorland wrestling, a pipe-smoking event, the ascent of a greasy pole and the singing of hunting songs.

walking, but only if you're prepared for a long day. The most challenging route in the area is the **Ennerdale Round**, an amazing horseshoe that takes in, among others, Red Pike, High Stile, Hay Stacks, Great Gable, Kirk Fell and Pillar. Not only is it long (between 22 and 25 miles, depending on which mountains you decide to include), but it involves about 8,000ft of lung-bursting ascent – and that means 8,000ft of knee-crunching descent too. There are some easy, grassy bits, but it's mostly on rough ground and the badly eroded paths on to and off of Kirk Fell are particularly difficult.

More than 500 individual archaeological sites have been recorded in Ennerdale, some of which are of regional and national importance. These include a bloomery where iron ore would have been smelted using charcoal during medieval times, a 600-year-old longhouse, an Iron Age settlement and the remains of shielings high up on the fells.

Wild Ennerdale

In 2003, Ennerdale's primary landowners – the National Trust, the Forestry Commission and United Utilities – formed a partnership called Wild Ennerdale, which aims to 'allow the evolution of Ennerdale as a wild valley for the benefit of people, relying more on natural processes to shape its landscape and ecology'. Just a few years into the project and the appearance of this valley is already changing – the regimented lines of conifers are disappearing, broadleaf trees are returning and the River Liza is being allowed to chart its own course unhindered.

Oak, birch, rowan and willow are among the species that can be seen today. Spruce is allowed to regrow for the sake of diversity, but it is removed if it starts dominating – as has happened close to the head of the valley.

No conifers have been planted since 2002, except juniper, which computer modelling shows probably once flourished here. The name of

Where to Stay in and around Ennerdale

The Shepherds Arms Hotel, Ennerdale Bridge, **t** (01946) 861249, *www.shep herdsarmshotel.co.uk* (*moderate*). Large TVs and dark wooden furniture are the order of the day in the comfortable, but slightly old-fashioned rooms in Ennerdale Bridge's only hotel. Bar meals available.

Ennerdale View, Kirkland, **t** (01946) 862311, *www.ennerdale-view.co.uk* (*moderate–budget*). This small B&B offers bright, cheery rooms at a reasonable price. Enjoy great views of Ennerdale while taking breakfast in the conservatory.

The Stork Hotel, Rowrah Road, Rowrah, Frizington, **t** (01946) 861213, *www.storkhotel.co.uk* (*moderate–budget*). Clean, simple rooms in a family-run hotel just outside the National Park. Provides a free pick-up and drop-off service for Coast to Coast walkers.

the dale itself, long thought to be connected to the name of a chieftain, Anund, might even come from the old Norse word for juniper – 'einir'.

Semi-wild Galloway cattle roam freely in Ennerdale. They were introduced in 2006 when ecologists advised the Wild Ennerdale team that the grazing and disturbance caused by large herbivores, mostly absent from British forests, was necessary to open the way for different plant species. Like everything else in the valley, they are mostly left to their own devices. Calves are born unaided – the mother going off to a secluded place to give birth before returning to the herd.

There are other mammals here too – otters have recolonized the valley; both red and roe deer frequent the area; and there have even been unconfirmed sightings of the elusive pine marten. The River Liza's substantial shingle beds are home to a rare type of stiletto fly. The larvae live just beneath the surface and can detect the vibrations of prey above. Stealthily, they position themselves underneath the prey and pierce it with stiletto-like mouthparts, injecting poison that instantly paralyses. They then drag their prey under the shingle.

When the River Liza changed course after two massive storms in the autumn of 2008 and overwhelmed a public right of way, a decision was made not to divert the new channel but to divert the path instead. This lack of human interference makes the wide, meandering River Liza one of the most natural rivers in England.

Wasdale

🔟 **Wastwater**

Wastwater in Wasdale achieved national fame a few years ago when it was named 'Britain's Favourite View' in a TV competition that culminated in a public vote. Who could fail to be moved by the image of England's highest and most dramatic mountains forming a backdrop to the calm, dark waters of England's deepest lake? Wasdale is, without a doubt, a very special place in a region that overflows with stunning views and spectacular scenery.

If you're coming from the north, the lively village of **Gosforth** forms the gateway to the dale. The churchyard of **St Mary's** makes for an interesting stop. It contains the tallest Norse cross in England. At 14ft, this remarkable artefact is also the country's tallest sandstone

Getting to and around Wasdale

By Train and Bus

Seascale railway station is about 11 miles from Wasdale Head, and Seascale is about 25 minutes from Whitehaven by **train**.

Gosforth Taxi Service runs **bus** service **13** between Seascale railway station, Gosforth and Wasdale Head on Thurs, Sat and Sun. This runs only if pre-booked. Call t (019467) 25308 before 6pm the day before travelling.

By Taxi

Gosforth Taxi Service, Gosforth, t (019467) 25308; C-Scale, Seascale, t (019467) 27967

monolith. Intricately carved with pagan and Norse symbols on one side and Christian motifs on the other, it is said to depict the victory of Christ over the heathen gods. The church's two 10th-century hogback tombstones carved with battle scenes are thought to cover the graves of Norse chieftains. The graveyard also contains Europe's most northerly cork tree, planted in 1833. Rather surprisingly, the church's tool shed is a listed building – it was built of Norse-inscribed stones from the original church.

Gosforth's economy used to be based on agriculture, but the largest employer now is the nuclear reprocessing plant at Sellafield, which occupies a site the size of a small town about two miles west of Gosforth. Whatever your view on nuclear energy, the **Sellafield Centre** contains some interesting and educational exhibitions, although many of the interactive displays that once drew the crowds have now gone.

Sellafield Centre
Sellafield,
t (019467) 28333,
www.sellafieldsites.com;
open Mon–Fri
10am–3.30pm; closed
public holidays

Heading away from the coast, and **Santon Bridge** hosts another of those quirky Cumbrian events. This time it's the **World's Biggest Liar** competition and, although it can't lay claim to the sort of long history that the Egremont Crab Fair has, its roots go back a fair while. Will Ritson, the first of the great liars, ran the inn at the head of Wasdale in the 19th century. A popular publican, he was nevertheless known among his regulars for his tall tales. Did you know, for instance, that he once mated a foxhound bitch with a golden eagle? The resulting pups, he told his customers, had eagle's wings and had no problem getting over the drystone walls during a hunt. And what about Wasdale's amazing giant turnips – so large, in fact, that the locals carved them out to make housing for the sheep. Ritson's memory lives on at the **Bridge Inn** (*www.santonbridgeinn.com*), which hosts the competition every November. People come from all over the world to tell their tall tales and, in 2006, comedienne Sue Perkins made history when she became the first woman to win the title with a tale of flatulent sheep – 'muttons of mass destruction' – causing a hole in the ozone layer.

Nether Wasdale is an unlikely sight on the edge of such dramatic scenery – a typical English village with two pubs, a church and a surprisingly large green with a maypole on it. This was put up in 1897 to mark Queen Victoria's diamond jubilee (60 years of reign), and is now a listed building. The community gathers here every year to celebrate May Day with traditional maypole dancing, children's fancy dress, Morris dancing and afternoon teas.

Wastwater and Wasdale Head

'The traveller will see as noble a group of mountains closing in on Wastdale, as he can look upon from any one spot of the district.'

Harriet Martineau

Approaching Wasdale proper, you are greeted by a magnificent view of the mountains with the iconic Great Gable dominating the scene. It's an almost perfect panorama, each fell with its own distinctive character and profile; so good, in fact, that it has become the symbol of the National Park.

Wastwater, as every attentive schoolchild knows, is England's deepest lake. But it won't be those still waters that draw the eye as you reach its shores; instead, the impossibly steep scree slopes, known simply as **The Screes**, on the other side of the lake, are the focus of attention. Local poet Norman Nicholson described The Screes as being 'like the inverted arches of a gothic cathedral'. These dramatic stone- and boulder-covered slopes plunge almost vertically, it seems, down into the water from a height of more than 1,700ft. And, occasionally, they do literally plunge into the water – avalanches of rock come thundering down the slope, particularly in the early spring. There is a public right of way crossing the base of The Screes, close to the water's edge, but it makes for uncomfortable and potentially dangerous walking – one awkward turn of the ankle and you could end up in the icy waters below.

The lake is 260ft deep, making it a popular destination for scuba divers. If you're a fan of the murky, cold depths and decide to take the plunge yourself – assuming, of course, that you are experienced – don't worry if you start seeing gnomes at a depth of about 48ft. No, you are not hallucinating, this is the lake's once secret, but now famous gnome garden. Police were called in a few years ago to remove the gnomes – and their lovely little picket fence – after a number of divers died, supposedly because they were spending too long in the deep water searching for the garden. But, as every owner knows, gnomes will always find their way home – and they have started reappearing in the lake. Rather peculiarly, one is sitting on a wooden aeroplane while another, affectionately named Gordon, has a lawnmower. Wastwater isn't the only lake with unusual artefacts on its bed – divers have managed to create a bathroom complete with toilet and bath tub on the bottom of Coniston Water too.

The small settlement at the head of the valley is known as **Wasdale Head**. Here, visitors will find an inn, a few dwellings, the tiny St Olaf's church – and the end of the road. Exploration from this point has to continue on foot, but what an area it is to explore. Walkers doing the national Three Peaks challenge (Ben Nevis, Snowdon and Scafell Pike) launch their assault on England's highest mountain from Wasdale Head.

The summit of **Scafell Pike**, which sits at 3,208ft above sea level, isn't the most inspiring of mountain tops – it is a bleak expanse of shattered, grey rock debris – but the views, as you'd expect, are among the best in the Lake District, if not the country. In his *Guide to the Lakes*, Wordsworth quotes a letter from his sister Dorothy, telling of an ascent of the mountain in 1818: 'Side by side with Eskdale, we now saw the sister Vale of Donnerdale terminated by the Duddon Sands. But the majesty of the mountains below, and close to us, is not to be conceived. We now beheld the whole mass of Great Gavel [Gable] from its base, –

Joss Naylor

One of Wasdale's most famous sons is the legendary Joss Naylor. He is generally regarded as the greatest fell-runner of all time, having achieved peak-bagging records that no other runner has been able even to get near. In 1975, he set a record for the number of Lake District peaks scaled inside 24 hours – he managed 72. The distance, incidentally, was more than 100 miles and the total climb was an excruciating 37,000ft. Aged 50, he slogged up all 214 of the summits listed in Alfred Wainwright's pictorial guides in just seven days, shaving three days off the previous record – and all of this while working as a sheep farmer. To celebrate his 70th birthday in 2006, he decided to run up and down 70 'small' mountains, another epic that covered more than 50 miles and included more than 25,000ft of ascent – in a mere 21 hours. His exploits, many of them for charity, have earned Naylor an MBE and two honorary university degrees.

But what makes Naylor's story all the more impressive is the difficult start he had in life. As a child, he had a serious back condition and was unable to take part in sports at school. He was deemed unfit for National Service and, when he was 18, an operation left him with a knee that still doesn't work properly. A few years later he had to have two discs removed from his back. Over the years, many doctors have tried to persuade Naylor to give up running, but each time he has defied their gloomy predictions to achieve ever greater things.

the Den of Wasdale at our feet – a gulf immeasurable: Grasmire [Grasmoor] and the other mountains of Crummock; Ennerdale and its mountains; and the sea beyond!'

Great Gable, Kirk Fell, Yewbarrow, Lingmell and Sca Fell can also be climbed from Wasdale Head. This is serious walking country, with some routes graded as scrambles, so make sure you seek local advice.

Every November, the summit of Great Gable is the scene of a moving Remembrance Day service. Just after World War One, the Fell and Rock Climbing Club purchased much of the mountain as a memorial to members who had died during the horrific conflict. Since then, whatever the weather, hundred of walkers and climbers have made their way every year to the top of this famous, dome-shaped fell to remember those who died while serving their country. A plaque, bearing a relief map of the area and the names of the fallen, can be found on the north side of the summit rocks.

Coleridge's first climb

Coleridge's well-documented ascent of England's second highest mountain Scafell – and subsequent descent of Broad Stand – in August 1802 is regarded by many as the first recorded climb for leisure purposes. He climbed it from Wasdale via Broad Tongue, a relatively easy, crag-free route until near the top. In a letter to his friend Sara Hutchinson, he wrote of the summit: 'O my God! What enormous mountains these are close by me... But o! What a look down under my feet! The frightfullest cove that might ever be seen. Huge perpendicular precipices... two huge pillars of lead-coloured stone – I am no measurer but their height and depth is terrible.'

The map he was carrying fell a long way short of the high standards of today's Ordnance Survey maps, and it was a miracle that he lived to tell the tale of his descent from Scafell down the dreaded Broad Stand. Today, this remains an accident blackspot in the mountains. Wasdale Mountain Rescue Team records more call-outs to this steep, rocky and

Walk: Pillar and Red Pike

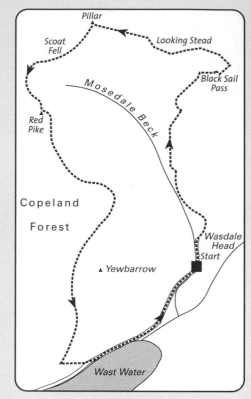

Start and finish:
The green at Wasdale Head (grid reference, NY186084)

Distance:
9.7 miles/15.6km

Total ascent:
3,514ft/1,072m

In brief:
This long, tough outing visits two peaks on the Mosedale Horseshoe – Pillar and Red Pike. Starting from Wasdale Head, it includes steep climbs on rough ground and some descents that will put your knees to the test. Having said all that, it is a walk to be savoured – with imposing crags, grassy plateaus and views that are hard to beat. It's one that you won't forget in a hurry.

Route description:
Follow the road to the **Wasdale Head Inn**. Take the path around the side of the pub, passing the **Barn Door Shop** on your right and then veer right. Go through the small gate and, ignoring the bridge on your left, follow the beck upstream.

The path splits about 350 yards beyond the pub; bear left here to continue alongside **Mosedale Beck**. The bridleway now goes through the right-hand of the two gates just ahead.

Keep to the clear track as it skirts the base of the steep western slopes of Kirk Fell. It's a relatively gentle climb into Mosedale at first, and you get plenty of time to enjoy this peaceful valley.

Soon after passing a large cairn to the left of the path, you will see a faint path going off to the left – heading deeper into Mosedale. Ignore this; keep to the main track as it continues to climb at an increasingly tiring angle.

Having forded **Gathersone Beck**, you begin a zig-zagging ascent. From **Black Sail Pass**, you can see across to the fells above Buttermere. Looking up Ennerdale, Green Gable is in view, but Kirk Fell hides the top of Great Gable.

Turn left at the pass. When you reach the cairn at the base of the first set of crags, the path splits in three. The one on the right marks the start of the climbers' route to **Pillar Rock**. Take either of the other two. They both ascend the ridge steeply, although the one to the left avoids the worst of the scrambling.

As the gradient eases, you can look across the valley to the left to the craggy NE face of Red Pike. As the crow flies, it doesn't look far, but lowly walkers have to go the long way round.

Unfortunately, the short rest is soon over and the long, uphill trudge restarts as you pick your way up through a rocky landscape. The path disappears at times among the boulders, but the route is cairned and you can also use the old fenceposts as guides.

The formidable northern face of Pillar includes a chaotic jumble of shattered crags, boulders and scree, so take some time to stop occasionally and peer over the edge.

Finally, you reach the summit – a grassy plateau occupied by a trig pillar, shelters...and those views! What can't you see from the top of Pillar? All of the major Lake District peaks are there, as are the Pennines, the Scottish hills, the Isle of Man, Morecambe Bay... but, thankfully, Haycock prevents this panorama from being spoiled by the sight of Sellafield. If you want to see the famous Pillar Rock, simply walk to the small shelter to the north of the trig point and then descend the rough path for a few feet. You'll soon be gazing down on the conspicuous lump.

Pillar Rock is one of the Lake District's most popular climbs. The first recorded ascent was made in 1826 by John Atkinson, of Crowfoot, Ennerdale. He is said to have climbed it by the Old West Route, which is today graded moderate. In 1891, Walter Parry Haskett-Smith, who was also the first man to climb Napes Needle on Great Gable, became the first to tackle the imposing north face. Other famous names in the history of Lake District climbing have also put up routes, including the Abraham brothers, Keswick photographers towards the end of the Victorian era, and Harry Kelly.

Continuing the walk, head SW from the trig pillar, following a line of cairns that quickly leads to a clear path. Take care on this steep and often loose descent!

Having dropped into the Wind Gap saddle, you now have to clamber steeply up a jumble of boulders to the cairn on top of **Black Crag**. Beyond is a lovely, grassy plateau – a welcome relief after your recent efforts.

As you saunter across this saddle, enjoying the uninterrupted view across to the Scafell group, you begin to climb at a leisurely angle to a fork in the path. Bear left (S veering SE) to skirt the top of steep, rough ground to the left. Don't be tempted by the grassy, level path that comes away from the edge a little later – it bypasses the summit. The top of Red Pike is marked by a small cairn, from which you can see almost all of the route you have walked so far.

Still hugging the edge of the precipice, descend the grassy slope to meet up with a path coming in from the right. Keeping to the left of a cairn-topped pile of rocks at the end of the summit ridge, you pick up a clearer path as you begin to descend more steeply (SSE).

The descent to **Dore Head** at the base of Yewbarrow is completed via a series of alternating rocky drops and grassy shelves. From Dore Head, turn right (SSW) on a faint, grassy path. Losing height at a barely perceptible rate, you pass through a gate in a wall and soon meet another wall. Cross the ladder stile and turn sharp right to descend steeply on grass with **Wastwater** straight ahead.

Passing one stile in the fence on your right, swing left to drop to another stile. Ignore this one too and turn left along a grassy path. This drops gently to a stile. Cross this and walk with the fence on your left until you reach the road. Now turn left and follow the road back to Wasdale Head.

often slippery short-cut between Scafell and Scafell Pike than to any other location. In what has become a classic of mountain writing, Coleridge recalls his descent of Broad Stand the following day:

'When I find it convenient to descend from a mountain, I am too confident and too indolent to look round about and wind about 'till I find a track or other symptom of safety; but I wander on, and where it is first possible to descend, there I go – relying upon fortune for how far down this possibility will continue. So it was yesterday afternoon... the first place I came to, that was not direct Rock, I slipped down, and went on for a while with tolerable ease – but now I came (it was midway down) to a smooth perpendicular rock about seven feet high – this was nothing – I put my hands on the ledge and dropped down – in a few yards came just such another – I dropped that too, and yet another, seemed not higher – I would not stand for a trifle so I dropped that too – but the stretching of the muscles of my hands and arms, and the jolt of the fall on my feet, put my whole limbs in a tremble, and I paused, and looking down, saw that I had little else to encounter but a succession of these little precipices – it was in truth a path that in a very hard rain is, no doubt, the channel of a most splendid waterfall. So I began to suspect that I ought not to go on, but then unfortunately tho' I could with ease drop down a smooth rock seven feet high, I could not climb it, so go on I must and on I went....'

Where to Stay and Eat in and around Wasdale

Gosforth Hall Inn, Gosforth, t (019467) 25322, *www.gosforthhallinn.co.uk* (*expensive–moderate*). Plenty of original features in this 17th-century hall, including spiral stone stairways and a priest's hole. The house is said to have been built using timbers from ships wrecked along the coast.

Westlakes Hotel and Restaurant, Gosforth, t (019467) 25221 (*expensive–moderate*). The neat, white tablecloths and heavy-framed mirrors give this restaurant a bit of a stuffy look, but eating here is a friendly, relaxed affair. Try the turbot fillet on a white bean and pancetta broth and basil aioli.

Lutwidge Arms Hotel, Holmrook, t (019467) 24230, *www.lutwidgearms. co.uk* (*moderate*). Friendly, family-run hotel where the owners will bend over backwards to make sure you are comfortable. Good value for money.

Rainors Farm, Wasdale Road, Gosforth, t (019467) 25934, *www.rainorsfarm. co.uk* (*moderate*). The two spacious and rather sumptuous yurts on Rainors Farm are an atmospheric

place to stay. They are fully carpeted, insulated with organic sheep felt lining and are equipped with woodburners, providing a surprisingly cosy environment. Of course, if you want something a little more conventional, there are standard en suite rooms indoors.

Strands Inn, Nether Wasdale, t (019467) 26237, *www.strandshotel. com* (*moderate*). Downstairs, the Strands has all the charms of a 19th-century coaching inn with a dark, beamed bar and toasty, open fires; but upstairs, guests get bright, airy rooms with pastel shades and pine furniture. Good food is also available.

Wasdale Head Inn, Wasdale Head, t (019467) 26229, *www.wasdalehead inn.co.uk* (*moderate*). First-time visitors to Wasdale inevitably make for this prominent hotel dominating the settlement at the head of the valley. Popular with walkers and climbers, the rooms are generally small, but cosy. The bar is crammed with climbing memorabilia and the food at **Abraham's Restaurant** has a good reputation. Try the roast lamb chump on braised Canadian lentils with honey and redcurrant sauce.

Eskdale

Eskdale's mountain scenery may not be quite on the same scale as Wasdale or Ennerdale, but it's a beautiful valley nonetheless with its own, unique charms and a peacefulness that's hard to find in other, busier areas of the Lake District. Maybe it's the location that puts visitors off – if you're not prepared to tackle the hair-raising **Hardknott Pass**, Eskdale is a very long drive from anywhere. And don't, for one minute, imagine that Hardknott Pass is an easy option, just another mountain road. It's got a gradient of one in three, making it one of the two steepest roads in England. Approaching it from the east, drivers are faced with a dizzying series of steep, tight bends, all in quick succession. Ice often makes the road impassable in winter, and, obviously, it's totally unsuitable for caravans or long vehicles. That didn't stop the misguided driver of an articulated lorry trying to use it as a shortcut from Whitehaven to Preston a few years ago. The lorry, needless to say, became stuck and the road had to be closed for 24 hours while rescue vehicles removed it.

The original road across the pass was built by the Romans. They used it to shift supplies from their port at Glannaventa, now Ravenglass (*see* p.186), to their fort at Galava, modern-day Ambleside. Protecting the wind-swept pass and the road from attack by the Scots and Brigantes was another fort, Mediobogdum. This was built on a grassy spur below the dark crags of Border End several hundred feet above Eskdale – and its substantial ruins still remain to this day, making it one of the most dramatically positioned Roman structures in the entire country. Passing through the fort's southwest gate, you can't fail to be impressed by the thickness of its walls, now nearly 1,900 years old. Mediobogdum, or **Hardknott Castle** as it is known today, was built by the Emperor Hadrian to house 500 infantry soldiers from Croatia, Bosnia-Herzegovina and Montenegro. It's difficult to imagine how hard life must have been for these men, living so far from their homelands in wooden barracks in an inhospitable environment 815ft above sea level.

⭐ **Hardknott Castle**

Some of the structures have been partly rebuilt from fallen masonry. These include the commandant's house, the headquarters, a pair of granaries and the bathhouse, which lies to the southeast of the walls. The Roman parade ground, to the east of the fort, is still clearly visible as is the 'tribunal' (today just a raised mound with a pile of large stones) from where the commandant would have inspected his men.

The fort can be reached easily from the road, although there is very little parking nearby. There are no fences around it, no admission charges, no opening restrictions – just wander as you please.

Woolpack Inn
www.woolpack.co.uk

Strung out along the valley bottom are the pubs, farms and homes that make up the dale's two villages – **Boot** and **Eskdale Green**. Despite its size, Boot has three pubs – the Brook House Inn, the Boot Inn and the **Woolpack Inn**, which has a microbrewery and hosts a beer festival.

Eskdale Mill
Boot,
t *(019467) 23335,*
www.eskdalemill.co.uk;
open Apr–Sept daily
11.30am–5.30pm; closed
some Mondays and
Saturdays; adm

Boot is also home to one of the few remaining corn mills in the country. **Eskdale Mill**, built in 1547, has two overshot water wheels powering a complex arrangement of wooden hoppers, hoists and millstones. As well as an exhibition of milling equipment and other

Getting to and around Eskdale

By Train and Bus

Ravenglass is on the main line between Carlisle and Barrow via Whitehaven (journey time to Whitehaven, 30 minutes). From here, visitors can catch the **Ravenglass and Eskdale Railway** or **La'al Ratty** narrow-gauge railway into Eskdale, t (01229) 717171, *www.ravenglass-railway.co.uk*. It stops at Muncaster Mill, Irton Road, The Green, Fisherground, Beckfoot and Dalegarth for Boot. Total journey time, 40 minutes.

The **X6/6 bus** links Ravenglass/Muncaster with Whitehaven (journey time, 74 minutes). There are only a few services per day. There are no buses serving Eskdale.

By Bicycle

Bikes can be hired from Budgie Bike Hire at Dalegarth Station, near Boot, t (019467) 23226.

Fold End Gallery
Boot,
t (019467) 23335;
telephone for opening
hours

artefacts from the valley, resident miller Dave King gives visitors a demonstration of how the machinery works.

Nearby, just over the packhorse bridge across Whillan Beck, is the small **Fold End Gallery**, which includes displays of local paintings, ceramics, sculptures and hand-blown glass.

Pretty **St Catherine's Church**, on the banks of the River Esk, is a short walk from the centre of Boot. It's worth a visit, if only for its peaceful, riverside location.

St Catherine's marks the end point of the old **Wasdale to Eskdale corpse road**. Before St Olaf's Church at Wasdale Head was licensed for burials, coffins had to be carried on horseback to St Catherine's in Eskdale. This was once a common occurrence in Cumbria, and there are corpse roads all over the Lake District, often crossing bleak and lonely fells. The Wasdale to Eskdale route is almost six miles long and climbs to a high point of about 1,000ft as it passes close to moody Burnmoor Tarn and then crosses remote Eskdale Moor. Now a bridleway, it makes for an interesting walk, although you wouldn't want to be up there when the mist descends. Aside from the obvious danger of getting lost, it's in foggy weather that the hoofbeats of a ghostly horse are said to be heard. Locals will tell you that, on one stormy winter's day many, many years ago, the horse carrying the coffin of a young Wasdale man suddenly took fright and disappeared into the mist near Burnmoor Tarn. The distraught bearers then had the awful task of having to tell the dead man's mother that his body had been lost, but the shock proved too much for the old woman and she died soon afterwards. A coffin was again strapped to the back of a horse and the party set off for Eskdale. Again, the group experienced bad weather and, again, the horse bolted. It was never seen again – and nor was the coffin.

If you are brave enough to face the moors to the north of Boot, you will be able to see extensive Bronze Age remains, including cairns and five stone circles on Brat's Hill. The little-visited moors of west Cumbria are home to dozens of enigmatic sites like this – stone rows, ancient settlements, cairn fields and mysterious stone circles. But, because reaching them often involves a long walk across pathless, often boggy ground, few people make the effort. They're missing out!

One of the most spectacular natural features of Eskdale is **Stanley Force**, a 60ft waterfall hidden away in a dark, dramatic gorge. This is one of Lakeland's lesser-known waterfalls, but it's one of the best. The hike up to the falls from Dalegarth Station is magical, passing through rainforest-like vegetation before walkers have the option of clambering the final few yards for a close-up view.

The waterfall is named after the Stanley family, who live at nearby Dalegarth Hall. The unusual chimneypots of this 16th-century building can be spotted over the wall as you walk to and from the station.

The **Discover Eskdale Centre** in St Bega's Church, Eskdale Green, plays host to an illustrated display of the people and landscape of Eskdale.

La'al Ratty

⭐ **La'al Ratty – Ravenglass and Eskdale Railway**
Ravenglass, t (01229) 717171, www.ravenglass-railway.co.uk; open all year, limited winter timetable

Eskdale is the glorious setting for one of the most picturesque railway lines in the whole of Britain. The **La'al Ratty** (or **Ravenglass and Eskdale Railway** to give it its proper name) opened in 1875 to carry iron ore from the mine at Boot to the main railway line at Drigg. After the mine's closure in 1882, the line continued to carry passengers until 1908 when it was closed, then reopened, then closed and reopened. For a while in the 1950s it served the quarries at Beckfoot. It was finally bought in 1960 by the Ravenglass and Eskdale Preservation Society.

The tiny steam train chugs its way up the valley for seven miles – from Ravenglass on the coast to Dalegarth, near Boot, stopping along the way at Muncaster Mill, Irton Road, The Green, Fisherground and Beckfoot. The 40-minute journey makes for a lovely, relaxed way to see Eskdale, especially if you're sitting in one of the open carriages on a hot summer's day. Keen walkers sometimes choose to walk back to Ravenglass via Muncaster Fell, and the line is also proving increasingly popular with cyclists now that every train is equipped to carry bicycles. (Cyclists need to pre-book at least 24 hours before their journey to guarantee a space for their bike.) There are also bicycles available for hire at Dalegarth Station and there is an easy 8.5-mile, fully way-marked cycle route from Dalegarth all the way to Ravenglass. Known as the Eskdale Trail, it is relatively flat and suitable for all ages.

Where to Stay and Eat in Eskdale

Brook House Inn, Boot, t (019467) 23288, *www.brookhouseinn.co.uk (expensive–moderate)*. Comfortable rooms with bright décor and spotless bathrooms. Great location. Good quality food also available.

⭐ **The Bower House Inn** >
The Bower House Inn, Eskdale Green, t (01946) 723244, *www.bowerhouseinn.co.uk (expensive–moderate)*. Homely rooms of all shapes and sizes fill this quaint 17th-century coaching inn. Free Wi-Fi. Large beer garden. The **restaurant** *(moderate)* prides itself on using mostly local produce, including home-grown herbs and salads.

Boot Inn, Boot t (01946) 723224, *www.bootinn.co.uk (moderate)*. Traditional inn – with log fire – just a few hundred yards from the Brook House. Small rooms with good views. Good quality food also available.

Stanley House Bed and Breakfast, Boot, t (019467) 23327, *www.stanley ghyll-eskdale.co.uk (moderate)*. Large Victorian house that stands out like a sore thumb among the delicate dwellings of Eskdale. Recently refurbished to a good standard, the bedrooms are spacious and there are comfortable communal areas and a pretty garden. Close to Beckfoot Station on the La'al Ratty.

Whitehaven and the Coast

Whitehaven

The main town along this part of the coast is Whitehaven, which was once the third largest port in England. A thriving place during the Industrial Revolution, its wealth was built on iron and coal as well as the trade in tobacco, illicit liquor and slaves. The town's development owes much to Sir John Lowther, who, inspired by Sir Christopher Wren's ideas for rebuilding London after the Great Fire, designed the original grid system of streets and specified the type of houses he wanted to be built. Although much of Whitehaven's former grandeur is now considerably faded, many of the impressive townhouses from this period remain and there are several excellent visitor attractions.

One of the town's more unusual claims to fame is that it is said to have inspired *Gulliver's Travels*. Jonathan Swift (1667–1745) is said to have first dreamt up Lilliput as he gazed down from the cliffs of Whitehaven on to the tiny figures below. The Dublin-born poet and satirist spent the first few years of his life in Whitehaven, living in **Bowling Green House** – which later became the Red Flag Inn and is now a private house – close to the candlestick chimney overlooking Whitehaven Harbour. He returned to the town on occasions as a grown man and admitted that he loved the place as if he had been born there.

Whitehaven Harbour has seen plenty of action over the years. In 1915, it was shelled by a German U-boat. There was some damage to buildings, but no one was killed. An earlier attack came at the hands of John Paul Jones, the man regarded today as the founding father of the American navy. Born in Scotland, he actually served his apprenticeship as a sailor in Whitehaven, but became a senior lieutenant in what was to become the American navy at the start of the American War of Independence. He returned to the Cumbrian coast in 1778, attacking a few towns and setting fire to several ships in Whitehaven Harbour. The people of Whitehaven didn't forgive the attack until 1999 when, during the town's Maritime Festival, the harbourmaster and an officer from the American navy signed a joint proclamation which gave the Americans the freedom of the harbour.

John Paul Jones isn't the town's only link with the American War of Independence; George Washington's grandmother Mildred is buried in Whitehaven's St Nicholas churchyard on Lowther Street. A widow living in Virginia, she married merchant George Gale in 1699. He brought her and her three children to live in his home port, Whitehaven, but when Mildred died in 1700, her sons returned to Virginia. One of them, Augustine, went on to father the first president of the United States.

Steep steps lead down to the impressive harbour conservation area where major refurbishment in the late 1990s and early part of this century have created an attractive waterfront. The first jetty, now known as the **Old Quay**, was built in 1634 by Sir Christopher Lowther. It is one of the oldest coal wharves in Britain. Later piers were added in 1741 and then in the 1830s.

Getting to and around Whitehaven and the Coast

By Train and Coach

Whitehaven is on a direct **train** line to Carlisle in the north (journey time, 70 minutes) and Barrow in the south (70 minutes). Trains also stop at Ravenglass, Drigg, Seascale, St Bees, Workington and Maryport. **National Express** runs a daily service (**570**) between Whitehaven and London (10 hours and 15 minutes).

By Local Bus

The hourly **300/301** bus service runs between Carlisle and Whitehaven (one hour and 50 minutes). The **X6/6** bus links Whitehaven with Gosforth (45 minutes) and Muncaster via Ravenglass (74 minutes). There are only a few buses every day. The **20** bus runs between Whitehaven and St Bees (23 minutes). There are also a number of other services linking Whitehaven with surrounding villages and towns. Some of these do not run on Sundays.

By Taxi

L&G Taxis in Whitehaven, t (01946) 66644; White Line Taxis, t (01946) 66111; Abbey Cabs, t (01946) 63000; KLM Cabs, t (01946) 66007.

The Beacon
West Strand,
t (01946) 592302,
www.thebeacon-
whitehaven.co.uk; open
all year Tues–Sun and
Bank Holiday Mondays
10am–3.45pm; adm

The Rum Story
Lowther St,
t (01946) 592933,
www.rumstory.co.uk;
open daily
10am–3.45pm; adm

The people of Whitehaven are clearly proud of their maritime history and **The Beacon** is just one of the places where you learn all about this fascinating past. Located in the harbour itself, this award-winning visitor attraction houses some great interactive displays that adults and children alike will love. As well as getting a taste of life during the Industrial Revolution and experiencing a shipwreck, visitors can present their own TV-style weather forecasts in the Weather Zone.

Another award winner is the **Rum Story**. Located in the original 1785 shop, courtyards, cellars and bonded warehouses of the Jefferson family, the imaginatively designed and vivid displays bring to life the story of the rum-smuggling that once went on along the Cumbrian coast. Visitors travel through a tropical rainforest, complete with sound effects, and a slave ship to learn about the implications of the trade. Interestingly, the Jeffersons' office was used as Mr Heelis's office in the film *Miss Potter*, which was set and filmed largely in Cumbria.

St Bees

A few miles south of Whitehaven is the village of St Bees, the start of Wainwright's *Coast to Coast*. This long-distance walkers' route crosses northern England, from St Bees on the Irish Sea coast in Cumbria to Robin Hood's Bay on the North Sea coast in North Yorkshire. Its popularity – and people come from all over the world to complete it – lies mostly in the fact that it crosses three National Parks (the Lake District, the Yorkshire Dales and the North York Moors), almost undoubtedly the best scenery that England has to offer.

St Bees is said to be named after Bega, the daughter of an Irish king, who fled from the prospect of a forced marriage to a Viking chieftain. The story of her life and miracles appears in the 13th-century manuscript, *Life and Miracles of St Bega*, kept in the British Museum.

There are many legends associated with St Bega, including the story that she sailed single-handedly across the Irish Sea and became shipwrecked. Others claim she came with a group of nuns and asked the Lord of Egremont for land on which to build a nunnery. He is supposed to have said that she could have as much land as was covered by snow the following day. Despite it being midsummer, snow did fall that night and she got to build her nunnery. It was founded in the middle of the seventh century.

The nunnery was destroyed by Danes in the 10th century, but the Normans built a priory on the same site in the 12th century. All that remains of the priory today is the gorgeous parish church of **St Mary and St Bega**, which dates from about 1120. It has a magnificent Norman doorway as well as some earlier stone fragments. The **Beowulf Stone**, which depicts St George killing the dragon, is thought to pre-date the Norman Conquest, and another stone, located between the churchyard and the vicarage, is thought to be eighth century. It may even have come from the original nunnery.

The other striking red sandstone buildings of St Bees belong to the independent school, centred on a courtyard opposite the church's chancel. It was founded in 1583.

You can't wander around the village or take a stroll along the coast without noticing the striking red-coloured rock that dominates here. Red St Bees sandstone is a form of new red sandstone from the Triassic period, not to be confused with the slightly older new red sandstone that is found in the Eden Valley. In the 12th century, it was used to build St George's Chapel at Windsor Castle.

Just to the north of the village, the rock culminates in an exposed headland, the 320ft-high **St Bees Head**. On a coastline that is generally bereft of high cliffs, St Bees Head stands out in more ways than one. A walk from the village along the coast to the lighthouse is an invigorating one – with views, on a clear day, out to the Isle of Man. Just before you reach the lighthouse, watch for a stile in the fence on your left. This leads to a RSPB viewing area, where, armed with binoculars, you can watch the many species of birds on the guano-whitened cliffs. An information panel lists some of the most common ones, including kittiwakes, herring gulls, cormorants, puffins and razorbills. St Bees Head is also the only breeding site in England for black guillemots. Offshore are skuas and shearwaters. You may even be lucky enough to spot the odd dolphin or porpoise.

Ravenglass

If you have time to visit just one place along the coast, make it Ravenglass, the only coastal village within the National Park boundary. Situated on an estuary where three rivers meet – the Esk, the Irt and the Mite – it was once an important port. The Romans were the first to see its potential and built a fort here. Men and supplies from all over the empire landed here and then crossed Hardknott Pass to reach the fort at modern-day Ambleside. Not much remains of the Roman settlement now, except the impressive walls of the old bathhouse. These stand more than 11ft high, making them among the tallest and best preserved of Roman constructions in the north of England. Now known as **Walls Castle**, the remains can be found just outside the village, to the east of the main railway line.

Ravenglass was also once a base for brandy and tobacco smugglers as well as an important centre for pearl fishing. Today, it's a quieter spot, the port having silted up many centuries ago. With the La'al Ratty narrow gauge railway starting here, visitors use it as a jumping-off point for Eskdale.

The **main street**, which narrows at both ends to help contain the animals that were once brought here to the market, consists of a motley collection of well-kept old cottages. With little traffic to speak of, walking from the railway station to the slipway on the River Esk is like stepping back in time.

The extensive dunes to the north and south are home to Europe's largest colony of black-headed gulls and the salt marshes provide an important habitat for the rare natterjack toad. More than 250 species of wildflower, including the heart's-ease pansy, wild thyme, pyramidal orchid and the easily identified bee orchid can be found among the marram grass here. Sea lavender, thrift, sea purslane and glasswort grow on the saltmarsh. The large variety of flowers attracts a variety of insects, and dark-green fritillary, gatekeeper, common blue and meadow brown butterflies can be seen in the summer. Come winter and birds such as wigeon and goldeneye arrive from further north.

Muncaster Castle

Muncaster Castle
Ravenglass,
t (01229) 717614,
www.muncaster.co.uk;
castle open end
March–end Oct Sun–Fri
12–4.30pm; gardens,
maze and World Owl
Centre open end
March–end Oct daily
10.30am–6pm, Nov–Dec
daily 11am–4pm; adm

The Pennington family home since at least the 13th century – if not earlier – **Muncaster Castle** and its extensive, colourful gardens are open to the public throughout the summer, providing plenty of family entertainment.

Much of the majestic building that you see today is the product of extensive alterations in the 18th and 19th centuries, although it was built around a 1325 peel castle, supposedly on Roman foundations. With a building as old as this, you'd expect a few legends – as well as a ghost or two – and Muncaster doesn't disappoint. One of the family's greatest treasures is an enamelled green glass bowl, known as the 'Luck of Muncaster'. The story goes that, at some time in the 1460s, Sir John Pennington gave shelter to an exhausted Henry VI, who was found wandering nearby by shepherds after being defeated in a battle. As a token of his appreciation, on leaving, the king presented Sir John with his drinking bowl, saying that, as long as it remained intact, the Penningtons would prosper. The family still have it – all in one piece.

And ghosts? Well, there are many. The most famous is Tom Fool, the castle's 15th-century court jester and the source of the expression 'Tomfoolery'. When passersby used to stop at the castle and ask for directions to London, Tom would point them in the direction of the quicksands rather than the ford. He continues to create much mischief around the place today. A more sinister spirit is said to inhabit the Tapestry Room. People who have stayed the night here complain of disturbed nights or feeling inexplicably chilled. Some say they have heard babies crying or seen a dark figure leaning over them in bed.

Even if you're not 'lucky' enough to spot one of the Muncaster ghosts, a tour of the castle will allow you to see some gorgeous classical furniture, fine wood carvings and paintings by renowned artists such as Reynolds and Gainsborough.

A maze of paths, some of them quite steep, criss-crosses Muncaster's 70 acres of gardens and wooded slopes. If you're coming for the gardens, come in the spring when one of Europe's largest collection of rhododendrons is in flower. This magnificent riot of colour adds a touch of the exotic to this beautiful corner of the Lake District. There is also a good collection of magnolias, camellias and maples, as well as hydrangeas and unusual trees, such as the nothofagus, which originate from South America. The terrace is particularly impressive, with its lovely views across the fells.

There's plenty for children to do too, including the **Meadow Vole Maze**, two small playgrounds and the interactive suite with games and quizzes. The castle grounds are also home to the **World Owl Centre**, run by the World Owl Trust. There are more than 40 species of these fascinating birds on display and, every day at 2.30pm, weather permitting, some of the stars of the collection fly on the front lawns.

Where to Stay in Whitehaven and on the Coast

(i) **Whitehaven Tourist Information Centre**
Market Hall, Market Place t (01946) 598914 www.rediscoverwhitehaven.com. Open April–Oct Mon–Sat 9.30am–5pm, Sun 11am–3pm during school holidays only; Nov–Mar Mon–Sat 10am–4.30pm.

(★) **The Georgian House Hotel** >

Moresby Hall, Moresby, Whitehaven, t (01946) 696317, www.moresbyhall. co.uk (expensive). There are lots of nice touches in the four large bedrooms of this beautifully converted manor house – hydro-massage power showers and steam enclosure, huge four-posters, fluffy dressing gowns and high-quality bed linen. Everything about the place says 'class', even the delightful walled garden.

Fleatham House, High House Road, St Bees, t (01946) 822341, www. fleathamhouse.com (expensive– moderate). Beautiful, secluded woodland setting; friendly welcome; popular with holidaying politicians, including Tony Blair and family.

The Georgian House Hotel, Church Street, Whitehaven t (01946) 696611, www.thegeorgianhousehotel.net (expensive–moderate). Quality rooms in a large, attractive town–centre house on a quiet side street close to the harbour.

The Pennington, Main Street, Ravenglass, t (01229) 717222, www. penningtonhotels.com (expensive– moderate). Luxury accommodation in

a new hotel in a 16th-century inn close to the seafront.

Abbey Farm House, St Bees, t (01946) 823534, www.abbeyfarm-stbees.co.uk (moderate). Modernized farmhouse with lots of character. Comfortable, homely rooms, some with log fires, one double with separate private lounge area.

Queens Hotel, Main Street, St Bees t (01946) 822 287, www.marstonspubs. co.uk (moderate). Another one of Cumbria's lovely, 17th-century inns. Cosy bar has velvet settles around the edge and red lamp shades; 14 simple bedrooms.

Rosegarth, Main Street, Ravenglass t (01229) 717275, www.rosegarth.co.uk (moderate). Fairly small, but comfortable and bright rooms in this charming Victorian house. Plenty of storage space and great sea views.

Glenfield Guest House, Whitehaven, t (01946) 691911, www.glenfield- whitehaven.co.uk (moderate–budget). Good, friendly guesthouse with six comfortable rooms, all individually decorated and furnished but generally in a traditional style.

The Bay Horse, Main Street, Ravenglass, t (01229) 717015, www.bayhorseravenglass.co.uk (moderate–budget). Good value accommodation in a carefully restored

18th-century house with oak lintels, wooden doors, exposed beams and open fireplaces. Lovely guest rooms with wood panelling.

Where to Eat in Whitehaven and on the Coast

(★) Zest Restaurant >

Zest Restaurant, Low Road, Whitehaven t (01946) 692848, *www.zestwhitehaven.com (moderate)*. Loved by visitors and locals alike, it is best to book a table at this smart restaurant, probably the best in Whitehaven, serving dishes like wok-fried chilli and garlic baby squid; pan-roasted Scottish salmon fillet with chilli and lemon mash and wilted spinach. Everything is as delicious as it looks. *Closed Sun–Tues.*

Zest Harbourside, West Strand, Harbour, Whitehaven t (01946) 66981, *www.zestwhitehaven.com (moderate–budget)*. The snazzier, more relaxed sister act to Zest Restaurant. Superb location. Simple dishes, including lots of pasta and huge salads.

Courtyard Café, The Rum Story, Lowther St, Whitehaven t (01946) 592933, *www.rumstory.co.uk (budget)*. Airy café with glass roof and pleasant balcony serves good value lunches.

Entertainment in Whitehaven

Rosehill Theatre, Moresby, Whitehaven, t (01946) 692422, *www.rosehilltheatre.co.uk*. Small but popular theatre and musical venue about a mile north of Whitehaven off the A595. Varied programme.

Solway Coast

The Solway Firth – where the River Eden, after its journey from the North Pennines, meets the Irish Sea – is one of the country's biggest estuaries. On the northern side of the water is Dumfries & Galloway, and the hills of the Southern Uplands are clearly visible from the Cumbrian side. A designated Area of Outstanding Natural Beauty, it is home to a wide range of rare habitats, including vast salt marshes and sprawling sand dunes.

One of the most unusual features of the estuary is its tidal bore. A tidal bore occurs when the leading edge of the incoming tide forms a wave as it is funnelled into a shallow, narrowing river via a broad bay. In some conditions the tidal bore on the Eden reaches a height of about 3ft and travels at seven knots. At these times, the wave is clearly visible and the sudden rush of the water can be heard from quite some distance.

Maryport

Once a thriving industrial town and a port of national importance, Maryport is a quieter place these days. At the beginning of the 18th century, it was little more than a fishing creek at the mouth of the River Ellen, consisting of a few huts and a farmhouse that is now the Golden Lion Hotel. Then along came Humphrey Senhouse and his grid plan for a new town. Its wealth was based largely on coal and iron, and by 1777 there were three shipyards here. The greatest period of development and growth was the 19th century, particularly after the town was linked by rail to Carlisle in 1846.

Maryport's sad decline began in the Depression of the 1930s. It seemed that it would never recover when the harbour was finally closed in 1961 and the mines were run down over subsequent decades. For some time, an air of dereliction hung over the town, but there have been successful attempts to revive the place in recent years. A new, attractive marina has been built and some of the impressive Georgian buildings have been given a lick of paint.

Probably the most famous person to have been born in Maryport was Thomas Henry Ismay, the founder of the White Star Line shipping company, best known for its ill-fated flagship RMS *Titanic*. The young Ismay spent a lot of time down at the harbour, learning about navigation, and his first job was at his grandfather's shipyard in town.

Aside from the Senhouse Roman Museum (*see* below), which is the only must-see museum, there are a few other attractions in Maryport. The award-winning **Lake District Coast Aquarium**, always entertaining for the children, specializes in native British aquatic life, but also has three tropical tanks that are home to sea horses and banded humbug fish among others.

The small **Maritime Museum** tells the story of the docks, the shipbuilding industry and some of Maryport's most famous inhabitants, such as Ismay and Fletcher Christian's family. One of the most fascinating displays is a copy of HMS *Bounty*'s logbook. The museum also houses the town's tourist information centre.

Lake District Coast Aquarium
South Quay,
t (01900) 817760,
www.lakedistrict-coastaquarium.co.uk;
open daily 10am–5pm; adm

Maryport Maritime Museum
Senhouse St,
t (01900) 813738;
Mon–Sat 10am–4pm

Roman Maryport

Long before Humphrey Senhouse came along, the place that we now call Maryport was a Roman port. This section of the coast formed part of the Roman Empire's northwestern frontier. Although Hadrian's Wall ended at Bowness-on-Solway, the defences didn't stop there. The section of coast between Maryport and the wall was a particular problem for the Romans because of its close proximity to Scotland. To combat this weak link, they built a series of fortlets interspersed with small towers. The full extent of these defences is unknown, but there are remains of mile-fortlets all the way between Port Carlisle and Maryport. Maryport itself, known as Alauna in Roman times, is likely to have been the command headquarters for these coastal defences as well as a major supply depot for some of the Hadrian's Wall forts.

Senhouse Roman Museum
Sea Brows,
t (01900) 816168,
www.senhousemuseum.co.uk;
Apr–June Thurs–Sun and Tues 10am–5pm; July–Oct daily 10am–5pm; Nov–Mar Fri–Sun 10.30am–4pm; adm

The **Senhouse Roman Museum**, housed in a Victorian battery overlooking the harbour, is well worth a visit. It has a large collection of inscribed altar stones. The collection, one of the largest private archaeological collections in the country, was started in 1570 by John Senhouse, Lord of the Manor of Ellenborough. He gathered inscribed stones from the Roman fort and civilian town lying along the coastal ridge above the Manor House and set them within the walls of the family mansion. The stones would have once belonged to auxiliary regiments, most notably the First Cohort of Spaniards, who were garrisoned here between AD 132 and 138. A new altar would have been dedicated annually on the emperor's birthday – usually to Jupiter, the god of war – and the old disposed of. The inscriptions give potted biographies of the auxiliary commanders, including name, birthplace, rank, previous postings and time spent at Maryport. One commander,

Getting to and around the Solway Coast

By Train

Maryport is on the **Carlisle to Barrow-in-Furness line**, which serves Cumbria's coastal towns and villages. Journey time to Carlisle, where there are then trains to Glasgow, London, Newcastle, Leeds, Manchester and Birmingham, is approximately 35 minutes. Journey time to Whitehaven is about 25 minutes.

By Local Bus

The hourly **60 bus** links Maryport with Silloth and Skinburness (journey time 30 minutes). The **58** bus between Maryport and Cockermouth runs every two hours (45 minutes). The hourly **300/301** bus service, which runs between Carlisle and Whitehaven, stops at Maryport. The journey time to Carlisle is about one hour; to Whitehaven, about 50 minutes. Silloth is also served by the **38** to Carlisle via Wigton (six buses daily, total journey time 40 minutes). Bowness-on-Solway and Burgh By Sands lie on the route of the **93** bus to Carlisle (five buses daily, journey time from Bowness to Carlisle 45 minutes). Most local buses do not run on Sundays. An additional service, the **AD122** or **Hadrian's Wall Bus**, visits Bowness-on-Solway and neighbouring villages three times a day every day between Easter and the end of October.

By Taxi

Keith's Kabs in Maryport, t (01900) 818686; Able Taxis in Silloth, t (01697) 731508.

Marcus Maenius Agrippa, was known to have been a personal friend of Emperor Hadrian, so Maryport must have been a prestigious posting.

Also within the museum grounds is an observation tower, a superb addition that allows visitors to get a clear view of the earthworks. These are all that remain of the Roman fort *in situ*.

Up the Coast to Silloth

The Solway Coast Area of Outstanding Natural Beauty was designated in 1964 and stretches from Maryport in the south to Rockcliffe in the north. It contains a wide range of fragile habitats, including the sand dunes along this section of the coast. These are home to wildflowers such as wild thyme, lady's bedstraw, restharrow, birds-foot trefoil and harebell. Take a walk through the dunes, which are mostly access land, and there is a good chance you will see large flocks of curlew, oystercatcher, little terns, bartailed godwit and little plover. Some nest in the strandline vegetation; others, like the curlew, head inland to nest on the moors of the North Pennines (*see* p.212). The area is also home to the rare natterjack toad, and the gorse and scrub has to be managed to improve the habitat for these noisy amphibians.

St John's Church, Crosscanonby contains items dating back to Norse times. Inside the porch are a cross shaft and cross head. A small grave-marker, bearing an incised cross, lies on a windowsill in the south aisle. Unfortunately, the church is normally locked, but you can also see part of a 10th-century hogback tomb in the churchyard, near the porch.

Nearby, just a little further up the coast, are some of the best preserved **saltpans** in the area. For almost 700 years, salt was extracted from seawater by filtering the water into a lagoon and then boiling it to extract the salt. Before the development of refrigeration, salt was used in large quantities by the local fishing industry. At one time, salt production was the third most important industry behind agriculture and fishing, and there was a chain of saltpans stretching from the head of the Solway all the way down the Cumbrian coast to Millom.

Allonby, an 18th-century seaside resort and once an important herring fishing centre, still has some interesting Georgian and Victorian buildings, including the Old Baths, an impressive colonnaded building in what was once the main street. There is also a Reading Room dating back to the 1860s, designed by Alfred Waterhouse, who designed Manchester's Town Hall and London's Natural History Museum.

In certain conditions, the beach becomes a good spot for both wind- and kitesurfers. At the first hint of warm weather, north Cumbrians flock to Allonby to take part in what has become almost a spring tradition in this part of the county – a stroll along the long, sandy beach with a Twentyman's ice cream in hand. This tasty treat has been handmade in the village to a secret recipe since the 1920s. Try the Allonby Whopper – an enormous cornet of ice cream and fruit.

A few miles up the coast, you come to **Silloth**, a surprisingly grand and airy Victorian seaside resort with elegant, tree-lined cobbled streets and 36 acres of grassy open space known as 'The Green'. An impressive promenade runs for more than a mile from Silloth to Skinburness, on the edge of the Solway marshes. Take a stroll along the front in the late evening to appreciate the wonderful sunset over the Scottish hills to the west, so fine that even the landscape painter Turner was inspired to capture it on canvas. You may even catch sight of one of the porpoises that frequent these waters.

The Solway Marshes

Turning your back on the sea and heading east from Silloth, you travel across a flat landscape composed mostly of farmland and lowland peat bogs, fringed by salt marshes that go on for miles. Every winter, the entire population of barnacle geese from the Svalbard archipelago in the Arctic Ocean descends on the English and Scottish marshes of the Solway Firth – between 25,000 and 30,000 birds, impressive both to see and hear. Thousands of other swans, ducks and geese also take advantage of the relatively mild Solway winters, as do snow bunting, twite and glaucous and Iceland gulls. The Solway is also a major migration route for seabirds such as the pomarine skua in the spring and shearwaters and storm petrels in late summer. If you're hoping to see the birds, the minor road from Cardurnock to Bowness-on-Solway has several lay-bys that provide excellent viewing opportunities. The RSPB reserve at **Campfield Marsh** also has a wheelchair-accessible hide looking out over an area of wet grassland where lapwing, redshank and snipe breed in the summer and thousands of geese and swans spend the winter.

The complex system of tall aerials that you can see from all along this part of the estuary is located at Anthorn. These are used to communicate with NATO submarines. This transmitter is also the home of the National Physical Laboratory's three atomic clocks, which provide the UK's time signal, the source of the 'pips' heard on BBC radio.

Bowness-on-Solway marks the western end of Hadrian's Wall. Although little can be seen of the wall or its associated defences west of Carlisle, the popular 84-mile Hadrian's Wall Trail terminates in this unassuming little village. There used to be a viaduct here, linking Bowness with Scotland, but, following years of storm damage, it was deemed unsafe and demolished in 1934.

Another failed transport scheme resulted in the building of nearby Port Carlisle. A 29-mile canal was built between Carlisle and this place, then known as Fishers' Cross, in 1823, improving the city's links with Liverpool in particular. Within just a few years though, it was experiencing financial difficulties, and the subsequent growth of the railways was the final nail in its coffin.

Further east, having taken the long, straight road across the Burgh Marsh, you come to pretty **Burgh by Sands** with its impressive church, where King Edward I's body lay in state in 1307. Edward had been at war with the Scots since 1295, leading his army into battle on several occasions – hence his nickname, Hammer of the Scots. He died of dysentery while camped on Burgh Marsh, close to the place where his army was hoping to cross the River Eden at low tide to enter Scotland. A monument was first built on the marsh in 1685 to mark the site where he died. There is also a bronze statue of the king on the village green close to the Greyhound Inn. This was unveiled in 2007 to commemorate the 700th anniversary of the king's death.

A few miles south of Burgh is Great Orton where a group of local people have established an 200-acre nature reserve on a former airfield that was also used as a burial ground for culled livestock during the 2001 foot and mouth outbreak. The **Watchtree Nature Reserve** has hay meadows, wetlands and woodlands that are home to more than 60 species of bird, red squirrels, hares, five species of bat and a variety of unusual invertebrates and amphibians. The Friends of Watchtree organize guided walks and other events. Cycles adapted for disabled people to use on the disused runways and on a specially built trail are also available, providing access to several bird hides around the reserve.

Watchtree Nature Reserve
01228 712539,
www.watchtree.co.uk

Holme Cultram Abbey

Much of the farmland on the Solway Plain was shaped by the Cistercian monks of Holme Cultram Abbey in Abbey Town. They set up their abbey in 1150 under the rule of Melrose Abbey in Scotland. Its foundation charter was granted by David I of Scotland, but the land soon passed into English hands. Ironically, the abbey's Scottish origins did not protect it from the unwanted attentions of Scottish raiders and Robert the Bruce devastated it in 1319, even though his own father, Robert de Bruce, the Earl of Carrick, was buried in the grounds.

In 1536, at the time of Henry VIII's Dissolution of the Monasteries, the abbot, Thomas Carter, joined the Pilgrimage of Grace, the uprising against the king's seizure of church lands. When it failed, the king wreaked savage retribution against the abbeys that had taken part.

Consequently, all that remains of the abbey today is the parish church, **St Mary's**, and this is only standing thanks to the pleas of local people, who claimed it was the only building in the area that provided adequate protection against Scottish raids. The nave dates from the 12th century, but the walls were built in the 18th century. Much of the interior of the church and its roof were sadly destroyed by an arson attack in 2006, but restoration is expected to be completed soon.

The monks of Holme Cultram also built St John's in nearby Newton Arlosh, a fine example of the fortified churches built in the border area in the 14th century. Access to the castellated pele tower was via a narrow doorway in the thick wall. In times of attack, the villagers would round up their animals, and take refuge inside.

(★) Hesket House

>>

(i) Silloth Tourist
Information Centre
*Solway Coast Discovery
Centre, Liddel Street
(opposite Texaco garage),
t (016973) 31944, www.
solwaycoastaonb.org.uk;
open daily 10am–4pm.*

Festivals and Events on the Solway Coast

Every summer, Maryport plays host to an international **blues festival** (*www.maryportblues.co.uk*) which, in the past few years, has attracted names like Van Morrison, Dionne Warwick, Chuck Berry and Jools Holland.

Every summer, Tarns near Silloth plays host to one of the most family-friendly music festivals around. The atmospheric and laid-back **Solfest** (*www.solwayfestival.co.uk*) has a special area dedicated to under-fives and their parents, supervised by qualified staff. Past acts have included Supergrass and The Charlatans.

Where to Stay on the Solway Coast

Hunday Manor Hotel, Hunday, near Workington, t (01900) 61798, *www.hunday-manor-hotel.co.uk* (*expensive*). Imposing 18th-century hall surrounded by four acres of beautiful, well-kept grounds with mature trees and great Solway sunsets. Immaculate rooms, all individually decorated and some with reproduction furniture, refurbished in 2008. Large lounge bar area and good á la carte **restaurant.**

Golf Hotel, Criffel Street, Silloth, t (016973) 31438, *www.golfhotelsilloth. co.uk* (*expensive–moderate*). Popular with golfers and close to the seafront, this hotel was partly refurbished in 2008. Superior (refurbished) rooms have bright, simple décor and large beds. Older rooms are slightly old-fashioned but spacious. Great views across Solway Firth from front rooms.

Hesket House, Port Carlisle, t (016973) 51876 or 07980 857 086, *www.hesket house.com* (*moderate*). A warm, friendly welcome awaits visitors to this bright and cheerful 18th-century house. The owners have clearly devoted a lot of time and imagination to furniture and décor. Lovely views.

The Queen's, Park Terrace, Silloth, t (016973) 31373, *moregain@tiscali. co.uk* (*moderate–budget*). What looks like a grand, old Victorian hotel from the outside turns out to be a simple, but pleasant B&B inside. High ceilings in the two airy rooms.

Where to Eat on the Solway Coast

Oily's, Winscales, near Workington, t (01900) 66655, *www.oilyspub.co.uk* (*moderate*). This bright, modern pub has a small patio area for al fresco dining with views across to the fells. Traditional meals include pan-fried duck breast and Cumberland sausage. Also a good range of pasta dishes and risotto. Decent vegetarian selection.

The Hope and Anchor Inn, Port Carlisle, t (016973) 51460, *www.hope andanchorinn.com* (*budget*). Simple but tasty pub meals (lamb shank, steak and kidney pudding, salmon-and-dill fish cakes) in a comfortable and friendly setting.

Entertainment on the Solway Coast

The Wave Centre, Irish Street, Maryport, t (01900) 811450, *www.thewavemaryport.co.uk*. Modern complex with a 234-seat theatre and cinema.

East Cumbria and Hadrian's Wall

If the eastern fringes of Cumbria were anywhere but right next to the Lake District, they would draw tourists by the bucketload. As it is, few venture this far from the National Park, leaving locals to delight in the fact that they have this beautiful area of the country all to themselves. The River Eden meanders majestically through an ever-changing panorama – with the land rising to the eerie border forests in the north and to the lonely moors of the North Pennines and the Yorkshire Dales in the east. Much of this is border country, where Hadrian built his famous wall to keep out the 'barbarians', and villages and towns, most notably Carlisle, were ravaged by centuries of warfare between the English and the Scots.

12

Don't miss

⭐ **Visit the historic border city**
Carlisle p.197

⭐ **Wander around a beautiful priory**
Lanercost Priory p.200

⭐ **Discover hidden sections of Hadrian's Wall**
Birdoswald Roman Fort p.200

⭐ **Climb to the highest point in the Pennines**
Cross Fell p.213

⭐ **Enjoy a peaceful market town**
Sedbergh p.215

See map overleaf

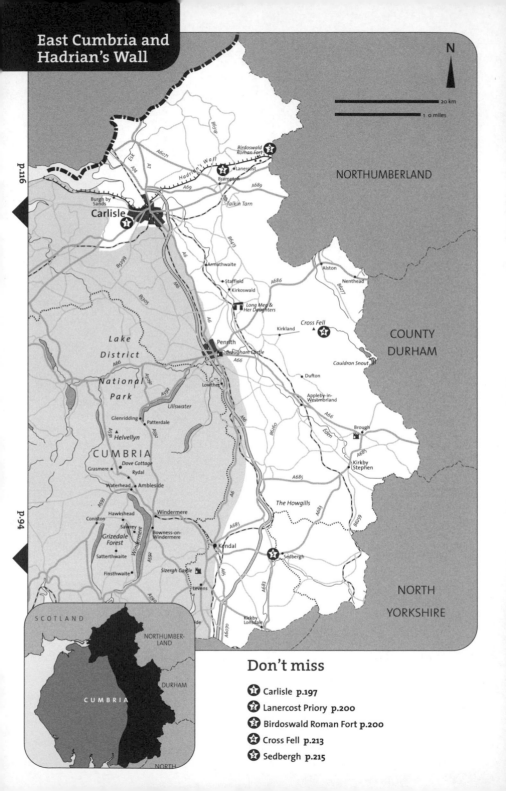

N

20 km

1 0 miles

p.116

p.94

NORTHUMBERLAND

COUNTY
DURHAM

NORTH

YORKSHIRE

Birdoswald
Roman Fort
Lanercost
Brampton
Hadrian's Wall
Burgh by
Sands
Carlisle
Talkin Tarn
Armathwaite
Alston
Nenthead
Staffield
Kirkoswald
Long Meg &
Her Daughters
Kirkland
Cross Fell
Penrith
Brougham Castle
Cauldron Snout
Dufton
Lowther
Appleby-in-
Westmorland
Lake
District
National
Park
Ullswater
Glenridding
Patterdale
Brough
Kirkby
Stephen
Helvellyn
CUMBRIA
Dove Cottage
Grasmere
Rydal
Waterhead
Ambleside
The Howgills
Hawkshead
Windermere
Coniston
Sawrey
Bowness-on-
Windermere
Grizedale
Forest
Kendal
Sedbergh
Satterthwaite
Finsthwaite
Sizergh Castle
Levens
Kirkby
Lonsdale

A6071
A7
A689
A69
A595
A6
A686
A66
A590
A592
A591
A685
A683
A6099
A6070
B6318
B6413
B6412
B6277

SCOTLAND

NORTHUMBER-
LAND

DURHAM

CUMBRIA

NORTH

Don't miss

Carlisle and Hadrian's Wall

⭐ **Carlisle**

With a population of about 70,000, Carlisle is Cumbria's largest settlement and its only city. It has been an important administrative centre for nearly two millennia – since the Romans established Luguvallium here and then built Hadrian's Wall, which crossed the River Eden at Carlisle. In the troubled centuries that followed Roman rule, control of the city passed from Celts to Anglians to Scots to English to Scots to English to Scots to English... Carlisle's history from at least the 11th century onwards is the history of England's border with Scotland, a troubled, very often bloody history. No other English city has endured so many assaults on it, and its red fortress was held by the Scots as recently as 1745. Today, it's a more peaceful place – a small city where well-kept hanging baskets adorn the beautiful sandstone buildings that once witnessed so much bloodshed, and dozens of bustling cafés cater for the many day-trippers who drop in while walking Hadrian's Wall or travelling on the Carlisle-to-Settle railway line.

Opposite the railway station, forming a grand southern entrance, are the two huge oval towers of the **Citadel**, once home to the assize courts and a prison. Although not generally open to the public, there are guided tours of the western tower throughout the summer. For details, contact the Tourist Information Centre in the old Town Hall.

Carlisle Guildhall
Green Market,
t (01228) 618718,
www.tulliehouse.co.uk;
open daily Apr–Oct
12pm–4.30pm; adm

The **old Town Hall**, built in 1770, is right on the edge of the historic heart of the city. Opposite is the modest **Guildhall Museum**. Dating from the 14th century, it is one of Carlisle's four oldest structures. Each floor of the half-timbered building projects out over the one beneath, a way of using less ground to create a larger home. The house was used as a meeting place for the town's eight medieval trade guilds, and the museum today contains items relating to those guilds and the general history of Carlisle. Visitors can also see much of the building's original timber structure as well as rare wattle-and-daub walls.

Carlisle Cathedral
Carlisle,
t (01228) 548151,
www.carlislecathedral.
org.uk; open Mon–Sat
7.30am–6.15pm, Sun
7.30am–5pm; donations
welcome

Just around the corner is the beautiful red sandstone **cathedral**. Founded in 1122 as an Augustinian abbey church, the interior is less austere than many of England's larger cathedrals and includes some fine tracery in the 14th-century east window and impressive medieval craftsmanship in the form of 15th-century choir stalls and misericords. And just look up at that wonderful painted ceiling – blue and starry, it's quite a sight. Some visitors may be disappointed at the cathedral's size, but its diminutive stature is due to the fact that six bays of the nave were carted away during the Civil War to repair the castle's walls.

Tullie House Museum and Art Gallery
Castle St,
t (01228) 618718,
www.tulliehouse.co.uk;
open Nov–March
Mon–Sat 10am–4pm,
Sun 12pm–4pm;
April–June and
Sept–Oct Mon–Sat
10am–5pm, Sun
12pm–5pm; July–Aug
Mon–Sat 10am–5pm,
Sun 11am–5pm; adm

Between the cathedral and the castle is the award-winning **Tullie House Museum and Art Gallery**. Housed in a 17th-century building with a modern frontage, this excellent museum contains lots of cleverly designed exhibits that tell the fascinating story of the city in an interesting, accessible way. Roman artefacts and Norse burial goods are among the items on show. Bloodcurdling tales of the Border Reivers and the Jacobite rebellion of 1745 keep visitors enthralled. Downstairs, the galleries house fine art including some Pre-Raphaelite gems. The museum also has a good restaurant and gift shop.

12 East Cumbria and Hadrian's Wall | Carlisle and Hadrian's Wall

Getting to and around Carlisle

By Train and Coach

Carlisle is on the West Coast Main Line, with direct **trains** to Glasgow, Crewe, Manchester, Birmingham and London Euston. The **Cumbria Coast and Furness lines** link Carlisle with Barrow-in-Furness before going on to Lancaster. There are also rail links between Carlisle and Newcastle via Brampton (roughly every hour; journey time, one hour and 25 minutes) and between Carlisle and Leeds via the scenic **Carlisle-to-Settle railway line** (about six trains a day; journey time, two hours and 45 minutes).

National Express runs several daily services from London to Carlisle (average journey time, seven hours). There are also at least six **coaches** (service **334**) every day linking Carlisle with Glasgow (journey time, two hours), Manchester (four hours) and Birmingham International Airport (seven hours).

By Local Bus

Buses converge on Carlisle from all over the county. A particularly useful service for tourists is the **Hadrian's Wall Bus AD122**, which runs between Carlisle and Newcastle during the summer, stopping off along the way at all the major sites along Hadrian's Wall (see p.201).

By Taxi

Radio Taxis, t (01228) 527575; Beeline Taxis, t (01228) 534440; Metro Taxis, t (01228) 522088; Carlisle Drivers, t (01228) 590590; and City Taxis, t (01228) 520000 – all in Carlisle.

By Bicycle

Scotby Cycles on Caldewgate (opposite McVitie's), t (01228) 546931, *www.bikebike.co.uk*. Closed Sun.

The underground Millennium Gallery links the main part of Tullie House with the castle. This is home to the **'Cursing Stone'**, which has been blamed for the city's devastating 2005 flood. The curse against the reivers, now written on a granite boulder, was made by the clearly unhappy archbishop of Glasgow in 1525: 'I curse their head and all the hairs of their head; I curse their face, their brain (innermost thoughts), their mouth, their nose, their tongue, their teeth, their forehead... ' It goes on – for more than 1,000 words, in fact.

Carlisle's original motte-and-bailey castle was built by William Rufus in 1092 on the site of a Roman fortress. The oldest surviving part of

Carlisle Castle
t (01228) 591922, www.englishheritage.org. uk; open daily Apr–Sept 9.30am–5pm, Oct–Mar 10am–4pm; adm

Carlisle Castle today is the keep, begun in the 12th century by Henry I of England and completed by David I of Scotland, a good illustration of how control over the border city was constantly changing hands. The keep is the highlight of any visit today – its basement dungeons home to the spine-chilling 'licking stones', the damp walls that thirsty Jacobite rebels had to lick for moisture to stay alive. Upstairs are some equally fascinating carvings made by prisoners in the late 15th century. Interesting displays tell the story of the castle's role in an horrendous, eight-month siege during the Civil War, the Jacobite uprising of 1745 and Mary Queen of Scot's 'imprisonment'.

Also contained within the castle grounds, in Queen Mary's Tower, is the **King's Own Royal Border Regiment Museum**, telling the 300-year-old history of the area's infantry regiment. Free entry to the museum is included in the castle admission fee.

Below the castle, on the south side of the River Eden is Bitts Park, a pleasant combination of open spaces, tree-lined avenues and colourful gardens. On the northeast side of the river is the more natural Rickerby Park. A riverside route, muddy in places, leads all the way from Rickerby

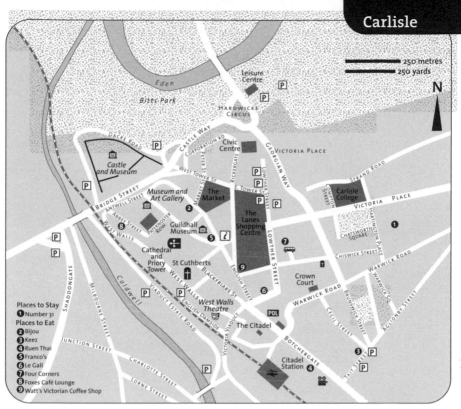

Carlisle

250 metres
250 yards

N

Eden

Leisure Centre

Bitts Park

HARDWICKE CIRCUS

DACRE ROAD

CASTLE WAY

CORPORATION RD

Civic Centre

GEORGIAN WAY

VICTORIA PLACE

Castle and Museum

WEST TOWER ST

PETER ST

RICKERGATE

LOWTHER STREET

STRAND ROAD

COMPTON STREET

Carlisle College

VICTORIA PLACE

HARTINGTON PLACE

BRIDGE STREET

ANTWELL STREET

Museum and Art Gallery

The Market

E TOWER ST

CHATSWORTH SQUARE

ABBEY STREET

PATENORTH ROW

Guildhall Museum

The Lanes Shopping Centre

LOWTHER STREET

CHISWICK STREET

WEST WALLS

Cathedral and Priory Tower

St Cuthberts

WEST WALLS

BLACKFRIARS ST

ENGLISH STREET

Crown Court

WARWICK ROAD

WARWICK SQ

SHADDONGATE

Coldwell

VIADUCT ESTATE ROAD

WEST WALLS

West Walls Theatre

ENGLISH DAMSIDE

POL

WARWICK ROAD

BRUNSWICK STREET

CECIL STREET

AGLIONBY STREET

MILBOURNE STREET

JUNCTION STREET

The Citadel

VICTORIA VIADUCT

BOTCHERGATE

CHARLOTTE STREET

LORNE STREET

Citadel Station

TAIT STREET

Places to Stay
1 Number 31
Places to Eat
2 Bijou
3 Keez
4 Ruen Thai
5 Franco's
6 Le Gall
7 Four Corners
8 Foxes Café Lounge
9 Watt's Victorian Coffee Shop

Park to the salt marshes at the mouth of the River Eden near Rockcliffe, more than nine miles away. Walkers may be lucky enough to see kingfishers and otters along this stretch of the river. The route passes close to several interesting historical sites, including the ruins of the '**fish house**' at King Garth. The Eden is an important salmon fishery and the king granted part of the fishery to the City of Carlisle in the 12th century. The 'fish house' was built in 1733 to house bailiffs and boats. Mayoral dinners were also held here until 1892 when the fishery was abandoned.

Around Carlisle

The unassuming village of **Wreay**, a few miles south of Carlisle, is home to a hidden gem of 19th-century church architecture. Shaped like a Roman basilica, **St Mary's Church** was built and paid for by local amateur architect Sara Losh in 1840–42. Sara was the daughter of a forward-thinking industrialist, a friend of William Wordsworth. She was brought up as her father's heir and received a well-rounded education – something which she put to good use when designing the church in memory of her beloved sister Catherine. The highly original building features crocodile gargoyles, an Italian green marble altar, an apse surrounded by an arcade of 14 pillars and a multitude of carvings – an extraordinary and fascinating mixture of styles. Outside is a replica of the Bewcastle Cross (*see* p.202).

About nine miles from Carlisle lies the peaceful market town of Brampton. The Tourist Information Centre is housed in the octagonal **Moot Hall**, built in 1817. Nearby is the parish church of St Martin, not a particularly attractive building in its own right, but inside are a set of glorious stained glass windows created by William Morris and Edward Burne-Jones. That great scholar and critic of British architecture, Sir Nikolaus Pevsner, described them as 'glowing with gem-stone colours'.

South of Brampton is **Talkin Tarn country park**, a beauty spot that is extremely popular with local people all year round – even when bitter winds blow in off the surrounding Pennines and the water in the tarn freezes over. Should you visit on such a day, there is a small café where you can get hot drinks and snacks.

Nearby, woodland paths wind through the gorge formed by the River Gelt. Here, the red sandstone cliffs are home to a rich variety of plant, bird and animal life as well as a host of fascinating local legends of bloody battles, cattle rustling and a sheep thief who fell from a crag to his death while trying to escape his pursuers. The gorge is also home to the Roman '**Written Rock of Gelt**'. Dating back to AD 207, it records the quarry workings of Roman soldiers belonging to the Second Legion.

Heading north, towards the great Roman wall, you quickly reach Lanercost, the site of one of the most beautiful of Augustinian priories.

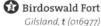 **Lanercost Priory**

Lanercost, Brampton, t (01697) 73030, www.englishheritage. org.uk; open Apr–Sept daily 10am–5pm, Oct–Nov Thurs–Mon 10am–4pm; adm

Located in a pretty vale beside the meandering River Irthing, **Lanercost Priory** was founded in 1166, but being so close to the Scottish border, it has had a turbulent history. The priory suffered its first raid in 1280 following a visit by Edward I, but the most damaging attack came in 1346 when King David II of Scotland ransacked the monastic buildings, desecrated the priory church and wasted the surrounding lands. Lanercost's unusual claim to fame is that, for five months at the beginning of the 14th century, a dying Edward I ruled his kingdoms from here, having summoned Parliament to Carlisle and moved the seals of the crown to Lanercost, effectively making it the capital. At the Dissolution of the Monasteries in 1536, the site was granted to Sir Thomas Dacre, who converted the west-range buildings into a private residence; and, in the middle of the 19th century, the ruins of the nave were restored and turned into an attractive parish church by the renowned architect Anthony Salvin. The substantial remains of the north and south transepts, the choir, the sanctuary and the cellarium are now in the care of English Heritage.

Hadrian's Wall passed through Lanercost, and there was a Roman camp on the high ground overlooking the site where the priory now stands. Very little of the Roman remains can be seen here today, but a

Birdoswald Fort

Gilsland, t (016977) 47602, www.englishheritage.org. uk; open daily Apr–Sept 10am–5pm, Oct–Mar 10am–4pm; adm

little further up the road is **Birdoswald**, the site of one of the best preserved forts along Hadrian's Wall. This would once have housed up to 1,000 soldiers. There has been a lot of building on the site since the Romans departed, including the turreted farmhouse that you can see today, but three main gates of the ancient fortress are still traceable, along with perimeter walls, towers, granaries and an unusual drill hall. An on-site visitor centre provides an interpretation of the site and engagingly describes the wall's history through a series of audiovisual presentations and archaeological artefacts.

Hadrian's Wall

Hadrian's Wall was constructed under the orders of the Emperor Hadrian after his visit to Britain in AD 122. He wanted, according to his biographer, to 'separate the Romans from the barbarians'. Over the next six years, professional soldiers, or legionaries, built a wall about 15ft high and 80 Roman miles long (73 modern miles) from Wallsend on the River Tyne in the east to Bowness-on-Solway in Cumbria in the west. Today, it is a UNESCO World Heritage Site.

As well as significant sections of the wall, which sometimes cross spectacularly rugged scenery, visitors can today see remains of some of the fortlets, or milecastles, that were positioned every Roman mile along the length of the Roman Empire's northwest frontier. Between each milecastle were turrets probably used for observation and signalling purposes. There were also 16 forts built to defend the wall, each housing between 500 and 1,000 troops. Birdoswald was just one of these. Other fort remains can be seen at Housesteads, just over the county border in Northumberland.

In May 2003, an 84-mile National Trail running the entire length of the wall was opened (www.nationaltrail.co.uk or www.hadrians-wall.org). The Hadrian's Wall Path has proved tremendously popular, bringing a welcome injection of tourism cash into the region but, at the same time, causing erosion. Unable to cope with the influx of walkers, rangers have, in fact, asked people to avoid using the trail during the winter when footpaths – and the underlying archaeology – are most at risk.

Below the fort, the River Irthing has carved an attractive, steep-sided valley with gorge-like sections that make for pleasant walking. Where Hadrian's Wall crossed the river, near Gilsland, visitors can see the substantial remains of the bridge abutments, complete with interpretative panels to help you make sense of the stonework.

If you are planning on visiting sites along Hadrian's Wall, in Cumbria or Northumberland, the **Hadrian's Wall Bus AD122** will prove very useful. Starting in Carlisle, with some services going as far as Newcastle, this little bus shuttles backwards and forwards between Lanercost, Birdoswald, Gilsland, the Roman Army Museum at Walltown, Haltwhistle, Vindolanda, Housesteads, Chesters and Hexham. The vehicle is equipped to carry bicycles and, at the height of the season, a guide provides a running commentary.

Hadrian's Wall Bus AD122
Hadrian's Wall Day Rover costs £8 for adult, £5 for children; 3-day and 7-day tickets also available

The tiny village of **Gilsland** sits right on Cumbria's border with Northumberland. In Victorian times, the foul-smelling spa waters here were almost as famous as those in Buxton and Harrogate, and a luxury hotel was built to cater for the needs of those who came to sample it. The spring is still there, housed in a stone alcove, right down in the bottom of the Irthing Gorge, a deep, dark ravine cloaked in thick woodland. The gorge has public rights of way running through it, and is a lovely place for a walk, especially in spring and autumn. A young Walter Scott proposed to his wife, Charlotte, here in 1797 after a whirlwind romance. The 'Popping Stone', where he is said to have popped the question, is on the Cumbrian side of the river, just north of the hotel. Charlotte, incidentally, said yes and the couple were married in Carlisle on Christmas Eve of the same year.

Beyond Gilsland are huge and lonely tracts of forest, a military site that was once cloaked in secrecy and thousands of acres of bleak and boggy moors. Settlements are few and extremely far between.

The military site referred to above is **RAF Spadeadam**, which once specialized in the development of Cold War defence technology. It was the test site in the 1950s and 1960s for the Blue Streak, the launch rocket for satellites and, more intriguingly, Britain's intended

Intermediate Range Ballistic Missile. Today, the site plays an important role in preparing UK and NATO air crews and ground-based air-defence units for combat in war zones such as Afghanistan. If you want to know more about the Blue Streak programme, rocket engines and a model of Spadeadam's rocket launch facility can be seen at the **Solway Aviation Museum** at Carlisle Airport.

One of the few settlements up here in the sparsely populated border area is **Bewcastle**, a scattering of lonely farmsteads. The church of **St Cuthbert** dates from the early 13th century, although much of the building you see today went up in the late 18th century. The church itself is pleasant enough, but it is the Anglo-Saxon cross in the graveyard that makes a trip to this far-flung outpost worthwhile. The 15ft-high shaft, now sadly missing its cross, dates from about AD 680. It bears several runic inscriptions, including one that mentions Jesus. The vine scrolls and intricately carved figures of Christ, St John the Baptist and various animals are remarkable. The Bewcastle cross and its cousin at Ruthwell on the Scottish side of the Solway coast, are among the finest to survive from Anglo-Saxon Britain.

Solway Aviation Museum
Aviation House, Carlisle Airport, Crosby-on-Eden, t (01228) 573823, www.solway-aviation-museum.co.uk; April–Oct Sat, Sun and Bank Holidays 10.30am–5pm; adm

East Cumbria and Hadrian's Wall | Carlisle and Hadrian's Wall

⭐ **Willowbeck Lodge** >>

ⓘ **Carlisle Tourist Information Centre**
Old Town Hall, Green Market, t (01228) 625600; open March–Oct Mon–Sat 9.30am–5pm, Sun 10.30am–4pm, Nov–Feb Mon–Sat 10am–4pm

ⓘ **Brampton Tourist Information Centre**
Moot Hall, Market Place, Brampton, t (016977) 3433; open Easter–Sept Mon–Sat 10am–5pm, Oct Mon–Sat 10am–4pm

Festivals and Events

The annual **Cumberland Show** (www.cumberlandshow.co.uk) is held every July with displays of farming, rural life and local products. Also in July, Brampton plays hosts to the biggest folk/roots festival in the north of England. The excellent **Brampton Live** (www.bramptonlive.net) attracts artists from all around the globe.

Where to Stay in Carlisle

Farlam Hall, Brampton, t (01697) 746234, www.farlamhall.co.uk (expensive–moderate). A family-run, rambling old manor house set in 12 acres of peaceful grounds at the foot of the Pennines. While some of the bedrooms are charmingly old-fashioned, facilities are anything but.

The Weary, Castle Carrock, t (01228) 670230, www.theweary.com (expensive–moderate). This rather cool establishment isn't what you'd expect to find in a sleepy little village at the foot of the Pennines. Luxurious rooms feature sumptuous beds, massive shower heads and inset TV screens that you can watch from the comfort of the deep bathtub. The classy **restaurant** (expensive) has an AA rosette (closed to non-residents Mon).

Willowbeck Lodge, Lambley Bank, Scotby, t (01228) 513607, www.willow beck-lodge.com (expensive–moderate). The words 'purpose-built' and 'hotel' don't normally sit well together, but Willowbeck Lodge is the exception to the rule. This exquisitely-designed house has bright, elegant guest bedrooms and a stunning dining area with an enormous window looking out on to the duck pond.

Bessiestown Farm Country Guesthouse, Catlowdy, Longtown, t (01228) 577219, www.bessiestown. co.uk (moderate). Remote but, well worth the effort it takes to get here. Each room has a fridge with fresh milk and chilled water – a simple touch, but appreciated. The hearty breakfasts are simply gorgeous.

Lanercost Serviced Apartments, Abbey Farm, Lanercost, t (016977) 41267, www.lanercost.co.uk (moderate). This has to be among the best-value accommodation in the whole of Cumbria. Lovely, modern rooms in recently converted farm buildings close to the gorgeous priory. Breakfast is served in the excellent **tearoom** next door (budget).

Number 31, Howard Place, Carlisle, t (01228) 597080, www.number31.co.uk (moderate). Each of the four, imaginative rooms in this lovely B&B has its own theme – a certain ooh-la-la in the black and fuchsia French-

themed junior suite and a Mediterranean feel in the cool Blue Room.
Willowford Farm B&B, Gilsland, t (016977) 47962, *www.willowford.co.uk* (*moderate*). This farmhouse B&B has under floor heating, large wet rooms, home-made soap and, the biggest surprise of all, an impressive section of Hadrian's Wall in the grounds.

Hall Hills, Raughton Head, Dalston, t (016974) 76779, *www.hallhills.co.uk* (*self-catering*). Five tasteful cottages recently converted from 17th-century farm buildings. The traditional features, such as solid oak floors and exposed beams are all there, but so are broadband connections and impressive integrated sound systems.

The Lodge, Hayton, near Brampton, t (01228) 670215, *www.the-lodge-holiday-cottages-cumbria.co.uk* (*self-catering*). From the headboard on the bed and the pictures on the walls to the welcome box of local beer and mouth-watering Toffee Shop fudge, a lot of thought has gone into absolutely everything in this beautiful self-catering cottage.

Where to Eat in Carlisle

(★) Number 10 >

(★) Watt's Victorian
Coffee Shop >>

Number 10, Eden Mount, Carlisle, t (01228) 524183 (*expensive*). Carlisle's best restaurant lies just to the north of the city centre. An unassuming exterior hides a cosy, friendly dining area that serves up superb modern British cuisine. The potatoes dauphinoise are just about the best you'll ever taste. *Closed Sun and Tues.*

Bijou, Carlysle's Court, Fisher St, Carlisle, t (01228) 818583, *www.bijou-restaurant.co.uk* (*expensive–moderate*). This tiny but top-notch restaurant is hidden away in a city-centre arcade and doubles up as a café during the day. An excellent menu and a relaxed setting. *Open for dinner Thurs–Sat.*

Keez, Cecil St, Carlisle, t (01228) 590670 (*expensive–moderate*). A relatively small, no-nonsense menu sits well with the smart, modern surroundings – cream walls with just a few small paintings scattered about; sleek, black chairs; and starched tablecloths. *Closed Mon.*

Blacksmiths Arms, Talkin, near Brampton, t (016977) 3452, *www.blacksmithstalkin.co.uk* (*moderate*). Traditional village pub serving fairly traditional pub food, but of a very high standard. The scampi is done in home-made beer batter and the salmon is cooked to perfection. Booking highly recommended.

Huntingtons, Marketplace, Brampton, t (016977) 3481, *www.huntingtons informaldining.co.uk* (*moderate*). A cosy, wine bar-cum-restaurant with a very relaxed feel. Go along on a Friday night to sample the seafood menu. *Closed Sun–Tues.*

Le Gall, Devonshire St, Carlisle, t (01228) 818388 (*moderate–budget*). Hugely popular café-bar with continental feel. Serves light meals until 7pm; 9pm on Fri and Sat.

Four Corners, Earl's Lane, Carlisle, t (01228) 598826 (*budget*). A great little daytime-only café near the bus station. Cute kitsch décor, art gallery upstairs and regular fresh specials board. The chef trained at Northcote Manor under Nigel Haworth. *Closed Sun.*

Foxes Café Lounge, Abbey St, Carlisle, t (01228) 536439, *www.foxescafe lounge.co.uk* (*budget*). Laid-back café-bar and gallery that's a popular lunch-spot. Also open Fri and Sat evenings for live music events and some of the best cocktails in town.

Watt's Victorian Coffee Shop, Bank St, Carlisle t (01228) 521545 (*budget*). Excellent Carlisle café. This one sells more than 20 different coffees, all roasted on the premises. *Closed Sun.*

Entertainment in Carlisle

The Sands Centre, Carlisle, t (01228) 625222, *www.thesandscentre.co.uk*. The city's leisure centre doubles up as a concert venue. Also stages occasional theatrical productions.

Vue Cinema, Botchergate, Carlisle t 08712 240 240, *www.myvue.com*. Mostly blockbuster movies.

West Walls Theatre, West Walls, Carlisle, t (01228) 523254, *www.carlisle greenroom.co.uk*. Home to Carlisle's amateur dramatic Green Room Club, which puts on half a dozen productions a year.

Eden Valley

The River Eden, one of the north of England's best salmon and trout rivers, rises in the Pennines, just south of Kirkby Stephen, before meandering its way north until it becomes the Solway Firth west of Carlisle. The valley it carves is an absolute delight, so worthy of the name Eden. Wooded gorges, gently rolling hills, tranquil villages and cosy B&Bs, all tucked in at the base of the Pennines, are typical of what visitors will discover here.

Working your way upstream from Carlisle, the first village you come to is **Wetheral**, a collection of fairly large houses built around a pleasant green. Lovely woodland walks alongside the river lead to **St Constantine's Cells**, a series of square caves cut deep into the sandstone cliffs. The caves are reputed to have been used by either a 6th-century prince or a 10th-century king as a hermitage, although there is no clear evidence to suggest that anyone ever lived in them. What is more likely is that they were used as storage chambers by the monks from nearby Wetheral Priory, possibly as a place to hide their valuables during cross-border raids.

Wetheral Priory Gatehouse
Wetheral, www.english-heritage.org.uk; open April–Sept daily 10am–6pm, Oct–March daily 10am–4pm

Wetheral Priory was set up by Benedictine monks in 1106, dedicated to the Holy Trinity and St Constantine. All that is left of the priory today is the well-preserved gatehouse, which was built in the 15th century and is now managed by English Heritage. It is located on a minor road just south of the main village. From the tunnel-vaulted entrance, a spiral stairway leads up to two storeys.

Sitting on the river bank, opposite the impressive 17th-century mansion of Corby Castle (not open to the public), is *Flight of Fancy*, a sculpture by Tim Shutter – one of 10 Eden Benchmarks. These sculptures, which also function as seats, were commissioned by the now defunct East Cumbria Countryside Project to celebrate the new millennium. Each by a different artist, they have been installed at various locations beside public paths along the entire length of the River Eden. The artists' brief was to produce sculptures that harmonized with the landscape and captured the essence of each locality. The first is *Water Cut* by Mary Bourne, located high on the wild moorland close to the source of the river at Mallerstang. The other nine are at Kirkby Stephen, Temple Sowerby, Appleby, Lazonby, Edenhall, Armathwaite, Wetheral, Bitts Park in Carlisle and Rockcliffe.

The next village is **Armathwaite**, another good base for walks along the Eden. There are particularly nice paths through **Coombs Wood** where some curious faces have been carved into the red sandstone. The unusual carvings also include a salmon and lines from Isaac Walton's *The Compleat Angler*. They are thought to be the work of William Mounsey, a local scholar and traveller of the 19th century who, in 1850, travelled the entire length of the Eden from his home on the Rockcliffe marshes at the river's mouth to its source in the Pennines.

Armathwaite is the first stop on the **Carlisle-to-Settle railway line** after Carlisle itself and features a colourful signalbox restored by the Friends of the Settle–Carlisle Line.

Work on the 72-mile line began in 1869 and lasted for seven years. About 6,000 men were involved in building it, the last mainline railway in England to be constructed almost entirely by hand. Many workers were killed during the construction; and many more died through outbreaks of diseases which spread quickly in the makeshift, unhygienic settlements in which they lived. The line opened to passengers on 1 May 1876 and includes 14 tunnels and 20 viaducts. It has famously survived two attempts to close it, in the early 1960s and in the 1980s.

Further upstream and on the other side of the River Eden is one of the most enigmatic sites in the whole of Cumbria – **Long Meg and Her Daughters**. This huge stone circle, which has a road running through it, consists of 59 stones, although there were originally about 70. The largest stone is Long Meg herself – a 12ft-tall standing stone that bears faint traces of mysterious cup and ring markings as well as concentric circles, which are thought to be 4,500 years old. Constructed of red sandstone quarried from the banks of the River Eden, she is positioned just outside the circle. Seen from the centre of the circle, she is aligned with the midwinter sunset.

Needless to say, there are a lot of spooky local legends associated with this site. The stones are said to be the petrified remains of a coven of witches who were turned to stone by Scottish wizard Michael Scot for profanities on the Sabbath. The site is supposedly endowed with magic, so that it is impossible to count the same number of stones twice. If you do manage to do so, then the magic is broken (or, alternatively, you are cursed by bad luck). A prophecy also states that if Long Meg were ever to be shattered, she would run with blood. It is said that when local squire Colonel Lacy attempted to destroy the stones in the early part of the 18th century, a terrifying storm broke out and the labourers fled in fear of black magic – and refused to return.

The same Colonel Lacy, who owned the Salkeld Hall estate, was responsible for the impressive caverns, known as **Lacy's Caves**, that have been hollowed out of the red sandstone embankments of the River Eden nearby. He created the five chambers in an attempt to impress his guests and supposedly even employed a man to live there as a hermit. The caves can be easily reached from a public footpath (*see* p.206), but visitors are warned to be careful; some of the caves open out on to sheer drops. This is not a place for unsupervised children.

The village of **Little Salkeld** is home to a working corn **mill** that still uses water power and traditional techniques to produce a range of stoneground organic flours. Originally built in 1745, it started life as a modest affair, but then prospered when the Carlisle-to-Settle railway line was built. The gorgeous buildings were lovingly restored by Ana and Nick Jones in 1975. They and their enthusiastic team run guided tours of the site, and the full range of flours is on sale next door in the delightful café. Visitors are advised to ring because guided tours may not be available if the mill is busy.

The next village upstream, **Langwathby,** holds some entertainment for the children. **Eden Ostrich World** houses wallabies, ostriches, racoons and the rare 'zebroid'. It is located on a working farm where youngsters can enjoy pony rides, a bouncy castle and, in the spring, get

Little Salkeld Watermill
Little Salkeld, near Penrith, t (01768) 881523, www.organicmill.co.uk; guided tours mid–Jan to mid–Dec Mon, Tues, Thurs, Fri 12pm, 2pm and 3.30pm, Sun 2pm and 3.30pm; adm

Eden Ostrich World
Langwathby Hall Farm, Langwathby, t (01768) 881771, www.ostrich-world.com; open daily 10am–3.30pm (closed Tues Nov–Feb); adm

Walk: Long Meg and Lacy's Caves

Start and finish:
Little Salkeld

Distance:
5.2 miles/8.4km

Total ascent:
731ft/223m

In brief:
This easy walk in the beautiful Eden Valley visits a tranquil village, the famous river, curious caves carved into the cliffs, a lonely church which has lost its village, and, the highlight of the excursion, one of the most impressive and mysterious stone circles in Britain. Using well waymarked paths throughout, it makes for an interesting yet peaceful afternoon stroll after a tasty lunch at Little Salkeld Watermill.

Route description:
With your back to the **old watermill** in Little Salkeld, turn right towards Glassonby. After just over a third-of-a-mile, turn left along a rough track. Bear left at a surfaced lane to reach **Long Meg and Her Daughters** (*see* p.205).

Having explored the stones, bear half-right just beyond them to make for the fence corner which houses three gates. Go through the small gate with a way-marker on it to walk with the fence on your right. On the other side of the field, choose the right-hand gate and then go straight through the small gate opposite.

Walking with field boundaries on your left, you pass through a series of gates until you reach a farm track. Once through the metal gate, go through the small gate in the church wall. This is **St Michael and All Angels**, Addingham, built on its present site in the 13th century. The original church and village of Addingham were washed away when the River Eden changed course in the 12th century.

Leaving the churchyard via gates on the other side of the building, turn left down a track. Turn right at the end. Turn left along the road. At **Daleraven Bridge**, turn left along a footpath. Bearing half-right after a stile, you find yourself standing on a steep precipice looking down on the River Eden.

What follows now as you bear left is a peaceful riverside stroll, sometimes across meadows, sometimes through pretty woodland. About 0.75 miles from Daleraven Bridge, you reach an area of sandstone cliffs. After the path drops down some steps, take a detour by turning right along a narrow trail through a cleft in the rocks. This brings you to **Lacy's Caves** (*see* above).

Continuing along the main path, you pass a disused **gypsum mine**. After an electricity sub-station, turn right along a concrete track, following signs for Little Salkeld. The track ends at a T-junction, where you turn left. Bear right at the next junction to return to the start.

to bottle-feed the lambs. And if you're still wondering what a 'zebroid' is – well, her mother was a Shetland pony and her father was a zebra. The site also has a tearoom, gallery and an adventure playground.

Gardens of Eden Valley

Acorn Bank Garden and Watermill
Temple Sowerby,
t (01768) 361893;
www.nationaltrust.org.
uk; open April–Oct
Wed–Sun 10am–5pm,
March Sat–Sun
10am–5pm; adm

The serene walled enclave of **Acorn Bank Garden and Watermill** is worth a visit. Sheltered from the worst of the weather by tall, ancient oaks, it is planted with 250 different types of medicinal and culinary herbs. Its orchards are well known for their traditional varieties and there is an 'apple day' every October to celebrate this. The day includes apple bobbing, storytelling, cookery demonstrations, children's music, craft workshops, a treasure hunt, Punch & Judy and Morris dancers. Outside the walls, follow the path through the woods and alongside Crowdundle Beck to the partially restored watermill. There is also a teashop on the site.

Winderwath Gardens
Temple Sowerby
t (01768) 88250; open
March–Oct Mon–Fri
10am–4pm, Sat
10am–12noon; adm

Not far from Acorn Bank in Temple Sowerby are the privately-owned **Winderwath Gardens**. This four-and-a-half acre site includes rockeries, herbaceous borders and mature trees, many of which were planted when the gardens were first laid out about 100 years ago. It is also home to many rare Alpine, Himalayan and New Zealand species.

Appleby

The lovely market town of Appleby makes for an interesting stop on the Carlisle-to-Settle railway. It has a very peaceful, laid-back feel to it and many interesting and rather charming historical buildings.

Looming over the town, built on top of a steep bank of the River Eden, is the **castle** (not open to the public). It dates from Norman times, and although much of it was rebuilt in the 17th century, the splendid keep, known as **Caesar's Tower**, dates from the 12th century. Like many castles in the area, and other buildings in Appleby, it owes its continuing existence to the efforts of Lady Anne Clifford, a strong-willed and passionate member of the local aristocracy during the 17th century. She was born in Skipton Castle in 1590, the sole heir of the third earl of Cumberland. She failed to inherit her father's Westmorland estates on his death and they eventually passed to her uncle and then her cousin. She fought hard to regain what was rightfully hers and even made a direct, although unsuccessful, appeal to the king. Eventually, her cousin died without a male heir, and Lady Anne won back her estates.

On the death of her second husband, she moved into Appleby Castle and began a massive project, restoring her castles at Brough (*see* 209), Brougham (*see* p.109) and Pendragon (*see* 209). She also built Appleby's St Anne's Hospital in Boroughgate, a lovely building for local women who were too ill to work.

Boroughgate, leading down from the castle, is a wonderfully wide main street flanked by lime trees and consisting of buildings from the Jacobean, Georgian and Victorian periods. At the bottom, north end of this truly grand thoroughfare is the Moot Hall, dating from 1596. Today, this is home to the Tourist Information Centre.

The Croglin Vampire

No visit to the villages scattered alongside the River Eden and at the base of the North Pennines would be complete without a retelling of the blood curdling tale of the Croglin vampire. Depending on which version of the story you hear, the terrifying events happened in the 19th century or just after the English Civil War and the scene of the vampire attack was Croglin Low Hall or Croglin Grange.

The owners of the house, the Fishers, had let it to two brothers and a sister – the Cranswells. One balmy summer night, the sister was savagely attacked by a mysterious creature that somehow managed to get into her bedroom and bite her throat. Several months later, the creature returned, but this time Miss Cranswell's terrified screams alerted her brothers and they came rushing to her aid with their pistols drawn. One of the brothers shot the creature in the leg and it fled, scrambled over the churchyard wall and disappeared into a vault.

The next day, the brothers and several brave villagers went into the vault and discovered that all but one of the coffins had been smashed to pieces. The one that remained intact turned out to contain shrivelled remains with the marks of a recent pistol shot in one leg. They set fire to the coffin and its contents, and the creature was never seen again.

The rose-hued church of **St Lawrence**, partly restored and rebuilt by Lady Anne Clifford, is entered here through a Gothic cloistered arcade. The lower part of the tower is the oldest part of the church, dating from the 12th century, but a lot of rebuilding took place in the 14th century – after the destruction caused during the border wars – and subsequently in the 17th, 18th and 19th centuries. The northeast chapel houses an impressive black marble monument to Lady Anne Clifford next to an alabaster figure of her mother. The church is also home to one of the oldest working organs in Britain, dating from the 1540s.

To the southwest of Appleby is the delightful **Lyvennet valley**, a little-visited area of quaint villages, low-lying limestone hills and ancient remains. The surprisingly large church of St Lawrence in **Crosby Ravensworth**, surrounded by ancient oaks, is a particularly impressive structure. Walkers can visit stone circles, ancient cairns and the sites of many prehistoric settlements on Crosby Ravensworth Fell and Crosby Garrett Fell. Between the two is the magnificent limestone pavement of Great Asby Scar. The disused railway through beautiful Smardale has been turned into a cycleway and footpath that crosses the awesome Smardale Gill Viaduct and passes through a National Nature Reserve.

Travelling east and southeast from Appleby, the gentle, pastoral surroundings of the lower Eden Valley are replaced by a bleaker, more austere and weather-beaten landscape as you head into the Pennines.

Brough

Between Appleby and Kirkby Stephen lies the village of Brough, split in two by the A66 as the dual carriageway climbs the bleak Pennine hills. Church Brough, to the south, is built on a Roman thoroughfare, and is where you will find the castle; Market Brough, on the northern side, is on the route of a medieval road. Despite sitting at almost 600ft above sea level and being exposed to some pretty dire winter weather, it was for years an important staging post for cross-border traffic. In the 18th and 19th centuries, there were more than 10 inns here. Even today, it occasionally finds itself hosting stranded motorists when winter storms force police to close the snow gates on the A66.

Brough Castle
Brough,
t 0870 3331181,
*www.english-
heritage.org.uk; open
April–Sept daily
10am–5pm, Oct–March
daily 10am–4pm*

The imposing **Brough Castle**, built on the site of a Roman camp, sits on a steep-sided mound beside a tributary of the River Eden. The oldest parts of it, including the foundations of the great keep and some of the walls, date from about 1100, but it has suffered some long periods of neglect during its 900-year history. The Clifford family, who came into possession of it in 1268, added the semicircular **Clifford's Tower**. It was ravaged by fire in 1521 and remained in ruins until Lady Anne Clifford inherited it more than 100 years later. As with her other properties, she quickly set about restoring it, but another fire, in about 1666, finished it off for good. The castle is now in the care of English Heritage.

Kirkby Stephen

Walkers will love Kirkby Stephen. With the moors of the North Pennines forming a dramatic backdrop, it is an important stopping-off point for people doing Wainwright's Coast to Coast walk. In addition, there are some wonderful walks in and around the town, enough to keep you occupied for several days.

Probably the most popular route is the hike up to **Nine Standards Rigg**, the site of the prominent cairns that stand guard high above the town. The origin of these nine 'stone men' is a mystery. One claim is that they were constructed by the Romans to look like troops from a distance; others say they are boundary markers. Major repairs on some of the cairns were carried out in 2005.

To escape from people entirely, get the train out to Garsdale and then walk the 12 miles back across lonely **Wild Boar Fell** (2,322ft). On a clear day, as you stride out along the ridge leading back into Kirkby Stephen, the views are among the best outside of the Lake District. England's last wild boar is said to have been killed on Wild Boar Fell by Sir Richard de Musgrave, who lived at Hartley Castle. A boar's tusk was found in his tomb in Kirkby Stephen church.

The people of Kirkby Stephen are clearly proud of where they live, and a lot of work has been done to improve paths and open up new routes. Part of the disused Stainmore Railway, originally constructed to carry coke from Durham to the blast furnaces in Cumberland and Barrow-in-Furness and then transport iron ore back to Cleveland, has been turned into a public footpath, with some of the viaducts restored by the Northern Viaduct Trust (*www.nvt.org.uk*). **The Poetry Path**, near the River Eden, features 12 short poems by local poet Meg Peacocke beautifully carved into a series of stones. A leaflet accompanying the walk can be picked up at the Tourist Information Centre.

The romantic ruins of **Pendragon Castle** sit beside the River Eden about four miles south of Kirkby Stephen. It was built in the late 12th century and later came into the possession of the Clifford family (*see* above). Local legend has it that Uther Pendragon, the father of King Arthur, originally founded the castle. He and 100 of his men are said to have been killed here when Saxons poisoned the well. The castle is on private land, but there is permissive access to the ruins. Visitors are asked to park considerately.

Festivals and Events in the Eden Valley

(i) **Appleby Tourist Information Centre**
Moot Hall,
t *(017683) 54206,*
www.visiteden.co.uk; open Easter–Sept Mon–Sat 9.30am–5pm; Sun 10.30am–2.30pm; Oct Mon–Sat 9.30am–5pm; Nov–March Mon–Sat, 10am–1pm

(i) **Kirkby Stephen Tourist Information Centre**
Market Place,
t *(017683) 71199,*
www.visiteden.co.uk; open Easter–Oct Mon–Sat 10am–4pm, Sun 11am–3pm

(★) **Augill Castle >**

For the last 300 years, Appleby has hosted the annual **Horse Fair** (*www.applebyfair.org*), one of the largest gypsy gatherings in Europe. Around 10,000 travellers descend on the tiny town each July. With youngsters washing their horses in the River Eden, ponies racing and trotting along Flashing Lane and some traditional, horse-drawn vehicles, it makes for a very colourful and lively spectacle.

Slightly more sedate is the **Appleby Agricultural Show, t** (01931) 714571, which takes place in August.

On the second Saturday of every month, Orton hosts one of Cumbria's biggest and best **farmers' markets** (*www.ortonfarmers.co.uk*) with more than 40 local producers.

Where to Stay in the Eden Valley

Augill Castle, South Stainmore, near Kirkby Stephen, **t** (01768) 341937, *www.augillcastle.co.uk* (*expensive*). This amazing turreted hideaway proves that staying in a castle doesn't have to be a stuffy, dusty affair. The exquisite rooms feature four-poster beds, bold décor and antique furniture. Despite its grandeur, there's a wonderfully relaxed feel to the place, and the owners go out of their way to make you feel at home.

Tufton Arms Hotel, Market Sq, Appleby, **t** (017683) 51593, *www.tuftonarmshotel.co.uk* (*expensive*). There's a sense of polish and refinement about the opulent bedrooms at this intimate little hotel. Contemporary fabrics, smart bathrooms and soft colours combine with antiques and chandeliers to provide both modern and classic luxury. The **restaurant** (*expensive–moderate*) serves up top-quality British classics such as home-made steak and ale pie.

A Corner of Eden, Low Stennerskeugh, Ravenstonedale **t** (015396) 23370, *www.acornerofeden.co.uk* (*expensive–moderate*). This isolated Grade II listed

farmhouse has been turned into a very classy but comfortable B&B. The décor is immaculate. Sadly there are no en suite rooms, but soft, fluffy bathrobes are provided for the short walk down the corridor to one of the bathrooms.

Acorn Bank, Wetheral, **t** (01228) 561434, *www.acornbank.co.uk* (*moderate*). Two elegantly designed and decorated rooms in a Georgian home in the pretty village of Wetheral. Excellent evening meals are available for residents.

Bank End House, Appleby, **t** (017683) 52050, *www.bankendhouse.co.uk* (*moderate*). Dazzlingly white rooms with smart, modern bathrooms. The Field Room is particularly bright and cheery and features a king-size oak bed and chaise longue.

Crake Trees Manor, Crosby Ravensworth, **t** (01931) 715205, *www.craketreesmanor.co.uk* (*moderate*). A delectable and friendly family-run B&B surrounded by lovely countryside. Rooms have sturdy iron-framed beds and exposed beams. Small, nicely furnished holiday cottage also available.

Marton House, Long Marton, **t** (017683) 61502, *www.martonhousecumbria.co.uk* (*moderate*). You get a lot of room for your money at cosy, comfortable Marton House. Lovely gardens are surrounded by some magnificent mature trees.

Meaburn Hill Farmhouse, Maulds Meaburn, **t** (01931) 715168, *www.cumbria-bed-and-breakfast.co.uk* (*moderate*). Expect a warm welcome from the award-winning landlady of this traditional B&B in the gorgeous Lyvennet valley.

Bracken Bank Lodge, Lazonby, **t** (01768) 898241, *www.brackenbank.co.uk* (*moderate–budget*). A trip back in time to an old-fashioned country estate. Hunting trophies adorn the dining room and the bathrooms have tartan walls. The lodge organizes clay-pigeon shooting lessons.

Wild Rose Park Wigwams, Ormside, Appleby **t** (017683) 51077, *www.wildrose.co.uk* (*budget*). Camping without the cold and the hassle. The 'wigwams' are small, warm, wooden cabins that include a sleeping platform, a fridge, kettle, toaster, microwave, TV and lockable door.

Green Barn Cottages, The Green, Ravenstonedale, t (015396) 23479, *www.greenbarncottages.co.uk* (*selfcatering*). This stone barn has recently been carefully converted into three well-appointed luxury cottages. Features include under floor heating, wood-burning stoves, French doors leading on to large patio areas, exposed stonework and whirlpool baths.

Where to Eat in the Eden Valley

Fantails Restaurant, The Green, Wetheral, t (01228) 560239, *www.fantails.co.uk* (*expensive*). A perennial favourite with locals, this traditional restaurant serves up the likes of shoulder of lamb, or fillet steak with a slice of haggis, wrapped in pastry and covered with a whisky and coarse-grain mustard sauce.

Kyloes Restaurant, The Highland Drove Inn, Great Salkeld, t (01768) 898349, *www.kyloes.co.uk* (*moderate*). Great Salkeld may seem a little off the beaten track for most tourists, but

Kyloes makes it worth the drive. A traditional-looking pub that verges on the gastro.

Black Swan, Ravenstonedale, t (015396) 23204, *www.blackswan hotel.com* (*moderate*). A simple, but good menu with a heavy emphasis on local produce. The bar has a good reputation for real ales and has won several CAMRA awards.

The Village Bakery, Melmerby, t (01768) 881811, *www.villagebakery.com* (*moderate–budget*). Whether it's breakfast, a light lunch or afternoon tea you're looking for, this is one of the best cafés in the whole of Cumbria. Totally organic, dishes include griddled haloumi with a black olive tapenade on huge chucks of toast, fresh, filling platters and a proper, big veggie breakfast, the likes of which you'll see nowhere else. Also has a good selection of wines.

The Watermill Tearoom, Little Salkeld, t (01768) 881523, *www.organicmill. co.uk* (*budget*). A rustic organic and vegetarian café that makes practically everything on the premises, including its delicious breads. Main meals such as quiche and rarebit are very filling, but you must leave room for the delicious scones, cakes and desserts.

 The Village Bakery >>

 The Watermill Tearoom >>

North Pennines

To the east of the Eden Valley, the land rises quite steeply to the highest part of the Pennine chain. Cross Fell (2,929ft), Little Dun Fell (2,762ft) and Great Dun Fell (2,781ft), with its golf ball-like civilian radar station, dominate the scenery and the only town, **Alston**, proudly boasts of being the highest market settlement in England. Three of the north's great rivers rise here – the Tees, the South Tyne and, just over the border in County Durham, the Wear.

There are two main ways to reach Alston from the west – along the A689 from Brampton, which winds up and over low moorland and then through the valley of the South Tyne; or, even better, via the A686 from Penrith. This amazing road, which is regarded as one of the most scenic drives in Britain, climbs steeply in a series of switchbacks to Hartside Pass. Here, motorists can take a break from the perils of the drive, and have a cuppa in the greasy café that is invariably full of motorcyclists. At 1,903ft, this can be a cold, windswept spot, but the views from the huge car park are wonderful. The mountains of the Lake District are clearly visible, including Helvellyn, Great Gable and Skiddaw, and the Scottish hills can be seen across the Solway Firth.

North Pennines Area of Outstanding Natural Beauty

This enormous area of high moorland and broad upland dales is the second biggest AONB and covers more ground than any of England's National Parks except the Lake District. It is the job of the AONB Partnership (*www.northpennines.org.uk*) to help conserve and enhance the natural beauty of the North Pennines.

The high moors are home to several bird species that you are unlikely to see anywhere else in England, most importantly the black grouse and the hen harrier. The black grouse, one of the UK's largest game birds, was present in every county of England 100 years ago. Today, it is confined to the North Pennines where its dove-like cooing and strange sneeze-like noise has an eerie way of filling the valleys and echoing off the hillsides. In the 1990s, its population was estimated to be declining at the shocking rate of 10 per cent per year as habitats were destroyed or fragmented, making it one of the most rapidly declining species in the UK. The North Pennines, however, has seen a slight resurgence in numbers in recent years, thanks in part to the co-ordinated efforts of farmers, estate managers and conservation organizations. The spring lek, when several males gather at dawn to show off their glossy plumage and lyre-shaped tails, is said to be one of the most impressive wildlife experiences in the UK.

The story of the hen harrier, sadly, lacks the hint of optimism that surrounds that of the black grouse. According to the RSPB, in 2008 breeding figures showed there were just 17 breeding pairs left in England and only 10 of these bred successfully. If you are lucky enough to spot a hen harrier, you could be in for a treat. The male bird performs a magnificent aerobatic display or 'sky dance' in the spring and provides food to his mate in spectacular food passes.

Other upland birds include Britain's smallest bird of prey, the merlin, the short-eared owl, red grouse, the elusive dunlin, meadow pipit and the beautiful golden plover. During the spring and early summer in particular, the lower grasslands are alive with the distinctive calls of the curlew and the lapwing.

Gossipgate Gallery
The Butts, Alston,
t (01434) 381806,
www.gossipgate-
gallery.co.uk; open
Easter–Oct Wed–Mon
10am–5pm

South Tynedale
Railway
The Railway Station,
Alston, t (01434) 381696,
www.strps.org.uk; services
run April, May and Oct
weekends only and
Sat–Thurs in school
holidays; June, July and
Sept Tues, Thurs, Sat and
Sun; Aug daily; adm

The Hub
Goods Shed, Station
Yard, Alston, t (01434)
381609, www.alston-
hub.org.uk; open
June–Sept daily
11am–5pm,
Oct–Christmas and
Easter–May Sat and Sun
11am–5pm

Beyond Hartside, the road crosses bleak moorland before dropping gradually to Alston. At almost 1,000ft above sea level, this remote, enchanting town can get cut off from the outside world after heavy snowfall. Its main street, steep and cobbled, has a distinctive market cross and several attractive old buildings. The Angel pub, for instance, is dated 1611. Visitors can spend a pleasant hour or two wandering the alleys and courtyards that were used in the filming of *Oliver Twist* (1999).

Tucked away on a quiet backstreet is the **Gossipgate Gallery**, which displays paintings, photography, ceramics, glassware, turned wood and jewellery. It also houses a pleasant café.

Alston is the home of the **South Tynedale Railway**, England's highest narrow-gauge railway. From 1840 to 1976, there was a standard-gauge branch line linking Alston with the Newcastle and Carlisle main line at Haltwhistle. It was originally built to carry lead from the mines of Alston Moor. After its closure, initial plans to preserve the line intact failed, but the South Tynedale Railway Preservation Society managed to build a 2ft gauge line on the standard gauge trackbed. The enthusiastic volunteers have put a lot of hard work into their baby, and have gradually extended the line over the Northumberland border to Kirkhaugh, 2.3 miles north of Alston. There are now plans to continue rebuilding track for a further 1.9 miles to Slaggyford. It's not a long journey, but a ride on the railway is fun, particularly when the steam engines are dragged out.

Next door to the station is **The Hub**, an interesting mish-mash of local history exhibits loaned or donated by local people. There are a lot of transport-related displays as well as old farming implements and photographs of wartime Alston.

Getting to and around the North Pennines

There are three buses (**service 680**) a day Mon–Sat from Carlisle to Nenthead via Brampton and Alston (total journey time, one hour and 15 minutes). Another service (**681**) links Alston with Haltwhistle twice a day, Mon–Sat (one hour). There is a once-daily Mon–Sat service (**888**) linking Alston with Newcastle and the Metro Centre in Gateshead (total journey time, two hours and 10 minutes). The **889** runs from Alston to Hexham via Nenthead once a day on weekdays only (one hour and 15 minutes).

For **taxis**, try Alston Taxis, **t** (01434) 381386.

Nenthead Mines Heritage Centre
Nenthead, near Alston,
t *(01434) 382726,*
www.npht.com; open
April–Oct daily
11am–5pm, Nov–March
open daily for pre-booked groups only; adm

Just over four miles east of Alston, before you reach the place where the borders of Cumbria, County Durham and Northumberland meet, is the **Nenthead Mines Heritage Centre**. Here you can find out all about the lead mining industry that once dominated this area of the North Pennines. The Romans were the first to mine lead here, when the ore could still be found fairly close to the surface, but the industry reached a peak in the 19th century when miners were also digging up substantial quantities of iron, zinc, copper and even some silver. At this time, the mine owners, the London Lead Company, were mostly Quakers (*see* below). Model employers, they provided their workers with homes, schools, medical care and recreational activities.

Some of the old mine buildings at Nenthead have been restored, and visitors are taken on a short underground tour of the workings. Self-guided trails enable you to get a good idea of just how far the mine spread, the Upper Nent Valley Trail, for instance, taking you out on to the moors where you will see the remains of a wheel pit.

The North Pennines offer some of the best **walking** in the country. The Pennine Way passes through Alston, having crossed Cross Fell on its 268-mile journey from Edale in Derbyshire to Kirk Yetholm in the Scottish Borders. **Cross Fell**, which is a long way from anywhere, can also be climbed from Garrigill to the south of Alston. An approach from the east inevitably means a long day on the hills, but it can be broken by staying overnight in Greg's Hut, a simple bothy with a sleeping platform and a wood-burning stove, but not much else. An old lead mining building, it was restored in 1972 in memory of John Gregory, who died in a climbing accident. A group of his friends adopted the hut and they still maintain it. It receives more than 600 visitors a year.

South of Cross Fell, one of the most impressive natural features of the Pennines is **High Cup**. This line of exposed whin sill rock forms a spectacular rim around the steep-sided, forbidding valley of High Cup Gill. It can be approached from Cow Green Reservoir on the Cumbria-County Durham border or from the red sandstone fellside village of Dufton near Appleby.

 Cross Fell

Where to Stay and Eat in the North Pennines

Lovelady Shield Country House Hotel, Lovelady Lane, near Alston, **t** (01434) 381203, *www.lovelady.co.uk* (*luxury–expensive*). The bright rooms in this elegant Georgian house include sofas, wide-screen TVs and good views across the three acres of gardens. Communal areas include a cocktail bar, library, lounge with log fires and a well-respected **restaurant** where diners are presented with an extensive, award-winning wine list.

(i) Alston Tourist Information Centre
Town Hall,
t (01434) 382244,
www.visiteden.co.uk;
open Apr–Oct Mon–Thurs
and Sat 10am–5pm, Fri
10am–7pm, Sun
10am–4pm

Nent Hall Country House, Alston, t (01434) 381584, www.nenthall.com (expensive–moderate). Eighteen en suite rooms, some with lovely four-poster beds and sumptuous sofas. For special occasions, the luxurious Tower Suite has five rooms.

Alston House Hotel, Townfoot, Alston, t (01434) 382200, www.alstonhouse hotel.co.uk (moderate). A friendly, family-run **restaurant** with a well-priced menu that puts local produce to good use: Cumbrian lamb shoulder, Alston sausage and mustard mash, locally-caught salmon. Also has comfortable rooms (moderate) at affordable prices.

Cumberland Hotel, Townfoot, Alston, t (01434) 381 875, www.alston cumberlandhotel.co.uk (moderate). Down-to-earth cooking at reasonable

prices in this handy, town-centre pub. Surprisingly extensive curry menu and budget children's meals.

Lowbyer Manor, Hexham Rd, Alston, t (01434) 381230, www.lowbyer.com (moderate). Hand-crafted quilts bring a splash of colour to this cosy guesthouse, close to the town centre.

The Miners Arms, Nenthead, t (01434) 381427, www.nenthead.com (moderate). Wood-fired pizzas, good, hearty pub meals and real ales are on the menu at this bright, friendly Pennine pub.

Alston Art Apartments, The Butts, Alston, t (01434) 382975, www.holiday cottagesalston.co.uk (self-catering). A set of three extremely stylish, open-plan cottages that have been convert-ed from stone barns and have won an award for their stunning design.

Western Dales and Howgills

Anyone who has driven north of junction 37 on the M6 or who has travelled beyond Oxenholme on the train will have seen the Howgills. As these major transport links slice through the Lune Gorge – and both radio reception and mobile phone coverage temporarily disappear – the Howgills are the compact group of grassy hills that loom to the east. The Yorkshire Dales National Park cuts right through the middle of these lonely, enchanting hills, although there are plans to extend the boundary north to take in the whole range. To the south and east of the Howgills, just within Cumbria's borders, are the pleasant towns of Sedbergh and Kirkby Lonsdale and two little-visited valleys, Garsdale and Dentdale.

The Howgills, like so much of Cumbria, make excellent walking country, but these brooding giants have their own special identity that sets them apart from both the Lake District fells and the Pennine moors. Smooth but steep slopes climb to a high, grassy plateau. At 2,217ft, the Calf is the highest point on this great dome of hills which Wainwright likened to 'a huddle of squatting elephants'. From here, lonely ridges – with some of the most far-reaching views in the whole of England – fan out in all directions, divided by steep-sided valleys. The Calf can be climbed relatively easily from Sedbergh, probably the most popular route. The only exception to the smooth regularity of these hills occurs on the eastern edge of the range where Cautley Crag, a mile-long series of crumbling buttresses, and Cautley Spout, a fine group of high waterfalls, come together to create a little more drama. A lung-burstingly steep path climbs from Cross Keys, but it gets you fairly close to the action, so it's worth the effort.

Just to the west of the Howgills, over the other side of the River Lune, the rough pastures are home to one of the most important sites in the history of the Quaker movement. On Sunday 13 June 1652, the

Getting to and around the Western Dales and Howgills

By Train and Bus

The stations of Garsdale and Dent on the scenic **Carlisle-to-Settle railway line** are within the Cumbrian part of the Yorkshire Dales National Park. Trains are reasonably regular.

As in the Eden Valley, this area of Cumbria is relatively poorly served by buses, seeing only one or two 'shoppers' services each week. There is a bus from Kendal to Sedbergh (**service 564, the Howgill Rambler**), which runs eight times a day on weekdays and four times a day on Saturdays (total journey time, 30 minutes). Some services continue to Kirkby Stephen (35 minutes). The **567** runs between Kendal and Kirkby Lonsdale every couple of hours on weekdays only (30 minutes).

By Taxi

Country Taxis, Garsdale **t** (01969) 667096; Twentyfourseven Taxis, Carnforth, **t** (015242) 73395.

By Bicycle

To hire bikes, try Sedbergh Bike Hire, **t** 07920 864586, *www.sedberghbikehire.co.uk.*

---

charismatic George Fox addressed about 1,000 people at this spot on Firbank Fell, now known as **Fox's Pulpit**, convincing many to follow his teachings. As a young man, he had become disillusioned with the religious status quo and, like other 'seekers', felt that the established church had become mired in ritual and politics. Believing that God spoke directly to each and every person, he wanted to live out the Christian message more simply. He began touring the country, taking his message to anyone who would listen – and he ended up in prison on several occasions for his dissenting views, regarded at the time as blasphemous. In June 1652, he had a vision on Pendle Hill in which God called him to gather a large group of believers. Fresh from this, he travelled north to Sedbergh to preach to the multitude on Firbank Fell, a significant turning point in the birth of the Quaker movement.

Quaker Meeting House
Brigflatts; open daily Easter–Sept 11am–6pm, Oct–Easter 11am–dusk

Northern England's oldest **Quaker meeting house** is located just to the south of Firbank Fell, at Brigflatts. Built in 1675, it still has many of its original oak furnishings. Visitors are welcome to drop in and soak up the calm, soothing atmosphere of this historic site.

 Sedbergh

If you're planning to explore the Howgills, the sleepy old market town of **Sedbergh** is a superb base. Its narrow streets and alleys are home to a fair few book shops, which have given it the accolade of England's Book Town. It also hosts a festival of 'books and drama' every September.

The famous public school, founded in 1525, occupies some attractive buildings on the edge of the town. Some of its most famous ex-students include former England rugby captain Will Carling, the pioneering geologist Adam Sedgewick and screenwriter Simon Beaufoy, who won an Oscar in 2009 for *Slumdog Millionaire*.

Farfield Mill Arts and Heritage Centre
*Garsdale Rd, Sedbergh, **t** (015396) 21958, www.farfieldmill.org; open daily 10.30am–5pm; adm*

Situated on the A684, about a mile east of Sedbergh, is the **Farfield Mill Arts and Heritage Centre**. Housed in an 175-year-old woollen mill, it includes working looms, heritage displays, art exhibitions and craft demonstrations. Visitors can see resident artists in their studios and, on most Wednesdays, they can watch the age-old skills of weavers as they work the looms.

East of Sedbergh are **Garsdale** and **Dentdale**, pretty valleys that lead deeper into the Yorkshire Dales. While Garsdale has an 'A' road passing through it, sleepy Dentdale has only a slow, winding road, making it a lot quieter and less frequented by visitors. The only tourists who come to Dentdale, it seems, are walkers doing the 78-mile Dales Way, which passes through the valley on its way from Ilkley to Bowness-on-Windermere. **Dent**, with its narrow cobbled streets, is the only village. Now a place of splendid peace and quiet, this lovely little village was once a busy spot with several thriving industries, including 'marble' quarrying, horse-breeding, coal mining and, most important of all, wool. It is said that, at one time, there were so many people knitting here that the clacking of their needles could drown out the noise of the men chipping away in the quarries. The marble, incidentally, wasn't real marble, but a limestone rich with fossils. The stone was turned into fireplace surrounds, one of which was installed in the Tsar of Russia's Winter Palace in 1843.

Dent Village Heritage Centre
Dent
t (015396) 25800,
www.dentvillageheritag
ecentre.com; open
Easter–Sept daily
11am–4pm, Oct–Easter
daily 11am–3pm; adm

There is a small but interesting **heritage centre** in the village which recalls the recent history of the dale. Domestic items and traditional farming implements are on show in re-created farmhouse rooms.

Dent Station, in a lonely spot more than four miles from the village that it serves, is 1,150ft above sea level, making it the highest mainline station in England. Both Dent and Garsdale stations provide a good starting point for several wild walks on the remote moors along the Cumbria/North Yorkshire border, including Wild Boar Fell (*see* p.214). Whernside, Yorkshire's highest hill, can also be easily accessed from Dent, although the more traditional (and busier) route starts from the next station along the line, Ribblehead.

Kirkby Lonsdale

The quiet market town of Kirkby Lonsdale, which sits on the western bank of the River Lune, is a delightful place with a rich history. Its quiet lanes are pleasant to wander in, its streets nose-dive at a crazy, photogenic angle down to the river, while the old churchyard deserves a rosette for all-round loveliness. The views over the river here are pretty special, and have attracted the attentions of the great and the good, including landscape painter J. M. W. Turner and John Ruskin, who waxed lyrical about this place, calling it 'one of the loveliest scenes in England – therefore in the world'.

Signs that mankind has been in the area for a long while include a **Neolithic stone circle** on Casterton Fell and the remains of Celtic settlements at **Barbon, Middleton** and **Hutton Roof**. The Romans were here too, and a Roman road followed the course of the River Lune, linking the forts at **Low Borrowbridge** (near Tebay) and **Over Burrow** (south of Kirkby Lonsdale).

The town itself developed at a river crossing point for several drovers' and packhorse routes, and is one of the few places in Cumbria that gets a mention in the Domesday Book, where it is described as Cherchibi (village with a church). It got its market charter way back in 1227, and market day (Thursday) continues to be a busy, bustling affair even now.

The Norman church of **St Mary's** stands close to the site of an earlier Saxon church. The oldest parts of it are the lower section of the tower and three sturdy columns in the nave, two of which feature diamond patterns that are thought to have been carved at the beginning of the 12th century.

Beyond the church, there's a nice little river walk, starting at Ruskin's View. From there, the **86 Radical Steps** (named after the liberal views of a Dr Francis Pearson, who had them built around 1830) go down to the river, and the path continues along the bank to **Devil's Bridge**, a handsome, double-arched stone bridge that was built in the 12th century. Local legend has it that it was constructed by the Devil himself. The story goes that a cow and horse belonging to a poor local woman, who lived on the banks of the river, had somehow managed to become stranded on the other side of the river. The woman was distraught because her survival depended on the animals. Hearing her lamentations, the Devil appeared and offered to build a bridge in return for the first soul to cross it. Of course, the Devil was expecting the woman to be the first to cross but, once the bridge was built, the wily widow reached into her bag and tossed a bun across it. Her dog immediately ran after the tasty morsel and the Devil was thwarted.

Just north of Kirkby Lonsdale is **Casterton**, home to a girls' school that was moved here from nearby Cowan Bridge, in Lancashire, in 1833. The Brontë sisters briefly attended the school in 1824–5 and Charlotte, remembering the miserable year she had there, turned it into Lowood, the infamous school in *Jane Eyre*.

Cumbria isn't exactly renowned for its potholes, but the caves under Ease Gill on the border with Lancashire – just to the northeast of Kirkby Lonsdale – form one of the longest and most complex systems in the whole of Britain. Potholers have been exploring this area since the late 19th century, and they have so far discovered almost 50 miles of underground passageways. Nearby Bullpot Farm, which provides the easiest road access to the valley, is the base of the Red Rose Cave and Pothole Club. Access to many of the caves, which is by permit only, is controlled by the Council of Northern Caving Clubs.

12

East Cumbria and Hadrian's Wall | Western Dales and Howgills

(i) Sedbergh Tourist Information Centre
Dales and Lakes Book Centre, Main St, t (015396) 20125; open Easter–Oct daily 10am–5pm, Nov–Easter daily 10am–4pm

Festivals and Events

Each June, this area plays host to the atmospheric **Dent Folk Festival** (*www.dentfolkfestival.co.uk*). This friendly, laid-back affair includes music, dance, workshops, guided walks, storytelling and street theatre. Having outgrown its original site, the popular festival is now held closer to Sedbergh.

Where to Stay in the Western Dales and Howgills

The Sun Inn, Market St, Kirkby Lonsdale, t (015242) 71965, *www.sun-inn.info* (*expensive–moderate*). Lightwood furniture and contemporary décor make for bright, refreshing rooms in this recently refurbished and welcoming 17th-century inn. The food and service in the award-winning **restaurant** (*expensive*) is excellent.

(★) The Highwayman >>

(i) Kirkby Lonsdale Tourist Information Centre: *Main St, t (015242) 71437; open Easter–Oct Mon–Fri 9.30am–5pm, Sat and Sun 10.30am–4pm; Nov–Easter daily 10am–3pm*

 (★) Church Brow Cottage >

St Mark's, Cautley, near Sedbergh, t (015396) 20287, *www.saintmarks.uk.com* (*moderate*). This 19th-century vicarage stands all alone beside the River Rawthey at the very foot of the Howgills, a beautiful location. Its studio regularly hosts textile workshops.

The Orange Tree Hotel, Fairbank, Kirkby Lonsdale, t (015242) 71716, *www.theorangetreehotel.co.uk* (*moderate*). Warm and inviting rooms in this cosy, friendly town pub. The annexe contains two particularly nice suites. Three nights for the price of two all year. The **restaurant** (*moderate*) serves up good, hearty meals, including some tasty steaks.

Blue Pig Bed and Breakfast, Mill Brow, Kirkby Lonsdale, t (01524) 273272, *www.bluepigkirkbylonsdale.co.uk* (*moderate–budget*). Small but comfortable rooms in this friendly B&B.

The Moorcock Inn, Garsdale Head, near Sedbergh, t (01969) 667488, *www.moorcockinn.com* (*moderate–budget*). Rooms in pubs on lonely moorland roads often tend to disappoint, but not the Moorcock. Here, the recently refurbished rooms are comfortable, stylish and superb value for money.

Church Brow Cottage, Kirkby Lonsdale t 0845 090 0194, *www.vivat-trust.org* (*self-catering*). This place really stands out from the crowd. A tiny, three-storey cottage, built to meet the 19th-century owner's image of a rural idyll, Church Brow stands close to Ruskin's View, with beautiful views over the Lune. The rooms have been elegantly furnished to create a period feel. It is let by the Vivat Trust, a charity dedicated to rescuing neglected historic buildings.

Where to Eat in the Western Dales and Howgills

The Dalesman Country Inn, Main St, Sedbergh, t (015396) 21183, *www.the dalesman.co.uk* (*expensive–moderate*). Customers can choose to eat in the cosy smithy or the more formal restaurant. Either way, the interesting menu makes use of a good range of trendy ingredients, such as ox cheek, monkfish tails and rare breed suckling pig.

The Highwayman, Burrow, near Kirkby Lonsdale, t (015242) 73338, *www.high waymaninn.co.uk* (*expensive–moderate*). Superb range of pub fare and enormous tasty platters proudly make use of the best of local produce. Head chef Michael Ward was named the UK's Pub Chef of the Year in 2009.

Avanti, Kirkby Lonsdale, t (015242) 73500, *www.baravanti.com* (*moderate*). A lively, modern restaurant and café-bar with a Mediterranean feel to it. Service starts early; you can go in for coffee, croissants and the daily newspaper from 9am onwards.

The Cross Keys Temperance Inn, Cautley, near Sedbergh, t (015396) 20284, *www.cautleyspout.co.uk* (*moderate*). A temperance inn may not be everyone's idea of a great night out, but this one does at least allow you to bring your own beer or wine. The inn's famous 'ham and eggs' has become the stuff of legend – a 16oz chunk of Wensleydale gammon griddled with two eggs and pineapple. Ask for a table in the glassed-in veranda for spectacular views of Cautley Spout.

The Pheasant Inn, Casterton, near Kirkby Lonsdale, t (015242) 71230, *www.pheasantinn.co.uk* (*moderate*). A traditional menu in a lovely village pub close to Kirkby Lonsdale. Serves up some old favourites such as prawn cocktail, breaded scampi and roast topside of beef with Yorkshire pudding and gravy.

Duo Café Bar and Bistro, Main St, Sedbergh, t (015396) 20552, *www.duo-sedbergh.com* (*moderate–budget*). Light bites, salads and paninis during the day and then a simple menu using good, fresh, local ingredients on Thurs, Fri and Sat evenings.

The Sedbergh Café, Main St, Sedbergh, t (015396) 21389, *www.thesedbergh cafe.com* (*budget*). A delightfully twee, old-fashioned tearoom in the centre of Sedbergh. Sandwiches, snacks and a few hot dishes. The beef and vegetable cobbler hits the spot.

Further Reading

Travellers' Tales

Gray, Thomas, *Journal of his Visit to the Lake District in October 1769* (Liverpool University Press, 2001). One of the first major literary figures to visit and write about the Lakes, Gray started in the east, had an extended stay in Keswick and Borrowdale - 'the Vale of Elysium' – and then travelled south to Grasmere, Windermere and Kendal.

Hudson, Roger, *Coleridge Among the Lakes and Mountains: From his Notebooks, Letters and Poems 1794-1804* (The Folio Society, 1991). The notebooks, letters and poems of the great Romantic poet brought together to provide an account of how he viewed the Lake District.

Martineau, Harriet, *An Independent Woman's Lake District Writings*, edited by Michael R. Hill (Humanity Books, 2004). A collection of perceptive, engaging and intelligently-written essays by the 19th-century journalist who eventually made her home in Ambleside. Her refreshing travelogues lack much of the rose-tinted romantic leanings of earlier writers.

West, Thomas, *A Guide To The Lakes* (Richardson and Urquhart, 1778). Probably the original travel guide to the Lake District, intended to help would-be visitors.

Wordsworth, William, *The Prose Works of William Wordsworth*, edited by W. J. B. Owen and Jane Worthington Smyser (Oxford University Press, 1974). Includes Wordsworth's *A Guide Through the District of the Lakes*.

History and Geography

Brooks, J. A., *Ghosts and Legends of the Lake District* (Jarrold, 1988). Spooky local legends from around the area.

Davies, Hunter, *A Walk Around the Lakes* (Frances Lincoln, 2009). The prolific Cumbrian writer describes a journey through the National Park and the people he meets. Using Wordsworth's life as a secondary narrative, his account is often amusing, always entertaining.

Davies, Hunter, *William Wordsworth* (Frances Lincoln, 2009). A detailed and fascinating biography of Lakeland's best-known poet.

Marsh, Terry, *Towns and Villages of Cumbria* (Sigma Press, 1999). A comprehensive guide to the history, folklore and customs of every town and village in Cumbria.

Prosser, Robert, *Geology Explained in the Lake District* (Fineleaf Editions, 2006). This guide takes a fairly straightforward approach to a complicated subject, using the author's own sketches and diagrams.

Ramshaw, David, *The English Lakes: Tales from History, Legend and Folklore* (P3 Publications, 1996). A collection of interesting stories from around the county.

Rollinson, William, *A History of Cumberland and Westmorland* (Phillimore and Co, 1996). A scholarly work written in an accessible style.

Wyatt, John, *Cumbria: The Lake District and its County* (Robert Hale, 2004). This huge, comprehensive tome covers Cumbria's history, geography and architecture. Written by the Lake District National Park's first warden who later became its chief ranger.

Index

Main page references are in **bold**. Page references to maps are in *italics*.